GETTING INVOLVED

Moral Development and Citizenship Education

'*Moral Development and Citizenship Education*' is a book series that focuses on the cultural development of our young people and the pedagogical ideas and educational arrangements to support this development. It includes the social, political and religious domains, as well as cognitive, emotional and action oriented content. The concept of citizenship has extended from being a pure political judgment, to include the social and interpersonal dynamics of people.

Morality has become a multifaceted and highly diversifi ed construct that now includes cultural, developmental, situational and professional aspects. Its theoretical modelling, practical applications and measurements have become central scientifi c tasks. Citizenship and moral development are connected with the identity constitution of the next generations. A caring and supporting learning environment can help them to participate in society.

Books in this series will be based on different scientifi c and ideological theories, research methodologies and practical perspectives. The series has an international scope; it will support manuscripts from different parts of the world and it includes authors and practices from various countries and cultures, as well as comparative studies. The series seeks to stimulate a dialogue between different points of view, research traditions and cultures. It contains multi-authored handbooks, focussing on specifi c issues, and monographs. We invite books that challenge the academic community, bring new perspectives into the community and broaden the horizon of the domain of moral development and citizenship education.

Getting involved
Global citizenship development and sources of moral values

Fritz Oser
University of Fribourg, Switzerland

&

Wiel Veugelers (Eds.)
University of Amsterdam / University for Humanistics Utrecht, the Netherlands

SENSE PUBLISHERS
ROTTERDAM / TAIPEI

A C.I.P. record for this book is available from the Library of Congress.

ISBN 978-90-8790-634-4(paperback)
ISBN 978-90-8790-6351 (hardback)
ISBN 978-90-8790-636-8 (e-book)

Published by: Sense Publishers,
P.O. Box 21858, 3001 AW
Rotterdam, The Netherlands

Printed on acid-free paper

CONTENTS

FRITZ OSER & WIEL VEUGELERS

INTRODUCTION

Dialogical Processes in identity development

'Getting involved' in society means becoming a human person by doing something for others and thus being connected to mankind and society. Youngsters who get involved, develop a feeling of agency. But 'getting involved' is not easy: society's growing cultural diversity makes connections between people more differentiated. The paradox is that in a modern, multicultural society 'getting involved' is even more important than in a traditional, more monocultural society. A society can only transcend if people are in a certain way connected. To live together in a true human sense, implies to participate actively in social life and in a peaceful, just and democratic way. From the perspective of the individual, there must be opportunities to get involved, to develop a sense of efficacy and to experience connectedness.

In today's societies 'getting involved' is a dynamic process that challenges people to enhance special social and civic competences, in particular attitudes. 'Getting involved' is not a natural development – learning processes are necessary to develop the capacity and the will to get involved. Youngsters should have possibilities in educational settings to experience sharedness, to get involved in a dialogue, to have common reflection and to act for and with others. Education, both in formal and in informal settings, can support children and adolescents in this development of identity.

'Getting involved' relates to various scientific orientations. Political, sociological, psychological and pedagogical questions are at issue, and all of these will be consulted in this volume. The main perspective however remains the issue of identity development relating to 'getting involved', and it will therefore be psychological. As most of the authors will show, this psychological development is always embedded within concrete social, cultural and political contexts and will therefore also be analyzed from political, sociological and cultural points of view. Developmental questions are about the capacities and justification strategies that children, adolescents and young adults are able to generate and the kind of differences in these capacities and the justifications that emerge. A main question is how educators can support this identity development. Which goals do educators find important and what kind of identity are they stimulating?

Recent thinking on 'getting involved' is related to the concept of citizenship. The concept of citizenship in contemporary social sciences and in discourses in society is not limited to the formal political level of engagement, but extends to the social and the interpersonal level. Modern conceptions of citizenship see 'getting involved' as a catalyst for a person to become a free, autonomous and participatory citizen. Citizenship education is therefore not limited to learning about politics, but to live a social and political life. Extending the notion of citizenship to the personal level means, in a democratic society, that youngsters must be given ample space for dialogical and social processes, and to empower and educate to what Dewey called a democratic way of life. Becoming a citizen is not a personal career but a collective effort of connected individuals.

Civil society, democracy and 'getting involved'

With the linking of the political and the personal, 'getting involved' has made 'civil society' a crucial arena of civic identity development. Since about 1980 'civil society' takes a central place in the debate about what politicians should support and stimulate and what political sciences can and should treat as central aspects of what we now call 'getting involved'. Civil societies encompass initiatives and spontaneous groupings of citizens, not only in problematic dictatorial societies like the former eastern communist countries, but also as energetic forces in democratic countries, which are in danger of losing their dynamism. Every society has its civil society; it depends on the relation between the political level and the broader society how civil society functions.

'Getting involved' and democracy need to be invented and built up continuously, and youngsters have to learn to be part of these processes. The modern state, with its structural fine-tuned intra-community supply of services, can only function if there is a counterweight of civil societal activities that are structurally free from absolute obligations, but are constituted in possibilities of political self-regulation of the society. The problem is that today the engagement of people to be active in traditional political, cultural, social or religious organizations is declining. And at the same time many people prefer to be active in small and manageable communities like community institutions for the poor, community churches, community hospitals, etc. Youngsters are very active in more modern communities like the internet, in music and style-related subcultures, and sometimes in local community actions.

In most introductions to political sciences, the authors distinguish between three forces that keep liberal market oriented societies going, namely the state, the market and the civil society. Whereas the market is responsible for the supply of all kinds of goods and the state regulates the conditions of any exchange of these goods, civil society regulates social, political, cultural and ecological problems through voluntary and solitary actions of citizens. These informal, but important groupings can influence either the market or the state in a quite intensive way. Civil society also effectively helps to intercede between state and other formal forces like law or financial capacities, takes the right to protect nature, gives security to children or supports art movements. This engagement is always voluntary, it is usually welfare oriented and it is self-organized.

Organizations in civil society engage people, but in a liberal market policy they are often representing only a certain group of people and a certain concern. Civil society is, in cases like this, market-oriented as well. In countries with a strong welfare state and in countries with a firm educational policy, the civil society can connect ideologically in another way to the political. In particular in countries with a strong democracy, the political level and civil society is interrelated. The political level in that case supports civil society, social justice for all, and diversity. Civil society in a strong democracy creates and supports a deliberative democracy with a concern for diversity and social justice. However each type of society, either a liberal market or a social justice oriented democracy, needs its citizens to 'get involved'.

Psychological foundations of 'getting involved'

In psychology and especially in social psychology, 'getting involved' is often treated as 'pro-social behavior' – that means behavior that is oriented towards helping or giving. Sometimes it is called 'supererogatory' acting, which means acting that goes beyond of what is necessary and societal demanded. To save someone who fell in a cold river is such behavior, but also to give a beggar a coin. We may think that this form of 'getting involved' is somehow too individualistic and is therefore not related to a common civil society; but we have to understand that it is a special element of it. And even if many psychologists speak about pro-social behavior as a moral act, the relationship between this helping behavior or empathy for others and morality is not at all clear. Indeed as Staub already states in his famous volume on 'Development and maintenance of pro-social behavior', although different approaches are somehow concerned with morality, 'the theoretical linkage received little attention' (Staub, 1984; p. XXVI). Staub argues that helpfulness, kindness, generosity and cooperation are behaviors or value-emotions that lead to 'the positive aspects of human morality, the *thou shalts*' (Staub, 1984; p. XXIII). However, neither the respective status of morality nor the analytical weight is reflected in these studies. Another source for 'getting involved' could be studies on altruism. The famous findings by Latané and Darley on the bystander syndrome, or the study of Lerner on the desire for justice and reactions to victims are examples of it. But these results are also quite general and not specifically embedded in morality. We do not know in fact how we can, in these examples, conceive the moral obligation and any moral sensitivity. Recently Seligman (2002), in his Authentic Happiness book, showed that engagement and involvement lead to more life satisfaction than 'wellness' and similar self-directed activities. But still the question is: what leads to 'getting involved' in the concern for others?

'Getting involved': Morality and social conditions

In this volume, when speaking about 'getting involved', we refer especially to three aspects of action frames, namely:

a) How young people get societal engaged,
b) The relationship between social engagement and moral thinking/feeling/sensitivity,
c) How societal conditions stimulate and inhibit the involvement of youngsters in voluntary social acts and movements.

a) Personal conditions for young people's involvement
Besides being in education and professional work, adolescents and young adults often participate a lot in leisure groups like drinking together, going shopping, hanging around, etc. Sociologists speak about the leisure generation, or even about leisure societies. The assumption is that these youngsters are not living consciously and do not reflect about their life and the world around them. This is not a new idea. Almost every older generation argues that the younger generation is not being serious enough and does not have the moral, reflective and dialogical competences and attitudes to live a meaningful life. Every older generation is partly blind for new forms of sense making and being in the world. However, every older generation does recognize the pedagogical task to educate youngsters and to continue society and mankind.

The question behind the leisure theory is not so much how youngsters could change such way of living, but how they learn to take responsibility for what happens around them, with others and with the ones who cannot participate in such endeavors. It seems that for the leisure generation the fragility of meaning making is high and shows up when life events like sickness, poverty, or loss of lives are at stake. Educationalists argue for more support for these youngsters to get involved. To 'get involved' is, according to us, also a way for embedding people into a more meaningful social system. Challenging youngsters to think about their life, enlarging their process of meaning making, and getting into a dialogue can result in 'getting involved'. From the point of view of society, the relational social gain is substantial and helps to understand how sense can be made. Youngsters who get involved have a different self-concept and a higher self-esteem than the ones that do not. They develop a social capital that helps sharing common understanding (Seligman 2002). Even if in a methodological sense we know how young people get involved, we still do not know what makes them 'getting involved'. In other words: what really are the sources of 'getting involved'?

b). Involvement and morality
What makes people 'getting involved'? As mentioned before it is not yet clear in which way helping behavior and other positive forms of social involvement are related to moral motivation. Morality in itself often refers to what not to do. Helping and getting engaged with others has a different source, namely to make the world a better place and give others a chance at an easier life. What are the moral elements for this social behavior? Is there a correlation between moral sensitivity and this pro-social enterprise? In the tradition of the Kohlberg paradigm, the judgment-

action bias does mostly mean moral judgment and the respective moral necessary act – for instance to prevent theft. Involvement with others is less compulsory and not directly related to such acts. Involvement needs a stronger sense of legitimation by the person involved. Nucci (2001) has made the important domain distinction of differentiating between domains that have a higher degree of freedom to act (social domain) and the ones with a lower degree (like morality).

Acting morally in the social domain is often justified by more universal categories like human rights, humanity, and cosmopolitism (Nussbaum, 1997; Hansen, 2008). These categories refer in a positive sense to human beings and the responsibility for humanity and the globe. It is an appealing discourse based on the idea of what connects us and what responsibilities we have, from a sustainability point of view in the cosmos.

A more political argument is given in discourses on democracy. Democracy is the peaceful living together of people with respect for minorities. In particular, more deliberate types of democracy (Gutmann, 1987) or strong democracy (Barber, 1984) needs citizens with the human capacities to reflect, to enter in a dialogue and to change praxis. Different kinds of society and different concepts of democracy ask for different kinds of citizenship. Veugelers (2007) makes a distinction between an adapted non-reflective type of citizenship, an individualistic type of citizenship and a critical-democratic type that combines autonomy and social concern. These types of citizenship refer to different values.

But what are the moral foundations of a more social oriented type of citizenship? Or in the tradition of Kohlberg: what motivates people to use the value of justice? Is it their human consciousness, their feeling that they should not do injustice? Is it a more social-psychological way of thinking of having an easy life without interpersonal and social tensions? Or is it a political living together driven by 'making the best of it' together? The crucial argument is when are people not thinking and acting from their own perspective, but do include the perspective of others. When are people getting socially involved?

c). Societal conditions for involvement

It needs to be analyzed under which conditions young people want to get involved. Research has not yet shown what it means to 'get involved' in a well organized world. In countries with a strong welfare state, it is difficult to help a beggar because such help is structurally regulated; in other countries however the openness towards poor people has exactly this spontaneous form that help others to overcome the next hours of hunger and misery. For many young members of western societies the necessity to help is not so obvious, and even to participate in social, cultural, political and religious groups is not always necessary.

Learning to participate in society, to 'get involved', is crucial. Education, and in particular schools, try to influence the identity development of youngsters. Schools socialize through a hidden curriculum and through explicit social goals. Schools may have their fundamental pedagogical goals like pro-social engagement, substantial helping and giving to others and they may have programs in which substantial getting involved for others is demanded. These programs can be directed at the society outside the schools, but help and cooperation can also be learned in the schools. Schools however are organized around selection and allocation, but more cooperative and democratic ways of learning are also possible. In schools we see many new forms of mentoring, in-service learning, community-based programs, etc.

Civil society as well offers many possibilities for caring. An orchestra of youngsters gives a concert in a home for drug addicts; students of a secondary school class organize a Christmas celebration in a prison; young members of a political party start a campaign against hunger in the world; members of the scout movement clean up a forest hoping to save it as a nature reserve, etc. All these activities show how much personal engagement of leaders, teachers and responsible educators must be realized in order to develop this vision in the next generation, namely to make caring the main goal of a societal life. These educational and civic programs can have different pedagogical goals, ranging from adapting to political action, and to achieve social justice (Westheimer & Kahne, 2004). Common in these programs is a concern for the other.

However, participating in programs like this doesn't guarantee a sustainable social orientation in youngsters. The focus should be on processes of personal identity development of youngsters in cultural practices. A psychological concern should be linked with a sociological analysis and driven by ethics and pedagogical goals. In this book we try to bring these perspectives together.

INTRODUCTION TO THE CHAPTERS

The main focus of this book is on how youngsters are 'getting involved' in society, the role of morality in this development and practices, experiences of educators working in families, schools and civil society, and effect studies of pedagogical interventions.

The volume is divided into six parts. The first part, 'Educating the good citizen: Civic engagement', deals with the relationship of civic education and moral education. The central question of the chapters in this part is about the interference of morality and politics. The second part, 'Moral development and social engagement', treats morality with respect to social and pro-social engagement. Elements like autonomy, context and discourse, are important. The third part, 'Teachers engagement for democratic schools', relates the 'getting involved' concept to schools, school-lives and school-structures. The issue of teacher's leadership is prevalent. Part four, 'Methods and strategies for fostering engagement in conflicting fields', includes many forms of pedagogically stimulating 'getting involved'; the main question is about how to influence what is going to engage young people. The psychological pre-conditions for such acting are analyzed. Part 5 focus on 'Research on religious involvement'. Religiousness can be an issue for engaging with others and for changing the world. 'Getting involved' was always a demand in religious denominations; we analyze if religiousness is still a motor for 'getting involved'. The sixth part, 'Conflicts between ethical involvement and economic engagement', finally is about the question of the relationship between economics and 'getting involved'. To speak about morality in business education means to introduce a different system of rules with respect to shareholder politics and profit and loss reporting.

We start the book with 'Educating the good citizen: Civic engagement'. In this first part contributions have been brought together that focus on the concept of citizenship and in particular the more affective engagement element of citizenship. All the chapters make clear that there are differences in the way citizenship and citizenship education is conceptualized theoretically and realized in practices.

Westheimer shows in his chapter 'On the relationship between political and moral engagement' that moral engagement can be interpreted differently. Westheimer presents research that shows that stimulating moral engagement is embedded in different kinds of pedagogical goals, educational practices and social and political relations. Westheimer and his colleague Kahne make a distinction between the personally responsible citizen, the participatory citizen and the social-justice oriented citizen. Most programs focus on the first type of citizen, the personal responsible citizen. Some programs focus on the participatory citizen. A democratic society needs, according to Westheimer, a social-justice oriented citizenship; educational programs that work on this kind of citizenship are however difficult to find.

Deakin-Crick presents in 'Pedagogy for Citizenship' a review of research on citizenship education and learning and achievement. She concentrates in her analysis on cognitive learning outcomes: meaning making, understanding and reasoning, higher order thinking skills, academic achievement, and communication skills. The learning processes that were identified as making a significant contribution to the five categories of cognitive learning outcomes were: engagement, promoting discussion, learner-centered teaching, meaningful curricula and developing personally. Deakin-Crick argues for a kind of citizenship education characterized by learners' own enquiry, rich interaction and effective two-way communication, attention to personal and social development, self-assessment and encouragement of reflective self-awareness in learners and their learning teachers.

Leenders, Veugelers and De Kat present in their chapter 'Moral education and Citizenship education in pre-university schools' an empirical research among teachers and students in schools about pedagogical goals, practices, experiences and outcomes in moral and citizenship education. They distinguish three types of citizenship and citizenship education: adapting, individualistic and critical-democratic. A school with a more adapting orientation has a dominant community concept of citizenship but with little concern for autonomy; their students however argue for more autonomy. A school with a more individualistic orientation lacks a link with an explicit social component. Also in this school, students ask for a better balance between autonomy and social commitment. A school with a critical-democratic orientation has a better balance between autonomy and social component, but the emphasis in the social domain is on social performance and not so much on participation in society. Students of all schools argue more then teachers for social issues and politics in the curriculum and for dialogue as method. Teachers are reluctant in teaching about politics.

Markoulis and Dikaiou focus in 'Being involved: theoretical and research approaches' on citizen's participation in actions and interventions to combat social problems in deprived communities. They show how social psychological phenomena can add to the understanding of participation in community context. Group history and inter-group relations are crucial elements in understanding the dynamic processes of participation especially when it refers to citizens from migrant minority groups.

Power and Power explore in 'Civic Engagement, global citizenship and moral psychology' some of the moral constructs involved in fostering global citizenship. In particular they focus on psychological prerequisites of citizenship like the moral self. Their empirical study among university students suggests that preparing students for global citizenship requires attention to the development of students' identity and moral judgment. If students are to become politically engaged, they must see themselves as related not only to other individuals but to their society and to the global community. The study of Power and Power points to the importance of moral judgment for responsible political engagement. Being a good citizen means committing oneself to the pursuit of justice and the common good.

The second part of the book is called 'Moral development and social engagement'. Chapters in this section focus on the moral component of citizenship. Morality is embedded in each type of citizenship, therefore citizenship development should be linked with moral development. The chapters in this part concentrate on more psychological concepts as moral self, emotional autonomy, sympathy, etc. These contributions show that affective components in the person's moral self and in the social interaction with others are influencing moral development. These components can support both a theoretical understanding and practical application for a psychological foundation of moral development and citizenship.

The first chapter in this part is by Higgins - D'Alessandro. She analyses in 'The judgment-action gap: A modest proposal' what research says about context and personal characteristics that can understand moral behavior. In particular she focuses on personal characteristics like moral self-processes that stimulate the moral self and moral identity. Higgins - D'Alessandro concludes that the notion of moral self-processes may be helpful as a developmental concept, allowing us to think about how moral ideas and values become incorporated into daily functioning and over time into one's sense of self. The wide variation in individuals' sense of the parameters of the moral domain may be accounted for by the idea that individuals develop different networks of moral self-processes based on individual life experiences.

Latzko presents in her chapter 'No morality without autonomy' an empirical study on the relation of autonomy and moral development. She makes a distinction in emotional autonomy between cognitive and affective autonomy. Her research shows that affective autonomy, for example the relationship with authorities like parents, influence moral development. There can however be a discrepancy between affective autonomy and cognitive autonomy. Latzko found a sub-group of adolescents who were rated as emotionally autonomous on a cognitive level of appraisal, not however with reference to the affective component. These adolescents found themselves in a transitional phase in the middle of the detachment process, whereby affective and cognitive components were not yet congruent.

Malti, Kriesi and Buchmann extend the focus on moral emotions. They analyze in 'Adolescent's pro-social behavior, sympathy, and moral reasoning' the role of sympathy and moral reasoning as motivational pre-requisites for pro-social action. Moral judgment seems to be a necessary but insufficient condition for moral education. Malti, Kriesi and Buchmann put forward sympathy as an important motive for pro-social behavior, in particular in the domain of friendship. Sympathy is defined as an understanding of another's situation and involves feelings of concern and involvement for the other. In their study they used a large sample of adolescents. They find that sympathy is an important stimulus for pro-social reasoning. The relationship between these components is however intermediated with the altruistic motive and it's relevance to a person's values and self-concept.

Thoma, Bebeau and Bolland present in their chapter 'The role of moral judgment in context-specific professional decision making' research on developmental processes in moral judgment of university students. In particular they looked at intermediate concepts that represent moral concerns that are described in terms of guiding ethical standards of the professional. They found a relation between moral judgment and these professional oriented intermediates. This relationship seems however more complex. Surprising was their finding of a decline in moral judgment development. In particular individuals that express strong personal interest reasoning show this decline. Thoma, Bebeau and Bolland conclude that professional ethics curricula should work more on reducing personal interest reasoning and enhance attention for professional situations.

Gibbs, Basinger, Grime and Snarey present in 'Globalization and cross-cultural studies of moral judgment development' a review of studies in which the Social-moral Reflection Measure instrument was used. The studies were done in different countries and cultures around the world. Gibbs and colleagues conclude that in line with the Kohlberg's view the social interaction, social participation, and, in particular social perspective-taking opportunities facilitate moral judgment development. Regarding cultural differences it is argued that in Snarey's pluralist-inclusionist stage model the higher stages must be broadened beyond Western philosophical traditions.

We end this part on moral development and social engagement with a contribution by Berkowitz, Althof, Turner and Bloch. In 'Discourse, development, and education' they show the importance of transactive discussion. Transactive discussion was defined as peer discussion where one discussant manifests discursive reasoning about another discussant's reasoning. They identified 18 different behaviors, ranging from just re-presentation to transformation of the other's reasoning. Based on a review of the research they conclude that more transactive discussion in adolescent peer moral discours resulted in greater moral reasoning development. These findings are, according to Berkowitz and colleagues, encouraging for educators who wish to reap the developmental benefits of discussion based pedagogies such as cooperative learning, class meetings, and moral dilemma discussions.

The third part is called 'Teachers engagement for democratic school'. Teachers play a very central role in moral and citizenship education. This chapter presents empirical work on teachers and moral leadership.

Vozzola and Long report in 'Teaching the political psychology of genocide' on their research on an educational program with university students. In their work they use the three types of citizens of Westheimer and Kahne.The research among their students shows that students were more involved in criticism than in action. They also find that the topic 'genocide' left students with a sense of despair rather than possibility. Vozzola and Long conclude that these kind of projects need to be complemented with stories of human engagement.

Lee presents in her chapter 'Students and teacher perception of moral atmosphere in Taiwan schools' a large empirical study. She uses the 'school as a caring community profile' scale of Lickona and Davidson. Taiwan students and teachers display a positive attitude toward their school, they score above the median. Students and teachers differ on some elements like 'perception of student respect for each other'; students were more positive. Students and teachers of elementary schools judge the atmosphere as being better than do students in high schools. The same is true for small schools. Interesting is the finding that in metropolitan schools students and teachers judge the atmosphere as being better than in the rural schools. Lee concludes that schools should encourage a stronger sense of identity and participation of students and teachers.

Schrader states in 'Teaching moral leadership: becoming moral leaders and being moral leadership' that all citizens should become consciously aware of what they are teaching and that they are teaching moral leadership. People in formal and informal positions of power exercise moral responsibility in both the means and the ends of interaction and participation. Moral leadership implies for Schrader that leaders have a special obligation for the growth and development of others, and the self, in social interaction. Developing self-reflective awareness and leading by moral example should be part of professional education programs.

In part 4 we bring together 'Methods and strategies for fostering engagement in conflicting fields'.

Montada argues in his chapter 'Moral education by conflict mediation' that social conflicts are at its core normative conflicts, and that even if justice is considered as an universal motive, the views of what is just and what is unjust are highly diverging. Montada therefore works on programs that teach people procedures and strategies to settle conflicts. He favors conflict mediation in which people learn to negotiate a social contract. Montada presents practical experiences with different strategies.

Lies and Block present in 'What does it takes to give?' an empirical study on moral identity, moral reasoning and religiosity as predictors of civic engagement in service-learning programs for upper-middle class students. They compare a group of students that participate in such a program with a group of students randomly selected. Lies and Bloch found that moral identity and moral reasoning are reliable predictors of participation in service-learning; religiosity was not.

Lapsley and Narvaez argue in 'Psychologized morality and ethical theory' that Kohlberg embraced the formalist ethical tradition and essentially lowered the fence between ethical theory and moral development. This affirmed the autonomy of morality, but at the expense of the autonomy of psychology. Lapsley and Narveaz advocate a more naturalist psychology approach that attempts to ground ethical theory by what is known about human motivation, the nature of the self, the nature of human concepts, how our reason works, how we are socially constituted, and a host of other facts about who we are and how the minds operates. These ideas imply a great shift in focus in research and educational practices; moral education should then focus more on psychological development.

Gross shows in 'Combating stereotypes and prejudice as a moral endeavor' how she works with Israeli Jewish and Arab students in a program on conflict management. The program gives voice and visibility for groups that were traditionally silenced at the university. The program focuses on exclusion and belonging, at inconsistency in attitudes and behavior, on how stereotypes are perceived, on how the transition from the general to the subjective occurs and on the impact of direct contact.

In part 5 we bring together 'Research on religious involvement'.

Walker and Primer argue in 'Being good for goodness' sake' that moral psychology suffers from a blind spot: the potential relevance of religion, spirituality, and transcendent faith to moral functioning. In a study on moral exemplars they find confirmation of their propositions: that transcendence acts to motivate and amplify moral functioning and that although morality may lead some individuals to concerns about transcendence, it will not do for everybody. Walker and Primer state that the relationship between morality and transcendence is much more complex and is mediated by many other factors.

Tirri, Nokelainen and Holm present a study on 'Ethical sensitivity of Finnish Lutheran 7th – 9th graders'. In this empirical study they use an ethical sensitivity scale questionnaire based on the work of Narvaez. Tirri, Nokelainen and Holm found that students who had more religious education at school and also were confirmed, assess themselves more as ethical sensitivity than their younger and non-confirmed educated peers. Female students estimated their ethical skills higher than their male peers. And more academically gifted students estimated their ethical skills as being higher than the opinions of average ability students.

In 'Phenomenography and the variation theory of learning as tools for understanding religion' Hella shows how the theory of Marton can help in understanding how the diversity of religious and secular traditions and variation in their beliefs and values can be dealt with as an understanding of religion and religious issues in education. Hella concludes that education should help students to engage with variation in the accounts of reality in order to make judgments between worldviews in relation to their own lives and to live responsibly with others as global citizens amongst the plurality of beliefs and moral values.

Part 6 focuses on 'Conflicts between ethical involvement and economic engagement'.

Beck studied 'Moral judgment in economic situations'. He collected moral judgment data from insurance apprentices and clerks over a period of six years. The results show that in the economic domain there is a tension between competition and cooperation. Ethically speaking it is of course unacceptable to sign the principle of seeking profit into an universal law. On the other hand it would be completely unacceptable as well to stigmatize this principle as morally deficient by nature. Beck concludes that instead of universalism we are in the economic domain in need of elaboration of a subsystemic relativism.

Minnamaier continues the debate between business and ethics. In 'Education for business ethics' he makes a clear distinction between situations in which direct moral action works and situations in which it is likely to be exploited so that these situations require changing the conditions of action. Conditions might be altered either in the sense of providing more opportunities for moral learning or setting suitable limits to the actions of morally incompetent individuals.

All together this book gives a broad overview of current research in the field of moral development and citizenship. It shows the diversity of concepts, research methodologies, and educational practices. The book in its diversity also shows the influence of local social, cultural and political contexts. Moral development is always articulated by local structures and cultural processes of giving meaning to life. 'Getting involved' is necessary for living together, creating democracy and sustainability of a global world.

This book is the first in the series 'Moral Development and Citizenship Education'. We hope this book will stimulate researchers in their work, in particular if they take positions, methodologies and theoretical traditions that are not or only marginally present in this book. You all are invited to contribute to our series.

REFERENCES

Barber, B. (1984). *Strong democracy: Participatory politics for a new age.* Berkeley: University of California Press.

Gutmann, A. (1987). *Democratic education.* Princeton: Princeton University Press.

Hansen, D.T. (2008). Curriculum and the idea of a cosmopolitain inheritance. *Journal of Curriculum Studies, 40,* 3, 289-312.

Nucci, L.P. (2001). *Education in the moral domain.* Cambridge: Cambridge University Press.

Nussbaum, M.C. (1997). *Cultivating humanity.* Cambridge MA: Harvard University Press.

Seligman, M. (2002). *Authentic happiness.* New York: Free Press.

Staub, E. (1984). *Development and maintenance of pro-social behavior: International perspectives on positive morality.* New York: Plenum Press.

Veugelers, W. & Oser, F.K. (2003) (Eds) *Teaching in moral and democratic education.* Bern: Peter Lang.

Veugelers, W. (2007). Creating critical democratic citizenship education: Empowering humanity and democracy in Dutch education. *Compare, 37,* 1, 103-119.

Westheimer, J. & Kahne, J. (2004). What kind of citizen? The politics of educating for democracy. *American Educational Research Journal. Summer, 41,* 2, 237-269.

Fritz Oser
University of Fribourg, Switzerland
Wiel Veugelers
University of Amsterdam; University for Humanistics, Utrecht, The Netherlands

PART 1

EDUCATING THE GOOD CITIZEN:
CIVIC ENGAGEMENT

JOEL WESTHEIMER

ON THE RELATIONSHIP BETWEEN POLITICAL AND MORAL ENGAGEMENT[1]

Ask people of any nation if they think children should learn how to be good, moral citizens and most will say "of course." Ask them if teaching children to get involved – locally, nationally, and globally – is a good idea, and, again, most will assure you that it is. But beyond the clichés, when teachers and education reformers wrestle with the nitty-gritty details of what will actually be taught about civic values, peace and war, nationhood and citizenship, global communities and global economies, the easy consensus starts to fray. What I'd like to do in this chapter is share some reflections on the role of schools in teaching students how to be democratic, politically-engaged, and ethical citizens. I'm going to draw on research that I have conducted with colleagues[2] over the past decade looking at programs that specifically aim to nurture "good citizenship" among youth and young adults. Specifically, in this chapter, I am interested in the relationship between political engagement and ideals of the "moral" citizen.

THE TROUBLE WITH MORALITY

I confess that my relationship with the field of moral education is fraught. As many within the field will be quick to note, the enormous range of goals, values, and ideological commitments represented in moral education curricula and the research programs that seek to assess and advance them often bewilders not only relative outsiders like myself but also longtime enthusiasts (Althof & Berkowitz, 2006). When educators with commitments as varied as those held by Lawrence Kohlberg, Ed Wynn, E.D. Hirsh, William Bennett, Nel Noddings, and John Dewey are all drawn on to support calls for moral education programs in schools, you know there is bound to be trouble. I have always been troubled by a particular strand of moral education that seems to stand in unwitting opposition to goals of independent thinking and critical engagement with ideas. Historically, the emphasis for some moral educators, has been on school practices that reinforce commonly accepted (but not necessarily just) social practices.[3] In contemporary terms, moral educators aligned with particular notions of "character" education – those that emphasize obedience over independent thinking – are, in my mind, too susceptible to pernicious anti-democratic tendencies that I will explain further on.

Moral education strategies can be valuable (especially as an antidote to the myo-

Fritz Oser & Wiel Veugelers (eds.), Getting involved, 17–29.

pic focus on math and literacy skills testing currently dominant in schools), but I worry about over-emphasis on conformity and "good" behavior. In fields outside of education – most notably literary criticism – scholars have often tended toward the use of the term "ethical" rather than "moral" to describe normative discourses of "goodness." The historically religious overtones of "morality" that suggest a kind of objective universality about life decisions and actions make a number of critics uncomfortable (think "moral majority"). For some, the term ethics signifies a more contextual analysis, a recognition that as circumstances and understandings change, so too must our definitions of "good" actions, "good" lives, and "good" societies. But with the exception of philosophers and some literary critics, in many works, the two terms "morality" and "ethics" are used loosely and often interchangeably. It is not my concern for this essay to enter into this important discussion; because the subject of this volume is global citizenship and moral values, I will use "moral" in the broadest sense and when the works I am addressing use "ethical," I will respond using that term instead.

Despite my reservations about the term "moral" and its associated assumptions, there is no doubt in my mind that consideration of one's conduct in the world is an important component of any proper education plan. As in other fields, education has a critical role to play in undertaking all of the big questions with which human beings have been preoccupied for thousands of years. In *The Way We Argue Now* (Anderson, 2006), literary theorist Amanda Anderson argues that her profession has most recently been marked by a "general turn to ethics" (p. 6) that makes central to literary criticism the question "How should I live?" I believe that education, too, must make such questions central. But, if the question "How should I live?" is increasingly central to theory, it has been less so in the last decade of practice in education reform. Moral educators, character educators, service-learning curriculum advocates, and those interested in humanistic and democratic approaches to teaching and learning have an obligation to direct the profession and the public to encourage exactly such inquiry.

For this chapter, I will examine a subset of this more general inquiry. I am concerned here with the role of schools in developing dispositions consistent with democratic habits of citizenship. Which norms of citizenship education typically practiced in schools are consistent with democratic participation? What are the ethical implications of emphasizing some strategies and affording less attention to others? Why are "politics" implicated in these questions and what is the relationship between the political and the moral? I am suggesting three related arguments that have implications for moral educators: (1) There are a variety of competing visions of citizenship; (2) These different visions have different political (and ethical) implications; (3) Programs that emphasize one of these kinds of goals do not necessarily fulfill – and may, in fact, work at cross purposes with – others.

WHAT KIND OF CITIZEN?

So much of school reform lately has been characterized by the elimination of any part of the curriculum that spurs thinking about big ideas, tackling controversial social and political issues, and asking sustained, philosophical questions. As a result, programs that aim to teach children about participation in civic and moral affairs of the community seem sorely needed. And many such programs are adopted in a growing number of North American schools. However, even when educators are expressly committed to teaching "good citizenship," there is cause for caution. When it comes to teaching democratic citizenship, there is generally quite a lot of head-nodding agreement about the importance of the goal. Yet the kinds of character traits and dispositions necessary are matters of great debate. Some parents, educators, and policy-makers perceive a diminishing sense of commitment, responsibility, and good "character" among students as threats to democratic life. They argue that students must be taught self-reliance, perseverance, and personal fortitude. Others are concerned with declining civic and political participation. Citing declining youth voter participation statistics, they hope schools might teach students the attitudes, skills, and knowledge necessary to participate as active and effective citizens in democratic life. When educators, policymakers, politicians, and community activists pursue democratic citizenship, they do so in many different ways and towards many different ends.

Students are no more in agreement on what good democratic citizenship means than are teachers, policy makers, or politicians. When asked what it means to be a good citizen, one student told us, "Someone who's active and stands up for what they believe in. If they know that something's going on that is wrong, they go out and change it." But another student from a different school told us that to be a good citizen, you need to "follow the rules, I guess, as hard as you can, even though you want to break them sometimes. Like cattle."[2]

My colleague Joseph Kahne and I spent the better part of a decade studying programs that aimed to develop good citizenship skills among youth and young adults. In study after study, we came to similar conclusions: the kinds of goals and practices commonly represented in curricula that hope to foster democratic citizenship usually have more to do with voluntarism, charity, and obedience than with democracy. In other words, "good citizenship" to many educators means listening to authority figures, dressing neatly, being nice to neighbors, and helping out at a soup kitchen – not grappling with the kinds of social policy decisions that every citizen in a democratic society needs to learn how to do.

In our studies of dozens of programs, we identified three visions of "good" citizens that help capture the lay of the land when it comes to citizenship education in the United States: the *Personally Responsible Citizen; the Participatory Citizen; and the Social-Justice Oriented Citizen* (Westheimer & Kahne, 2004). It is worth summarizing the differences here so we might better be able to situate various educational programs that emphasize moral values among these kinds of goals. They can serve as a helpful guide to uncovering the variety of assumptions that fall under the idea of citizenship education (see Table 1).

Table 1. Kinds of Citizens

	Personally Responsible Citizen	Participatory Citizen	Social-Justice Oriented Citizen
DESCRIPTION	Acts responsibly in their community Works and pays taxes Picks up litter, recycles, and gives blood Helps those in need, lends a hand during times of crisis Obeys laws	Active member of community organizations and/or improvement efforts Organizes community efforts to care for those in need, promote economic development, or clean up environment Knows how government agencies work Knows strategies for accomplishing collective tasks	Critically assesses social, political, and economic structures Explores strategies for change that address root causes of problems Knows about social movements and how to effect systemic change Seeks out and addresses areas of injustice
SAMPLE ACTION	Contributes food to a food drive	Helps to organize a food drive	Explores why people are hungry and acts to solve root causes
CORE ASSUMPTIONS	To solve social problems and improve society, citizens must have good character; they must be honest, responsible, and law-abiding members of the community	To solve social problems and improve society, citizens must actively participate and take leadership positions within established systems and community structures	To solve social problems and improve society, citizens must question and change established systems and structures when they reproduce patterns of injustice over time

From: Westheimer, J. & Kahne, J. (2004). What kind of citizen? The politics of educating for democracy. American Educational Research Journal. 41(2), 237-269.

Personally Responsible Citizens contribute to food or clothing drives when asked and volunteer to help those less fortunate whether in a soup kitchen or a senior-citizen center. They might contribute time, money, or both to charitable causes. Both those in the character education movement and those who advocate community service would emphasize this vision of good citizenship. They seek to build character and personal responsibility by emphasizing honesty, integrity, self-discipline, and hard work (Ryan, 1989; Lickona, 1991).[5] The Character Counts! Coalition, for example, advocates teaching students to "treat others with respect …deal peacefully with anger … be considerate of the feelings of others … follow the Golden Rule … use good manners" and so on. They want students not to "threaten, hit, or hurt anyone [or use] bad language" (Character Counts! 1996). Other programs that seek to develop personally responsible citizens hope to nurture compassion by engaging students in volunteer activities.

Other educators emphasize the vision of the *Participatory Citizen*. Participatory citizens actively participate in the civic affairs and the social life of the community at local, state/provincial, and national levels. Educational programs designed to support the development of participatory citizens focus on teaching students about how government and other institutions (e.g., community-based organizations, churches) work and about the importance of planning and participating in organized efforts to care for those in need, for example, or in efforts to guide school policies. While the personally responsible citizen would contribute cans of food for the homeless, the participatory citizen might organize the food drive.

A third image of a good citizen, and perhaps the perspective that is least commonly pursued, is of individuals who know how to critically assess multiple perspectives. They are able to examine social, political, and economic structures and explore strategies for change that address root causes of problems. We called this kind of citizen the *Social-Justice Oriented Citizen* because the programs fostering such citizenship emphasize the need for citizens to be able to think about issues of fairness, equality of opportunity, and democratic engagement. They share with the vision of the Participatory Citizen an emphasis on collective work related to the life and issues of the community. But the nature of these programs gives priority to students thinking independently, looking for ways to improve society, and being thoughtfully informed about a variety of complex social issues. These programs are less likely to emphasize the need for charity and volunteerism as ends in themselves, and more likely to teach about ways to effect systemic change. If *Participatory Citizens* organize the food drive and *Personally Responsible Citizens* donate food, the *Social-Justice Oriented Citizens* – some might also call them critical thinkers – ask why people are hungry, then act on what they discover.

Currently, the vast majority of school programs that take the time to teach citizenship are the kind that emphasize either good character (including the importance of volunteering and helping those in need), or technical knowledge of legislatures and how government works. Far less common are schools that teach students to think about root causes of injustice or challenge existing social, economic, and political norms as a means for strengthening democracy. If, like Lawrence Kohlberg, we agree that "social education is moral education and moral education is preparation for citizenship" (Kohlberg, 1976, p. 213), then the kind of citizenship preparation going on in schools is overwhelmingly oriented to individual service and rote "moral" inculcation of rules, rather than to collective forms of social conscience and action.

Interestingly, many large-scale evaluations of school-based programs showcase the same penchant for avoiding critical thinking and moral engagement with controversial issues. Research and evaluation of educational programs also reflect this individual-character based conception of personally responsible citizenship. Common survey items (the items use a five point Likert scale based on responses ranging from "1–strongly disagree" to "5–strongly agree") include:

— Taking care of people who are having difficulty caring for themselves is (everyone's responsibility including mine/is not my responsibility)
— Helping others without being paid is (not something people should have to do/ something every student should feel they have to do)

21

—· Recycling cans, bottles, and other things is (too much of a hassle for me to bother with/everyone's job, including mine)

These questions (and many more like them) emphasize individual character and charitable acts. They ignore other possible levers for ethical and engaged action in a democracy – participation in social movements, for example, or efforts to shape government policy on behalf of those in need.[6] These same surveys do not ask students questions that address issues such as whether there are enough jobs that pay decent wages for anyone who wants to work or how society should respond if there are not.

"MORAL" CITIZENSHIP DOES NOT ALWAYS MEAN DEMOCRATIC CITIZENSHIP

Programs that privilege individual acts of compassion and kindness often neglect the importance of social action and the pursuit of social justice. I believe it is fair to say that personal responsibility as represented in *some* moral education programs is an inadequate response to the challenges of educating a democratic citizenry. First, the focus on individual character and behavior obscures the need for collective and often public sector initiatives. Second, this emphasis distracts attention from analysis of the causes of social problems. Finally, volunteerism and kindness are put forward as ways of avoiding politics and policy.

In other words, it is not at all clear that character education, for example, will solve deep-seated social problems unless accompanied by important lessons in critical analysis and ethical reasoning. As John Holt (1995) observes in *How Children Fail,* "schools tend to mistake good behavior for good character." When we consider the implications for democracy, the consequences become even more stark. Government leaders in a totalitarian regime would be as delighted as those in a democracy if their young citizens learned the lessons put forward by many of the proponents of personally responsible citizenship: don't do drugs; show up to work on time; give blood; help others during a flood; recycle; etc. These are all desirable traits for people living in a community. But they are not about democratic citizenship. Efforts to pursue some conceptions of personal responsibility might even undermine efforts to prepare participatory and justice oriented citizens. Obedience and loyalty (common goals of character education), for example, may work against the kind of independent thinking that effective democracy requires. The hidden curriculum of too many character education programs is how to please authority, not how to develop convictions and stand up for them.

POLITICAL ENGAGEMENT AND MORAL ENGAGEMENT

Unfortunately, broader school reform has recently moved even further in this direction. In the past five years, hundreds of U.S. schools, districts, states, and even the federal government have enacted policies that seek to restrict the kind of critical analysis and independent thinking that is consistent with learning how to be an ethically-engaged moral person. For example, in June 2006, Florida became the first state to ban historical interpretation in public schools, thereby effectively outlawing critical thinking. The 2006 Florida Education Omnibus Bill includes language specifying that:

> The history of the United States shall be taught as genuine history.... American history shall be viewed as factual, not as constructed, shall be viewed as knowable, teachable, and testable.

Other provisions in the bill mandate "flag education, including proper flag display" and "flag salute" and require educators to stress the importance of free enterprise to the U.S. economy. But what some find most alarming is the stated goal of the bill's designers: "to raise historical literacy" with a particular emphasis on the "teaching of facts." For example, the bill requires that only facts be taught when it comes to discussing the "period of discovery" and the early colonies. Facts, that is, but not (ethical) interpretation.

Of course, historians almost universally regard history as exactly a matter of interpretation; indeed, the competing interpretations are what make history so interesting. Historians and educators alike have widely derided the mandated adherence to an "official story" embodied in the Florida legislation, but the impact of such mandates should not be underestimated – especially because Florida is not alone. In April 2008, the Arizona House of Representatives passed SB 1108 specifying that schools whose teachings "denigrate or encourage dissent" from American values would lose state funding. This drive to engage schools in reinforcing a unilateral understanding of history and policy shows no sign of abating. More and more, teachers and students are seeing their schools or entire districts and states limiting their ability to explore multiple perspectives to controversial issues. From a moral-reasoning perspective, Berkowitz (1988), Walker (1983), and others, have emphasized the importance of being exposed to multiple perspectives on the development of moral thinking. Moreover, role-taking exercises (limited under a growing set of legislative policies) have also been found to promote the development of moral reasoning (Day, 1991; Lind, 2000). As changes in the school curriculum reflect a growing intolerance for discussion, debate, and role-playing exercises, some educators are concerned with the devastating impact reforms like these could have on the health of democracy itself.

POLITICALLY-ENGAGED MORAL EDUCATION

There are many varied and powerful ways to teach children and young adults to engage the moral issues critical to the development of democratic societies. While a significant body of work has been written in this regard (for example, Greene, 2000; Kohn, 2004; Noddings, 2007; Veugelers & Oser, 2003; Shapiro, 2005; Veugelers, 2007), I want to focus here on a few examples of the possibilities for curriculum aimed in particular at civic engagement with dilemmas of ethical importance. For example, longtime teacher Brian Schultz's inspiring efforts with his 5th grade class in Chicago's Cabrini-Green housing project area included having his students conduct research on improving conditions in their own neighborhood, especially with regard to broken promises to build a new school. His students studied historical approaches to change and, rejecting passivity, demonstrated a deep attachment to their community and neighbors. Each step of the way, they grappled with ethical concerns as they related to the political and economic reality of their surroundings (Schultz, 2008).

Bob Peterson, a one-time Wisconsin Elementary Teacher of the Year, worked with his students at La Escuela Fratney in Madison to examine the full spectrum of ideological positions that emerged following the events of September 11, 2001 and the policies that followed. Instead of avoiding the challenging questions his 5th grade students posed, Peterson encouraged them, placing a notebook prominently at the front of the classroom labeled "Questions That We Have." As the students discussed their questions and the unfolding current events, Peterson repeatedly asked students to consider their responsibilities to one another, to their communities, and to the world. Through poetry (Langston Hughes's "Let America Be America Again"); historical readings (the Declaration of Independence, the U.S. Constitution, the 1918 Sedition Act); and current events (photographs of September 11 memorial gatherings, protests in the United States and abroad, newspaper editorials), Peterson allowed students to explore political events surrounding the September 11 attacks and their effect on American patriotism and democracy (Peterson, 2007; Westheimer, 2007).

El Puente Academy in the Williamsburg neighborhood of Brooklyn, New York, ties the entire school curriculum to students' and teachers' concerns about the community. Named a New York City School of Excellence, El Puente boasts a 90 percent graduation rate in an area where schools usually see only 50 percent of their students graduate in four years. El Puente principal Héctor Calderón attributes the school's success to a curriculum that engages students in efforts to realize democratic ideals of justice and equality, reverse the cycle of poverty and violence, and work toward change in their own neighborhood. Students study environmental hazards in the area, not only because they care about the health of the natural environment, but also because these hazards directly affect the health of the community to which they are deeply committed. El Puente students learn that ethical action requires more than following a list of rules or principles, but rather constant engagement with realities of neighbors, causes of problems, and political solutions. In one unit, students surveyed the community to chart levels of asthma and identify families affected by the disease. Their report became the first by a community organization to be published in a medical journal. Students and teachers also successfully fought a 55-story incinerator that was proposed for their neighborhood (Gonzales, 1995; North Central Regional Educational Laboratory, 2000; Westheimer, 2005).

These approaches to political engagement all force students and teachers to grapple with profoundly moral questions of justice, equality, and community. They share several characteristics with some but by no means all more traditional moral education programs. First, teachers encourage students to ask questions rather than absorb pat answers – to think about their attachments and commitments to their local, national, and global communities. Second, teachers provide students with the information (including competing narratives) they need to think about subject-matter in substantive ways. Third, they root instruction in local contexts, working within their own specific surroundings and circumstances because it is not possible to teach democratic forms of thinking without providing an environment to think about.

CHALLENGE FOR MORAL EDUCATORS

Many of the most popular moral education programs focus first and foremost on virtues – last month honesty, this month integrity, next month loyalty, and so on. As a recipe for unquestioning obedience, the rationale for this kind of educational approach might be compelling. But for those who want to develop ethical citizens, able to critically evaluate public policies and act on their beliefs, the challenge lies rather in creating a school environment in which the ethical life can flourish. This kind of school environment is under attack either directly or indirectly in many school reform policies. Indeed, many educators concerned with the ethical development of children and with societal improvement would find their goals well-represented by turn-of-the-20th-century progressives. John Dewey, for example, called for school activities to constitute a continuous engagement with social aim of the community. Under these conditions, he wrote in 1916, "the school becomes itself a form of social life, a miniature community, and one in close interaction with other modes of associated experience beyond school walls... All education which develops power to share effectively in [such a] social life is moral" (Dewey, 1916, p.360). The progressives, while concerned with the moral development of the individual, laid that concern squarely in the broader struggle towards a better society. Their hopes for change reflected the historical power of social movements and democratic participation in social and political movements. They sought "not to instill and reinforce specific virtues but to engage in the skills of democratic citizenship: deliberation, problem solving, and participation in governance of the group" (Berkowitz, 2004, p. 192). As Jeffrey McClellan (1999, cited in Berkowitz, 2004) observes, progressives,

> consistently gave more attention to great social and political issues than to matters of private conduct. Reversing the emphasis of earlier moral educators, they expressed little interest in the drinking habits or sexual conduct of individuals as long as such personal behavior did not impede the ability to operate as intelligent and productive citizens. (p. 57).

Education is without a doubt both a moral and a political enterprise. We all want to live next to people who do not lie, who pick up their trash, who are hard-working, cheerful, and who, for the most part, obey the law. But, as I have suggested and as many advocates of moral education observe, moral education too often through both omission and commission, advances a far darker side of individual character, one that works towards neither democratic, nor global, nor – many would argue – moral behavior. Although there are many who are careful to define their work in moral development in terms that embrace the goals of democracy, diversity, and social justice, when it comes to schools, they are often found locked in opposition, or worse in uneasy but oddly productive cahoots with those who equate morality with the status quo and with the most conservative neo-liberal forces this world has seen in more than a century. There is good reason to worry that the more we allow cultural, social, and political problems to be defined exclusively as individualistic and moral ones, the more we further the work of this latter group.

Often when I have spoken about these issues, I have inadvertently conveyed a sense that I am somehow against the idea of schools teaching personal responsibility (or what some readers might consider "character" or "virtues." I have never intended to suggest that there is something wrong with developing a sense of personally responsible citizenship in young people (except to the extent it conflicts with critical thinking). I am only suggesting that personally responsible citizenship is only a partial response. We also need citizens to be able to talk about visions of the good society and think critically about policies that help or hinder their goals. And we need citizens who can take action on ideas they believe in to help improve society. But personal responsibility is still an important disposition to teach, as I will illustrate with a personal story.

I am from New York City. On the morning of the September 11 terrorist attacks, I stood with my wife and daughter on a street corner 18 city blocks away from the World Trade Center. We watched as the second plane hit the South tower. Soon after, we watched both buildings collapse into the impossibly dense financial district streets below. I can't properly describe for you the haunting silence, shock, and grief in the minutes that followed. It spread across our fellow New Yorkers – who stood with us on that corner and on countless other corners, in cafés, and in living rooms throughout the city. It was not long after the second tower fell that the first office workers arrived at our corner covered in dust and debris and carrying first-hand accounts of what had happened. As rumors of gas explosions spread and as the enormity of the events slowly revealed themselves, we raced home to fetch bicycles and pedal uptown to Washington Heights, the northern Manhattan community where my mother lives – still close by but removed from the noxious air that ensued for months after the attacks. We spent the next few days, like most New Yorkers, communing with others on the streets, in local restaurants, and in parks, trying to make sense of the unthinkable. I tell this here because I want to draw your attention to the fact that I fully considered only weeks after September 11: While we were standing on that street corner, tens of thousands of schoolchildren in lower Manhattan were with their teachers. In fact, until we went to get my daughter, she too was in a pre-school.

In the book *Forever After: New York City Teachers and 9/11*, dozens of teachers tell stories of being put in impossible situations, many of them on their 3rd or 4th day of teaching. These teachers picked a vocation defined by responsibility for the young. But they never could have imagined what that responsibility would entail. The teachers responded in all different ways: had children sing songs; draw pictures; get in lines; escorted them outside; grabbed hands and ran as fast as they could. Some children saw people jump from the burning towers; some children and teachers were covered in debris. Some were frightened; others confused. Teachers didn't really know what to do. Nobody did. But every one of those teachers – on their fourth day of the school year – knew that they were teachers and that they held enormous personal responsibility for those children. Patricia Lent, one of the teachers whose story is told in this book, was a third grade teacher who taught at PS 234, right under the collapsing towers – she ran with her children uptown to PS 41 and to safety. Eight months after that harrowing day, she asked her young students "what do you remember most about September 11?" And one of the little boys said, "what I remember most is that you held my hand and never let go." Let's hope that none of us are ever put into a similar situation. But in many ways – big and small – as educators, we all hold personal responsibility for the people we teach. And as citizens, we all hold personal responsibility for each other.

At the same time, moral educators interested in developing the ethical predispositions long associated with democratic citizenship have a responsibility to advance at least the three dimensions of citizenship I have described. Personal responsibility is not the same as participation in the civic and political life of the community. Similarly, personal responsibility and participation do not guarantee an orientation towards justice. For those interested in schooling's civic purposes, it is not enough to argue that moral values as important as traditional academic priorities. We must also ask what kind of values. What political and ideological interests are embedded in varied conceptions of citizenship and moral behavior? How do these values encourage or discourage deep thinking about social problems? How do these different values encourage or discourage action? Through questions such as these, we can assess whether students will be ready to take action to make our world more humane and more just. That is a goal for moral education that I believe we should all be able to support.

NOTES

1   This chapter is adapted from a keynote address delivered at the annual conference of the Association For Moral Education (Freiburg, Switzerland), July 2006. The author would like to thank Fritz Oser and John Snarey for the invitation to present at the conference. The research for this chapter was supported by generous grants from the Social Sciences and Humanities Research Council of Canada, the Center for Information & Research on Civic Learning & Engagement (CIRCLE), and the University Research Chair Program at the University of Ottawa. Wiel Veugelers gave thoughtful feedback on an earlier presentation of these ideas.
2   Most notably, research conducted with my longtime colleague Joe Kahne of Mills College in Oak-

land, California but also with Sharon Cook, Gina Bottamini, Alessandra Iozzo, Kristina Llewellyn, Alison Molina, and karen emily suurtamm at the University of Ottawa.

3 Historically, school-based moral education programs relied on "codes of conduct" to convey a set of core values to children (McClellan, 1999) and many contemporary character education programs continue to follow in this tradition. The Children's Morality Code, published in 1917 by William Hutchins, for example, suggested that children be taught ten laws of "right living." These included: self-control, good health, kindness, sportsmanship, self-reliance, duty, reliability, truth, good workmanship, and team work. Similarly, contemporary programs that emphasize the popular "Six Pillars of Character" (from the Josephson Institute of Ethics): trustworthiness, respect, responsibility, fairness, caring and citizenship.

4 Westheimer & Kahne, (2004).

5 See also Schudson, The Good Citizen, 1998 for his discussion of 'colonial citizenship' "built on social hierarchy...and the traditions of public service, personal integrity, [and] charitable giving..." (294).

6 See Kahne, Westheimer, & Rogers (2000).

REFERENCES

Althof, W. & Berkowitz, M. (2006). Moral education and character education: their relationship and roles in citizenship education. *Journal of Moral Education, 35*, 4, 495–518 .

Anderson, A. (2006). *The Way We Argue Now*. Princeton, NJ: Princeton University Press.

Berkowitz, M. (1988). Try and catch the wind: Dialogue, dialectics and development in Kohlberg's life and legacy. *Journal of Counseling and Values, 32*, 179-186.

Character Counts (1996). *Character Counts*. Washington DC: Character Counts! Coalition.

Day, J. M. (1991). Role-taking revisited: Narrative and cognitive-developmental interpretations of moral growth. *Journal of Moral Education, 3*, 20, 305-315.

Dewey, J. (1916/1966). *Democracy and education*. New York: Macmillan.

Gonzales, D. (1995, May 23). Alternative schools: A bridge from hope to social action. *New York Times*, p. B2.

Greene, M. (2000). *Releasing the imagination: Essays on education, the arts, and social change*. New York: Jossey-Bass.

Holt, J. (1995). *How Children Fail*. New York Press: Da Capo Press.

Kahne, J., Westheimer, J. & Rogers, B. (2000). Service learning and citizenship: Directions for research. *Michigan Journal of Community Service Learning*.

Kohn, A. (2004). *What does it mean to be well educated?* Boston, MA: Beacon Press.

Kohlberg, L. (1976). This special section in perspective. *Social Education*, 213-215.

Lickona, T. (1991). *Education for character: How our schools can teach respect and responsibility. New York: Bantam Books.*

Lind, G. (2000). The importance of role-taking opportunities for self-sustaining moral development. *Journal of Research in Education, 10*, 9-15.

McClellan, B. E. (1999). *Moral education in America*. New York: Teachers College Press.

Noddings, N. (2007). *Critical lessons: What our schools should teach*. Cambridge: Cambridge University Press.

North Central Regional Educational Laboratory. (2000). *Viewpoints: Vol. 7: Small by design—Resizing America's high schools*. Naperville, IL: Learning Points Associates.

Peterson, B. (2007). La Escuela Fratney: A journey toward democracy. In M. Apple & J. Beane (Eds.), *Democratic schools: Lessons in powerful education* (pp. 30–61). Portsmouth, NH: Heinemann.

Ryan, K. (1989). In defense of character education. In Larry P. Nucci, ed., *Moral development and character education: A dialogue*. Berkeley, Calif.: McCutchan, 1989.

Schudson, M. (1998). *The good citizen: A history of American civic life*. New York: Free Press.

Schultz, B. D. (2008). *Spectacular things happen along the way: Lessons from an urban classroom.* New York: Teachers College Press.

Shapiro, H. S. (2005). *Losing heart: The moral and spiritual mis-education of America's children.* New York: Lawrence Erlbaum.

Veugelers, W. & Oser, F.K. (2003) (Eds) *Teaching in moral and democratic education.* Bern: Peter Lang.

Veugelers, W. (2007). Creating critical democratic citizenship education: Empowering humanity and democracy in Dutch education. *Compare, 37,* 1, 103-119.

Walker, L. J. (1983). Sources of cognitive conflict for stage transition in moral development. *Developmental Psychology, 19,* 103-110.

Westheimer, J. & Kahne, J. (2004). What kind of citizen? The politics of educating for democracy. American Educational Research Journal. *Summer. 41*(2), 237-269.

Westheimer, J. (2005). *Real world learning: El Puente Academy and educational change* (Democratic Dialogue occasional paper series). Ottawa, Ontario: DemocraticDialogue.com.

Westheimer J. (2007). (Ed.). *Pledging allegiance: The politics of patriotism in America's schools.* New York: Teachers College Press.

Joel Westheimer
University of Ottawa, Canada

RUTH DEAKIN-CRICK

PEDAGOGY FOR CITIZENSHIP

INTRODUCTION

Citizenship education became a statutory requirement for secondary schools in England from September 2002 and a recommended subject for primary schools with guidelines in the form of a framework for personal, social and health education and citizenship. The history of the development of this policy initiative spans the 1990s and has been informed by the requirements of the 1992 Education Act, which required OFSTED to report on the spiritual, moral, social and cultural development of students in schools. Significant among the resulting policies were developments in personal, social and health education; and a range of initiatives, which addressed the personal and social aspects of student development, including the National Forum for Values in Education and the Community[1]. All these initiatives have been informed by growing societal concerns about values and the personal development of young people. Resources for citizenship education are provided from within the voluntary sector and from government departments.

Alongside these policy developments, there has been a much greater emphasis on improving standards in education, focusing mostly on measurable learning outcomes but, more recently in the UK, a significant emphasis on the processes of learning, and the use of assessment for learning rather than simply of learning outcomes. These policy initiatives are generally seen as distinct and separate from the initiatives surrounding citizenship and values. However, evidence from a systematic review (Deakin Crick et al., 2004) suggests that when schools address citizenship education, defined in its broadest sense, then there are implications for the core tasks of schooling and in particular for the context and manner in which students learn. This paper reports on the findings of a second systematic review which focused on the relationship between citizenship education and learning and achievement (Deakin Crick et al., 2005).

DEFINITIONAL AND CONCEPTUAL ISSUES

Within England, and to some extent the five nations of the UK, the Crick Report (1998) provides the current framework for citizenship education. Crick defined citizenship education as including three distinct strands: moral and social responsibility, community involvement and political literacy. The programmes of study for the National Curriculum appear to focus more on political literacy, but many of the outcomes are in the domain of personal development. Citizenship is linked in these documents to whole school ethos and organisation, to values education and to the spiritual, moral, social and cultural development of students. While much discretion is left to individual schools, it is clearly expected that citizenship education will appear in discrete curriculum time, across the whole curriculum and in extracurricular activities and be related to the school's particular vision and values.

The report identified four distinct elements of Citizenship Education, which it suggested should be reached by the end of compulsory schooling. These are key concepts, values and dispositions, skills and aptitudes, and knowledge and understanding. The skills in particular relate to cognitive and social learning processes, while the values and dispositions relate to moral concerns some of which are reminiscent of Smith and Spurling's (1999) moral components of lifelong learning.

The first systematic review addressed the question of the impact of citizenship education on the processes and structures of schooling (Deakin Crick et al., 2004). The findings of that review, based on 14 studies from around the world, indicated that citizenship education does have a significant impact on school processes and structures. The implications of this are important for school leaders as they address policies relating to teaching and learning; leadership and management; school ethos and context; external relations; and community and curriculum construction and development.

The combined findings relating to these themes are summarised here:
- – The quality of dialogue and discourse is central to learning in citizenship education.
- – Dialogue and discourse are connected with learning about shared values, human rights, and issues of justice and equity.
- – A facilitative, conversational pedagogy may challenge existing power structures.
- – Transformative, dialogical and participatory pedagogies complement and sustain achievement rather than divert attention from it.
- – Such pedagogies require quality of teacher-student relationships that are inclusive and respectful.
- – Students should be empowered to voice their views, and to name and make meaning from their life experiences.
- – Contextual knowledge and problem-based thinking can lead to (citizenship) engagement and action.
- – Engagement of students in citizenship education requires educational experiences that are challenging, attainable and relevant to students' lives and narratives.
- – Opportunities should be made for students to engage with values issues embedded in all curriculum subjects and experiences.
- – A coherent whole-school strategy, including a community-owned values framework, is a key part of leadership for citizenship education.
- – Participative and democratic processes in school leadership require particular

attitudes and skills on the part of teachers and students.

—· Listening to the voice of the student leads to positive relationships, an atmosphere of trust and increased participation. It may require many teachers to 'let go of control'.

—· Teachers require support to develop appropriate professional skills to engage in discourse and dialogue, and to facilitate citizenship education.

—· Strategies for consensual change have to be identified by, and developed in, educational leaders.

—· Schools often restrict participation by students in shaping institutional practices but expect them to adhere to policies and this can be counterproductive to the core messages of citizenship education.

THE RELATIONSHIP BETWEEN CITIZENSHIP EDUCATION AND ACHIEVEMENT

On the basis of these findings, the Review Group undertook a second systematic review to focus on the relationship between citizenship education and learning and achievement. For the purposes of this review Citizenship education was understood as all of those planned experiences that school-based educators construct for their students in order to fulfil the different aims and purposes of citizenship education. These may be formal or informal, explicit or implicit, extra-curricular, cross-curricular or within particular curriculum strands. Citizenship education also includes the provision for pastoral and personal development of students and relates to both pedagogy and school ethos and culture.

The conceptual framework provided a starting point for the review was drawn from Crick (1998). This framework was selected because it was itself the outcome of considerable research, development and consultation, drawing on a wide range of processes that together were referred to at the time, as forming 'preparation for adult life' initiatives. It is also a framework that defines the scope of citizenship education in England and although its terminology is contested, it is 'maximal' in its scope and provided a broad framework around which to focus the study. However, internationally there are other terms which refer to aspects of citizenship education, and in order to capture the widest possible range of curriculum activities the terms described in Table 1 were used in searching and in keywording.

Table 1. Search terms for 'citizenship educaiton'

Citizenship Education	Educational programmes which are designed to:
Moral and social responsibility	Develop in learners' moral and social attitudes, values, beliefs and behaviours.
Community involvement	Engage learners in learning and service in the wider community or the school community.
Political literacy	Equip learners with the knowledge, skills, values, attitudes and know how to engage in public life.
Spiritual moral social and cultural development	Develop in learners any aspect of personal development which is not measured as a cognitive learning outcome.
Education for diversity	Nurture in learners an understanding of difference between groups and cultures and a capacity to engage positively with groups and cultures 'different in some way from me'. Includes race, disability, gender, religion, ethnicity, sexual orientation.
Character education	Contribute to the formation of a person's – values, virtues, character and behaviour – which is beneficial to self, others and society.
Emotional and social literacy	Develop the capacity to understand one's own emotions, others' emotions and to use that knowledge effectively.
Values education	Nurture learners in an understanding of and a personal engagement with values.
Service learning	Engage learners in learning which is constructed as service in the wider community or the school community.
Conflict resolution	Enable learners to understand and resolve personal and communal conflicts.
Peer mediation	Enable learners to support peers in resolving conflicts.
Human rights education	Lead to an understanding of human rights and an engagement with the values of human rights legislation.

LEARNING AND ACHIEVEMENT

The terms learning and achievement were used to capture both the processes and the outcomes of learning that may, theoretically, be associated with citizenship education. Learning processes include those cognitive, affective and volitional processes, attitudes and dispositions that operate in order for students to learn. 'Learning outcomes' refers to achievement, when that is determined by a summative assessment either by teachers, or by tests or examinations. The domains of achievement are not limited to cognitive outcomes, although these are the most readily understood, as, for example, in the knowledge, skills or understanding required for particular levels in a subject of the curriculum. Specific curricular outcomes, such as these, are often referred to as 'attainment'. For the purpose of this review, 'achievement' was understood as a learning outcome, which may be assessed by teachers or students and which may pertain to cognitive, personal, social, emotional, or moral/political domains of human experience.

Achievement in citizenship education, for example, could be determined by a portfolio or narrative account of particular service activities or experiences a student has recorded and evaluated. Less common, achievement measures could be a 'citizenship award' for particular service to the community, or the 'learner of the week' award in a classroom where the processes of learning are valued as much as the outcomes. It could also be a teacher or self-assessment of a students social skills, such as empathy or conflict resolution.

THE REVIEW METHODOLOGY

Funding for this review was provided by CitizEd – a professional resource network in the UK funded by the Teacher Development Agency (TDA) and by the EPPI-Centre, which was established in 1999 with UK Government funding to support groups in undertaking systematic reviews of research in education to inform policy and practice. Its aim is to provide, in the education sector, a resource that gives policy makers and practitioners access to constantly updated results from synthesised research evidence. As a condition of funding, reviews are undertaken by groups, using systematic protocols and procedures briefly described later, which provide precise parameters for the review specification[2].

The literature was restricted to studies conducted with students aged 4-18, and excluded further and higher education. The search for studies was completed in 2004 and any studies published after this date were not included. A further limitation was that the review included studies published in English, and although theoretically studies from all around the world could be included, it meant that studies published only in other languages were excluded.

Within this framework, the review included all types of studies, from a range of research genres. The term 'intervention' was used to describe any intentional pedagogical activity which met the criteria for citizenship education. The review attempted to appraise the weight of evidence of each study and this was based on a composite judgement of its methodological soundness, the relevance of the study type to the review and the extent to which the study addressed the review question. This overall judgement is review specific and does not represent a view of the quality of a study in its own right.

REVIEW QUESTION

The overall question addressed in the review was as follows:

What is the impact of citizenship education on student learning and achievement?

In order to achieve all the aims of the review, it was necessary to address the following further question:

What are the implications of the findings of the review for teacher education?

The term 'impact' was used in this review question with care. It could imply a linear, cause-effect relationship between an independent variable and a dependent variable. However, the Review Group was concerned that such a narrow definition might not do justice to the complexity of the two variables, and the iterative relationship between them.

LITERATURE SEARCH

Addressing these questions involved seeking out a range of studies of different types. Both intervention studies and non-intervention studies were relevant. Intervention studies were those in which a specific citizenship intervention programme was introduced in order to study the effect of citizenship education on student learning and achievement. These studies could be either researcher manipulated (e.g. the researcher had introduced the intervention), or naturally occurring (e.g. the citizenship programme was already occurring prior to any evaluation). These interventions took the form of quasi-experimental studies and some involved the comparison of results between groups who received the intervention and those groups who did not. Non-intervention studies did not involve intervention programmes but included surveys of existing conditions relating to citizenship education in order to describe and identify associations between citizenship programmes and learning processes and outcomes.

The review question served as a framework in the search for studies. All the relevant electronic databases, journals held in accessible libraries and those online were searched, citations in earlier reviews and obtained papers were followed up and personal contacts used to obtain further references. The number of studies relevant to the review question found in this way was 578.

APPLYING INCLUSION AND EXCLUSION CRITERIA AND KEYWORDS

Before obtaining the full text of the studies, inclusion and exclusion criteria were systematically applied to titles and abstracts of the articles. Studies were included if they were empirical studies, written in English, undertaken in a school context, involved citizenship education *and* learning or achievement. The full text of the 48 studies meeting those criteria were then obtained and read. A further 13 were excluded at this stage because of a mismatch between abstract and text, or because the reporting was of insufficient quality. The next step was to describe the remaining 35 studies in terms of a set of keywords relating to study type, source, age range and a set of review specific keywords describing which aspect of citizenship education and which aspects of learning and/or achievement the study addressed. The review specific key words are presented in table 2 below. A definition of each of the key words is provided in appendix one. The keywording and the application of inclusion and exclusion criteria were both undertaken by two reviewers working independently, and then moderated.

Table 2. Review specific keywords

Citizenship Education	Learning	Achievement
Moral and social responsibility Community involvement Political literacy Human rights education Education for diversity Spiritual moral social and cultural development Personal development Character education Emotional and social literacy Values education Service learning Active learning Conflict resolution Peer mediation Community participation Responsible action Civics Preparation for adult life	Creative thinking Critical thinking Meta-cognition Experiential learning Meaning-making Inter- and intra-personal awareness, including empathy Communication skills Collaboration Problemsolving/decision-making Values awareness	Cognitive outcomes (e.g. logical, linguistic, mathematical) Personal outcomes (e.g. inter and intra-personal development) Social outcomes (e.g. relationships with groups, societies, communities, organisations and the world) Moral and political outcomes (e.g. political literacy, political knowledge, ethical decision-making)

FINAL SELECTION OF STUDIES

At this point a detailed 'map' of the included studies was discussed by the review group. The resource implications and complexity of the map led to a decision to focus only on those studies which addressed cognitive learning outcomes, leaving the remaining studies for a future review process. Of particular interest to the group was the relationship between citizenship education and the development of knowledge, skills and understanding. The in-depth review question was therefore:

What is the impact of citizenship education on students' cognitive learning outcomes?

EXTRACTION AND EVALUATION OF EVIDENCE FROM STUDIES

Data extraction was carried out using the guidelines for coding and quality assessing educational research (EPPI-Centre 2003b) applying the EPPI Reviewer – the EPPI-Centre's software. This rigorous and quality assured process led to a set of research evidence which was then available for synthesis. In order to bring the studies together to form conclusions, the studies were reported initially in terms of evidence of cognitive outcomes, such as higher order, critical and abstract thinking, conceptual and creative thinking with the application of concepts and principles to situations, meta-cognition, meaning-making and making connections between concepts and experiences, communication skills, problem-solving/decision-making, the award of grades and academic achievement. Other significant outcomes, such as social and personal outcomes were reported on secondarily where relevant, because, while not being cognitive, these outcomes were recognised as making a fundamental contribution to the cognitive learning and achievement of the whole person.

The details of the findings of each study are reported in the full review text[3] while a summary of the studies is reported in table 3. At this stage the findings were then peer reviewed, both in a consultation meeting and in writing.

Table 3. Details of Selected Studies (see Appendix A for full references)

Study	Country	Study type	Citizenship education	Learning	Achievement	Overall weight of evidence	Age Group
Beyer and Presseisen (1995)	USA	Evaluation: Researcher-manipulated	Moral and social responsibility Spiritual moral social and cultural development Spiritual moral social and cultural development Values education Human rights education	Critical thinking Meaning-making Inter-personal awareness Values awareness	Cognitive outcomes Social outcomes Moral and political outcomes	Medium	Middle School
Black and Goldowsky (1999)	USA	Evaluation: Naturally occurring	Moral and social responsibility Spiritual moral social and cultural development Values education	Creative thinking Critical thinking Meaning-making Values awareness	Cognitive outcomes Personal outcomes Social outcomes Moral and political outcomes	Medium	High school
Clare et al. (1996)	USA	Exploration of relationships	Moral and social responsibility Spiritual moral social and cultural development Character education	Critical thinking Meaning-making Intra-personal awareness	Cognitive outcomes Moral and political outcomes	Medium	Primary
Day (2002)	England	Evaluation: Researcher-manipulated	Moral and social responsibility Spiritual moral social and cultural development Emotional and social literacy	Critical thinking Inter-personal awareness Collaboration Values awareness	Cognitive outcomes Personal outcomes Social outcomes Moral and political outcomes	Medium	Secondary

Study	Country	Study type	Citizenship education	Learning	Achievement	Overall weight of evidence	Age Group
Deakin Crick (2002)	England	Exploration of relationships	Moral and social responsibility Community involvement Spiritual moral social and cultural development Character education Values education Service learning	Creative thinking Critical thinking Meaning-making Inter-personal awareness Intra-personal awareness Communication skills Collaboration Values awareness	Cognitive outcomes Personal outcomes Social outcomes Moral and political outcomes	Medium	Secondary
Faubert et al. (1996)	USA	Evaluation: Researcher-manipulated:	Character education	Creative thinking Critical thinking Meaning-making Inter-personal awareness Intra-personal awareness	Cognitive outcomes Personal outcomes	Medium	Secondary
Garcia-Obregon et al. (2000)	USA	Evaluation: Naturally occurring	Moral and social responsibility Community involvement Spiritual moral social and cultural development Service learning	Experiential learning Meaning-making Inter-personal awareness	Cognitive outcomes Personal outcomes Social outcomes	Medium	Secondary
Laconte et al. (1993)	USA	Evaluation: Researcher-manipulated	Moral and social responsibility Character education	Intra-personal awareness Communication skills Problem-solving/ decision-making	Cognitive outcomes Personal outcomes Social outcomes	Low	

Melchior (1999)	USA	Evaluation: Naturally occurring	Community involvement Service learning	Experiential learning Meaning-making Inter-personal awareness Intra-personal awareness	Cognitive outcomes Personal outcomes Social outcomes Moral and political outcomes	Medium	
Polite and Adams (1997)	USA	Exploration of relationships	Moral and social responsibility Emotional and social literacy Values education	Creative thinking Critical thinking Experiential learning Meaning-making Communication skills Problem-solving/ decision-making	Cognitive outcomes Personal outcomes Social outcomes Moral and political outcomes	Medium	Secondary
Russell (2002)	Ireland	Evaluation: Naturally occurring	Moral and social responsibility Spiritual moral social and cultural development Emotional and social literacy Values education	Creative thinking Critical thinking Meta-cognition Meaning-making Inter-personal awareness Intra-personal awareness Values awareness	Cognitive outcomes Social outcomes Moral and political outcomes	Medium	Secondary
Tibbitts (2001)	Romania	Evaluation: Researcher-manipulated	Political Literacy Values education	Critical thinking Communication skills Collaboration Values awareness	Cognitive outcomes Personal outcomes Social outcomes Moral and political outcomes	Medium	Secondary
Wade (1994)	USA	Evaluation: Naturally occurring	Human rights education	Critical thinking Meaning-making Intra-personal awareness Values awareness	Cognitive outcomes Personal outcomes Social outcomes	High	Primary

KEY THEMES EMERGING FROM THE FINDINGS

The findings from the 13 studies were synthesised into five categories of cognitive learning outcomes and five learning processes. Although this review focused on the 13 studies that reported on evidence of impact on cognitive learning outcomes, these studies all reported evidence relating to other types of outcomes and a range of learning processes. The evidence suggests that it is the interrelatedness of affective, cognitive, and volitional learning processes, interacting together in a cohesive and well planned citizenship education programme (Melchior, 1999; Deakin Crick 2002), which has an impact on the achievement of the learner as a whole person, who then displays greater self-confidence and is a more potent learner (Faubert et al. (1996).

An overarching finding is that the effects of these variables are difficult to study independently of each other because they function together more in the manner of a complex 'ecology' rather than as a set of discrete entities. Thus the evidence suggests that learning and achievement in citizenship education is a complex domain, which cannot be reduced to a single variable. Student learning and achievement is associated with the nature and quality of the pedagogy of the subject. The following discussion will deal with these factors together to reflect this complexity.

COGNITIVE LEARNING OUTCOMES

The five categories of cognitive learning outcomes (table 4) drawn from across the 13 studies
- meaning-making
- understanding and reasoning
- higher order thinking skills
- academic achievement
- communication skills

Table 4. Emergent cognitive learning outcomes findings from in-depth review

Cognitive learning outcomes	Characteristics	Study
Meaning-making	Making connections, making sense of content, apply knowledge to personal experiences – in own world and society	Beyer and Presseisen (1995), Black and Goldowsky (1999), Clare et al. (1996), Day (2002), Deakin Crick (2002), Melchior (1999), Polite and Adams (1997), Russell (2002), Tibbitts (2001), Wade (1994)
Understanding and reasoning	Improved understanding, reasoning, decision-making, problem-solving	Beyer and Presseisen (1995), Black and Goldowsky (1999), Clare et al. (1996), Day (2002), Deakin Crick (2002), Faubert et al. (1996), Melchior (1999), Polite and Adams (1997), Russell (2002), Wade (1994)
Higher order thinking skills	Meta-cognition, abstract, complex, critical, analytical, reflective and conceptual thinking	Black and Goldowsky (1999), Deakin Crick (2002), Faubert et al. (1996), Polite and Adams (1997), Russell (2002), Tibbitts (2001), Wade (1994)
Academic achievement	Improved grades, increased achievement/ability, cognitive engagement/ functioning	Beyer and Presseisen (1995), Garcia-Obregon et al. (2000), Melchior (1999), Polite and Adams (1997), Wade (1994)
Communication skills	Self-expression, debate, listening	Black and Goldowsky (1999), Day (2002), Russell (2002), Wade (1994)

LEARNING PROCESSES

The following learning processes (table 5) were identified from the findings as making a significant contribution to the five categories of cognitive learning outcomes.
– engagement
– promoting discussion
– learner-centred teaching
– meaningful curricula
– developing personally

Table 5. Learning processes findings of in-depth review

Learning processes	Characteristics	Study
Engagement	Increased opportunities to participate and interactive participation, explore, student 'voice', self-expression, felt listened to and what they said mattered; student self-responsibility for own decisions, choices and own work; student self-reliance, student engagement.	Black and Goldowsky (1999), Clare et al. (1996), Day (2002), Deakin Crick (2002), Faubert et al (1996), Garcia-Obregon et al. (2000), Melchior (1999), Polite and Adams (1997), Russell (2002), Wade (1994)
Promoting discussion	Discussions, teacher-learner dialogue, conversational discourse, open-ended questions, communication and listening skills, cooperative learning environment, holistic teacher-learner relationship, learner-learner relationship.	Black and Goldowsky (1999), Clare et al. (1996), Day (2002), Deakin Crick (2002), Melchior (1999), Polite and Adams (1997), Russell (2002), Wade (1994)
Learner- centred teaching	Teacher technical skills to lead discussions, clarify and summarise, knowledge of student ability level and appropriateness of teaching material, learner-centred approaches/facilitators versus didactic traditional methods insufficient/teachers no longer reciters of wisdom; students learn through doing/relating content to own experiences, essays, research papers, writing and making presentations, group and individual work, journal-keeping, weekly written reflection exercises.	Clare et al. (1996), Day (2002), Deakin Crick (2002), Faubert et al (1996), Melchior (1999), Russell (2002), Tibbitts (2001), Wade (1994)
Meaningful curricula	Real-life contexts, connecting historical/abstract with real-life experience of students, theatre, role-play, festival presentations, simulation, drama, art and writing activities, seminar forums, formal, informal settings, programme length, quality of programme/delivery makes a difference.	Beyer and Presseisen (1995), Black and Goldowsky (1999), Day (2002), Deakin Crick (2002), Faubert et al. (1996), Laconte et al. (1993), Melchior (1999), Polite and Adams (1997), Russell (2002), Tibbitts (2001), Wade (1994)

| Developing personally | Improved attitudes, behaviour, better attendance, positive experiences, positive self-image and self-confidence, care and respect for others, ability to respond, conflict-resolution skills, increased interest in learning, beneficial impacts non-white, educationally disadvantaged, and students with learning difficulties. | Clare et al. (1996), Faubert et al. (1996), Garcia-Obregon et al. (2000), Melchior (1999), Polite and Adams (1997), Russell (2002) |

DISCUSSION OF FINDINGS: COGNITIVE LEARNING OUTCOMES

Meaning-making

There is strong support from the study findings that citizenship education can engage children to seek (cognitive) understanding for the meaning of their personal stories and experiences when acquiring conceptual knowledge and knowledge of others' situations (Beyer and Presseisen, 1995; Black and Goldowsky, 1999; Day, 2002; Polite and Adams, 1997). There is evidence that students' motivation to participate increased when topics were pertinent and relevant to their own experiences and they could make connections between the content and experiences in their personal lives (Wade, 1994; Polite and Adams, 1997). Students were able to apply knowledge of others' situations to make sense of:

- their own personal and social worlds making learning more meaningful (Black and Goldowsky, 1999; Deakin Crick, 2002)
- the implications of their own actions (Beyer and Presseisen, 1995)
- how they regarded people who may be in similar challenging situations (Day, 2002)

Meaning-making was linked to innovative learner-centred media, such as the use of theatre, role-play, simulations, conversational instructional discourse, discussion, journal-keeping and reflection exercises (Black and Goldowsky, 1999; Clare et al., 1996; Deakin Crick, 2002; Faubert et al., 1996; Melchior, 1999; Wade, 1994). The findings suggest that quality dialogue, thinking and talking and well-designed programmes make a difference and are likely to have an impact on student outcomes (Deakin Crick 2002; Melchior, 1999). Where students were given the opportunity to discuss events in relation to their personal experiences, this aided them in connecting their world with a curriculum content that they would otherwise have seen as disparate and unrelated to their life (Faubert et al., 1996).

The implication is citizenship education can enhance students' ability to make meaning of and connections between their personal stories and society.

45

Understanding and reasoning

Students' understanding and inductive and deductive reasoning, were enhanced and developed (Deakin Crick, 2002; Polite and Adams, 1997; Russell, 2002) in citizenship education through the use of meaningful curricula and learner-centred processes such as:

– dialogue and debate – class conferences, conversational discussions, seminars (Clare et al., 1996; Polite and Adams, 1997; Wade, 1994)
– increased participation – group and individual, presentation, research, discussion (Clare et al., 1996; Deakin Crick, 2002; Faubert et al., 1996; Polite and Adams, 1997; Russell, 2002)
– opportunities for reflection – watching theatre, journal-keeping, weekly written exercises (Day, 2002; Faubert et al., 1996; Melchior, 1999).

Students' understanding of the process of conceptual change can influence their understanding of lesson content and their cognitive engagement (Wade, 1994) leading to a better understanding of community (Melchior, 1999). It is evident from the studies that student reasoning skills about human relationships (Beyer and Presseisen, 1995) were helped and enhanced with students better able to reason about social, moral and ethical issues of different subjects, such as science, that may impact their lives (Black and Goldowsky, 1999). The evidence suggests that students were better able to comprehend problems (Clare et al., 1996), their thinking skills went beyond levels normal for their classroom (Deakin Crick, 2002; Russell, 2002) and that students developed a greater reliance on problem-solving (Faubert et al., 1996).

The implication is that citizenship education can improve students' understanding and reasoning skills.

Higher order thinking skills

There is support in the study findings by Polite and Adams (1997) that citizenship education can engage and encourage students in meta-cognitive processes and this is achieved through the processes of learner-centred pedagogy and meaningful curricula. Where teachers assisted students with developmentally appropriate questions, students' critical thinking skills in moral or social reasoning were increased (Clare et al., 1996). Students' conceptual thinking; ability to analyse, consider and grasp multiple ideas and abstract concepts (Deakin Crick, 2002; Tibbitts, 2001); their ability to make sense of the abstract notions of the lesson content and to reconsider their ideas in the light of new information (Wade, 1994) were all outcomes of these studies. Conceptual abstract thinking and thought provoking curricula increased students ability to link complex and moral issues (Black and Goldowsky, 1999), facilitating students to move beyond basic points and superficial understanding to explore the moral and emotional qualities of issues (Clare et al.,

1996). The provision of citizenship education can result in statistically significant positive changes in formal operational thought through movement from concrete literal thinking to abstract and scientific thinking (Faubert et al., 1996) resulting in higher levels of reflection.

The implication is that the provision of citizenship education can engage and enhance students' higher order thinking skills.

Academic achievement

Evidence from across the studies show that citizenship education improved students' grades and academic achievement. There was a positive impact on grades, with increased achievement, cognitive engagement and cognitive functioning (Deakin Crick, 2002; Melchior, 1999; Polite and Adams, 1997); the development of further knowledge (Wade, 1994); and gains in cognitive abilities (Faubert et al., 1996; Garcia-Obregon et al., 2000). There was some evidence that service learning had a stronger impact on academic achievement among non-whites, along with improved school performance (Melchior, 1999).

The implication is that the provision of citizenship education can enhance students' academic achievement.

Communication skills

There is evidence of increased communication skills (Black and Goldowsky, 1999; Day, 2002), which is closely related to participation and dialogue. Where students received increased opportunities to participate in dialogue and structured class discussions, they could express themselves freely and justify and explain their views (Wade, 1994). Citizenship education was found to enhance students' abilities to develop, debate and express complex moral and social themes (Clare et al., 1996) and encouraged students to respond to each other with a deepening ability to actively listen and reciprocate to others (Clare et al., 1996; Faubert et al., 1996; Russell, 2002)

The implication is that the provision of citizenship improved students' communication skills. Learning processes emerged as contributing to the achievement of cognitive learning outcomes.

Engagement

There is evidence from the studies that contextual knowledge, problem-based thinking and matching learning content with pedagogy seemed to result in increased student engagement, participation and action for individuals and groups (Clare et al.,

1996; Day, 2002; Deakin Crick, 2002; Faubert et al., 1996; Polite and Adams, 1997; Russell, 2002). The studies presented evidence that students learn in an experiential manner through 'doing' and through their own 'lived' experience and that they can apply what they have learned in this way to other situations to either express empathy or take action (Clare et al., 1996; Day, 2002). In addition, there was evidence of active programme participation having an impact on student career choice (Melchior, 1999), and that citizenship programmes can impact on student cognitive growth (Faubert et al., 1996).

The implication is that the provision of citizenship education through students' engagement and active participation can contribute to students' cognitive learning outcomes.

Promoting discussion

A common feature throughout the studies is the practice of increased opportunities for students to make a contribution such as in a group discussion, dialogue, conversational discourse or debate (Clare et al., 1996). These practices are highly characteristic of the processes of citizenship education and had an impact on student learning and achievement. Schools' involvement in transformative interactive dialogical pedagogies and democratic processes was not at the expense of, but complementary to, and enhancing of, academic learning and achievement. There was evidence from Russell (2002) and Clare et al. (1996) that a highly interactive and challenging dialogue process helped children refine their ideas and created an opportunity for comprehension and moral growth.

Dialogical pedagogies require quality of relationships, which are inclusive and respectful. When the learner was regarded as a whole person, with affective and volitional and cognitive needs, then teachers related differently to students (Deakin Crick, 2002). The findings show learning and teaching strategies that facilitated a conversational pedagogy, in which dialogue and discussion were the norm, because questioning and dialogue encouraged students in the processes of reflective searching for deeper meaning to issues and events (Clare et al., 1996; Day, 2002; Deakin Crick, 2002; Russell, 2002). Such strategies included weekly class conferences (Wade, 1994), student participation in formal and informal group discussions (Deakin Crick, 2002; Melchior, 1999) and Socratic dialogue (Polite and Adams, 1997).

The implication is that the provision of citizenship education promoted discussion and dialogue, which can contribute to students' cognitive learning outcomes.

Learner-centred teaching

Some of the studies provide evidence that teachers may need to change their pedagogies and will need support in order to develop a more facilitative role and enhance their competencies of questioning, listening and summarising (Clare et al., 1996; Wade, 1994). In cooperative learning environments, where the teacher lets go of control in order to listen to the voice of students, an atmosphere of trust and safety was created that enhanced teacher/student relationships and increased participation (Clare et al., 1996; Deakin Crick, 2002; Polite and Adams, 1997; Russell, 2002). When teachers possess the technical ability skilfully to question, listen, summarise and clarify what the student has said, the students are empowered because they feel listened to and what they have said mattered and was taken seriously (Clare et al., 1996; Polite and Adams, 1997; Russell, 2002). It is an acknowledgement of the student as a person with opinions, and those opinions and contributions are of value. This can in turn lead to a boost in student self-confidence because they think and feel that they have something to meaningful to offer and their stories are of value for others to hear and learn from. This is empowering for students, both cognitively and affectively (Faubert et al., 1996).

The implication is that the provision of learner-centred teaching through citizenship education can contribute to students' cognitive learning outcomes.

Meaningful curricula

The studies provided evidence where the content of the curriculum is relevant and pertinent to students' lives that there is increased motivation to participate (Russell, 2002; Tibbitts, 2001; Wade, 1994). The use of real-life contexts, which were highly relevant to students' personal life experiences, and the use of different media (such as plays and theatre forum), led to students being better able to apply and make connections between events and issues and their own experiences, leading to improved learning, an improved ability to reason about their own and the experiences of others, and an improved ability to reason about the impact of developments on their lives (Beyer and Presseisen, 1995; Black and Goldowsky, 1999; Day, 2002).

The development of meaningful curricula requires a change from traditional teaching methods (Clare et al., 1996; Tibbitts, 2001; Wade, 1994). Greater interactivity, through audience participation (Black and Goldowsky, 1999) and volunteer service in the community, affects students' ability to make meaning of the lesson content and provides a positive experience of participation (Melchior, 1999). When students are given opportunities to make contributions in a discussion or role-play scenario, they are more likely to initiate discussions (Clare et al., 1996) with students expressing a preference for seminar scenarios to the classroom environment (Polite and Adams, 1997), because they learned more than in a regular classroom environment (Wade, 1994). A facilitative pedagogy and meaningful curricula enable students to make deeper connections with lesson content and hence learn on deeper cognitive and affective levels than they might otherwise (Clare et al., 1996; Deakin Crick, 2002). The evidence suggests that more attention should be given to the use of different strategies to encourage greater student participation (Black and Goldowsky, 1999) and that highly interactive and challenging discussion approaches can be a useful tool for educators attempting to enhance comprehension (Clare et al., 1996; Deakin Crick, 2002; Wade, 1994).

The implication is that the provision of citizenship education can enhance students' cognitive learning outcomes through relevant learning experiences and the use of different media.

Developing personally

There is evidence from across the studies that the provision of citizenship education has an impact on personal and social affective outcomes, as well as on cognitive learning outcomes in areas such as the development of self-concept (Faubert et al., 1996), increased self-confidence (Russell, 2002) and more positive behaviour (Melchior, 1999). These were positive impacts on behaviour, with students displaying less risk behaviours and more positive attitudes to society (Melchior, 1999). Students displayed greater empathic and impartial reasoning (Faubert et al., 1996; Russell, 2002) and there were increases in student motivation levels to participate and get involved, in particular when the lesson content was relevant to the students' own experiences. Emotional salience played a significant role in conceptual change (Wade, 1994). Greater gains in self-concept development were evident with students taking greater responsibility for their own choices (Russell, 2002), developing a greater sense of autonomy, working diligently, increasing a firmer sense of self and presenting with poise and confidence (Faubert et al., 1996; Russell, 2002). Decreases in absence levels were reported with a lower number of referrals; more students were reported to be feeling better about themselves; and the programme interventions helped students get along with, and care about, others (Garcia-Obregon et al., 2000). Different learning-centred approaches allowed students to develop and apply conflict resolution skills; seminars gave students the opportunity to witness to other students' contributions (Polite and Adams, 1997) and engage in active listening (Russell, 2002), developing increased feelings of respect for others opinions and noticing differences in peer behaviour, with more polite behaviour commented upon (Polite and Adams, 1997).

The implication is that the provision of citizenship can impact on students' cognitive learning outcomes through helping them to develop personally.

CONCLUSIONS

The review into the impact of Citizenship Education on student learning and achievement offers us a different way of looking at teaching and learning – one that has the potential to improve performance, whilst recognising that the drive for improved performance in itself neither engages nor motivates learners, neither shapes nor energises learning. Four themes emerge from the implications of the review, which can certainly shape, energise, motivate and engage, but which profoundly challenge much familiar practice and policy in our schools. They are the themes of flexibility, relationships, process-orientation and holistic thinking.

Firstly, the review's findings imply the need for a pedagogy reflective of learners' needs, interests, current knowledge, life experience, circumstances, responses and capabilities. This echoes Miliband's definition of 'personalised learning' as 'something very simple... a system tailored to the needs, interests and aptitudes of every single pupil[4]. This Review suggests that such an aim requires flexibility in two important areas: flexible groupings of students, flexible sequencing of curriculum content, thereby allowing teaching and learning to respond to – and so enhance – students' emerging capacity for responsibility and decision-making.

Secondly, the review's findings underline the crucial part played by the quality of relationships in learning. Relationships need to be positive and open, so learning can grow through communication and interaction. They need to be supportive, so the environment is safe for risk-taking. They need to be strong, so misconceptions can be challenged without breakdown. They need to be trusted, for conceptual conflict to be embraced and illuminated without rancour and strongly-held convictions aired and re-considered in the light of new information. Relationships of this quality are incompatible with an authoritarian culture; they are fostered by teachers relinquishing control with confidence and clarity about the structures and ground rules of shared responsibility and mutual respect.

Thirdly, the review significantly challenges a 'didactic' view of curriculum and assessment design. The studies show what a difference it makes when learners have a conceptual 'map' of how their learning works - and why? - and an understanding of the processes of conceptual change. Instead of basing the curriculum on content and simply assessing related knowledge, skills and understanding, it argues for the new approach embodied by such projects as the RSA's 'Opening Minds' curriculum. This makes much more explicit to learners both *processes* of learning and *criteria* for assessment, by developing and self-assessing learning 'competencies' whilst using them to solve problems and access required knowledge through enquiries designed and driven by the learner. These approaches to curriculum design appear to have yielded dramatic improvements in motivation, achievement, continuity and progression between key stages. They do appear, however, to be incompatible with the current format of the National Curriculum and sit uneasily within its assessment framework.

Lastly, there is the repeated insistence on the need for holistic thinking. This comes up in several guises in the studies scrutinised for this Review. One of them speaks of the role of 'emotional salience in fostering motivation to learn and cognitive engagement'. At the heart of the Review's findings is the understanding that intellectual progress is inextricably bound up with feelings; insights come from personal identification with new learning; cognitive development goes hand in hand with emotional development. The 'personal' and 'academic' aspects of a student's progress, just like the 'intellectual' and emotional' components of 'meaning', are as inseparable and co-creative as shape and colour in a watercolour landscape.

The review's holistic theme develops this view of the learner as a 'whole person' by recognising the interplay of thought, feeling and action in all learning and emphasising the vital importance of linking learning with personal experience and story. One of the studies focussed on the positive impact of service learning on mathematics grades, for instance; another on how theatre made science more meaningful by dramatising the moral and ethical reasoning it provoked.

The message is as clear for researchers and policy-makers as it is for students and teachers: that improved academic performance is not best accomplished by being made the single, main or ultimate goal of learning. It would seem, though, that it is the virtually inevitable by-product of meaningful, integrated programmes characterised by learners' own enquiry, rich interaction and effective two-way communication; attention to personal and social development, self-assessment and encouragement of reflective self-awareness in learners and their learning teachers. In short, education for citizenship, done properly, enhances learning and achievement for everyone.

NOTES

1   http://www.nc.uk.net/nc/contents/values.htm
2   For a detailed explanation of the methodology see http://eppi.ioe.ac.uk/cms/
3   http://eppi.ioe.ac.uk/EPPIWeb/home.aspx?page=/reel/reviews.htm
4   David Miliband, then Minister for Schools, in speech to National College for School Leadership Annual Network Conference, October 2004.

REFERENCES AND BIBLIOGRAPHY

Those studies included in both the map and the synthesis are marked with an asterisk.

*Beyer, F.S. & Presseisen, B.Z. (1995). *Facing history and ourselves: Initial evaluation of an inner-city middle school implementation*. Philadelphia, PA, USA: Research for Better Schools, Inc.
*Black, D.R. & Goldowsky, A. (1999). *Science theater as an interpretive technique in a science museum*. Paper presented at the Annual Meeting of the National Association for Research in Science Teaching. Boston, MA, USA: March 28–31.
*Clare, L., Gallimore, R. & Patthey-Chavez, G. (1996). Using moral dilemmas in children's literature as a vehicle for moral education and teaching reading comprehension. *Journal of Moral Education* 25: 325–341.

*Day, L. (2002). 'Putting yourself in other people's shoes': The use of forum theatre to explore refugee and homeless issues in schools. *Journal of Moral Education 31:* 21–34.
*Deakin Crick, R. (2002). *Transforming visions, managing values in schools.* Bristol: Middlesex University Press.
*Faubert, M., Locke, D.C., Sprinthall, N.A. & Howland, W.H. (1996). Promoting cognitive and ego development of African-American rural youth: A program of deliberate psychological education. *Journal of Adolescence 19:* 533–543.
*Garcia-Obregon, Z., Trevino, J., Uribe-Moreno, S. & Zuniga, S. (2000). *The effectiveness of a school based service-learning program 'Community Connection' at a South Texas middle school.* Texas, USA: South Texas Research and Development Center.
*Laconte, M.A., Shaw, D. & Dunn, I. (1993). The effects of a rational-emotive affective education program for high-risk middle school students. *Psychology in the Schools 30:* 274–281.
*Melchior, A. (1999). *Summary report: National evaluation of Learn and Serve America.* Waltham MA: Center for Human Resources, Brandeis University. Available from: http://www.learnandserve. org/pdf/research/lsreport.pdf
*Polite, V.C. & Adams, A.H. (1997). Critical thinking and values clarification through Socratic seminars. *Urban Education 32:* 256–278.
*Russell, J. (2002). Moral consciousness in a community of inquiry. *Journal of Moral Education 31:* 142–153.
*Tibbitts, F. (2001). Prospects for civics education in transitional democracies: Results of an impact study in Romanian classrooms. *Intercultural Education 12:* 27–40.
*Wade, R.C. (1994). Conceptual change in elementary social studies: A case study of fourth graders' understanding of human rights. *Theory and Research in Social Education 22:* 74–95.

OTHER REFERENCES

Crick, B. (1998). *Education for citizenship and the teaching of democracy in schools: Final report of the Advisory Group on Citizenship.* London: Qualifications and Curriculum Authority.
Deakin Crick, R., Coates, M., Taylor M. & Ritchie, S. (2004). A systematic review of the impact of citizenship education on the provision of schooling. In: *Research evidence in education library.* London: EPPI-Centre, Social Science Research Unit, Institute of Education.
Deakin Crick, R., Taylor, M., Tew, M., Samuel, E., Durant, K. & Ritchie, S. (2005). A systematic review of the impact of citizenship education on student learning and achievement. In: *Research evidence in education library.* London: EPPI-Centre, Social Science Research Unit, Institute of Education.
EPPI-Centre (2003a). *Core keywording strategy: Data collection for a register of educational research. Version 0.9.7.* London: EPPI-Centre, Social Science Research Unit.
EPPI-Centre (2003b). *Guidelines for extracting data and quality assessing primary studies in educational research. Version 0.9.5.* London: EPPI-Centre, Social Science Research Unit.
Smith, J. & Spurling, A. (1999). *Lifelong learning: Riding the tiger.* London: Cassell.

Ruth Deakin-Crick
University of Bristol, United Kingdom

APPENDIX – DEFINITIONS OF KEYWORDS

Learning processes	*Definitions*
Creative thinking	This involves relating together principles, ideas, information and entities in new and original ways to generate new entities or ideas.
Critical thinking	This involves the evaluation of arguments or propositions in relation to evidence, reasoning, drawing conclusions.
Meta-cognition	Meta-cognition refers to higher order thinking that involves active control over the cognitive processes engaged in learning. Activities such as planning how to approach a given learning task, monitoring comprehension, and evaluating progress toward the completion of a task are meta-cognitive in nature.
Experiential learning	This is learning that comes from reflection on direct experience.
Meaning-making	This is a person's capacity to make personal meaning from information by integrating different kinds of knowledge. It is the ability to link information gained from different learning arenas and throughout a person's personal history which provides an integration of different kinds of knowing – at personal, group, societal and global levels and across life contexts (home, school and community).
Inter-personal awareness	This is concerned with the capacity to understand the intentions, motivations and desires of other people. It allows people to work effectively with others. Educators, salespeople, religious and political leaders, and counsellors all need a well-developed interpersonal intelligence, including empathy.
Intra-personal awareness	This entails the capacity to understand oneself, to appreciate one's feelings, fears and motivations. In Gardner's (1993) view, it involves having an effective working model of ourselves, and being able to use such information to regulate our lives.
Communication skills	This category includes the range of communication skills: for example, listening, speaking, writing, persuading and influencing etc.
Collaboration	This is the capacity to work with other people in a cooperative way, drawing and building on their ideas and willingly contributing their own.
Problem-solving/decision-making	This involves the whole process of arriving at a decision from generating a range of ideas, screening the ideas to select the most profitable one(s) and employing a mechanism for choosing a limited number for implementation.
Values awareness	This concerns increasing awareness of the values that are held and the implications those values have for life and learning.

Achievement	*Definitions*
Cognitive outcomes	Assessment evidence of achievement in higher order creative and critical thinking skills, problem-solving, analysis.
Personal outcomes	Assessment evidence of achievement in personal development, including values, attitudes, dispositions.
Social outcomes	Assessment evidence of achievement in social development, including empathy, engagement in community, service learning, collaboration and team work.
Moral and political outcomes	Assessment evidence of achievement in moral and political development, including ability to hold a particular point of view and to act on it.

Citizenship Education	*Educational programmes which are designed to:*
Moral and social responsibility	Develop in learners' moral and social attitudes, values, beliefs and behaviours.
Community involvement	Engage learners in learning and service in the wider community or the school community.
Political literacy	Equip learners with the knowledge, skills, values, attitudes and know how to engage in public life.
Spiritual moral social and cultural development	Develop in learners any aspect of personal development which is not measured as a cognitive learning outcome.
Education for diversity	Nurture in learners an understanding of difference between groups and cultures and a capacity to engage positively with groups and cultures 'different in some way from me'. Includes race, disability, gender, religion, ethnicity, sexual orientation.
Character education	Contribute to the formation of a person's – values, virtues, character and behaviour – which is beneficial to self, others and society.
Emotional and social literacy	Develop the capacity to understand one's own emotions, others' emotions and to use that knowledge effectively.
Values education	Nurture learners in an understanding of and a personal engagement with values.
Service learning	Engage learners in learning which is constructed as service in the wider community or the school community.
Conflict resolution	Enable learners to understand and resolve personal and communal conflicts.
Peer mediation	Enable learners to support peers in resolving conflicts.
Human rights education	Lead to an understanding of human rights and an engagement with the values of human rights legislation.

HÉLÈNE LEENDERS, WIEL VEUGELERS & EWOUD DE KAT

MORAL EDUCATION AND CITIZENSHIP EDUCATION AT PRE-UNIVERSITY SCHOOLS

SUMMARY

This survey investigates the objectives, practical application and learning outcomes of moral education at three pre-university (VWO) schools with differing views on citizenship. We explore teachers' and students' pedagogical, socialpolitical and moral development objectives, and how they deal with values and dialogue, and with diversity. We go on to investigate how the objectives materialize in practice, and teachers' and students' perceptions of the learning outcomes. The results show that moral education may be interpreted in a predominantly social way, as a combination of social and autonomy development, or with a clear emphasis on autonomy development. Students tend to differ little in what they want to learn from moral education. Differences in practical application and learning outcomes they mention happen to correspond with the school they attend. It is surprising that students and teachers emphasize different aspects. Indeed, students are more socially aware and politically engaged than teachers.

INTRODUCTION

Citizenship education is an important theme in current political initiatives and public debate, and the education sector has an important part to play. Governments in various countries have incorporated citizenship development into education in recent years (Torney-Purta & Barber, 2004). The Dutch Minister of Education submitted a legislative proposal in 2006 obliging schools to actively promote citizenship and social integration. The minister defines social integration as 'the participation of citizens in society and its institutions, as well as social participation and familiarity with and knowledge of Dutch culture' (Ministry of Education, Culture & Science (OCW) 2004, p.4). The government gives schools the freedom to interpret citizenship education in their own way.

We consider it important in view of the international debate on citizenship education in the political and academic worlds, and the cultural and social challenges facing Dutch society and its education system, to examine how moral education and citizenship are being implemented in secondary education. The freedom enjoyed by Dutch schools to interpret citizenship education makes it interesting to investigate

Fritz Oser & Wiel Veugelers (eds.), Getting involved, 57–74.

examples of differing approaches. This article presents the results of an empirical study into how three schools have interpreted moral and citizenship education. We investigate whether teachers succeed in putting their aims into practice and identify the learning outcomes they observe among students.

The reason that we focus on teachers is that they have the professional role of putting educational policy, the pedagogical concept of the school and their own cultural-pedagogical aims into practice. Teachers make the curriculum and, consciously or not, they tend to influence their students' moral development. It is important for teachers to be aware of the values they wish to encourage, the type of citizenship they are aiming for, and what form of practical support they give students in their personal moral development. Students' opinions are also important. They are, after all, the targets of citizenship education. Citizenship education philosophy sees them as active participants, who develop their identity through reflection and action. We have accordingly included the student perspective in the survey.

THEORETICAL FRAMEWORK

Citizenship

The current debate on young people's social development is imbued with the concept of 'citizenship'. Citizenship education may focus on transferring knowledge on democracy, its institutions and the structure of society (Cleaver, Ireland, Kerr & Lopes, 2005). Equally, the approach could be more on promoting particular social norms, or on an active construction of moral signification (Haste, 2004). We endorse the latter approach, in which both the individual's social performance and participation in society are of interest (Veugelers, 2003). Among the moral values to be developed are 'justice', 'respect', 'autonomy', and 'social and moral commitment'.

Citizenship is not restricted to the political aspect, but also relates to society as a whole, to the everyday relations between people and individuals' identity development (Banks, 2004). If citizenship education is to be more than merely an explanation of rights and duties, or a sort of behaviouristic conformity, then it has to be anchored in a firm foundation of *moral development*. There is a growing tendency to link moral development and citizenship development (Haste, 2004; Oser & Biedermann, 2004; Veugelers, 2007). The relationship between moral education, citizenship education and moral development is that the process of addressing value development controls the citizenship development. A morally founded citizenship education of this kind may encourage young people to actually apply their knowledge and skills, to act moral and social. Citizenship education may also become more reflective, and therefore susceptible to change, by improving moral reasoning and action (Veugelers, Derriks, De Kat, & Leenders, 2006).

We distinguish three components of moral development in this survey: 'dealing with different opinions and being capable of exchanging points of view'; 'having insight into social situations'; and 'sociomoral attitude' (Buxairras, Martinez,

Noguera & Tey, 2003). The point is therefore not only the more conditional and cognitively oriented exchange of points of view and social insight, but also the willingness to display insights into conduct (the attitude aspect of moral development).

The education minister is of the view that the educational objectives for active citizenship and social integration must address the cultural diversity in society. A place is thus given in education to *cultural and ideological diversity*, with values such as 'tolerance' and 'respect for differences' (Blum, 1999; Parker, 1996). Teachers attend to these matters in various ways. They might, for instance, use teaching material that presents the Netherlands as a multicultural society, or attempt to start a dialogue in their lessons between different cultures and world views.

We treat *socialpolitical objectives* with particular scrutiny in this survey, in the light of the bias in education policy towards social cohesion and social integration in citizenship education. Citizenship education addresses not only knowledge and skills, but also the development of willingness to use these skills. The point is not only the social skills, but also a social involvement. A key element in the sociopolitical objectives we investigate is attitude formation, which acts on two levels: 'social involvement' (solidarity with others, involvement with others) and 'political engagement' (the development of an attitude that promotes equality and democracy in society) (Veugelers, et al., 2006).

Teachers and values

'Values are an integral part of teaching, reflected in what is taught and also in how teachers and students relate to each other' (Arthur, 2003, p.317). Teachers express values through their choice of subject, the examples they use and in how they supervise their students (Gudmundsdottir, 1990). Teachers can convey values, but also create conditions in which multiple perspectives are presented, and so influence students' moral development, consciously or hidden. The education system simultaneously stimulates the development of certain values and the skills to enable students to form their own opinions.

Curriculum researchers point out that attention is needed in research for the underlying pedagogical objectives that control the actual teacher actions (Goodson, 2005). Research into teachers' pedagogical actions refers consistently to the importance of objectives, particularly in value-laden contexts (Hansen, 2001). We confronted teachers, students and parents in earlier studies with several pedagogical objectives based among others on the work of Oser (1994) and Berkowitz (1997). These studies produced a reliable and valid instrument for measuring the attention given to pedagogical objectives. The instrument itself covers 'social development', 'autonomy' (forming critical opinions) and 'disciplining'.

Teachers employ a specific pedagogical philosophy in which a certain type of citizenship may be dominant. We identified three types of citizenship in earlier studies of teachers' pedagogical objectives. The three types differ in the pedagogical objectives the teachers emphasize:

- Adapting citizenship (in which the teachers consider disciplining and social development more important than autonomy);
- Individualistic citizenship (in which the teachers consider disciplining and autonomy more important than social development);
- Critical-democratic citizenship (in which the teachers consider autonomy and social development more important than disciplining). (Leenders, Veugelers & De Kat, in press).

All these approaches stress specific aspects of values, which may relate to different pedagogical-didactic practices.

How do teachers address values in education, and how do they initiate and supervise students' moral development? In order to describe *teachers' pedagogical-didactic approach in moral education* we differentiate in this survey between one oriented to practical social conduct ('social conduct'), one which revolves around actual, predefined, values, ('value transfer'), and one in which values are the subject of reflection and communication ('value communication') (Veugelers & De Kat, 2005).

One of the ways students can work on their moral development in practice is through *moral dialogues in school*. We examine how values are communicated in the citizenship education class, distinguishing between the opinion-forming process ('discussion') and the more 'sociopolitical content of opinion forming'.

In summary, we examine the pedagogical objectives in citizenship education, in particular in the sociopolitical domain. We also examine the moral development objectives that are interwoven with citizenship education. How these objectives take shape in educational practice is also investigated, with particular attention to dialogues and diversity.

RESEARCH QUESTIONS

We formulated the following research questions based on the theoretical framework. How do schools (with different citizenship orientations) differ with respect to:

- The pedagogical and sociopolitical objectives that teachers and students consider important, and the learning outcomes they observe;
- The learning outcomes in moral development observed by teachers and students;
- The forms of practical application of moral education and the aspects considered desirable by teachers and students, with regard to:
  - the pedagogical-didactic approach;
  - moral dialogues;
  - cultural and ideological diversity.

Teachers shape moral education in a school in practice, and it is the students who experience it every day. We used questionnaires to investigate teachers' and students' objectives, moral education practice and assessment of learning outcomes. The survey was accompanied by observing lessons and interviewing teachers and students. The interviews involved the same moral education aspects as in the questionnaire, presented as open questions. We occasionally used data from the interviews when interpreting the findings.

We first investigated whether the schools we selected indeed differed in citizenship orientation in the way we expected. We then explored the opinions of teachers and students in the various schools on the objectives and practical application of moral education and the learning outcomes. We finally established how the differences between the schools are connected with theoretical conceptions of moral education and citizenship.

SURVEY INSTRUMENTATION AND EXECUTION

The questionnaire used in the survey was based on measurement instruments used in an earlier survey. The questionnaire is in six parts; 'Pedagogical objectives', 'Sociopolitical domain in the curriculum', 'Moral development', 'Pedagogical-didactic approach', 'Moral dialogues in school', 'Cultural and ideological diversity' and concludes with several questions on the respondents' 'Background characteristics'. Each part of the questionnaire involves one or more scales. The internal consistency of the scales used is good (Cronbach's alpha is between 0.72 and 0.93).

Teachers' and students' questionnaires

The questionnaires were oriented to teachers' and students' goals, the practical application of moral education and the reported learning outcomes. The content of the teachers' questionnaire and students' questionnaire were related. For example, if the teachers were asked to state the objectives they consider important and the extent to which they achieve them, the students were asked which objectives they consider important and how well they think they are achieved at school. The questionnaire consists of the following components.

Pedagogical objectives The pedagogical objectives comprise three scales: 'disciplining', 'social development' and 'autonomy'. These scales were derived from an earlier survey (Leenders et al., in press). The respondents were requested to rate the objectives they would like to achieve, and the extent to which they consider they have been achieved, on a 5-point scale.

Sociopolitical domain in the curriculum Teachers' objectives in the social domain were measured with the 'concern for others' scale from the Child Development Project (Watson, Battistich & Solomon, 1997). This scale measures teachers' attention to 'social involvement': solidarity with others, concern for and involvement with others. We also developed a more politically oriented scale. Our 'political engagement' scale measures teachers' attention to the development of an attitude oriented to creating equal opportunities for all, and a critical attitude towards inequalities in society. We also investigated how well teachers consider these objectives to have been achieved (learning outcomes).

Moral development　Moral education can contribute to students' moral development. We asked teachers what they thought students had learned in moral development, for which we used the 'Dimensions of Moral Personality Questionnaire' (Buxairras et al., 2003; see Veugelers & De Kat, 2005). The scales concerned were 'exchange of points of view', 'insight into sociomoral situations' and 'sociomoral attitude'.

Pedagogical-didactic approach　We examined teachers' pedagogical-didactic actions on three scales: 'value transfer', with items such as 'I convey defined values and standards to the students'; 'social conduct', with items such as 'I ensure that students behave in a social way'; and 'value communication', with questions such as 'I am happy for students to have different views on matters'. For 'social conduct' we use the 'Promotion of social understanding and prosocial values' scale from the Child Development Project (Watson, Battistich & Solomon, 1997). We developed the other two scales ourselves, and have used them in an earlier survey (Veugelers & De Kat, 2003).

Moral dialogues in school　We investigated how communication on values took place in the class and what people wanted based on the two scales, 'discussion' and 'sociopolitical opinion forming'. The questions were derived from the 'Elicitation of student thinking and active discussion' scale from the Child Development Project (Watson et al., 1997) and the 'Attitudes to open classroom climate' scale from the IEA *Citizenship Education Study*. The CDP scale is oriented to the opinion-forming process, with items such as 'I respond with more questions to students' answers' and 'I establish connections between students' different points of view'. The IEA scale is oriented to the sociopolitical content, with items such as: 'I encourage students to form their own opinion on political and social issues'.

Cultural and ideological diversity　In order to determine how much attention teachers wish to give to cultural and ideological diversity, and how much they actually do, we present them with statements such as 'I give the students in my lessons an opportunity to speak about their own culture or religion' (Veugelers & De Kat, 2005).

Background characteristics　We asked teachers their age, gender and what subject they teach. We asked students their age, gender, personal beliefs, country of origin and school grade, and their chosen subjects. We wish to investigate whether the students of the three schools differ in these characteristics, and whether there might be a relationship between the student characteristics and their opinion on moral education.

Participating schools, teachers and students

We selected three pre-university (VWO) schools that we expected to have different approaches to moral education. Our earlier study into teachers' objectives with moral education (Leenders et al., in press) revealed that schools can differ in citizenship orientations. We selected schools for this survey such that the four teachers participating had the same citizenship orientation. We selected one school for each orientation.

The first school, where we expected that many teachers would aim for an adapting orientation, is a Protestant school in the east of the Netherlands. The second school, where we expected that many teachers would have a critical-democratic orientation, is a Roman Catholic school in the south of the Netherlands. The third school, expected to have teachers aiming for a predominantly individualistic orientation, is a nondenominational school in the east of the country (private but public paid). All three schools are medium-sized, with approximately 100 teachers, half of which teach the final years of pre-university education. The second school has a somewhat larger pre-university structure than the other two. All three have a school population of predominantly Dutch national students, with fewer than 5% non-Dutch origin students in the VWO departments.

Questionnaires were distributed to all teachers at each school teaching the VWO final years. A total of 149 questionnaires were distributed (43 at the first school, 61 at the second and 45 at the third). 56 teachers returned the questionnaire (16, 25 and 15 teachers, respectively), which is a response of 37% at the first school, 41 % at the second and 33% at the third, and 38% in total. Each school's response contained contributions from teachers of a variety of subjects. The ratio of older to younger teachers and of women to men largely corresponded with the actual proportions in the schools.

The students of VWO years 4, 5 and 6 completed the questionnaire in a lesson. A total of 392 questionnaires were administered by the mentors at school (109, 177 and 106 students, respectively). We found no large differences between the schools in terms of the age of students participating in the survey, the ratio of boys to girls, their cultural background, or their chosen profiles. However, the schools did differ in terms of their students' religious background. 49% of the student participants at the Protestant school were Protestant, 12% Catholic and 29% non-religious; at the Roman Catholic school 43% were Catholic, 2% Protestant and 49% non-religious; and 76% of the students at the nondenominational school stated that they had no religious belief. 3% of the participants in all three schools adhered to Islam or Hinduism. However, we found no statistically significant link between the students' religion and their scores on the dependent variables.

Data analysis

The schools were selected on the basis of an expectation that they would differ on the three a priori identified citizenship orientations, and consequently in their approaches to moral education. A person-centred hierarchical cluster analysis was used to allocate the teachers to groups. The data for the desired pedagogical objectives were analysed with a three cluster single solution in which the scale scores (desired) 'disciplining', 'social development' and 'autonomy' were used as criterion variables. A one-way analysis of variance was used to investigate whether the three groups of teachers indeed differ in the importance they attach to the various learning objectives, and that the issues they accordingly emphasize correspond with the citizenship orientations we postulated. The differences between the schools were investigated with a one-way analysis of variance.

RESULTS

Differences in types of citizenship

The distribution of the 56 teachers who completed the questionnaires is as follows:

– 12 teachers (21%) consider disciplining (M=4.85) and social development (M=4.80) to be more important than autonomy (M=4.05). These teachers are of the adapting citizenship type;
– 11 teachers (20%) consider disciplining (M=4.27) and autonomy (M=4.25) to be more important than social development (M=3.39). These teachers are of the individualistic citizenship type;
– 33 teachers (59%) consider social development (M=4.47) and autonomy (M=4.41) to be more important than disciplining (M=3.96). These teachers are of the critical-democratic citizenship type.

A one-way analysis of variance confirms that the three groups of teachers indeed differ in the importance they attach to the various learning objectives ($p < 0.01$ for all differences) and that the points they accordingly emphasize correspond with the citizenship orientations we postulated.

Most of the 135 VWO teachers in the earlier, national, study happened to aim for critical-democratic citizenship (61%), one fifth for individualistic citizenship (22%) and a small minority for adapting citizenship (17%). These results agree reasonably with the structure we found in the current survey. It is relevant for the current survey to examine the distribution of the three types of teacher in the three schools involved. Is there such a thing as a 'more adapting school', a 'more individualistic school', and a 'more critical-democratic school', as we expected? Indeed there is, apparently.

- School 1: 33% of the teachers aim for adapting citizenship, 17% individualistic oriented, and 50% critical-democratic. Compared with the survey, this school has a relatively large number of adapting teachers. This school is referred to below as '**A**' ('more Adapting');
- School 2: 17% of the teachers are of the adapting type, 8% are oriented to individualistic citizenship, and 75% to critical-democratic citizenship. This school has predominantly critical-democratic teachers and is referred to below as '**C**' (more Critical-democratic');
- School 3: 7% of the teachers are adapting, 40% individualistic, and 53% critical-democratic. This school has a relatively large number of individualistic teachers and is referred to below as '**I**' ('more Individualistic').

This survey examines the differences between these schools and the teachers' and students' opinions in greater depth.

Differences between the three schools: teachers and students.

The differences between the schools were investigated with a one-way analysis of variance. For all the differences mentioned in the text, $p < .05$. The average scores of the teachers and the students at the three schools are shown in Table 1.

Desired pedagogical objectives and the sociopolitical domain   Teachers and students at all schools state that disciplining, social development and autonomy are 'important'. We expect the school with a relatively large number of adapting teachers to have a higher teacher score for disciplining and social development and a lower score for autonomy; the school with mostly critical-democratic teachers a lower score for disciplining; and the school with a relatively large number of individualistic teachers a lower score for social development. Although this tendency is discernible (albeit that the desired disciplining at school A has a lower score than expected), the differences are not statistically significant.

The schools differ in the desire to develop social involvement and political engagement. The teachers at school A are more strongly oriented to the development of social involvement than their counterparts at school I. We observe a strikingly large difference for political engagement. The teachers at schools A and C state that they are more oriented to the development of political engagement than their counterparts at school I. This means that the teachers at schools A and C put more effort into developing a critical attitude to inequalities in society than their counterparts at school I. Whereas we observe differences among the teachers, the students of the three schools differ little in their desire to learn social involvement and political engagement at school. The students of school I want considerably more attention to be given to political engagement than their teachers do.

In the sociopolitical domain, school I differs markedly from the other two schools.

Table 1. Differences between the three schools

Instruments	schools	Teachers (N=56)						Students (N=392)					
		Desired		Practice		Learning outcomes		Desired		Practice		Learning outcomes	
		M	SD	M	SD	M	SD	M	SD	M	SD	M	SD
pedagogical objectives													
disciplining	A	3.98	0.60			3.38*	0.47	3.92	0.54			3.21	0.70
	C	4.15	0.66			3.76	0.53	3.82	0.73			3.28**	0.66
4 items, α =0.72	I	4.28	0.30			3.80**	0.47	3.82	0.74			3.08*	0.60
social development	A	4.40	0.43			3.70	0.50	4.06	0.63			3.14	0.68
	C	4.36	0.85			3.76	0.73	4.04	0.65			3.15	0.56
7 items, α =0.90	I	4.14	0.72			3.60	0.45	3.96	0.69			2.99	0.60
autonomy	A	4.19	0.38			3.47*	0.48	4.09	0.66			3.43	0.71
	C	4.53	0.56			3.83**	0.61	4.11	0.62			3.39	0.67
4 items, α =0.79	I	4.48	0.43			3.98**	0.55	4.16	0.61			3.39	0.73
Sociopolitical													
social involvement	A	3.98**	0.50			3.38**	0.53	3.58	0.63			2.82	0.65
	C	3.68	0.88			3.12	0.77	3.56	0.75			2.66	0.76
7 items, α =0.90	I	3.15*	0.82			2.56*	0.69	3.36	0.86			2.73	0.76
political engage-ment	A	3.44**	0.49			2.61**	0.69	3.34	0.81			2.50	0.71
	C	3.15**	0.96			2.48	0.67	3.31	0.83			2.32	0.79
4 items, α =0.76	I	2.38*	0.62			2.02*	0.67	3.19	0.88			2.40	0.77
Moral development													
exchange of points	A					3.48	0.40					3.34	0.58
of view	C					3.81**	0.52					3.21	0.65
6 items, α =0.82	I					3.32*	0.48					3.28	0.67

Scale		M	SD	M	SD	M	SD	M	SD	M	SD	M	SD
socialmoral insight	A					3.35	0.48					3.31	0.53
	C					3.64	0.58					3.20	0.70
5 items, α =0.76	I					3.32	0.57					3.28	0.62
socialmoral at-titude	A					3.34	0.42					3.20	0.52
	C					3.54	0.54					3.12	0.69
5 items, α =0.75	I					3.23	0.55					3.16	0.60
Ped-didactics													
social conduct	A	4.11	0.53	3.54	0.46			3.72	0.64	3.04**	0.63		
	C	4.06	0.81	3.67	0.63			3.56	0.74	2.80*	0.71		
6 items, α =0.85	I	3.60	0.62	3.29	0.46			3.55	0.78	2.92	0.62		
value transfer	A	4.00	0.47	3.61	0.41			3.66	0.60	3.14	0.63		
	C	4.11	0.70	3.88**	0.59			3.49	0.77	3.07	0.64		
5 items, α =0.76	I	3.80	0.42	3.43*	0.38			3.51	0.77	3.02	0.61		
value communica-tion	A	3.61	0.41	3.37	0.73			3.14	0.63	2.74	0.58		
	C	3.88**	0.59	3.25	0.76			3.07	0.64	2.57	0.67		
6 items, α =0.93	I	3.43*	0.38	3.01	0.89			3.02	0.61	2.65	0.66		
Dialogues													
discussion	A	4.33	0.44	3.90	0.47			3.91	0.59	3.45	0.71		
	C	4.29	0.63	4.03	0.51			3.79	0.67	3.23	0.80		
7 items, α =0.88	I	4.18	0.64	3.88	0.79			3.76	0.77	3.38	0.75		
sociopolitical opinion.forming	A	4.31	0.45	4.03	0.50			3.84	0.62	3.32**	0.72		
	C	4.06	0.80	3.82	0.68			3.73	0.74	3.00*	0.80		
5 items, α =0.85	I	3.81	0.96	3.56	0.96			3.84	0.68	3.23**	0.75		
Diversity													
cultural.and ideo-logical diversity	A	3.37	0.81	2.86	0.95			3.31**	0.82	2.55**	0.74		
	C	2.79	0.83	2.26	0.75			3.00	0.92	2.11*	0.80		
7 items, α =0.90	I	2.77	0.94	2.44	0.96			2.97*	0.97	2.28	0.75		

Note. Differences between * and ** in the schools are statistically significant (p < 0.05). Significant differences between teachers and students in a school are not indicated by symbols in the table, but are commented on in the text.

The teachers at school I consider social involvement and political engagement to be less important than their counterparts at the other two schools, whereas the students of this school actually want attention to be given to these aspects.

Reported learning outcomes for the pedagogical objectives and in the sociopolitical domain   Teachers state that a discrepancy exists between the importance they attach to the various objectives and the learning performance that they yield, and students demonstrate a similar discrepancy. Schools differ on the teachers' views of the pedagogical objectives (disciplining, autonomy and social development) and the sociopolitical objectives that are most completely achieved. The teachers at school A consider themselves to be less successful than their counterparts at both other schools in developing students' capacity to form autonomy. With respect to disciplining, it is again the teachers of school A that have a lower estimate of the effect of their efforts, in which they differ strongly from school I. However, it is striking that the student estimates of school I's learning outcomes on disciplining are actually the lowest of all.

Whereas the teachers at school A estimate that they are poorly on achieving the pedagogical objectives, they actually score well on sociopolitical aspects. The results show that these teachers estimate the learning outcomes on social involvement higher than their counterparts at school I. This means that their teachers think that the students of school I scarcely learn solidarity with others and concern for others. The students of the participating schools do not differ in their assessment of the learning outcomes on social involvement – they all consider it to be fairly low.

The teachers at school A estimate the learning outcomes on political engagement higher than their counterparts at school I, but the related scores are low for all schools. Their teachers consider that the students in the schools investigated achieve at most 'a tiny gain' in critical attitude towards inequalities in society. Students share this opinion – irrespective of the school they attend.

The moral development of students   The clusters that we identified for moral development were exchange of points of view, socialmoral insight and socialmoral attitude. We asked only about learning outcomes that teachers and students considered had been achieved. The survey shows that teachers consider that students learn to differentiate between different perspectives somewhat better than they develop social insights and sociomoral attitudes. There are considerable differences between the schools in this regard. Only on exchange of points of view do the teachers at school C estimate the learning outcomes they achieve higher than their counterparts at school I. We found no statistically significant differences between the students of the three schools. There is conspicuously little difference between teachers and students at schools C and I in their estimates of learning outcomes for moral development, whereas the differences at school C were substantial for all three clusters.

The pedagogical-didactic approach of moral education   The pedagogical-didactic approach of moral education can be oriented to teaching practical social conduct, or can address the actual values. When the values are predefined, we refer to 'value transfer', and when they are subject of reflection we refer to 'value communication'. All three pedagogical-didactic approaches appear to be important, but it is striking that value transfer and encouraging social conduct achieve higher scores than the more reflective value communication. We observed this tendency in both the desired and the actual practical application, and among both teachers and students. However, if we ask about the practical application of dialogues in moral education then teachers and students are keen to have many discussions in the class as well as attention to forming sociopolitical opinions. In practice both teachers and students say that this attention is now reasonably in evidence.

If we look at the differences between the schools, it would appear that the teachers at school C want to give more attention to value communication than their counterparts at school I, whereas the teachers at school C actually give more attention in practice to value transfer than their counterparts at school I. The teachers at school C apparently believe that value communication is somewhat neglected in their practice in comparison with value transfer. The students also differ in their assessment. The students of school A stated that more attention was given in practice to social action at their school than the students of school C.

We found no differences between the teachers at the three schools on attention to moral dialogues in school and attention to cultural and ideological diversity, in either the attention they wish to give to these aspects, or how they perceive their practical application. We do observe differences between the students. The students of schools C and I state that somewhat more attention is given to forming sociopolitical opinions at their school than the students of school A. The students of school A state that somewhat more attention is given in practice to cultural and ideological diversity at their school than the students of school C. This means that the students of all three schools report that only 'a tiny bit' of attention is given to this theme.

The findings by school

We assume that attention is given in the education system to all the aspects of moral education investigated in this survey. When we arrange the findings below by school, this is the criterion of our analysis and suggestions.

School A: the school with a relatively large number of adapting teachers   The survey indicates that moral education at this school has a markedly social bias. The social domain (social development, social involvement, social action) is important in the aims, in practice and in the reported learning outcomes. This school also has the highest score of all three schools on the sociopolitical aspects of moral education, but this means that students acquire only a modest portion of political engagement at school. The students state that they wish more attention to be given to learning to deal with cultural and ideological diversity. The students both recognize and value the social signature of their school. On the other hand, they consider the most important pedagogical aim should not be social development, but autonomy. The teacher scores showed that the learning effects for autonomy are relatively low.

In our opinion, all three areas are important. If this school were to pay more attention to the development of communicative and reflective skills, moral education might show a better balance between conformity and autonomy. This desire also exists at school: both teachers and students state that in practice they want to give more attention to discussion. Teachers could teach students to formulate personal opinions, to justify divergent opinions and to cope with criticism more than is now the case; they could respond with more questions to students' answers and help them clarify their thinking. Doing so might bring about more reflection on values and standards.

School C: the school with predominantly critical-democratic teachers Moral education at this school is a balance between social development and autonomy development. The survey shows that although this school's scores are generally lower than those of the first school, they are more evenly distributed. Like the first school, much attention is given to the social domain, but forming autonomy is also important. This school is conspicuous in moral education practice in the considerable attention to discussion and the importance that teachers attach to value communication. Teachers appear to achieve their aims, according to their positive assessment of learning outcomes for autonomy, social development and moral development alike. However, the students are less positive about the learning outcomes.

Strikingly enough, there is a relatively large amount of value transfer at this school. The teacher interviews show that knowledge transfer is considered important, and that class management plays a part. Another striking point is that little explicit attention is given at this school to important social topics: forming sociopolitical opinions and cultural and ideological diversity. The students are aware of this: they are fairly critical of the little attention given to forming sociopolitical opinions and diversity. This is apparent from the questionnaires and is also revealed in the student interviews. The students in the interviews praise the social character of their school and the intellectual challenge, but they state that they perceive insufficient social preparation.

School I: the school with a relatively large number of teachers of the individualistic type Moral education at this school is shaped by a clear emphasis on autonomy development. The teachers give much weight to self discipline and taking personal responsibility, while the students –as they confirm in the interviews – consider that while they learn to plan their work well at their school, no sense of community exists, which they regret. The students state clearly in the questionnaires that they want more attention to be given to social development. The score they give the current attention to this aspect is the lowest of all students. Indeed, the school has a conspicuously low score on social aspects: the teachers say that little attention is given to social development, and relatively modest learning experiences are reported for social conduct and social involvement. The survey also shows that this school has a high score on autonomy but a relatively low score on discussion and value communication. Furthermore, both teachers and students would like most attention in practice to be given to autonomy development (teachers in particular have a high score on this point).

In our opinion, it is important that values are included consciously in the learning process. If this school were to link communicative skills more strongly with values, students might perhaps be better able to develop morality. The school is already strong in autonomy development and the personal responsibility of the student in the learning process. If values were to be better integrated into the learning process, students' moral development could be strengthened.

CONCLUSIONS AND DISCUSSION

This survey shows how schools with distinct citizenship orientations can differ in the way in which teachers shape moral education and the learning outcomes they observe, but similarities also exist between the schools. We first consider the similarities, and then the differences.

The survey shows that both teachers and students state that they want more attention to be given to aspects of moral education than actually happens in practice in the class. Teachers and students attach importance to pedagogical and sociopolitical objectives. However, the reported learning outcomes are invariably much lower than envisaged. We found this earlier in the national survey of teachers (Leenders et al., 2005), and we observe it here among the students too. An important difference between teachers and students is that teachers consider that they give more attention in practice in their classes to the various aspects of moral education and achieve better learning outcomes than do the students. Students apparently perceive this attention less than the teachers themselves. It is most surprising that students stress different aspects of the content than teachers: their interest is both more social, socially involved and politically engaged. The survey shows regarding moral development that teachers and students consider that learning to make a clearer distinction between different perspectives has more effect than developing social insights and sociomoral attitudes.

Citizenship education can equip young people to participate in the social and political domains, and could also motivate young people to make the necessary effort. This survey shows that young people are also willing to learn this aspect at school, and that their schools are now lagging behind in the development of sociopolitical opinions and dealing with cultural and ideological diversity. Students differ little in the pedagogical objectives and sociopolitical objectives they find important. They do observe clear differences in learning outcomes – differences that are related with the school they attend.

If we look at teachers' pedagogical-didactic approach, it is striking that value transfer and stimulating social conduct attain higher scores than the more reflective value communication. We observed this tendency in both the desired and the actual practical application, and among both teachers and students. However, if we inquire into the desired practical application of dialogues in moral education, teachers and students are keen to have many discussions in the class and attention to be given to forming sociopolitical opinions. Both teachers and students say that this attention is now reasonably in evidence in practice. A possible explanation for the difference in attention given to value communication and discussion as opposed to forming sociopolitical opinions is that teachers and students view values more as something you have to adhere to, and accordingly make hardly any distinction between values and standards. The reasoning seems to be 'you don't communicate about values, you have to adhere to them'. Teachers and students do think that social topics and sociopolitical education can and must be discussed, and students must form an opinion. The low score on value communication would suggest that moral values are not much to the fore in this discussion and in forming these opinions.

Differences between schools

The ministry's citizenship education policy gives schools the freedom to apply their own accents to the content and their own pedagogical-didactic structure. These differences are already visible in practice, each with their specific advantages and disadvantages. If we link the findings of this survey with teachers' and schools' various citizenship orientations, we can conclude that a school with a more adapting orientation may be characterized by much attention to togetherness, social development and other social aspects compatible with a community concept of citizenship, but with little regard to developing the skills to be able to reflect on values and to develop values independently. The risk exists in moral education oriented to adapting citizenship that the personal autonomy of the student will be insufficiently developed (Leenders & Veugelers, 2006).

A more individualistically oriented citizenship orientation can also lack balance. The bias is then on personal autonomy, based on optimism that the power of rationality can improve human existence, and faith in people's power to overcome individual differences and define and serve the general interest. However, the survey shows that a strong individual determination coincides with the risk of losing sight of the social aspects. If autonomy is not linked with an explicit social component, the result can be individualism. We referred to this as 'the reform pedagogic myth': the assumption that students in their own pursuits and based on their own experience will develop self discipline, a sense of responsibility and self-knowledge, against the background of the class and the school as a microcommunity. However, social commitment is not created spontaneously.

The social can also coincide with the critical, as is the case in critical-democratic citizenship. We applaud a school aiming for a balance between students' personal development (autonomy and critical thinking) and their social development. However, this is not sufficient in itself to prepare students properly for society. Both the social performance of students and their future participation in society are important in citizenship education. Education must therefore be concerned not only with values such as reliability, respect and individual responsibility, but – from the perspective of social performance – also with values such as social and moral responsibility, and, as an extension, with tolerance and respect for differences. Our survey shows that none of the schools prepares its students thoroughly and appropriately for an active and democratic participation in our multicultural society. It is both striking and a source of optimism that it is the students who are arguing most vigorously in this direction.

REFERENCES

Arthur, J. (2003). Editorial: Professional value commitments. *British Journal of Educational Studies, 51*, 4, 317-319.

Banks, J. A. (2004). *Diversity and citizenship education. Global perspectives.* San Francisco: Jossey-Bass.

Berkowitz, M. W. (1997). *Integrating structure and content in moral education.* Paper presented at AERA 1997, Chicago.

Blum, L. (1999). Race, community and moral education. Kohlberg and Spielberg as civic educators. *Journal of Moral Education, 28*, 2, 125-134.

Buxairras, M. R., Martinez, M., Noguera, E., & Tey, A. (2003). Teachers evaluate the moral development of their students. In W. Veugelers & F.K. Oser (Eds.), *Teaching in moral and democratic education* (pp.173-192). Bern / New York: Peter Long.

Cleaver, E., Ireland, E., Kerr, D., & Lopes, J. (2005). *Citizenship education longitudinal study: second cross-sectional survey 2004. Listening to young people: citizenship education in England* (DfES Research Report 626). London: DfES.

Goodson, I. F. (2005). Change processes and historical periods: an international perspective. In W. Veugelers & R. Bosman (Eds.), *De strijd om het curriculum (The struggle for the curriculum)* (pp.19-29). Antwerp/Apeldoorn: Garant.

Gudmundsdottir, S. (1990). Values in pedagogical content knowledge. *Journal of Teacher Education, 41*, 3, 44-52.

Hansen, D. T. (2001). *Exploring the moral heart of teaching.* New York: Teachers Lecture Press.

Haste, H. (2004). Constructing the citizen. *Political Psychology, 25*, 3, 413-438.

Leenders, H., & Veugelers, W. (2006). Different perspectives on values and citizenship education. *Curriculum and Teaching, 21*, 2, 5-20.

Leenders, H., Veugelers, W., & Kat, E. de. (2005, April). *Teachers' views on moral education. Goals and practices.* Paper presented at the annual meeting or the American Educational Research Association, Montreal.

Ministry of Education, Culture & Science. (2004). *Legislative proposal and explanatory memorandum W2624K-2.* The Hague: OCW

Oser, F. K. (1994). Moral perspectives on teaching. *Review of Research in Education, 20,* 57-127.
Oser, F. K., & Biedermann, H. (2003). *Jugend ohne Politik.* Zürich: Rügger.
Parker, W. C. (1996). 'Advanced' ideas about democracy: towards a pluralist conception of citizenship education. *Teachers Lecture Record, 98,* 1, 104-125.
Torney-Purta, J., & Barber, J. (2004). *Democratic school participation and civic attitudes among European adolescents. Analysis of data from the IEA civic education study.* Strasbourg: Council of Europe.
Veugelers, W. (2003). *Waarden en normen in het onderwijs. Zingeving en humanisering: autonomie en sociale betrokkenheid (Values and standards in education. Giving meaning and humanization: autonomy and social involvement.* Utrecht: University for Humanistics (inaugural lecture).
Veugelers, W. (2007). Creating critical democratic citizenship education: empowering humanity and democracy in Dutch education. *Compare, 37, 1,* 105-119
Veugelers, W. & Kat, E. de (2003). Moral and democratic education in secondary schools (193-214). In W. Veugelers & F.K. Oser (Eds.), *Teaching in moral and democratic education* (pp.173-192). Bern / New York: Peter Long.
Veugelers, W., & Kat, E. de. (2005). *Identiteitsontwikkeling in het openbaar onderwijs. (Identity development in public education).* Antwerp / Apeldoorn : Garant.
Veugelers, W., Derriks, M., Kat, E. de, & Leenders, H. (2006). *Burgerschap in het Algemeen Bijzonder Onderwijs (Citizenship in private nondenominational education).* Amsterdam: Instituut voor de Lerarenopleiding.
Watson, M., Battistich, V., & Solomon, D. (1997). Enhancing students' social and ethical development in schools: An intervention program and its effects. *International Journal of Educational Research, 27,* 7, 571-586.

Hélène Leenders
Fontys Hogeschool, Sittard, The Netherlands
Wiel Veugelers
University of Amsterdam; University for Humanistics, Utrecht, The Netherlands
Ewoud De Kat
University of Amsterdam, The Netherlands

DIOMIDIS MARKOULIS & MARIA DIKAIOU

BEING INVOLVED:

Theoretical and Research Approaches

ABSTRACT

The concept of citizen's participation in actions and interventions seeking to combat social problems in deprived communities is discussed in this paper. Utilizing a number of applied research studies and action programs related to the needs of migrant and minority street children, this chapter seeks to contribute to debates about the role of citizen's participation in social change by suggesting how social psychological phenomena can add to the understanding of participation in community context. It is suggested that group history or inter-group relations are crucial elements in understanding the dynamic processes of participation especially when it refers to citizen from migrant minority groups. The chapter shifts thereafter to the discussion of the dynamics behind citizens' mobilization in the context of the wider society, focusing on instrumentality, identity and ideology.

INTRODUCTION

The recent worldwide outburst of protest against actions of war and of all forms of unfair discrimination renders the phenomenon of citizen mobilization extremely topical, bringing into the arena discussions of forms of united actions and the effects they have on world peace. Given the general admission that these times we live in can be characterized by political indifference and lack of social mobilization, yet the emergence of terrorism and increase of violence is apparent, such involvement in protest actions provides the basis for the development of a new form of unified pressure and influence on an international scene.

Forms of collective citizen mobilization have always been of concern to social theory and attracted the interest of philosophers, historians and political scientists (Vincent and Plant, 1984; Heather, 1990; Fukuyama, 1992) and educationalists (McLaughlin, 1992; Crick, 1998) and are relevant to citizens' rights and obligations and the maintenance of democracy and world peace. This paper, having such collective phenomena as its central focus, views the citizen as a gregarious being and central player and carrier of actions that occur within and between social groups.

In particular, this chapter, after first outlining the ways in which the socio-psy-

Fritz Oser & Wiel Veugelers (eds.), Getting involved, 75–87.

chological literature deals with the topic of "citizen mobilization" will thereafter shift to the examination ideology and identity might exert on a citizen's decisions to "be involved".

CITIZEN MOBILIZATION IN SOCIO-PSYCHOLOGICAL THEORY AND RESEARCH

It has become commonplace over the last few years to hear terms such as mobilization and participation of the citizen circulating in discussions of concern to the community, whether referring to the social policy of a united Europe or the national policy of each individual member state. Similar discussions exist in countries on the other side of the Atlantic from which it seems that specific proposals about kinds of citizen mobilization have already been processed, thus again bringing to light issues of citizens offering to volunteer and those of activism by members of non-privileged groups (Wittig and Bettencourt, 1996; Snyder, 2000; Penner, 2002). At the same time, in an effort to support social policy that takes such a direction, the United Nations in making a special reference, emphasized the need for active involvement of the citizens in issues of concern to the general community, and to the non-privileged in particular (United Nations General Assembly, 2002).

It is often pointed out (Stukas and Dunlap, 2002) as a universal request, treated, however, with skepticism by social scientists. Many studies, while making reference to the purposes, the methods and the prospects of mobilization in various countries, take the line that the whole discussion surrounding the activism of citizens is nothing more than an avoidance of real responsibility on the part of the state, and a fobbing off of the responsibilities onto the weaknesses of the welfare state to face the needs of special segments of the populations (e.g., Austin & Hasenfeld, 1985). Others, taking a different line (Owen, 1986; Stukas & Dunlap, 2002), suggest that the existence of non-paid provisions of services and the contribution citizens make to the society constitutes real, practical evidence of the power that people have to intervene in and have an influence on the society, at the same time making the shortage that exists in the provision of social services public knowledge.

A final point worth making in this section is that the viewpoints and reviews cover a wide range of reactions, reactions that are reflected in research. So, for example, the urging of citizens to get involved in issues that concern local communities in the United States of America is depicted in the various areas of interest of the social scientist: the promotion of the idea of volunteering (Snyder, 2000) to give one example, and the encouragement of the organizing of independently operating social activism (Wittig & Bettencourt, 1996), to give an example of a different kind.

Collective action as a way of educating citizens about exercising their democratic rights (Lawson, 2001; Turner, 2001; Jarvis, 2002), and the range of phenomena connected to the citizenship of women (Deligianni, 1998; Arnot et al., 1996), and youth (Haste, 2001; Van Hoorn, Komlosi & Samelson, 2000), are some of the main strands of research in Europe.

The majority of scientists actively researching at the present time, while apparently differing about the meanings and importance that they give to mobilization, seem to agree about the need of such mobilization and the involvement of citizens in social issues.

RESEARCH DEVELOPMENT AND THEORETICAL MODELS

Although in psychological research there is not exact agreement about the term mobilization, a substantial chunk of socio-psychological literature over the last few years reveals interest in topics that are related to it: Raising awareness of being active citizens and social participation and involvement in the community are among the more common terms met in applied social research that is interested in people 's intervention in the community, whether looking at the issue from the scientists' viewpoints or from those of the citizens'. From a conceptual point of view, by placing the three terms in a strict socio-psychological framework, it would be possible to state that they are independent, each describing different stages of the same process. As it will hopefully be apparent, whether a person is or is not involved in collective action and the way he/she perceives of and deals with social problems are connected to the concept to which we turn.

THE CONCEPT OF THE CHARACTERISTIC OF THE CITIZEN

The perception we have of the rights and obligations that a citizen derives in his/her relationship with the state in democratic societies, provides the base for forming the definition of what the characteristic of a citizen is. To follow a historical path, the definition and the multi-varied interpretations given to that quality, vary according to the times and the socio-political directions of the studies (Ichilov, 1998; Torney-Purta, Schwille & Amadeo, 1999; Van Horne, Komlosi, Sduchar & Samelson, 2000). So, for example, the views put forward by Marshall (1950), on the political and social dimensions that influence the forming of the characteristic of the citizen in the 1950s, were extended under the pressure of the social events of the following decades to include other dimensions, such as the economic and cultural ones (Turner, 2001). Such changes are reflected in the research.

Taking Marshall as a starting point, a substantial amount of research in Europe and in the more general western world centered on the dimension of the role of the state, interpreting the term politics as a straightforward exercise in political rights. In such a frame, research looked for ways of training young people to participate more effectively in political life. In realizing a more conservative interpretation of the meaning of the term "citizen" the associated research initially focused on typical patterns of electoral behavior (high or low turn outs, especially of young people, in the procedures associated with electing or being elected) as well as the processes of initiation and joining of individuals into closed political circles. Three important historical developments that occurred in the period from 1967 to 1987, the students' uprising, the Vietnam war and the peace movement brought about, according to

Haste (2001), a change in the direction of the research, having in mind the need for investigation of political activities that contained conflict and the psychological factors that accompanied such actions. The new political model that came out of that period describes a citizen of activism having a strong sense of effectiveness and control, a citizen who not so much participates, but is an instigator of social events (March, 1977; Haste, 1993). With the coming of the end of the social movements and of the cold war, the emphasis changed to the investigation of skills, such as those of taking on leadership and responsibility, that were responsible for the involvement of young people in collective actions, the nature of which involved dialogue and discussion. Leaving behind the framework of conflict, the prime factors in the family, the social and educational environments that from a social change point of view were responsible for the above activities, become the focus of investigation (Hamilton & Fenzel, 1988; Lenhart & Rabiner, 1995). In the last decade, the desire to search deeply for a reason for the existence or the absence of political interest by the populations in Europe and America, have acted as an excuse to revitalize interest in the issue of citizen mobilization, mainly within the area of education directed towards achieving human rights (Ichilov, 1998). In Great Britain a recent educational plan emphasized the need to create the model of an active as opposed to a passive citizen, one who will have the power not only to participate, but also, and more importantly, be able to propose and bring about alternative solutions to all the problems that concern him/her (Crick, 1998).

It is clear that the characteristic of a citizen in no way matches any kind of predetermined model of what it is to be human, but quite the reverse, is subject to historically formed patterns that we can scan for and carry out research on. In working with such a line it also becomes obvious that the ways in which researchers conceive of the characteristic of the citizen vary from period to period, thus resulting in a great range both of the models and skills of the citizen undergoing research each time, and of the special programs that are devised to serve these models. Different models of thinking about the desirable or non-desirable characteristics of a citizen lead, for example, to different conceptions of what citizen mobilization is, especially when it is associated with concepts such as the active participation and involvement of the citizen in the community.

COMMUNITY: PARTICIPATION AND INVOLVEMENT

A look should be taken at the ways in which researchers handled the above terms. Two characteristic of the studies stand out in this section. At a theoretical level, participation in the community is identified with positive forms of social behavior such as offering to volunteer, providing help and working without payment (Wilson, 2000). The main aim of such kinds of participation is the improvement of the community, achieved either directly through certain practical actions, or indirectly through creating, for example, a social support network between the citizens (Putman, 2000). The active citizen is associated with the concept of altruism, an increased sense and awareness of collective responsibility concerned with solving the practical problems of the community or the groups of the population with special problems (e.g. of health, poverty or illiteracy). At a research level, most studies center on active action and the different realizations of it when community participation is involved.

In particular, a brief run through the literature reveals that the importance accorded to the expression "citizen participation and involvement" varies according to what the research is looking for and the aims of the researcher. Therefore, within the framework of applied social research "participation" and "involvement" are two terms linked with the organizers behind the action in each case and the procedures in which they are involved, with reference at times to the research procedures designed and realized by the social scientists, and at other times to the procedures that the self-same citizen him/herself takes on with no guidance from the scientists. In the first case the reference is to actions that, in conjunction with the authorities of the community, are taken by the social scientists to deal with a specific issue that creates a social problem for the citizens of a community. A characteristic example of such a position is the drawing of active research needed when there is an attempt to reorganize the community or some aspect of it (e.g. Bryton-Miller & Tolman, 1997; Lykes, 1997; Chataway, 1997), along with the design of special programs that aim to educate the citizen about providing services to the community. A special sub-branch of this category concerns the educational programs that connect academic knowledge with practice in the community, so preparing the students to offer services to the community (Kendrick, 1996; Markus, Howard & King, 1993). Such programs have been springing up internationally at all levels of education throughout the last decade (e.g. Stanton, Giles, Gruz, 1999). In Greece, the self-help post graduate program of the psychology department of the Faculty of Philosophy of the Aristotle University of Thessaloniki is an attempt to work in this direction (Zafiridis, 2001). Similar attempts exist today in many European countries, where the idea of educating the citizen seems to be gaining more ground, while at the same time the juxtapositions about the usefulness of such education in relation to social change are deepening (Torney-Purta, Schwille & Amadeo, 1999; van Hoorn, Komlosi, Suchar & Samelso, 2000).

The research related to the actions citizens take on provides one of the most interesting sections of modern socio-psychological reading, as it brings to light findings that concern the ability of the citizen to organize him/ herself. One of the editions of the "Journal of Social Issues" (Stukas & Dunlap, 2002), recognizing the importance of the topic, concentrates, making reference to a series of various topics, on the ways in which citizens can take action. This edition promotes the view that social issues and problems such as, for example, labeling, prejudice and discrimination, and the protection of the environment, even given the various forms that characterize them, offer the citizen the chance to act, either as an individual, or by becoming a member of a group or organization, or by participating as an activist in social movements. The interest of the research collected in the above edition lies in its focus on the individually acting citizens themselves, investigating either their motives and values (Glary & Snyder, 2002), or the characteristic of the environment and wider socio-political procedures (such as the distribution of wealth and power, and the various possible effects that such a distribution can have as a source for providing help), that encourage or discourage their actions (Putnan, 2000).

In examining the consequences of the above terms of participation in social actions that people make, a large chunk of the research focuses on the benefits to and satisfaction of the individual as opposed to the benefit or not that the community acquires (Kraft, 1996; Zlotowski, 1998; Stukas, Clary & Snyder, 1999; Dunlap, 2000). While accepting that the aims of the two sides, whether of the community or the individual, are not always in agreement, today it is recognized that the participation of the citizen in community actions is, over all, a process as beneficial for the individual as for the community. Such is the conclusion of the discussions taking place in the United Europe that wish to promote participation and describe and analyze the pros and cons associated with the established and official forms of social policy.

Besides giving a simple outline of the good and bad points, it is necessary to clear up what is meant by the term community. To begin with, it is valuable to stress that, especially between psychologists, there is no agreement as to which is the definition or criteria necessary to establish the limits of what is meant by community (Garcia, Giuliani & Wiesenfeld, 1999). Many put forward that communities can be divided into *local* communities making reference to gatherings of people in a geographical area such as a neighborhood, province or city, and *international* ones, meaning the networks that people develop depending on their interests and abilities. Somehow, most studies emphasize the nature and arrangement of the existing geographical communities while not offending equally important approaches such as that of examining the socio-psychological dimensions that have to do mainly with a subject's perceptions of the characteristics of others who may or may not be similar. It is not essential for this similarity to coincide with a geographical entity (McMilan & Chavis, 1986), especially in our times when population movements create new needs to do with integrating into the populace and a resetting of identities. The view set in this paper is that the meaning of the term community has to be extended to include all of the above elements in order to result in a framework of mobilization for today's citizen. A citizen of Europe faces various problems as a result of changes in the financial, political, social and cultural aspects of life. It is well-known that the political and economic integration of European countries into a United Europe, the dissolution of once-established alliances (the ex-Soviet Union, Yugoslavia, Czechoslovakia) mass migration, the increased waves in request for asylum, along with mass unemployment are some of the factors that exclude millions of people, even some of those in the richer states, from their full integration into the community of the state. Given the above reality, the issue today is not about the integrating of the above-mentioned groups into the already existing socio-cultural communities, but about resetting the boundaries of each of the communities to include the new forms of divergence. One of the most interesting questions being asked internationally today is about the types and roles of participation by citizens of different national-cultural groups in the above resetting of communities and identities.

THE DIMENSION OF MASSIVE INVOLVEMENT

If we move beyond the community framework as defined above to the wider social context we will observe that massive political participation has become more frequent during the last decades. As Meyer and Tarrow (1998) observe the diffusion of protest does not only apply to growing numbers of those involved but relates to broader sectors of society as well, breaking through gender lines, age groups, socio-economic positions and occupations.

The reasoning behind this diffusion of protest varies. Klandermans (2003) distinguishes between two lines of explanation; the first attributes the diffusion of massive mobilization to the fact that western societies have become less hegemonic. According to the second, the relative effectiveness of mobilization encourages similar actions, functioning in other words as an incentive for political participation, be it conventional or unconventional, though such a distinction has become obsolete given the recent developments in the field of collective action. A number of studies have shown that politically active citizens employ an extended repertoire of political activities, falling into both kinds of collective social movements. From a strict theoretical standpoint it is more useful "to distinguish between individual and collective forms of political action, because the motivational dynamics of collective action are different from those of individual action" (cf. Klandermas, 2003, p. 673).

As we mentioned earlier, the dynamics of mobilization have for a long time attracted the attention of researchers from a variety of disciplines. An approach suggested by Snow and Benford (1988, 2000) refers to collective action frames considered as frames of collective beliefs, values and world views which give meaning to massive participation. In a somehow similar vein, Klandermans and Oegama (1988) and Klandermans (2003) broke the process of action mobilization into four separate steps, each of which brings the supply and demand of collective political action closer together "until an individual eventually takes the final step to participate" (p. 677). Behind this process there exist three motives, their relative weight of which has not been assessed in a single study. We will draw upon Klandermans' (2003, p. 679 ff) analysis of the three motives, shifting thereafter to the discussion of ideology (moral ideology in particular) in order to ascertain its possible effects on being involved.

A number of theories have been proposed to relate each of the three motives with collective participation in social-political movements (Tarrow, 1998). In Klandermans' "additive" model, participation is more likely to be the case if all three motives are present. The model implies that the motives may compensate one another or they may interact. A strong identification or ideology, for instance, "might alter cost-benefit calculations... Similarly a strong ideology may reinforce levels of identification ..." (p. 679).

The first motive, *instrumentality*, constitutes an attempt on the part of the individual to achieve some external good, i.e. to influence his/her social and political environment. A demand for change originates from experiences of inequality, feelings of injustice, moral indignation or imposed grievances. The crucial question faced by scholars was not so much why people are aggrieved but why aggrieved people participate in political mobilizations.

Olson's (1968) explanation that rational actors will not contribute to the achievement of a collective good unless specific incentives persuade them to do so, was considered inadequate on the grounds that it explains why people do not participate but it fails to explain why people do participate. Irrespective, therefore, of the fact that specific (or selective) incentives are not irrelevant to political involvement, they do not provide a sufficient explanation, the main criticism being that Olson 's model assumes that the individuals make their decisions in isolation, as if there are no other people with whom they consult, with whom they feel solidarity..." (Klandermas, 2003, p. 681).

The second motive, *identity*, manifests the will of an individual to become identified with a reference group. It is conceived in terms of the various places the person occupies in society: a student, worker, housewife, football player, politician etc. (cf. Simon, 1999). All these different roles and positions form the personal identity. But, since we don't live in isolation, the places a person occupies are, at the same time, shared with other people- a fact which creates the collective identity. To put it another way, personal identity is general, characterized by a variety of roles, whereas collective identity is specific, related to a specific place. Such a definition implies that personal identity is always collective identity at the same time.

The impact of personal and collective identities on massive mobilization can be searched for within the basic tenet of self-categorization theory (cf. Turner, 1999), namely that people are prepared to employ a social category and hence they are more willing to act as a member of that group. According to Huddy (2001-cited in Klandermans, 2003) identifying more or less strongly with a group may make a real difference especially in political contexts. This assumption is strongly supported by the available empirical evidence, ranging from the workers' involvement in their respective unions' demands to the feminists' movements.

Ideology as a search for meaning and expression of one's views is the third motive. In classic studies of social movements the basic distinction made, with regard to social mobilization, was between instrumental protest, that aimed at an external goal, and expressive movements in the frame of which participation was a goal in itself. Recently, this idea has been revived with the emphasis given on the creative, cultural and emotional aspects of social movements (cf. Goodwin, Jasper & Polletta, 2001).

Ideology in political science is usually conceptualized along the left-right spectrum. By social psychologists it is defined as a cohesive set of cognition, attitudes and feelings, with a salient affective component. From this perspective, ideology is considered as fundamental pivot for movement participation. As Goodwin et al.

(2001) have argued emotions that are politically relevant play a crucial role in the growth and unfolding of social movements and political protest. For these emotions cultural and historical factors are the tools for the interpretation of a given state of affairs. Furthermore they can be manipulated, as the activists and the politicians are well aware of, through the utilization of moral outrage and the cultural, historical and religious memories or feelings of a given group or wider society. Protests and rallies, for instance, against the war in Serbia, few years ago, were in the agenda, while 95% of the Greek citizens deplored the war against a country with which they felt solidarity originating from historical and religious ties.

THE DIMENSION OF THE MORAL REASONING IDEOLOGY

A fundamental assumption of structural-developmental theories of moral reasoning (or moral sophistication) is that the developmental process reflects the reorganiza-tion of thinking pertaining to socio-moral issues (Kohlberg, 1976; Kohlberg, Levine & Hewer, 1983; Colby and Kohlberg, 1987; Rest, 1979). The process in Kohlberg's theory is exemplified with reference to levels and stages of moral development. Each stage acquires a progressive adequacy of the social perspective taking, a cogni-tive ability related to resolving conflicts of interest. The progressive reorganization of sociomoral reasoning can be evidenced by the differentiation of the sociomoral perspective supposedly characterizing conventional and post-conventional think-ers. This construct "which underlines both role-taking and sociomoral judgment" (Kohlberg, 1976, p. 33) refers to the point of view the individual adopts with regard to social facts and sociomoral values. In this respect the conventional thinker can-not yet adopt a generalized system perspective, in contrast to the post-conventional individual whose "prior-to-society" perspective allows him to move beyond the conventions of the particular society in which he/she happens to be.

Kohlberg's conception of morality, in comparison to other relevant approaches (cf. Turiel's, 1983 domain theory and Rest's, 1984 four components model), raises in a more succinct way ideologically charged concerns which touch upon the issue of political reasoning and action. The most obvious implication of the model's basic assumptions is that evidence linking moral reasoning and political reasoning and action is most appropriately interpreted in terms of moral maturity (cf. Markoulis, 1989; Weinreich-Haste, 1986). Viewed in these items, political attitudes are the de-pended variables whose framework for the appropriate or inappropriate political behavior (i.e. involvement or not in a political issue), is set by the evolving capacities in the moral-cognitive realm.

Several earlier and relatively more recent studies (Haan, Smith & Block, 1968; Alker & Poppen, 1973; O' Connor, 1974; Candee, 1976; Nassi & Abramovitz, 1979; Rest, 1979; Tygart, 1984; Gross, 1996; Xila, 2005; Emler, Tarry & James, 2006) have found correlations between sociomoral reasoning and political participation and/or political ideology. Despite methodological shortcomings a repeated finding connects conventional sociomoral reasoning with right-conservative ideology while post-conventional reasoning was associated with lest-wing or liberal ideology. The explanation of this kind of evidence has also been a matter of controversy. As Gross (1996) has noted, in the worse case the evidence casts doubt on the structural integrity of cognitive developmental theory "suggesting instead that the stages of moral reasoning are not content free but reflect a commitment to, or bias for, liberal democratic norms" (p. 318).

In an effort to overcome methodological inadequacies found in previous studies, Muhlberger (2000) sought o show, using Rest's Defining Issues Test (DIT), that moral sophistication is relevant to a "broader category of participation: present day public interest group involvement" (p. 669). As the author argues the findings of the study are important in several respects. For one thing they establish in a more valid way that ethical considerations matter for political behavior. The rationale behind this assertion lies on the fact that the study provided for the control of factors which made the results of previous studies less convincing. Previous research supportive of the impact of sociomoral reasoning on political participation decisions used behavioral intentions or recollected past behavior as proxies for behavior. Second prior studies did not analyze the process by which sociomoral reasoning affects political participation. They "assume a linear positive relationship between moral reasoning and activism, a relationship for which there is no good theoretical rationale" (Muhlberger, 2000, p. 670). Third the author defends his findings against criticisms that the P score of DIT simply measures ethical self-presentation, invalidating thus the results reported in his study. Nevertheless this is a controversial issue that had not as yet found its final answer, if there is one. (For the respective arguments and the research evidence on this issue, see Emler, Renwick & Malone, 1983; Emler, Palmer-Canton & James, 1998; Emler, 2002; Emler, Tarry & James, 2006; Thoma, 1993; Thoma, Barnett, Rest & Narvaez, 1999).

A CONCLUDING REMARK

Citizen's mobilization is undoubtedly a complex social-psychological process and as such it raises a number of questions and methodologies pertaining directly or indirectly with the conceptual demarcation of the mobilization processes and of the social-psychological phenomena penetrating these processes. Further investigation of the economic, social and cultural factors that encourage or hinder the citizen's involvement in the socio-political system, seems also to be a necessity. At a general level mobilization is in essence a socio-political activity which, depending on the target, the group of people involved and the framework in which it takes place, acquires different socio-psychological features.

Among the basic motives behind many kinds of involvement, identity and ideology deserve more attention. As Klandermans (2003) observes solid empirical studies on identity are still rare. The same picture is also true for ideology and its relationship with emotions. The study of moral sophistication as a cognitively loaded component of ideology could contribute in a more clear manner to the explanation of evidence that issues closely associated with deeper ethical concerns, as it is the case of the environment, motivate less the low-sophisticated persons.

REFERENCES

Alker, H. A., & Poppen, P. J. (1973). Personality and ideology in university students. *Journal of Personality, 41*, 652-671.

Arnot, M., Araujo, H., Deligianni, K., Rowe, G., & Tome, A. (1996). Teachers, gender and the discourses of citizenship. *International Studies of Sociology of Education, 6* (1), 3-35.

Austin, D., & Hasenfeld, Y. (1985). A prefatory essay on the future administration of human services. *The Journal of Applied Behavioral Science, 21*, 351-364.

Bryton-Miller, M., & Tolman, D. (1997). Transforming psychology: Interpretive and participatory research methods. *Journal of Social Issues, 53* (4), 597-811.

Chataway, C. (1997). An examination of the constraints on mutual inquiry in a participatory action research project, *Journal of Social Issues, 53* (4), 747-765.

Clary, E., & Snyder, M. (2002). Community involvement: Opportunities and challenges in socializing adults to participate in society. *Journal of Social Issues, 58* (3), 581-592.

Candee, D. (1976). Structure and choice in moral reasoning. *Journal of Personality ana Social Psychology, 34*, 1293-1301.

Colby, A., & Kohlberg, L. (1987). *The measurement of moral judgment, Vol. 1. Theoretical foundations and research validation.* NY: Cambridge University Press.

Crick, B. (1998). *Education for citizenship and the teaching of democracy in schools.* New York: Free Press.

Deligianni, K. (1998). *Women and citizenship.* Thessaloniki: Vanias Publ. (in Greek)

Dunlap, M. (2000). *Reaching out to children and families: Students model effective community service.* Lanham, MD: Rowman & Littlefield.

Emler, N. (2002). Morality and political orientations: An analysis of their relationship. *European Review of Social Psychology, 13*, 259-291.

Emler, N., Renwick, S., & Malone, B. (1983). The relationship between moral reasoning and political orientation. *Journal of Personality and Social Psychology, 45*, 1073-1080.

Emler, N., Palmer-Canton, E., & St. James, A. (1998). Politics, moral reasoning and the Defining Issues Test. A reply to Barnett et al., 1995. *British Journal of Social Psychology, 37*, 457-476.

Emler, N., Tarry, H., & James, A. (2006). Post-conventional moral reasoning and reputation. *Journal of Research in Personality*, 1-14.

Fukuyama, F. (1992). *The end of history and the last man.* New York: Free Press.

Garsia, I., Giulani, F., & Wiesenfeld, E. (1999). Community and sense of community: The case of an urban barrio in Caracas. *Journal of Community Psychology, 27*, 727-740.

Goodwin, J., Jasper, T. & Polletta, F. (2001). Why emotions matter. In J. Goodwin, J Jasper & F. Polletta (Eds), *Passionate politics, emotions and social movements* (pp. 1-24). Chicago: University Press of Chicago

Gross, L. M. (1996). Moral reasoning and ideological affiliation: A cross-national study. *Political Psychology, 17* (2), 317-338.

Haan, N., Smith, M. B., & Block, J. (1968). Moral reasoning of young adults: Political-social behavior, family background, and personality correlates. *Journal of Personality and Social Psychology, 10*, 183-201.

Hamilton, S., & Fenzel, I. (1988). The impact of volunteer experience on adolescent social development. *Journal of adolescent research, 3* (1), 65-80.

Haste, H. (1993). Moral creativity and education for citizenship. *Creativity Research Journal, 6*, (1&2), 153-164.

Haste, H. (2001). The new citizenship of youth in rapidly changing nations. *Human Development, 44*, 375-381.

Heather, D. (1990). *Citizenship: The civic ideal in world history, politics and education.* London and New York: Longman.

Ichilov, O. (1998). *Citizenship and citizenship education in a changing world.* London: the Woburn Press.

Jarvis, P. (2002). Globalization, citizenship and the education of adults in contemporary European society. *Compare, 32* (1), 5-19.

Kendrick, J. (1996). Outcomes of service-learning in an introduction to sociology course. *Michigan Journal of Community Service Learning, 3,* 72-81.

Klandermans, B., & Oegema, D. (1987). Potentials, networks, motivation and barriers: Steps toward participation in social movements. *American Sociological Review, 5,* 519-531.

Klandermans, B. (2003). Collective political action. In D. O. Sears, L. Huddy & K. Jervis (Eds), *Oxford handbook of political psychology,* (pp. 670-709). Oxford NY: Oxford University Press.

Kohlberg, L. (1976). Moral stages and moralization: The cognitive-developmental approach. In Th. Lickona (Ed.), *Moral development and behavior: Theory, research and social issues,* (pp. 31-53). New York: Holt, Rinehart & Winston.

Kohlberg, L., Levine, C., & Hewer, A. (1983). *Moral stages: A current formulation and a response to critics.* New York: Karger.

Kraft, R. (1996). Service learning: An introduction to its theory, practice, and effects. *Education and Urban Society, 28,* 131-159.

Lawson, H. (2001). Active citizenship in schools and the community. *The Curriculum Journal, 12* (2), 163-178.

Lenhart, L., & Rabiner, D. (1995). Social competence in adolescence. *Developmental Psychopathology, 2,* 543-561.

Lykes, M. B. (1997). Activist participatory research among the Maya of Guatemala: Constructing meanings from situated knowledge. *Journal of Social Issues, 53* (4), 725-746.

March, A. (1977). *Protest and political consciousness.* London: Sage.

Markus, G., Howard, J., & King, D. (1993). Integrating community service and classroom instruction enhances learning: Results from an experiment. *Educational Evaluation and Policy Analysis, 15,* 410-419.

Markoulis, D. (1989). Political involvement and socio-moral reasoning: Testing Emler's interpretation. *British Journal of Social Psychology, 28,* 203-212.

Marshall, T. H. (1950). *Citizenship and social class and other essays.* Cambridge: Cambridge University Press.

McLoughlin, T. (1992). Citizenship, diversity and education: A philosophical perspective. *Journal of Moral Education, 21* (3), 121-145.

McMillan, D., & Chavis, D. (1986). Sense of community: A definition and theory. *Journal of Community Psychology, 14,* 6-23.

Meyer, D., & Tarrow, S. (1998). *The social movement society: Contentious politics for a new century.* Boulder, CO: Rowman and Littlefield.

Muhlberger, P. (2000). Moral reasoning effects on political participation. *Political Psychology, 21* (4), 667-695.

Nassi, A., & Abramowitz, S. (1979). Transition or transformation? Personal and political development of former Berkley Free Speech Movement activists. *Journal of Youth and Adolescence, 8,* 21-35.

O' Connor, R. E. (1974). Political activism and moral reasoning: Political and apolitical students in Great Britain and France. *British Journal of Political Science, 4,* 79-107.

Olson, M. (1968). *The logic of collective action. Public goods and the theory of groups.* Cambridge: Harvard University Press.

Owen, D. (1986). Opening address: Social formal and informal patterns of care. *British Journal of Social Work, 16* (supplement), 15-22.

Penner, L. (2002). Dispositional and organizational influences on sustained volunteerism: An interactionist perspective. *Journal of Social Issues, 58* (3), 447-468.

Putnan, R. (2000). *Bowing alone: The collapse and revival of American community.* New York: Simon & Schuster.

Rest, J. (1984). Morality. In P. H. Mussen (Ed.), *Handbook of child psychology, vol. III*, pp. 556-627. New York: Wiley.

Simon, B. (1999). A place in the world: Self and social categorization. In T.R. Tyler, R. M. Kramer, & O. P. John (Eds), *The psychology of the social self* (pp 47-69). Mahwah, NJ: Erlbaum

Snyder, M. (2000). *Doing good for self and others: Volunteerism and the psychology of individual and collective action.* Paper presented at the biennial meeting of the Society for the Psychological Study of Social Issues, Mineapolis, MN. A.

Stanton, T., Giles, D., & Cruz, N. (1999). *Service learning: A movement's pioneers reflect on its origins, practice, and future.* San Francisco: Jossey-Bass.

Stukas, A., Clary, E., & Snyder, M. (1999). Service learning: Who benefits and why. *Social Policy Report, 13,* 1-19.

Stukas, A., & Dunlap, M. (2002). Community involvement: Theoretical approaches and educational initiatives. *Journal of Social Issues, 58,* 411-427.

Thoma, S. (1993). The relationship between political preference and moral judgment development in late adolescence. *Meril-Palmer Quarterly, 39,* 359-374.

Thoma, S., Barnett, R., Rest, J., & Narvaez, D. (1999). What does the DIT measures? *British Journal of Social Psychology, 38,* 103-111.

Torney-Purta, J., Schwille, J., & Amadeo, J. (Eds), (1999). *Civic education across countries; Twenty-four national case studies from the IEA Civic Education project.* Amsterdam: The International Association for the Evaluation of Educational Achievement.

Turner, B. S. (2001). The erosion of citizenship. *British Journal of Sociology, 52* (2), 189-209.

Turner, J. C. (1999). Some current issues in research on social identity and self-categorization theories. In N. Ellemers, R. Spears & B. Doosje (Eds), *Social Identity* (pp. 6-34). Oxford: Blackwell

Tygart, C. E. (1984). Moral autonomy and social-political activism among the faculty and staff of a West Coast University. *Sociological Inquiry, 54,* 16-25.

Turiel, E. (1983). *The development of social knowledge: Morality and convention.* Cambridge: Cambridge University Press.

United Nations General Assembly (2000). *Further initiatives for social development.* Resolution (A/RES/S-24/2) adopted at the Special Session of the United Nations General Assembly, Geneva, 26 June-1 July. Available at http://www.un.org/esa/socdev/geneva2000/.

Van Hoorn, J. L., Komllosi, A. & Samelson, D. (2000). *Adolescent development and rapid social change.* Albany: SUNY Press.

Vincent, A. & Plant, R. (1984). *Philosophy, politics and citizenship.* New York: Blackwell.

Weinreich-Haste, H. (1986). Kohlberg's contribution to political psychology: A positive view. In S. Modgil &C. mogdil (Eds), *Lawrence Kohlberg: Consensus and commentary,* (pp. 337-360). Brighton: Falmer Press.

Wilson, J. (2000). Volunteering. *Annual Review of Sociology, 26,* 215-240.

Wittig, M., & Bettencourt, B. (Eds.), (1996). Social psychological perspectives on grassroots organizing. *Journal of Social Issues, 52* (1).

Xila, H. (2005). Internal and external factors of political socialization during adolescence. In D. Markoulis & M. Dikaiou (Eds), *Political psychology: Problems and prospects* (pp. 305-344). Athens: Dardanos Publications (in Greek).

Zafiridis, F. (2001). Mental health and self-help. *Psychiatric Papers, 73,* 22-29.

Zlotkowski, E. (1998). *Successful service-learning programs: New models of excellence in higher education.* Boston, MA: Anker.

Markoulis Diomedes & Dikaiou Maria
Aristotle University, Thessaloniki, Greece

F. CLARK POWER & ANN MARIE R. POWER

CIVIC ENGAGEMENT, GLOBAL CITIZENSHIP AND MORAL PSYCHOLOGY

In this chapter we explore some of the moral psychological constructs involved in fostering global citizenship. We do so by examining the relationship between "getting involved" or what is typically called "civic engagement" and moral responsibility. "Getting involved" is a part of one's moral responsibility as a citizen. Getting involved also is a way of cultivating a sense of moral responsibility because it one's engagement that one forms a sense of self as a citizen, connected with one's society. The path to global citizenship seems at first glance to proceed from becoming a good citizen of one's city or nation to becoming a citizen of the world. The path to global citizenship also seems to be a moral path leading from the particular to the universal, from socio-centrism to globalism.

If we are to promote global citizenship as a moral ideal, we must ask what citizenship means in a global context. This is not an easy question because the concept of citizenship refers to a particular city or state and not to the international human community (the English word, citizen, is derived from the French word, *cité*, which means city). When we speak of a global citizenship then, we are using the notion of citizenship analogously. Global citizenship does not confer particular rights or imply particular duties. On the other hand, global citizenship does recognize universal rights and universal moral duties.

WHAT IS GLOBAL CITIZENSHIP?

Global citizenship comes from the recognition that one is a member of the human family or of an emerging transnational community and that as a member one has certain responsibilities to that community. Although the global community is not a formal political entity, it functions psychologically and sociologically in many ways similarly to a formally constituted state or nation. As a global citizen, one experiences a sense of connection and even identification with others across national boundaries. This sense of connection and identification goes beyond recognition of a common personhood or of common human rights to a sense of responsibility for global community as an interdependent whole. In the absence of a formal transnational governmental entity that represents all nations and people (other than the United Nations, which has very limited power) the concept of a global community is still an ideal. On the other hand, ever expanding economic, technological, and

Fritz Oser & Wiel Veugelers (eds.), Getting involved, 89–101.

communication systems are creating networks making national boundaries increasingly permeable. Although the political structures for a global community are still in the making, the forces of globalization are well underway.

These forces are making the people of the world increasingly interdependent and vulnerable. For example, it is becoming clear to people all over the world that technological and economic advances threaten the biosphere and the future habitability of our planet. The behavior of any one nation threatens the welfare of all. The only effective response to a catastrophe, such as global warming, is for individuals and for nations to acknowledge their common destiny and to work together for the sake of the common good. Responsible citizenship is global citizenship.

In a highly provocative and often cited essay, "The Tragedy of the Commons," Hardin (1968) argues that in the absence of a regulative authority individuals will to exploit the commons to advance their private interests. Although one may dispute whether individuals are as selfish or as shortsighted as Hardin claims, it is difficult to dispute the social phenomenon of the exploitation of common resources in the absence of any effective regulatory agency. While it is true, that many individuals and organizations are vigorous proponents of protecting the global environment, it is also true that they can effect little meaningful change without international cooperation. Such cooperation entails support for a governing body at the international level with the regulatory power to compel responsible energy use and care for common resources. This governing body is necessary to address other threats requiring international solidarity and cooperation power for their solution, such as extreme poverty, war, terrorism, and the abuse of human rights. The energy needed to bring about such a radical change in the way nations relate to one another must comes from citizens around the world, who recognize the moral imperative of international cooperation and work for such cooperation through the democratic processes in their countries.

THE PSYCHOLOGICAL PREREQUISITES OF CITIZENSHIP

What can we, as psychologists and educators, say about the cultivation of a global citizenship capable of taking moral responsibility for the planet? What constructs might we advance that would serve as a framework for a new kind of citizenship education? Before one can be a global citizen, it appears that one has to be an engaged citizen of a particular political entity. Good citizens take an interest in the common welfare and work on behalf of the group as a whole as well as the members in it. Likewise, global citizens care about global welfare and bettering the conditions for all people of the world. Just as individual members of a group align their private interests with those of their group, so too do global citizens align their interests with those of the world community.

Although there are many similarities between being a good citizen of a particular nation and being a good citizen of the world, we acknowledge that a good citizen of a particular nation may well put the interests of that nation above those of other nations and above global welfare more generally. We have numerous examples in our world today in which individual countries pursue policies that advance their national interests at the expense of others and even at the expense of their own future generations. Being a global citizen requires a sense of justice that takes into account the perspectives of other nations and people. How would such a perspective be cultivated? Might it be too much to expect that such a perspective be fostered in the typical civic education curriculum?

In our view global citizenship requires an approach to citizenship education based on principles of justice and concern for the common good. Such a citizenship education must foster respect for all persons as persons regardless of national origin and high regard for the political processes necessary to protect human rights and promote the welfare of all. When one considers the interdependence of the people and nations of the world, being a good citizen of one's country also requires being a good citizen of the world. Yet in the United States today we are witnessing a crisis of citizen disengagement that threatens the foundations of our democratic society and dims the prospect of fostering global citizenship. Before we can hope to foster global citizenship on a widespread level, we must first find a way of engaging America's youth in its democratic political structures.

CITIZENSHIP EDUCATION

In recent years there has been a revival of interest in civic education (e.g., Altof and Berkowitz, 2006; Colby, Ehrlich, Beuamont, and Stephens, 2002; Galston, 2001; Neimi and Jun, 1998; Sherrod, 2002). Yet the most recent assessment of the civic knowledge of American students in the 4th, 8th, and 12th grades, (Lutkus and Weiss, 2007), indicates that in spite of efforts to reform civic education in the schools, serious problems persist. Only 27% of students in the 12th grade have reached the level of proficiency. Perhaps more alarming is the finding that 34% are not even at the basic level. Most students in the 12th grade are either at or within a year of voting age.

Although civic knowledge does not necessarily lead to engagement, the two are related (Galston, 2001). The better informed students are about the values and processes of their democratic government; the more likely they are to participate in political life. The reverse, however, also appears to be true; civic knowledge follows from engagement in civic life. If students do not have a vital interest in democratic governance, what motivation is there for them to acquire civic knowledge? In an international study of the effects of a civic education curriculum, Vontz, Metcalf, and Patrick (2000) found that involving students in public policy analysis and decision-making is an effective way of developing their knowledge base and willingness to participate in civic life. Similarly, Baldi, Perie, Skidmore, Greenberg, and Hahn (2001), Campbell (2005), Torney-Purta (2002), and Veugelers and Oser (2003) have found that civic education courses with open classroom discussion have a positive effect on the civic competence of students. In sum, recent research demonstrates that civic engagement is best nurtured fostered through classroom engagement using constructivist teaching practices. We have reason to be concerned, however, that without the motivation supplied by being a member of a civics education class, many high school graduates simply lose interest in politics.

A CRISIS OF CIVIC ENGAGEMENT

Social scientists and policy-makers in both Europe (e.g, Oser and Reichenbach, 2003) and the United States (e.g., Colby and Ehrlich, 2003; Putnam, 2000) have expressed a concern about striking decline in the level of participation in civic life over several decades. There are many indicators in the United States of a generational decline in almost all every form of political involvement (Putnam, 2000; Zukin, Keeter, Andolina, Jenkins, and Carpini, 2006). For example, Zukin et al. (2006) report that in contrast to older cohorts, the DotNets (those born after 1976), the most recent cohort to come of voting age, are the least interested or engaged in politics. Next to the DotNets, the GenXers (those born between 1965 and 1976) are the next least involved and the trend continues with the Boomers (those born between 1946 and 1964) and Dutifuls (the born before 1946).

Putnam (2000) claims that the decline in engagement goes further than political participation to social networks themselves. He finds that Americans are not coming together they way they used to in clubs, organizations, and even in informal dinner parties and sports outings (like bowling!). If Putnam is correct, and his evidence is very persuasive, then the crisis of civic engagement is rooted in an erosion of the social bonds that sustain social as well as political life. In line with Putnam's findings, McPherson, Smith-Lovin, and Brashears, M. (2006) show that over the past two decades Americans have experienced a dramatic decrease in their number of confidants, such that the modal American has no confidants with whom to discuss important matters, whereas in 1985, the modal American had three. How are millions of Americans going to manage to face the trials and tribulations of daily life alone? How can American society maintain a modicum of mental health let alone political health amid such isolation?

The picture of civic life that Zukin et al. (2006) present is not as dire as that of Putnam (2003) or of McPherson, Smith-Lovin, and Brashears (2006). Zukin et al. (2006) make an important distinction between civic and political engagement. By civic engagement, they mean organized voluntary activity "focused on problem solving and helping others" (p. 7). In contrast, by political engagement they mean activity directed at influencing government and public policy. Zukin et al. (2006) show when it comes to civic engagement, the DotNets do well in comparison with other generations. Although the percentage of those volunteering regularly is slightly less than the GenXers and Boomers, the percentage of those volunteering occasionally is much higher. On the other hand, the DotNets are at the bottom of most indices of political engagement.

The DotNets' relatively strong participation in voluntary service may be due in part to their schooling. During the 1990s, increasing numbers of schools across the

United States sponsored service programs. Although sponsorship leveled off from 1999 to 2004, over 60% of public schools continue to maintain service programs (Scales and Roehlkepartain, 2004). These programs are of two types: 1) extracurricular community service and 2) curricular-related community service (service learning). Although research has clearly established the benefits of the service learning model (e.g. , Youniss and Yates, 1997), less than half (26%) of the schools with extracurricular community service projects offer service learning programs (Scales and Roehlkepartain, 2004). The DotNets high rate of volunteering but low rate of political engagement may to some extent reflect the fact that so many schools failed to provide the academic support needed to relate their service to the political sphere. Moreover, as Zukin et al. (2006) speculate, school sponsored service programs may have a negative effect on political engagement if they convey the message that service can substitute for political engagement.

Although extracurricular service may not lead directly to political engagement, service, nevertheless, appears to be a much needed form of civic engagement, particularly at a time when the social fabric appears to be unraveling. Yet we should be cautious about attributing too much significance to the DotNet's volunteer rates. A recent report shows a decline in volunteering from 2005 to 2006, particularly in the youngest cohort (Corporation for National and Community Service, 2007). More disturbingly that same report notes that one out of three volunteers in one year dropped out the following year. Although the DotNets may be volunteering in relatively impressive numbers, many are not staying involved. This could be remedied making service a part of the curriculum. Zukin et al. (2006) find that discussions about volunteer work double the likelihood that students will continue their service. Why should discussion make a difference? Discussions can certainly make students more aware of the need for and value of their work so that service is seen less as an act of charity and more as a moral duty. Viewing service as a civic duty is the only attitude that Zukin et al. (2006) find significantly correlated to students' level of activity. Youniss and Miranda (1999) note that discussions about service not only lead students to integrate their activity within a larger moral framework but to reflect on their future responsibilities in society.

POLITICAL ENGAGEMENT

As we think ahead to the demands of global citizenship, the DotNets level of volunteer service hardly compensates their lack of their political engagement. Although most attention has been paid to low voter turnout, the DotNets conspicuously absent themselves from all kinds of political involvement whether it is working for a political campaign to taking part in a political discussion. The DotNets also appear strikingly uninterested in politics and current affairs. Only 25% say that they "follow politics and government … most of the time" (Zukin et al., p. 81). Perhaps more revealing is the statistic that only 34% of college first year students find it "essential or very important" to "keep up with political affairs" (Zukin et. al 2006, p. 83). The fact that students do not find value in keeping up with politics suggests not only that they believe that politics are irrelevant to their lives but also that political affairs make no moral claim on their attention. The data on civic and political engagement indicate that the majority of the DotNets do not understand why they should become involved in the public domain.

How should we think of the morality of political engagement? Is political engagement a moral duty? Although political engagement is desirable and even necessary for the health of a democratic society, is participation mandatory? While under ordinary circumstances it would be wrong to steal or to lie, would it be wrong not to vote or not to become involved in the political process? Although participation may not be a moral duty in the strict sense, Citizenship education desperately needs a conception of political engagement based on a moral framework. We suggest that this framework might start with the notion that in general, political engagement is a moral responsibility in a democratic society. The responsibility for engagement arises not only from the fact that the members are so interconnected that their society cannot function for the good of all without their participation but also from the fact that as citizens of a democracy, they are charged with governing their society. Democratic governance imposes the burden of legislative responsibility on its members.

Sherrod, Flannagan, and Youniss's (2002) research suggests that many young adolescents believe that that their duties as citizens do not extend much beyond obeying the laws or being a good person. Similarly, Zukin et al. (2006) report that only 38% of the DotNets agree that citizenship entails "special obligations" and 58% think that "being a 'good person' is enough" (p. 100). Studies by the Tarrance Group (2000) and Higher Education Research (2001) note that a high percentage of college first year students have little or no grasp of the political demands of citizenship and are simply not related to about the public sphere. Taken together, these findings point to the influence of a culture of privatism focused on personal and family aspirations. Parker (2002) rightly argues that in a democracy citizens are expected to play an active role in governance. Yet in a 1999 study, only 9% of high school seniors could list two benefits from citizens' active participation in a democratic society (National Assessment of Education Progress). This finding reveals the depth of the crisis of engagement. Many young people appear to be so detached from the political institutions of the United States that they simply cannot relate their role as citizens with the welfare of society. In other words, many young people lack a meaningful sense of democratic agency with respect to the public sphere. They simply do not see themselves as responsible for the public sphere even though they are aware that they live in a democratic society.

In psychological terms, the problem of engagement seems to us to be rooted in self understanding and identity development. As young people are developing a sense the person they hope to become, they appear to focus almost exclusively on private concerns. This is not to say that they are necessarily narcissistic or selfish. Our research shows that the majority of children and adolescents (Power and Khlmelkov, 1997; Roney, Power, and Power 2006) include at least one moral quality in their descriptions of their real and ideal selves. These children and adolescents aspire to be a person who is kind to others, particularly to friends and family members. Relatively few, however, extend their circle of concern beyond family and friends. From a cognitive developmental framework (e.g, Damon and Hart,1988); Kohlberg, 1984), we are not surprised that children's social and moral words would be so limited. On the other hand from a cognitive developmental framework, most adolescents are capable of relating to a social organization or a society as an entity distinct from its individual members. If adolescents do not envision their ideal selves as related in some way to society, we should not be surprised if they are not politically engaged (cf. Youniss and Miranda, 1999).

Youniss and Yates (1999) draw on the work of Blasi (1984), Colby and Damon (1995), and Hart and Fegley (1995) among others to argue that they key to civic engagement is to be found in the self and not in moral judgment. In our view, Youniss and Yates (1999), like Bergman (2002), so emphasize the importance of the identity in explaining moral action that they fail to consider instances in which moral judgment is also required. Although we agree with Youniss and Yates and others that civic and political engagement arise out of a sense of self rather than out of a "rational calculation" (Youniss and Yates, 1999, p. 373), identity alone is not sufficient for the exercise of the legislative demands of democratic citizenship. Responsible moral citizenship entails deliberation about particular policies, deliberation that in turn requires moral reasoning and decision-making. Moral self and moral judgment constructs are both necessary for an adequate account of the moral dimension of citizenship. Individuals attach to society through their identities or sense of self. Their identities, however, are necessary but not sufficient for making decisions about what is best for society or the world.

We propose that research on citizenship and political engagement start with an assessment of what we call the ideal self (Power and Khmelkov, 1997). We define the ideal self as the self that one aspires to become. We speculate that individuals develop a sense of their ideal selves as they experience a wide array of relational and cultural influences. In our view, many of those influences appear to lead in the direction of privatism, which focus on what is good for oneself and one's family rather than on the common good. Developing a sense of self that includes a concern to help others outside of one's immediate circle of family and friends may be particularly challenging today. Apart from developing a moral sensitivity to the needs of other individuals, young people must also become aware of awareness of the political order and of their responsibilities as democratic citizens. Caring for others as individuals is not enough. Citizenship in its fullest sense requires caring for one's society. This kind of caring requires an engagement with issues of justice and human welfare at a structural level. In order to distinguishing between these two kinds of caring, we define two types of moral selves: a moral self that is oriented to interpersonal concerns and a moral self that is oriented to social-structural concerns. We hypothesize that individuals with moral selves oriented to social-structural concerns are most likely to become engaged in political activities.

From a moral point of view, the mere engagement in political activities is not enough. Individuals may engage in political activities to advance their own interests or to advance the interests of a favored group. They may even engage in political activities to advance what they consider to be moral purposes, but do so in overly simplistic ways. For example they may support candidates who seem to be virtuous people without considering their policies. Popkin and Dimok (1999) find that individuals who do not adequately understand political processes use "estimates of personal character" as a "proxy for political character" (p. 127; see also Galston, 2001). If political engagement is to moral, it must be done with the ends of justice and the common good in view.

In emphasizing the crisis of disengagement, we may have paid too little attention the further issue of the morality of the ends being pursued through the political process. Encouraging young people to vote is simply not enough. We should be preparing young people to exercise their moral judgment when they vote. Global citizenship depends upon more than identifying with the world community but deliberating about policies that will most effectively promote the good of all.

In the study that follows, we use distinct measures of the moral self and moral decision-making to explore civic and political engagement and the concept of global citizenship. We hypothesize that a more differentiated conception of the moral self (one that distinguishes interpersonal and societal orientations) will help to explain why some young people become politically involved while others do not. We also hypothesize that the moral self construct alone is not sufficient to explain the legislative demands of citizenship at a national or a global level.

METHOD

Sample

The sample is composed of 112 students and graduate students from a mid-size university in the Midwestern United States with an unusually high rate of community service volunteerism. The sample was split evenly between male and female students; sixteen percent of the sample was minority (African American and Latino/a).

Method

Civic Engagement was measured by the scale developed by Keeter, Zukin, Andolina, & Jenkins (2002). Participants answered 15 questions on a 4 point scale from never (1) to many (4) on how frequently they engaged in the civic behavior in the past two years. Items included questions pertaining to civic activity (e.g., volunteering, donating time or resources to the community), electoral activity (voting),and political discussion (e.g. discussing political issues with friends, participating in online political dsicussions).

Civic Efficacy and Responsibility was measured with a scale taken from Keeter,

Zukin, Andolina, & Jenkins's (2002) questionnaire for assessing civic attitudes. Sample items include *It is my responsibility to get involved to make thing better for society,* and *Every citizen should take the time to find out about current events even if it means giving up spare time.* Cronbach's α coefficient for this scale is .76 (LaVoi and Power, 2006).

The Moral Self was measured by coding responses to the following: How would you describe the person that you want to become? Describe the characteristics of your ideal self. Responses were categorized as having no moral content (I want to be successful in my chosen profession); some interpersonal moral content (e.g., I aspire to be a person who always treats others with kindness), and some societal moral content or moral content that invokes social structures (e.g., I want to be an active and engaged citizen by working with groups opposed to human trafficking). Moral focus was coded by dividing the number of moral characteristics used to describe the self by the total number of descriptive characteristics.

Legislative Perspective was assessed by coding answers to the question: How should a person make up his or her mind in voting on a difficult issue or for a political candidate? What considerations are most important in making voting decisions? Legislative Perspective was categorized according to whether only the interests of the self are taken into account, whether the interests of the self are balanced by the interests of others, or whether the common good is given priority.

Global Welfare was assessed by coding responses to the question: In dealing with the issues of the environment and armed conflict, which should take priority – the interest of the United States or the interests of all nations? Answered were coded according to three categories: 1) Put the United States first; 2) Balance the interests of the United States with other nations, and 3) Put Global interests first.

Results

A very high proportion of the participants (85%) were coded describing their ideal selves with some moral content. Of these, 63 % were coded as interpersonally-oriented and the remaining 37% as societal-oriented. Those categorized as societal-oriented used a significantly greater number of moral characteristics to describe their selves (moral focus).

When we turn to key engagement variables, we find that the content of the ideal moral self is not significantly related to voting behavior or community service, but is significantly related to political involvement (e.g., volunteering for a political organization, working for a for a political candidate) and to engaging in political discussion (See Table 1). Those with a societal-oriented moral ideal self are significantly more engaged in these areas than those with an interpersonal or no moral self.

The level of legislative perspective is not significantly related to the ideal self. In a regression analysis, legislative perspective and the ideal self independently contribute to engaging in political discussion (see Table 2). The legislative perspective is also significantly correlated with staying politically informed (r=.39, p<.01).

Table I. Relationship of moral self to political engagement

Moral Self	Political Involvement M (SD)	Political Discussion M (SD)
No Moral	5.64 (2.62)	3.12 (1.58)
Interpersonal Moral	5.90 (1.89)	3.33 (1.24)
Societal Moral	7.80 (3.42)	4.34 (1.83)
	F = 6.92, P = .001	F = 6.119, P = .003

Table II. Results of Multiple Regression using the ideal self and the legislative perspective variables to predict the frequency of participation in political discussions

Variable	beta	t
Ideal Self	.298*	2.66
Legislative Perspective	.316**	2.82

Total R^2 = .164
Adjusted R^2 = .139

*P = .01, **P<.001.

The extent to which one identifies as a citizen of the world does not relate to any of the engagement variables with the exception of being informed about political issues. Asked about their perspective on issues concerning the environment and armed conflict, almost half (49%) of the participants put global interest first, 28% sought a balance between Global interest and U.S. interest, and 23% put the U.S.'s interest first. Taking a global perspective was significantly correlated to the level of legislative perspective (r=.40, p=.001). We found no relationship between the ideal self and global versus U.S. interest.

DISCUSSION

The results of this study indicate that the moral self and legislative perspective are related to political and global citizenship. Moreover, they suggest that the concept of global citizenship may differ from national citizenship in several important ways. In exploring the relationship between the ideal self and civic engagement, we found that differentiating between two kinds of a moral self, interpersonal-oriented and societal-oriented, makes a difference when one considers different kinds of civic engagement. We found that those with a societal-oriented ideal self are more likely to engage in civic engagement that requires interaction with others through either political discussion or participation in a political organization than those with an interpersonal-oriented moral self. Although those with a societal-oriented ideal self used more moral descriptors to describe their ideal selves (moral focus), moral focus did not predict to participating in political discussions or political organization. This suggests that what counts in explaining the relationship of the moral self to specifically political kinds of activity is whether or not there is at least some connection of the self with a socially oriented moral concern. We find it worth noting that those who describe themselves with at least one societal-oriented characteristic tend to use a higher percentage of moral characteristics (both interpersonal-oriented and societal-oriented) in describing themselves. Perhaps those who develop a societal-oriented moral self are generally more concerned about others in directing their lives. We need longitudinal investigation to understand the pathways to the development of a societal-oriented moral self.

The findings that legislative perspective is not related to the ideal self or to any of the civic engagement variables except those having to do with political discussion and staying politically informed indicate the importance of attending to the role of moral cognition in understanding the motivation for politically kinds of civic engagement. Individuals may participate in politics in order to advance their own interests. This pursuit of private interest over the public or common good is, according to Parker (2005), a serious threat to democratic societies and a form of "idiocy" understood in the sense of its Greek root *idios* as self-centered.

We do not find a relationship between identifying as a citizen of the world and the ideal self. Those with a societal-oriented moral self are no more likely to describe themselves as citizens of the world than those with non-moral or interpersonal-oriented ideal self. The lack a relationship between identifying as a global citizen and the moral self may well have to do with the way in which we measured identifying as a global citizen. Asking respondents to place themselves on a continuum between being a citizen of the United States and a citizen of the world forces them to choose between two kinds of relationships that need be seen as competing. It is possible to identify strongly as both a citizen of one's country and a citizen of the world. In fact, having a strong sense of moral responsibility for the behavior of one's country in international affairs may be a prerequisite for responsible global citizenship.

The question asking how respondents resolve conflicts between national and global interests may reveal more about their sense of global citizenship than their sense of global identification. The level of global perspective-taking is significantly correlated with the level of legislative perspective but the level of global perspective-taking is not related to the ideal self. This is not a surprising finding when one considers the parallelism between the legislative and global perspective measures. Legislative perspective assesses the extent to which individuals put the public good over private good; global perspective assesses the extent to which individuals but the global welfare over national welfare. Both kinds of perspective-taking thus have to do with making moral judgments and are cognitive variables. The ideal self variable is not, strictly speaking, a cognitive variable although individuals' stage of moral reasoning may be necessary although not sufficient for the orientation of the moral self as we have defined it. We have shown in the context of discussing citizenship at a national or local level that the ideal self variable was related to certain kinds of political engagement but not to one's legislative perspective on particular issue. Participating in political discussions and becoming involved with political organizations are kinds of activism that often do involve international concerns. Insofar as we have shown a link between the societal-oriented moral self and these forms of political engagement, we have some basis for claiming that the moral self is related to the engagement presumed in the notion of global citizenship. On the other hand, we believe that global citizenship must include the active pursuit of global welfare over national interest. Global citizenship thus appears to require the development of moral judgment as well as the development of the moral self.

Our study suggests preparing students for global citizenship requires attention to the development of students' identity and moral judgment. If students are to become politically engaged, they must see themselves as related not only to other individuals but to their society and to the global community. This may mean that civic education courses need to help students to see the limitations of the privatism so prevalent in American culture. Our study also points to the importance of moral judgment for responsible political engagement. Political engagement does not necessarily make an individual a good citizen. Being a good citizen means committing oneself to the pursuit of justice and the common good.

REFERENCES

Altof, W. & Berkowitz, M. (2006). Moral education and character education: their relationship and roles in citizenship education. *Journal of Moral Education* 35: 495-518.

Baldi, S., Perie, M., Skidmore, D., Greenberg, E. & Hahn, C. (2001). *What democracy means to ninth-graders: U.S. results from the International IEA Civic Education Study*. National Center for Educational Statistics.

Bergman, R. (2002). Why be moral? A conceptual model from developmental psychology. *Human Development, 45*, 104-124.

Campbell, D.E. (2005). Voice in the classroom: How and open classroom environment facilitates adolescents' civic engagement. *Circle Working Paper 28*. College Park, MD: Center for Information and Research on Civic Learning and Engagement, University of Maryland.

Colby, A. & Damon, W. (1992). *Some do care: Contemporary lives of moral commitment*. New York: Macmillan.

Colby, A. Ehrlich, T.; Beaumont, E. & Stephens, J. (2003) *Educating citizens: Preparing America's graduates for lives of civic and moral responsibility*. San Franciso: Jossey-Bass.

Corporation for National and Community Service,. (2007). *Volunteering in America: 2007 State trends and rankings in civic life*. Washington, DC: Office of Research and Policy Development.

Damon, W., & Hart, D. (1988). *Self-understanding in childhood and adolescence*. Cambridge: Cambridge University Press.

Galston, W.A. (2001) Political knowledge, political engagement and civic education. *Annual Review of Political Science* 4: 217-234.

Hahn, C.L. & Torney-Purta, J. The IEA Civic Education Project: National and international perspectives. *Social Education* 63: 425-431.

Hardin, G. (1968). The tragedy of the commons. *Science* 162: 1243-1248.

Higher Education Research. (2001). 2000 Annual Freshman Survey: Looking inward, freshman care less about politics and more about money. *Chronicle of Higher Education*. January 22, 2001.

Kohlberg, L. (1984). *Essays on moral development. Vol. 2: The Psychology of moral development*. San Francisco: Harper & Row.

Lutkus, A. & Weiss, A. (2007).*The Nation's Report Card: Civics 2006* (NCES 2007–476). U.S. Department of Education, National Center for Education Statistics. Washington, D.C.: U.S. Government Printing Office.

Maiello, C., Oser, F. & Biederman, H. (2003) Civic knowledge, civic skills and civic engagement, *European Educational Research Journal*, 2(3), pp. 384-395.

McPherson, M., Smith-Lovin, L. & Brashears, M. (2006). Social isolation in America. *American Sociological Review* 71, 353-175.

Niemi, R.G. & Junn. J. (1998). *Civic education: What makes students learn*. New Haven, CT: Yale University Press, 1998.

Oser, F. & Reichenbach (2000). *Political and civic education in Switzerland: Final report*. Berne: Swiss Conference of Canton directors.

Popkin, S.L. & Dimok, M.A. (1999) Political knowledge and citizen competence. In S.K.Elkin and K. E. (Eds.), *Citizen competence and democratic institutions* (214-238). University Park: Penn. State Univ. Press.

Power, F.C. & Khmelkov, V. T. (1997). The development of the moral self: Implications for moral education. *International Journal of Educational Psychology*, 27 (7) 539-551.

Putnam, P.D. (2000). *Bowling Alone*. New York: Simon and Schuster.

Roney, K, Power, A.M.R. & Power, F.C. (2006). *Orienting to the common good: Developing a moral self in the middle school years*. American Educational Research Association, San Francisco.

Scales, E.C. & Roehlkepartain, P.C. (2004). *Community service and service learning in U.S. public schools 2004*. St. Paul, MN: National Youth Leadership Council.

Tarrance Group. *New millennium project part 1: American youth attitudes on politics, citizenship, and voting*. NASS New Millennium Project, 1999.

Torney-Purta, J., Lehmann, R., Oswald, H. & Schulz, W. (2001). *Citizenship and education in twenty-eight countries: Civic knowledge and engagement at age fourteen*. Amsterdam: The International Association for the Evaluation of Educational Achievement.

Youniss, J. & Yates, M. (1997). *Community service and social responsibility*. Chicago: University of Chicago Press.

F. Clark Power & Ann Marie R. Power
University of Notre Dame, USA

PART 2

MORAL DEVELOPMENT
AND SOCIAL ENGAGEMENT

ANN HIGGINS-D'ALESSANDRO

THE JUDGMENT-ACTION GAP:

A Modest Proposal

INTRODUCTION

The moral judgment-action gap continues to be of real interest for practical and theoretical reasons. Practically, the concern about this gap focuses on society's desire to predict and count on moral behavior, especially consistency in moral actions across situations and time, as well as its desire to predict and prevent immoral, or at least antisocial, behavior in wide range of circumstances. Society entrusts moral and character educators and school teachers as well as families, religious and youth organizations and the law with the positive development and correction of its citizens. Theoretically, it is of interest because the nature of morality is unique among domains of human endeavors; thus, moral behavior is unique as well. Two general ideas have been introduced as influential in either deepening or closing this gap, specific social and time-bound circumstances and individual characteristics, including ideas such as the will, identity, sense of self, commitment, and abstract personality characteristics that put people at risk for immoral behavior. Research (Blasi, 2004; Kohlberg & Candee, 1984; Oser, 1996; Power, Higgins, & Kohlberg, 1989, to select just a few) has shown that context and personal characteristics are often critical dimensions in understanding moral and immoral behavior; however, the gap remains – in most studies and for most people in their real lives.

This chapter suggests that there is a barrier to further understanding moral behavior; the barrier is that moral reasoning, the social situation, and individual characteristics are theoretically considered similar in the sense that when they are operationalized in research, they are most often considered to be constructs at the same level of analysis. Instead, it may be useful to consider a multilevel approach that would include higher order concepts such as moral reasoning competence, micro or concrete concepts such as designated chunks of behavior, mid-level concepts that represent interactions of moral reasoning and personal characteristics influenced by past experience and self-awareness, and situationally-bound behaviors. This view is consistent with Walker's (2004) working definition of moral functioning as fundamental and pervasive in human life, consisting of interpersonal and intrapsychic components; that it is multifaceted, involving the dynamic interplay of thought, emotion, and behavior.

For many, by definition, morality is intentions and motivations as much as it is

Fritz Oser & Wiel Veugelers (eds.), Getting involved, 105–118.

judgment and action, denoting a person who intends to act, a self (e.g., Blasi, 2005; Hart, 2005; Kohlberg, 1981; Higgins-D'Alessandro & Power, 2005; Power, Power, & Kmehlkov, 1998). Moreover, intentions and motivations are not strictly cognitive, having an emotional side revealed by the potential various actions individuals whose personalities and character differ could make to the same situation. The idea of a fully integrated relationship between morality and the self is captured in the term, moral identity, and gives it its power. Blasi (2005) and Carlo and Hardy (2005) have each developed ideas of moral identity in adulthood and Hart (2005) has addressed the development of moral identity in youth. I would like to move back in developmental time and think about precursors of moral identity, more specifically to suggest that mid-level moral self-processes emerge in the relationship of the self to moral decisions and behavior from early childhood.

In this chapter I interpret findings from several studies done by our research group (Kuther & Higgins-D'Alessandro, 2000 Markman, 2002; MacLaine, 2007) as well as longitudinal just community research (Gross-Lipshitz, 2001; Power, Higgins, & Kohlberg, 1989) as suggestive of mid-level concepts, what I call moral self-processes. Research studies in the areas of self-esteem (Bouchey & Harter, 2005; Harter, 1996; Harter & Whitesell, 2003) and self-concept (Marsh & Craven, 2006; O'Mara, Marsh, Craven & Debus, 2006) have demonstrated that children and youth parse self-concept and self-esteem into very specific domains, such as self-concept related to school subjects (Bouchey & Harter, 2005; Marsh & Craven, 2006) and self-esteem related to physical characteristics, intellectual ability, relations with peers and with parents, etc. (Harter, 1996). Using this research as an analogy, I suggest that children and youth have specific ideas of themselves as moral that result from as well as inform future moral self-processes. Moral self-processes arise from interrelationships among moral reasoning competence, the person's view of himself in a particular domain, personal characteristics, and the action choice or course of action taken in a specific situation. This is a multilevel and dynamic view of morality and the development of moral behavior and is consonant with an organismic-contextualist perspective (Overton, 2006). This chapter represents one attempt to address the question: 'If a moral action can only be known by knowing the intent of the actor, then how does the self function in moral action?'

THE JUDGMENT-ACTION GAP

The judgment-action or competence-performance gap has been identified as a problem in the fields of moral theory and moral education for almost 40 years, ever since Kohlberg (1971) clarified that stages of moral reasoning in his theory represent an individual's competence – the best moral reasoning of which one is capable given a hypothetical fully constrained moral dilemma and no real life contingencies. If one's best moral reasoning represents moral competence, an abstract idea, then how does moral reasoning competence inform performance? Theoretically, Kohlberg (1981) argued that to know whether an action is moral, we must know that the actor had moral intentions, that is, that an individual intends her action to be moral or have a moral outcome. In real life situations that pose moral issues that require action, whether verbal or behavioral, one's intentions represent not only some kind and level of moral reasoning, but also characteristics often assigned to the self or person, characteristics such as responsibility, courage, insight, being a skillful negotiator, etc. In this view, the constraints of specific circumstances of time, place, and others involved in the morally problematic situation are critically important because they can elicit several and even conflicting intentions. How trustworthy are individuals' self-reports of their moral intentions?

When reasoning about hypothetical moral dilemmas none of the above constraints apply but when reasoning about real life moral dilemmas in which one is situated, they all apply. This produces a gap between producing a position and rationally defending it when responding to hypothetical dilemmas and acting when confronted by or when one perceives a situation demands some moral response. In the latter case, rationally defending one's actions are done after the fact. An action may be taken almost without thinking, from habit, or without being aware of the moral dimensions of the situation. Furthermore, explanations offered after the fact about why one acted as she did almost always include references situatioinal and time constraints. Less often individuals discuss their strengths and weaknesses, personality, background, and/or habits as influential.

Reflections on Moral Action

I conducted a study showing that a sample of 60 people from 10 to 80 years old could be classified into moral types. Participants were interviewed; first they were asked to describe themselves in a way that fundamentally captured who they were, second they were they asked what guidelines or rules they lived by and the characteristics of the person they admired most that they sought to develop in themselves, and third to recount four situations they faced that posed dilemmas for them in terms of following or not following one of their life guidelines or not expressing a virtue they were trying to cultivate. They were asked to discuss two situations in which they failed according to their own guidelines and ideals and two in which they succeeded in upholding or expressing them. The self-descriptors were coded in isolation and inductively organized. The same was done for guidelines and admired characteristics. Four types of self-awareness emerged and confirmed with cluster analyses. These 4 types are: self-reflectively moral, self-reflectively social and moral, descriptively social, and descriptively aesthetic or non-moral. Less than 10% described their core sense of self as reflectively moral, 2% as only aesthetic or non-moral, with 40% percent in each of the two social types, reflectively social and moral and descriptively social.

The types were unrelated to moral stage as assessed by the Moral Judgment Interview (Colby & Kohlberg, 1987) and age. The participants used their views of themselves and the guidelines and virtues they admired to judge the seriousness of the situations they recounted and their own behavior in those situations. One strong result was that all participants reported their "moral failures" as resulting from a combination of their own emotional blindness, the suddenness and sometimes unexpectedness with which the moral issue arose, and/or situational demands for an immediate response. They did not say that if given the time or the personal will, they would not have known what was the right or good thing to do. In this chapter, I focus on the interrelationship of self with moral reasoning in circumstances considered moral or immoral by the persons involved.

RESEARCH IN SUPPORT OF MORAL SELF-PROCESSES

In conducting research with my students on the relationship of moral reasoning to actions taken in particular circumstances, it has been true that while moral reasoning is often a significant explanatory variable, it is certainly not the full explanation (Turiel, 1998). I suggest that a theoretically parsimonious explanation to increase understanding of the judgment-action relationship is to recognize higher-order, mid-level, and concrete concepts, in the following studies these are respectively, moral reasoning competence and moral domain assignment, inferred moral self-processes and self-representations, and specific action choices or behavior.

Claiming Moral Authority

The research conducted by Power, Higgins, and Kohlberg (1989) in the just community high school program that examined the gap between judgment and action, garnered evidence that the social environment, specifically the school culture, played a critical role in moral behavior. When students felt they had some ownership and a real voice in creating their school culture, their behavior as a group became more consistent with the norms and values underlying the rules made by the community of students and teachers. Student practices of cutting, vandalism, and stealing and of teasing and isolating unpopular students as well as the social separation based on skin color lessened dramatically over 4 years in the Cluster School, one just community program with the 60+ students and 5 teachers, as they made and reworked rules for their community (Power et al., 1989). In addition, democratic discussions and decision-making about their community's functioning was related to students' making higher stage and more community and contextually grounded responses to a set of hypothetical school moral dilemmas than did a group of comparison students attending the same large high school. Longitudinally, higher stage responses to the hypothetical school dilemmas led to higher stage responses to Heinz and the other dilemmas of the Moral Judgment Interview (MJI; Colby & Kohlberg, 1987). The experiences in the school infused and fostered student moral reasoning, decisions about their school community, and their own decisions to quit cutting, vandalizing, etc.

Although Power and colleagues (1989) had conceived of a positive moral school culture as promoting moral reasoning development, they did not hold any hypotheses that suggested that students' reasoning on school dilemmas would lead their reasoning on the MJI dilemmas. Quite the contrary, they thought that because school dilemmas were designed to evoke students' real lives, that their highest stage of moral reasoning competence would not be elicited. In fact, results from the comparison group of students showed what we expected to find. Comparison students reasoned at higher stages on the MJI dilemmas and at lower stages, on average preconventional, on the school dilemmas. We interpreted these results to show the power of a democratic, one person-one vote, environment, rich in opportunities for perspective-taking, negotiation, compromise, and leadership to directly promote moral reasoning. Weekly community meeting transcripts were analyzed for the development of norms and community valuing over the four years (Power et al., 1989). These analyses revealed new rules were made or weaker ones made stronger, when some students became speakers for the community, when they spoke for the community using "we" and when they spoke in terms of reaching for an ideal (Don't we want to be a community where you can leave your stuff around, where you don't have to worry about someone stealing your stuff?) or meeting an obligation (We should pay for the dock, some of us let it float away.)

We did not analyze differences on any dimension between those students who as leaders spoke for the community and others who advocated for their own ideas or who did not speak, but the willingness of some to have spoken for all seems to imply that they felt they had the moral authority to do so. We (Higgins, Power, & Kohlbert, 1994; Power et al., 1989) discussed these findings in terms of judgments of responsibility, aretaic judgments that the person speaking was willing to take personal responsibility to act through advocacy or action. Claiming moral authority seems to imply that these students both accepted a moral viewpoint as legitimate and took on that moral viewpoint as an expression of themselves. Different students were community spokespersons on different issues demonstrating that they saw their moral authority as grounded in a specific action rather than seeing themselves as moral authorities in general. Further evidence of the specific nature of their moral authority lay in the fact that other students would support a spokesperson on a specific moral position but not generally; students did not look to "leaders." They were adamant about their democratic equality. Looking at our research from the perspective of students' claiming moral authority suggests that they did so on specific issues and that their statements in meetings were acts of moral advocacy or statements of their particular present or intended moral behavior, as such, suggest that students appealed to an idea of themselves as moral in specific instances. Claiming moral authority as illustrated here is an example of a moral self-representation; there is no claim or evidence of a global moral self or moral identity.

Evidence of Claiming Moral Authority

How students speak and to whom are indicators of claiming moral authority in just community weekly community meetings. An analysis of 77 community meeting transcripts over a 5 year period in the Scarsdale Alternative School, a just community high school program now in its 30th year, offers information about how students expressed moral authority. Over a five year period, 15 community meeting transcripts per year were analyzed for direct responses between students during discussions and for use of moral argumentation and moral language, and for statements about community normative expectations and values (Gross-Lipshitz, 2001). Direct and accurate responses in which references were made to another's position or argument during a discussion in which many points of view were being expressed Gross-Lipshitz and I interpreted as an indicators that the students had engaged in perspective-taking. Using moral language and making moral arguments and advocating for community ideals and welfare indicated taking moral authority. Direct responses occurred in 55% of the meetings. Moral arguments and language were used in two-thirds of the meetings, about equally split between advocacy (we should do this…) and recriminations (we failed to do what we decided we should…). Statements about community expectations and values, made in 48% of the meetings, were also fairly equally split between encouraging the community to move toward some ideal or to uphold a rule and chastising it for what it was not or when it failed to give consequences to those who violated rules. During an average meeting, 28% of the statements were direct responses between students discussing an issue, eight percent were moral statements or arguments, and 13% focused on community normative expectations and values. These numbers indicate lively moral discussions rooted in the real life issues facing the school community (Gross-Lipshitz, 2001). The outcomes of such discussions were votes on new rules, on the consequences for breaking rules, creating explicit expectations for relations with the rest of the school and with each other as community members, etc.; all issues which personally affected every student. These figures suggest that in just community schools, ownership and moral authority were the order of the day. Furthermore, the low percentages of use of moral language and argumentation and language focused on community norms and values demonstrates that students moralized specific issues or positions – that they exerted their moral authority as specific acts and about particular behaviors of themselves and/or others in the contexts of particular discussions – they did not do so usually and nor regardless of topic.

This evidence of the specificity of moral authority suggests that a mid-level notion such as moral self-processes may be useful for understanding how moral ideas and ideals become aspects of a person's thinking about himself through development and over time. A reasonable developmental hypothesis suggests that these aspects or moral self-processes become interrelated and informative of wider domains of experience as contexts and experiences of moral authority multiply over time.

Moral Motivation

The following research that my students and I conducted examined moral domain judgments, motivation, and behavior in the first study and moral domain judgments, moral reasoning, and behavior in the second and third studies. Markman's (2002) research on the same just community school outside of NYC, the Scarsdale Alternative School, found that students (n=54) attributed moral reasons as motivating their academic work--attending school, working to get good grades, and being prepared and participating in class. Students in a comparison group (n=178) from the larger parent high school did not moralize their academic work. Differences were highly significant. Both just community and comparison group students moralized their reasons for how they treated their friends and others in social situations to the same degree. Moralizing homework and class preparation may seem unusual but having a moral attitude can be interpreted as an indicator of the presence of moral self-processes related to schooling and schoolwork.

Prosocial Helping and Self-esteem

Markman (2002) also found that students in both the just community school and the comparison group were equally likely to complete a prosocial task. The task was designed as a legitimate example of prosocial behavior that could be measured. The prosocial task was presented as helping the researcher by completing a packet of surveys outside of school time and mailing them back to her. The task was inspired by earlier research (Kohlberg & Candee,1984). Markman found that high school students from both the just community (n=18) and comparison group (n=16) who completed the prosocial task also responded significantly more positively on only two subscales of a self-esteem scale – those that measured valuing oneself and reporting that one uses principles/guidelines to judge one's actions. This finding suggests links between self-valuing, judging and deciding upon a course of action by using principles or guidelines, and following through with that course of action. I interpret these links as soft evidence of a moral self-processes.

Moral domain, Moral Reasoning, and Risk Behaviors

We have also conducted research to specifically address the judgment-action gap often noted between adolescent moral reasoning and their engagement in at-risk or risky behaviors (Kuther & Higgins-D'Alessandro, 2000; MacLaine, 2007). In the first study, adolescents from the Scarsdale just community school (n= 68) and a comparison group from the parent high school (n=122) completed the Defining Issues Test (DIT; Rest, 1986), used as the indicator of moral reasoning understanding, made assignments of risky behaviors to personal, conventional, and moral domains as discussed by Turiel (1983; 1998), and gave self-reports about the frequency of engaging in the same risk behaviors (theft, violence, substance use-alcohol, marijuana, illicit drugs, and selling illicit drugs).

The results showed that students did not view risk behaviors as issues of convention. Since they did not assign any risk behaviors to the conventional domain, analyses focused on the moral and personal domains. Students assigned each risk behavior to either to the moral domain, the personal domain, or a mixture of moral and personal. While just community students preferred post-conventional moral reasoning significantly moreso than did comparison students, there were no differences in level of moral reasoning understanding in terms of which students reported that they engaged in risk behaviors or in their assignment of such behaviors to the moral and personal domains. When theft and violence were considered moral issues, students in both groups who reported that they did not engage in those activities demonstrated *post*-conventional moral reasoning understanding on the DIT. When illicit drug use and selling were considered moral issues, those who said that they engaged in these activities preferred *pre*-conventional reasons on the DIT. When any of the risk behaviors were seen as personal issues or as personal and moral mixed, there was no relationship between moral reasoning understanding and the frequency with which students said they engaged in those risk behaviors.

Taken together, these results suggest that seeing an issue as moral may motivate higher level moral competence and be a motivating condition for restraint, that is, for not being involved in risk behaviors. Thus, knowing whether an adolescent perceives a behavior or activity as moral helps to explain the judgment-action relationship. When adolescents or anyone assign behaviors or activities to the moral domain, they are saying two things: one, that those behaviors and activities have a unique nature or status – that they are grounded in obligation and responsibility; and two, that they as an individual recognize that when they engage in those behaviors and activities they knowingly or intended to engage in a moral (or immoral) behavior. Since domain assignment is self-conscious, it links one's self to actions taken in the moral domain. Thus, this study's finding of a three-way linkage between moral reasoning understanding, moral domain assignment, and engagement in risk behaviors suggests in part why moral reasoning alone is insufficient for understanding moral behavior. It can be inferred from these results that the self is directly involved in moral or immoral behavior at a concrete level of specificity. It seems reasonable that involvement of the self is at a fairly specific level; that is, that there is involvement of specific self-processes of decision-making and action, in this case, moral self-processes that could be evidenced as moral self-representations had students been interviewed regarding their risky behaviors.

The Case of Truancy

The last study, a recent dissertation completed by MacLaine (2007), found that considering truancy as being in the moral domain, using Turiel's categorization scheme (1983), related strongly to actual truancy, whether measured by self-report or taken from school records. The sample of 206 middle school students, 85% Latinos who had immigrated or whose parents had immigrated from the Dominican Republic and 15% African-Americans, were from the Bronx, the poorest among New York City's five boroughs. Research has shown that the middle school years mark the time when adolescents are at greatest risk for truancy (Rudolph, Lambert, Clark,

& Kurlakowsky, 2001). In the United States, Latino-American students drop out of high school at four times the rate of white students and twice the rate of African-American students. Since truancy is the gateway to dropping out of school, Ma-cLaine hypothesized that knowing how students think about truancy would help in understanding truant behavior. In addition, she thought that impulsivity would be a mediator of truant behavior since research has established a link between impulsivity and delinquent and antisocial behavior (Romero, Luengo, & Sobral, 2001). Responses to two school-related dilemmas about truancy and one dilemma about petty stealing were given to the students. Responses to the dilemmas included moral, conventional, or personal domain assignments to both "should the protagonist" and "would I" go truant or steal. Students also chose among stage-related reasons for not going truant or not stealing. The outcome measures were students' reports of the frequency of their own truancy and school records showing each student's truancy. Knowing the domain assignment and the preferred moral reasoning stage were very good predictors of both measures of truancy Results showed that two-thirds of the adolescents considered truancy to be in the moral domain. For those who said truancy was a personal preference, greater impulsivity related to higher truancy. Contrary to the risk behaviors studied by Kuther and Higgins-D'Alessandro (2000), higher truancy was reported by students who assigned it to the conventional as well as personal domain. As in the previous study, judging truancy to be in the conventional domain was not related to stage of moral reasons for not going truant and not stealing. Students who chose higher moral reasoning statements (stages ¾ and 4) for not going truant and not stealing were most likely to have assigned truancy to the moral domain; whereas those who chose lower moral reasoning statements (stages 2 and 2/3) most often assigned truancy to the personal domain.

Truancy increased as impulsivity increased for students who chose lower moral stage statements (stages 2 and 2/3). Truancy decreased as impulsivity increased for students who chose higher moral stage statements (stages 3 and ¾). Thus, moral stage moderated the relationship between impulsivity and truancy, such that the rate of truancy actually decreased as impulsivity increased in the context of a preference for higher stage moral reasoning.

Together, the findings on domain assignment and on impulsivity and moral stage for predicting either self-reported truancy or truancy based on school records again suggests that higher moral reasoning when applied to a behavior a person sees as moral fosters the ability of that person to regulate his own behavior in spite of characteristically high levels of impulsivity. Of course, in part this is likely due to the change in understanding reasons for adhering to societal norms that occurs in the transition to Kohlbergian conventional reasoning (stages 3 and 4). Second, it is in part due to the increasing push for consistency or motive to act consistently with one's judgment. Third, that this motivation for consistency is sufficient to overcome a high level of impulsivity shows engagement of self-processes. These linkages suggest articulating mid-level self-processes in future research may be profitable for understanding how and when people will restrain from engaging in negative behaviors.

A MODEST PROPOSAL: MORAL SELF-PROCESSES

How morality influences the self as interpreted in the studies just discussed is the crux of a modest proposal that a mid-level concept between moral reasoning, moral identity, or moral self and specific moral or immoral acts or behaviors may open opportunities for new thinking and research. I have termed such mid-level concepts moral self-processes and moral self-representations. Moral self-processes function as coordinators between judgment and action and as facilitators of moral action in specific circumstances (e.g., helping a researcher by sending back completed surveys, going truant or not on a particular day, or student behavior in just community weekly meetings). To say this another way, moral self-processes are involved when specific moral ideas (e.g., domain judgments, moral reasoning understanding) inform a particular behavior or course of action, and especially so when contraindicative personal characteristics (e.g., impulsivity) exist that make the moral course of action more difficult.

Moral self-processes are neither a moral self, moral identity, nor a moral self-concept. However, theoretically some or all of one's moral self-processes may become organized over developmental time into such higher order concepts. In an earlier presentation (AME 2006) I used the term moral self-concepts instead of moral self-processes. This term was confusing because the reference is to a mid-level construct that involves the creation of interrelationships among higher and lower order concepts, such as moral reasoning competence generally or in response to a specific dilemma, assignment of a specific behavior or course of action to the moral domain, and specific behaviors in context. It also seems reasonable to hypothesize that as young children develop, many moral self-processes also develop which have their origins in the behavioral interactions of the child with her social life experiences. Moral self-processes, then, should be sensitive to developmental changes in individual cognitive and social cognitive capacities and have a developmental progression or progressions of their own. Lastly, moral self-processes, I hypothesize, is a useful construct for bringing the self into relationship with contextually specific behaviors. Moral self-processes engage the moral ideas and principles that a person holds as his own and as such interrelate with specific acts and domains of life experience. Although not fully articulated here, this idea is consonant with an organismic-contextualist dynamic systems perspective.

Metatheoretical Perspective

The proposal of moral self-processes is in keeping with a metatheoretical perspective as reviewed by Witherington (2007) and discussed by Overton (2006) as an organismic-contextualist dynamic systems perspective. This view allows for a multiple levels of analysis which inform and are informed by each other. It allows both macrodevelopment of higher order concepts with their own patterns and structures and as not reducible to microdevelopmental processes, even though they give rise to them. Thus, moral self-processes would be emergent properties of actions taken intentionally to create outcomes that a person judges as in the moral domain. Additionally, higher order concepts such as moral self or moral identity would emerge from and be constrained by moral self-processes. These interrelationships are dynamic and circular over time.

This metatheoretical approach "attempts to join the formal abstractions of organicism with the real-time particularities of contextualism by acknowledging the explanatory significance of both" (Witherington, 2007, p. 143). If the gap between judgment and action or competence and performance is seen as a gap between formal abstractions and real-time particularities, then moral self-processes comprise aspects of the dynamic interplay between them. It is also then reasonable to hypothesize that networks or interrelations among moral self-processes would have their self-organization and developmental patterns in keeping with an organismic contextualist metatheory. The dynamic organization of moral self-processes over time could constitute at any one point in time a moral self if measured at an abstract formal level.

THE SPECIFICITY OF SELF-CONCEPTS

Another argument for the idea that moral behavior may be better understood using a notion of specific moral self-processes rests on making an analogy with work in academic self-concepts which is burgeoning. The analogy can be clearly made using examples of this research from Marsh (Marsh & Craven, 2006; O'Mara et al., 2006) and Harter (Bouchey & Harter, 2005; Harter & Whitesell, 2003) whose research has demonstrated that self-concepts vary by academic areas and by situation.

Marsh and Craven (2006) found empirical support for a multidimensional idea of self-concept that becomes differentiated and integrated as children develop. They showed that young children have self-concepts, that is, ideas and evaluations about themselves, when those ideas and evaluations are hooked to concrete and specific areas of a child's life. For instance, they found that children 5 to 8 years old have differing mathematics and verbal self-concepts. Their longitudinal research showed that a positive self-concept in a specific academic area contributed uniquely to a child's later positive academic performance in that same area. They also showed the reciprocal effect, doing well contributed to a later more positive self-concept in the area. Thus, self-concept at time 1 predicted performance a year later at time 2, controlling for performance at time 1. A second important finding from his research is that there is little generalization. Positive mathematics self-concept did nothing to promote verbal performance nor influence verbal self-concept. Lastly, they showed some, but not strong, evidence that *unrelated* self-concepts became even more unrelated as children grew older and *related* self-concepts became even more related, leading him to theorize that academic self-concepts become organized into a multidimensional and hierarchical structure with global self-concept at its apex.

Harter (1996) was one of the first to examine self-esteem in children and adolescents related to specific domains of life, such as scholastic competence, intellectual ability, peer acceptance, sense of humor, relationship with parents, close friendship, etc. Morality is a domain in her scheme as well. The overall finding of recent research by Bouchey and Harter (2005) on reflected appraisals, academic self-perceptions, and math and science performance in early adolescence are similar to those of Marsh and colleagues. Using structural equation modeling, they found that prior achievement as well as reflected appraisals of parents and teachers, but not peers, seemed to serve as temporal precursors of students' academic self-perceptions and performance (grades) in math and science courses.

Since these studies as well as other have found that very specific academic self-concepts relate to performance only in the same area/course and not others, they suggest that students develop and understand themselves as a self constructed of separate and different parts. The research by Harter, Marsh, and their colleagues supports the idea that children different and separate moral self-representations that indicate different and separate moral self-processes. In this chapter, I have argued that this is likely the case in the moral domain as well. However, instead of having a hierarchical model with global moral self or moral identity at the apex as Marsh and Craven (2006) hypothesized for self-concept, I have conceived of specific ways in which children and adolescents function morally as aspects of dynamic interrelationships among concepts at different levels of theory and analysis.

In an interesting study on variation in high school students' self-worth related to different relationships, parents, teachers, male classmates, and female classmates, Harter and Whitesell (2003) found that students had different perceptions of self-worth in different relational contexts or situation-specific self worth. This may be commonplace when thinking about moral issues. For example, high school students could consider the same action to be morally wrong when discussing it with their parents because they know their parents' view, and to be something they approve when talking with peers because they know their peers' view. Harter and Whitesell found that 75% of the students reported discrepant self worth across different relationships. They also found that self-worth in the most salient relationship for the adolescent was more highly correlated with global self-worth than was self-worth in the other relationships. This was true whether self-worth was high or low in that salient relationship. In keeping with our example, moral self-processes are likely also influenced by the saliency of relationships involved in specific situations. This aspect was not considered in this chapter but would be an important consideration in fleshing out the notion of moral self-processes as coordinators and facilitators between an individual and her chosen courses of action in her lived experience.

CONCLUSION

The notion of moral self-processes may be helpful as a developmental concept, allowing us to think about how moral ideas and values become incorporated into daily functioning and into one's sense of self over time. It may also help to explain why most adults have a strong sense of themselves as moral beings even when morality is not a central or core aspect of who they see themselves as being. Moreover, it allows the roles of culture and convention, gender, social class, and family dynamics to have real influence. The wide variation in individuals' sense of the parameters of the moral domain may be accounted for by the idea that individuals develop different networks of moral self-processes based on individual life experiences.

REFERENCES

Blasi, A. (2004). Moral functioning: Moral understanding and personality. In Daniel K. Lapsley & Darcia Narvaez (Eds.) *Moral development, self, and identity* (pp.335-348). Mahwah, NJ: Lawrence Erlbaum Associates, Publishers.

Bouchey, H. A. & Harter, S. (2005). Reflected appraisals, academic self-perceptions, and math/science performance during early adolescence. *Journal of Educational Psychology,* 97(4), 673-686.

Carlo, G., & Hardy, S.A. (2005). Identity as a source of moral motivation. *Human Development,* 48(4), 232-256.

Colby A. & Kohlberg, L. (1987) *The measurement of moral development, Vols. 2: Standard issue scoring manual.* NY: Cambridge University Press.

Gross-Lipshitz, S. (2001). Analysis of student participation in just community meetings over 5 years in the Scarsdale Alternative School. Predoctoral thesis. Department of Psychology, Fordham University, Bronx, NY.

Hart, D. (2005). The development of moral identity, In G. Carlo & C. P. Edwards, (Eds.) *Moral motivation through the life span,* (pp. 165-196). Lincoln, NE: University of Nebraska Press.

Harter, S. (1996). Historical roots of contemporary issues involving self-concept.. In B.A. Bracken (Ed.). *Handbook of self-concept: Developmental, social, and clinical considerations,* (pp. 1-37). Oxford, England: John Wiley & Sons.

Harter, S. & Whitesell, N. R. (2003). Beyond the debate: Why some adolescents report stable self-worth over time and situation, whereas others report changes in self-worth. *Journal of Personality, 71(6), 1027-1058.*

Higgins-D'Alessandro, A. & Power, F. C. (2005) *Character, responsibility, and the moral self.* In D. Lapsley and F.Clark Power (Eds.). *Character Psychology and Character Education.* (pp.101-120). Notre Dame, IN: University of Notre Dame Press.

Higgins, A., Power, F. C. & Kohlberg, L. (1994). The relationship of moral atmosphere to judgments of responsibility. In Bill Puka (Ed.) *New research in moral development. Moral development: A compendium, Volume 5.* (pp. 190-222). New York, NY: Garland Publishing.

Higgins, A., Power, F. C. & Kohlberg, L. (1984) The relationship of moral judgement to judgments of responsibility. In W. M. Kurtines, & J Gerwitz (Eds.), *Morality, Moral Development and Moral Behavior: Basic Issues in Theory and Research.* New York: Wiley.

Higgins-D'Alessandro, A. (2006) Youth development, morality, identity in citizenship, relationships, and work: Reflections inspired by the idea of moral identity. Association for Moral Education Annual Conference, Fribourg, Switzerland, July 5-7.

Higgins-D'Alessandro, A. & Power, F. C., (in press) The just community approach to moral education and the moral atmosphere of the school. In D. Lapsley & D. Narvaez, (Eds.). *Handbook of moral and character education.*Notre Dame, IN: University of Notre Dame Press.

Kohlberg, L. (1971). From is to ought: How to commit the naturalistic fallacy and get away with it in the study of moral development. In W. Mischel (Ed.),*Cognitive development and epistemology* (pp. 57-88). NY: Academic Press.

Kohlberg, L. (1981). *Essays on moral development: Vol. 1. The philosophy of moral development: Moral stages and the idea of justice.* San Francisco, CA: Harper & Row.

Kohlberg, L. (1984). *Essays on moral development: Vol.2. The psychology of moral development: The nature and validity of moral stages.* San Francisco, CA: Harper & Row.

Kohlberg, L. & Candee, D., (1984). The relationship of moral judgment to moral action. In L. Kohlberg, *Essays on moral development: Vol.2. The psychology of moral development: The nature and validity of moral stages* (pp. 498-581). San Francisco, CA: Harper & Row.

Kuther, T. L. & Higgins-D'Alessandro, A. (2000). Bridging the gap between moral reasoning and adolescent engagement in risky behavior. *Journal of Adolescence,* 23 (3), 409-422.

MacLaine, C. (2007). *Moral development, impulsivity, and truancy.* Department of Psychology, Fordham University, Bronx, NY.

Markman, L. B. (2002). The impact of school culture on adolescents' prosocial motivation. *Dissertation Abstracts International: Section B: The Sciences & Engineering, 62,* 6024.

Marsh, H. W. & Craven, R. G. (2006). Reciprocal effects of self-concept and performance from a multidimensional perspective: Beyond seductive pleasure and unidimensional perspectives. *Perspectives on Psychological Science,* 1(2), 133-163.

O'Mara, A. J., Marsh, H.W., Craven, R. G. & Debus, R. L. (2006) Do self-concept interventions make a difference? A syngeristic blend of construct validation and metha-analysis. *Educational Psychology,* 41(3), 181-206.

Oser, F.(1996). Kohlberg's dormant ghosts: The case of education. *Journal of Moral Education,* 25 (3), 253-277.

Overton, W. F. (2006) Cognitive-developmental and behavioral-analytic theories: Evolving into complementarity. *Human Development,* 49(2), 143-172..

Power, F.C., & Power, A.M. R. & Khemlkov, V. T. (1998). Discipline and community in moral and character education, *Journal of Research in Education* 8(1), 16-25.

Rest, J. R. (1986). Moral development: Advances in research and theory. NY: Praeger.

Romero, E., Luengo, M. A. & Sobral, J. (2000). Personality and antisocial behavior: study of temperamental dimensions. *Personality and Individual Differences,* 31, 329-348.

Rudolph, K. D., Lambert, S. F., Clark, A. G. & Kurlakowsky, K. D. (2001). Negotiating the transition to middle school: The role of self-regulatory processes. *Child Development,* 72, 929-946.

Turiel, E. (1983). *The development of social knowledge: Morality and convention.* Cambridge: Cambridge University Press.

Turiel, E. (1998). The development of morality. In W. Damon & N. Eisenberg (Eds.), *Handbook of child psychology, Fifth edition: Vol. 3: Social, emotional, and personality developmenet* (pp 863-932*).* NY: Wiley

Walker, L. J. (2004). Gus in the gap: Bridging the judgment-action gap in moral functioning. In D. K. Lapsley & D. Narvaez (Eds.) *Moral development, self, and* identity (pp.1-20). Mahwah, NJ: Lawrence Erlbaum Associates, Publishers.

Witherington, D.C. (2007) The dynamic systems approach as metatheory for developmental psychology. *Human Development,* 50(2-3), 127-153.

Ann Higgins-D'Alessandro
Fordham University, New York, USA

BRIGITTE LATZKO

NO MORALITY WITHOUT AUTONOMY:

The Role of Emotional Autonomy in Moral Development

This chapter discusses the role of emotional autonomy in moral development. A study addressing the empirical validity of a two-component model of emotional autonomy is presented. 16 adolescents were interviewed. The assumption of an affective and a cognitive component can be confirmed. The results serve as basis to discuss the relation of emotional autonomy and moral development. Finally, implication for moral education in families and schools are derived.

INTRODUCTION

My main research interest in the context of moral development in adolescence is to conceptualize the relationship between autonomy and authority in terms of moral development. From that perspective, this chapter focuses on the role of emotional autonomy in moral development. The exploration of moral development in adolescence leads us unavoidably to the subject of autonomy development during adolescence. Despite the fact that both research lines hardly take notice of each other, there are not only terminological but also some theoretical links: In Kohlberg's (1984) account, for instance, the development towards the stage of autonomous moral judgment could be described as a process of reorganization of the relationship between the subject and social systems like peers, parents, the society itself or its values. In Turiel's (1983) words, the topic of moral development is the distinguishing between moral, conventional and personal domains. Morality is constructed out of reciprocal individual environment interactions. Put briefly, it is always a battle between autonomy and authority. In this way, I attempt to discuss the relationship between emotional autonomy and moral development on the basis of empirical findings. First of all, I will present some data of an empirical study addressing emotional autonomy in adolescence. On the basis of these data, I will go on to discuss the relationship between the development of emotional autonomy and moral development. Finally I will derive some implications for moral education in families and schools.

THE STUDY ON EMOTIONAL AUTONOMY IN ADOLESCENCE

The construction of an autonomous identity is undisputably a central developmental task during the period of adolescence (Erikson, 1968; Fend, 2005; Havighurst,

Fritz Oser & Wiel Veugelers (eds.), Getting involved, 119–129.

1952). The development of autonomy was and continues to be, as can be seen by the abundance of empirical work on the subject, a prevailing topic within the framework of psychological theory and research surrounding adolescence. An inventory of relevant literature reveals however, that within this field of research the theoretical concepts and corresponding operationalisations are of a very heterogenerous nature (e.g., see Latzko, 2006; Zimmer-Gembeck & Collins, 2003). Beyers, Goossens, Vansant und Moors aptly characterise the current debate concerning autononmy as "conceptual confusion" (2003, p. 352).

Whilst general concensus is to be found regarding the theoretical frame of reference for individuation, whereby the transformation of parent-child relationship is described as a dual process of separation and connectedness (Youniss & Smollar, 1985), the specification of the individual concepts varies considerably: separation is understood on the one hand more in the sense of it's original meaning and from a psychoanalytical perspective as being an emotional detachment from the parents (Blos, 1979; Steinberg & Silverberg, 1986), and on the other hand from a perspective whereby cognitive and behavioural aspects are emphasised (e.g. Hofer, 2003; Masche, 2006; Noack, 1993; Papastefanou, 2000; Pikowsky, 1998).

The focus on cognitive elements is particularly highlighted by Hofer's summary (2003). With the exception of few studies (e.g. Frank, Avery & Laman, 1988; Papini, Farmer, Clark, Micka & Barnett, 1990) emotional autonomy as an explicit research-subject appears to have taken a back seat. This is almost certainly due to the conceptual and methodological criticism (see Hill & Holmbeck, 1986; Ryan & Lynch, 1989; Schmitz & Baer, 2001; Latzko, Kim, & Hoppe-Graff, 2002) which has been formulated in connection with the classical instrument for measurement of emotional detachment during adolescence, namely Steinberg and Silverberg's Emotional-Autonomy-Scale (1986).

In view of pathological development however, it is a successful emotional detachment which is so crucial for the formation of identity and personality during adolescence and early adulthood (see Barber & Harmon, 2002; Heuves, 2005; Resch, 1999; Stierlin, 1994). For this reason it is essential that in the course of applied developmental psychology, the phenomenon of emotional detachment is differentially viewed as a precondition for the development of an autonomous identity.

Consequently this study will aim to introduce the development of a theoretical definition of emotional autonomy, in addition to a methodolgical approach which will enable the process of emotional detachment to be represented together with all relevant developmental-psychological determinants. Regarding my main topic – the relationship of autonomy and authority – the conceptualization of emotional autonomy in the following two-component model is used as a way to tap into the construct of autonomy.

PILOT STUDY

In an initial step, Landgraf (2003) and Latzko, Hoppe-Graff und Kim (2003) were able to demonstrate that emotional autonomy is not only manifest in the formation of self-determined domains, but also in the subjective appraisal of these domains. According to these findings, the process of emotional detachment is not adequately described by the increasing establishment of one's own private spheres independent of one's parents. Rather than being represented on the lower level of content, the given process can be represented at the level of reasoning which includes both cognitive and affective components: thirty adolescents, aged fifteen, were presented the task of completing the EAS. A semi-structured interview based upon items from the questionnaire was additionally carried out. By means of the interview it was possible to examine the reasoning behind particular viewpoints of the adolescents and furthermore the emotions connected with these viewpoints.

An analysis comparing answers from the questionnaire with those from the interview reveals that a statement at the level of content receives a whole new meaning as soon as the level of reasoning is encorporated. For example, two adolescents who both respond in the same manner to the EAS item "there are some things about me that my parents don't know ", can by all means cite very different reasons their statement. A content analysis of these reasons revealed two categories of argumentative patterns: adolescents claimed to keep things to themselves, either because they fear the reaction of their parents or rather to avoid unpleasant consequences, or, they argued under the conviction that they have the right to keep certain areas of their life to themselves.

The result of this analysis refers back to an important developmental-psychological distinction formulated by Piaget (1965) in connection with moral development: initial orientation towards external entities, authorities, and penalties linked with moral judgments are displaced by one's own convictions in the sense of co-constructing moral norms in social interactions (Kohlberg, 1984; Turiel, 1998) and internalizing as Grolnick, Deci and Ryan (1997) put it.

The central idea of heteronomy and autonomy is reflected in adolescents' reasoning behind emotional autonomy: patterns of argumentation which indicate emotional autonomy are characterised by the fact that they demonstrate a passing through the process of co-construction and internalization (see above). It is this process which increasingly enables adolescents to recognise and proclaim for themselves, psychologically relevant elements of autonomy development. Consequently adolescents develop an understanding of their need for private spheres through the process of individuation.

This insight is not to be found in patterns of argumentation which infer a lower level of emotional autonomy. Such patterns are instead characterised by the fact that adolescents set their parents and their parents' reactions as a reference point for their reasoning and not themselves with their own personal convictions. This important distinction is not apparent when adolescents are classified as being either "emotionally autonomous" or "less emotionally autonomous" solely on the basis of information provided by the questionnaire, since the classification then takes place at content-level and the relevant level of reasoning is left unconsidered.

A content analysis of answers to the question concerning emotions, revealed a difference in subjective experience between individual adolescents who had been classified, according to the procedure described above, as "emotionally autono-mous". It was not the case that positive emotions accompanied the given cognitive appraisal for all adolescents. Negative emotional reactions could be interpreted as evidence that endorsement of private spheres has only taken place at a cognitive and not an affective level.

It thus becomes clear that affective as well as cognitive components must be ac-knowledged as being of significant value in the conception of emotional autonomy. The subjective experience of adolescents is the deciding factor when it comes to distinguishing emotional and for example cognitive autonomy. Affective elements show how adolescents perceive the establishment of private spheres on an emo-tional level.

To summarise, the results of the pilot study suggest that emotional autonomy be conceived as a quality of emotions which reflects the general stage of autonomy de-velopment, experienced by adolescents. This quality of emotions can be described using a two-component model (see figure 1), combining a cognitive and an affec-tive element. The cognitive component refers to the ability to declare and argue for oneself that private spheres be established. It is insubstantial, in terms of content, in what form these private spheres are manifested. Regardless whether they consist of values, political world-views, finances or friends, an autonomous structure of reasoning must demonstrate that the individual, in the course of becoming an adult, has developed an understanding for the function of autonomous domains.

The affective component shows which emotions adolescents connect with their cognitive convictions. Within this context it is not necessary to adopt an attitude or behaviour which is contrary to that of the parents, as the theoretical fundament of the EAS would suggest. The core of emotional autonomy lies within self-determi-nation. The ability to determine for oneself is proved – in particular regarding af-fective components - especially when the individual is able to persist in a viewpoint which is opposed to that of the parents (see Beyers et al., 2003).

It is only when congruence between cognition and emotion exists that emotional autonomy can be concluded. This explicitly entails that emotionally autonomous adolescents do not experience a bad conscience or self-doubt when argumentatively representing their own (especially parent-opposed) convictions; ranging from choice of their own clothing and friends, to self determined political points of view. Viewed in this light, the process of emotional detachment should not be seen as a quantative increase in emotionally autonomous spheres, but rather a qualitative change in the experience of the adolescent, connected with an increase in autonomous domains. Emotional autonomy is therefore not an area clearly defined in terms of content and existing alongside other areas, but rather as an evaluative aspect, it is a kind of structural characteristic of all domains which are relevant to autonomy and which can, in terms of their content, be clearly distinguished from one another.

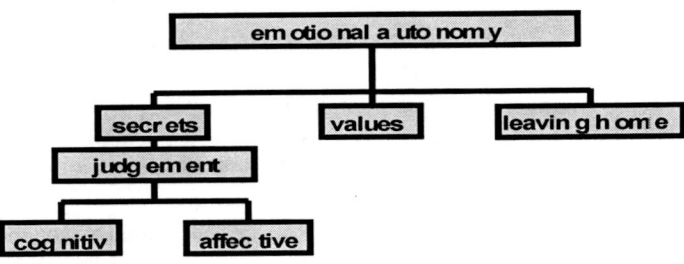

Figure 1. Two-component-model of emotional autonomy

MAIN STUDY

The theoretical framework of emotional autonomy, as introduced above, was tested at an empirical level in the form of interviews. The key question which the interviews aimed to address was whether adolescents can be classified as either "emotionally autonomous" or "less emotionally autonomous", as postulated in the theoretical conception of the two-component model.

Participants

The sample consisted of six girls and ten boys with a mean age of 14.7 years (SD = .55; range = 14 – 16). Half of the sample lived in single-parent-families with a mother and the other half in traditional two-parent-families with a mother and a father. With the exception of one family, all mothers had jobs. The families came from working and middle class backgrounds, whereby the adolescents either attended a Mittelschule (secondary modern school) or Gymnasium (grammar school) according to their given background.

Measure

The two-component model to be tested consists of a cognitive and an affective component. At a methodological level both components should be apparent in the answering of questions relevant to autonomy. Whilst the cognitive component should be manifest in the reasons given by adolescents for their standpoint, the affective element includes emotions which are explicitly displayed.

The semi-structured interview is an optimal instrument for investigating structures of reasoning. Through directly addressed questions, the interview additionally enables affective appraisals to be exhaustively examined. Content material relevant to autonomy was operationalised using the item "having secrets from your mother". The relevance of secrets in the development of autonomy is widely supported in literature surrounding the topic (Beyers et. al. 2003; Finkenauer, Engels & Meeus, 2002; Hofer, 2003; Seiffge-Krenke, 1988). Furthermore, the formulation of this item leads the adolescents to take a stance and make their position clear. It is required of them that they decide whether areas of their life exist which they intentionally do not share with their parents.

Based upon these considerations, an interview-structure was developed for the adolescents which targeted their secrets (content level), the reasoning behind their secrets (cognitive level of appraisal), and the corresponding emotions (affective level of appraisal). Information concerning the mothers' emotions as seen from the perspective of the adolescents was also gathered within the interview.

Procedure and scoring

Subjects were recruited via a youth club and were not personally known to the investigators. The interviews were carried out in the adolescents' homes by a trained interviewer, collecting data for his Master's thesis (Koch, 2004). The analysis of the interview transcripts was based upon Mayring's structured content-analysis (2002) and was carried out by the author. The data analysis process focused on testing whether the empirical data collected conformed with the theoretical framework presented above.

Classification of the adolescents to the categories "emotionally autonomous" and "less emotionally autonomous" occurred on the basis of the following theoretically derived indicators: in step one autonomous and less autonomous structures of reasoning were distinguished from one another. Grasping to external authorities or unpleasant consequences in the argumentation was coded as an indicator of an externally orientated structure of reasoning. Opposingly an internally orientated structure of reasoning was characterised by a pattern of argumentation emphasising personal convictions and viewpoints which demonstrated that the adolescent was aware of the importance - in this case of having secrets - for his/her development. At the same time the judgment is guided by responsibility towards the belongings and feelings of all family members. Their perspectives are taken into account.

In step two, the affective level of appraisal was examined in light of whether adolescents named positive or negative emotions in connection with their secrets. Positive emotions indicate emotional autonomy and negative emotions less emotional autonomy. On an affective level positive emotions reflect the fact that the individual is convinced of their standpoint in the sense of an internal orientation. Negative emotions show that doubt is present and therefore indicate that the development of emotionally autonomy has not been completed. A classification as "emotionally autonomous" thus depends on the fulfilment of two criteria: an internally orientated structure of reasoning and the naming of positive emotions.

Results

All adolescents claimed to have secrets from their parents, whereby general consensus was found in terms of the subject areas: being in love, sexuality, friendship group and use of free time. Eight adolescents were classified as "emotionally autonomous". Congruence between their cognitive and affective appraisals was evident and they clearly detached their own emotions from the emotions of their mothers. Eight adolescents were classified as "less emotionally autonomous". Within this category two of the eight subjects differed from the rest in that they fulfilled the criteria of an autonomous structure of reasoning, not however of a positive emotional appraisal. Whilst these adolescents were able to argumentatively represent their viewpoint, they both reported feelings of unease with reference to their mother. There was no effect of sex and social class of the adolescents on the classification of emotional autonomy. The kappa-coefficient for interrater reliability was $\kappa = .875$. For the purpose of clarifing the classification procedure, examples from interviews can be found in table 1.

Table 1. Examples from interviews with adolescents for clarification of the indicators used within the classification procedure.

Classification criteria	Example from interview
Non-autonomous structure of reasoning	„because I don't dare tell her, because I'm scared what kind of a reaction I will get. [....] I'd just rather everything be harmonious" (subject 1b)
autonomous structure of reasoning and negative affective appraisal	„[…] because I think that they don't have anything to do with anyone else. To put it one way, it's my life and I can do what I want with it. […] I'd say not so good. You really should speak openly with your parents […] Because I then feel funny. […] Like I said, being scared that the other person has a different opinion" (subject 12b)
autonomous structure of reasoning and positive affective appraisal	„[…], every person should have a certain amount of privacy, that includes children from their parents, that should be respected, by parents too. […] I need time to think about whether I should say it or not. […] Secrets are important to me. […] I feel like I'm more respected when I have some privacy" (subject 9b).

DISCUSSION

The results support the empirical validity of the two-component model of emotional autonomy. Adolescents who took part in the interviews of the present study could indeed be classified into emotionally autonomous and less emotionally autonomous categories (see table 1) on the basis of theoretically derived indicators. Given the finding that all subjects claimed to have secrets, it is evident that the degree of emotional autonomy is not determined by the simple establishment of private spheres alone. It is only when the analysis of structures of reasoning is combined with affective appraisals that a differential and theoretically plausible classification can take place.

It is interesting that a sub-group of adolescents could be identified who were rated as emotionally autonomous on a cognitive level of appraisal, not however with reference to the affective component. These adolescents were able to argumentatively justify their viewpoint, reported at the same time however negative emotions (see table 1). This result might be interpreted as suggesting that these individuals found themselves in a transitional phase in the middle of the detachment process, whereby affective and cognitive components were not yet congruent. As emotional autonomy increases it can be assumed that cognition and emotion are progressively unified. Future research should look to examine whether the transitional phase observed above is correlated with age and the two-component model therefore able to encorporate developmental processes.

The role of emotional autonomy for moral development

The two-component model indicates that emotional autonomy plays an important role in adolescents' moral development:

In comparing the categories for describing the development of emotional autonomy (in terms of the two-component model) with moral development there is evidence for similarities. Both, the status of "emotional autonomy" and moral autonomy according to Piaget (1965) and Kohlberg (1984) as well as the internalization of moral values (see Grolnick, Deci and Ryan 1997) are characterised by autonomous structures of argumentation which in turn are marked by the fact that the individual has reflexively spent time taking a good look at the given subject matter. The close connection between emotional autonomy and moral autonomy in terms of judgment shows that the core of both developmental lines is the same. We draw the conclusion that emotional and moral autonomy influence each other in a reciprocal relationship. It follows from this argument that parent's and teacher's autonomy support contributes to moral development and vice versa. Having the freedom of self-determinated decision-making as well as being involved in dilemma discussions foster autonomous reasoning. (It doesn't matter if these are dilemma discussions in the Kohlbergian tradition or real life discussions about actual familiy conflicts). Therefore education has to focus on critical reflection and personal responsibility rather than to engage in drill and obedience.

In the broader context of identity development as described by Erikson (1968) the status of "identity achievement" is also characterised by an autonomous structure of argumentation. The status of "foreclosure" and "less emotional autonomy" within the scope of the two-component-model, are on the other hand distinguished by an external orientation. These similarities imply that emotional autonomy should be given a central position within the formation of a moral identity. In order to more precisely clarify the relationship between emotional autonomy and moral identity it would be possible in a further study, to carry out the interview for investigating emotional autonomy together with the moral judgment interview (Colby & Kohlberg, 1987) and the identity status interview (Marcia, 1980). The theoretically plausible correlative relationship could, on the basis of data collected from these tree interviews, be empirically tested.

Due to the finding that the classification as "emotionally autonomous" takes both into account, an internally orientated structure of reasoning and the naming of positive emotions, the two-component model strengthens the meaning of emotions for adolescence development. As Gibbs (2003) argues that "Kohlberg's and Hoffman's theories need to be taken together for a comprehensive understanding of moral development" (p. 238), our data support an integrative conception of cognition and emotion for developing moral identity in adolescence (see also Blasi, 1993). Finally, further research should also address the issue how to educate emotions in adolescence in the field of moral development.

Overall this chapter rises up the question how moral development interacts with different developmental contexts in adolescence. The overlap of emotional autonomy and moral development shows the relevance to investigate the links among different developmental lines in order to contribute to a better understanding of identity development.

REFERENCES

Barber, B. K. & Harmon, E. L. (2002). Violating the self: Parental psychological control of children and adolsescents. In B.K. Barber (Ed.), *Intrusive parenting: How psychological control affects children and adolescents* (pp. 15-52). Washington, DC: American Psychological Association.

Beyers, W., Goossens, L., Vansant, I. & Moors, E. (2003). A structural model of autonomy in middle and late adolescence: Connectedness, separation, detachment and agency. *Journal of Youth and Adolescence, 32,* 351-365.

Blasi, A. (1993). The development of identity: Some implications for moral functioning. In G.G. Noam & T.E. Wren (Eds.), *The moral self* (pp. 99-122). Cambridge, MA: MIT Press.

Blos, P. (1979). *The adolescent passage.* New York: University Press.

Erikson, E. H. (1968). *Identity: Youth and crisis.* New York: Norton.

Fend, H. (2005). *Entwicklungspsychologie des Jugendalters* [Developmental psychology of youth] (3rd. Ed.). Wiesbaden: VS Verlag für Sozialwissenschaften.

Finkenauer, C., Engels, R. C. M. E. & Meeus, W. (2002). Keeping secrets from parents: Advantages and disadvantages of secrecy in adolescence. *Journal of Youth and Adolescence, 2.* 123-136.

Frank, S. J., Avery, C. B. & Laman, M. S. (1988). Young adults' perceptions of their relationships with their parents: Individual differences in connectedness, competence and emotional autonomy. *Developmental Psychology, 24,* 729-737.

Gibbs, J.C. (2003). *Moral development and reality: Beyond the theories of Kohlberg and Hoffman.* Thousand Oaks, CA: Sage.

Grolnick, W.S., Deci. E.L. & Ryan, R.M. (1997). Internalization within the family: The self-determination theory perspective. In J.E. Grusec & L. Kuczynski (Eds.), *Parenting and children's internalization of values: A handbook of contemporary theory* (pp. 135-161). New York: John Wiley & Sons.

Havighurst, R.J. (1952). *Developmental tasks and education* (3rd. Ed.). New York: Longmans, Green and Co.

Heuves, W. (2005). Junge Adoleszente: Entwicklung und Behandlung [Early adolescents: Development and treatment]. In V. Green (Ed.), *Emotionale Entwicklung in Psychoanalyse, Bindungstheorie und Neurowissenschaften* [Emotional development in the field of psychoanalytic and attachment theory and neuroscience] (pp.257-283). Frankfurt am Main: Brandes & Apsel.

Hill, J.P. & Holmbeck, G.N. (1986). Attachment and autonomy in adolescence. In G. J. Whitehurst (Ed.), *Annals of child development, 3,* (pp. 145-189). Greenwich, CT: JAI Press.

Hofer, M. (2003). *Selbständig werden im Gespräch. Wie Jugendliche und Eltern ihre Beziehung verändern* [Becoming independent in communication. How adolescents and parents change their relations]. Bern: Hans Huber.

Hoffman, M.L. (1983). Affective and cognitive processes in moral internalisation. In E. Higgens, A. Ruble & W. Hartup, (Eds.), *Social cognition and social development: A sociocultural perspective* (pp. 236-274). Cambridge: Cambridge University Press.

Koch, C. (2004). *Emotionale Autonomie aus der Sicht von Jugendlichen und deren Müttern* [Emotional autonomy in the view of adolescents and their mothers]. Unpublished thesis, University of Leipzig, Germany.

Kohlberg, L. (1984). *Essays on moral development: Vol.2. The psychology of moral development: The nature and validity of moral stages.* San Francisco: Harper & Row.

Colby, A. & Kohlberg, L. (1987). *The measurement of moral judgment. Vol. 1: Theoretical foundations and research validation.* New York: Cambridge University Press.

Landgraf, J. (2003). *Emotionale Ablösung im Jugendalter: eine Methodenstudie* [Emotional detachment in adolescence: An empirical study]. Unpublished thesis, University of Leipzig, Germany.

Latzko, B. (2006). Adolescents' perception of emotional autonomy – Theoretical considerations and empirical data for a re-defined concept. *Zeitschrift für Sozialisationsforschung und Erziehungssoziologie, 26,* 36-51.

Latzko, B., Kim, H.-O. & Hoppe-Graff, S. (2002). Emotionale Autonomie im Jugendalter: Dekonstruktion einer Skala und Rekonstruktion eines Konzeptes [Emotional autonomy in adolescence: de-construction of a scale and re-construction of a concept]. In E. van der Meer, H. Hagendorf, R. Beyer, F. Krüger, A. Nuthmann & S. Schulz (Eds.), *Bericht über den 43. Kongress der Deutschen Gesellschaft für Psychologie in Berlin* [Report of the 43rd Congress of the German Society for Psychology in Berlin] (p. 115). Berlin: Pabst Science Publishers.

Latzko, B., Hoppe-Graff, S. & Kim, H.-O. (2003, September). *Emotionale Ablösung im Jugendalter: Ein Methodenvergleich* [Emotional detachment in adolescence: A comparison of different methods]. Paper presented at the 16th Congress of the German Society of Psychology, Section Developmental Psychology, Mainz, Germany.

Marcia, J. E. (1980). Identity in adolescence . In J. Adelson (Ed.), *Handbook of adolescent pschology* (p. 159-187). New York: Wiley.

Masche, J. G. (2006). Eltern-Kind-Beziehung und Elternverhalten bei 13- und 16jährigen: Individuation oder Ablösung [Parent-child relations and parenting behaviors with children at the age of 13 and 16: Individuation or detachment]. *Zeitschrift für Sozialisationsforschung und Erziehungssoziologie, 26,* 7-22.

Mayring, P. (2002). *Qualitative Inhaltsanalyse:* Grundlagen und Techniken [Content analysis: Basics and methodology]. Weinheim: Deutscher Studien Verlag.

Noack, P. (1993). Zusammenhänge zwischen Familieninteraktionen und Beziehungsqualitäten aus Sicht der Familienmitglieder [Relations between family interaction and the quality of relationship in the view of the family members]. *Zeitschrift für Familienforschung, 5,* 115-133.

Papastefanou, C. (2006). Ablösung im Erleben junger Erwachsener aus verschiedenen Familienstrukturen [Young adult's experience of separation from parents – A comparison between traditional families and single parent families]. *Zeitschrift für Sozialisationsforschung und Erziehungssoziologie, 26,* 23-35.

Papastefanou, C. (2000). Die Eltern-Kind-Beziehung in der Auszugsphase – Die neue Balance zwischen Verbundenheit und Abgrenzung [The parent-child relationship in the launching phase- the new balance between connectedness and autonomy]. *Zeitschrift für Sozialisationsforschung und Erziehungssoziologie, 20,* 379-390.

Papini, D. R., Farmer, F. F., Clark, S. M., Micka, J. C. & Barnett, J. K. (1990). Early adolescent age and gender differences in patterns of emotional self-disclosure to parents and friends. *Adolescence, 25,* 959–976.

Piaget, J. (1965). *The moral judgment of the child.* New York: The Free Press.

Pikowsky, B. (1998). Konfliktgespräche jugendlicher Mädchen mit Mutter, Schwester und Freundin [Conflict discussions between young girls, their mothers, sisters and friends]. *Zeitschrift für Pädagogische Psychologie, 12,* 179-190.

Resch, F. (1999). *Entwicklungspsychopathologie des Kindes- und Jugendalters – ein Lehrbuch* [Developmental psychopathology of child and youth] (2., überarb. u. erw. Aufl.). Weinheim: Beltz. PVU.

Ryan, R. M. & Lynch, J. H. (1989). Emotional autonomy versus detachment: revisiting the vicissitudes of adolescence and young adulthood. *Child Development, 60,* 340-356.

Schmitz, M. F. & Baer, J.C. (2001). The vicissitudes of measurements: A confirmatory factor analysis of the Emotional Autonomy Scale. *Child Development,72,* 207-219.

Seiffge- Krenke, I. (1988). Geheimnisse und Intimität im Jugendalter: Ihre Bedeutung für die Autonomieentwicklung [Secrets and privacy in adolescence and the meaning for autonomy development]. In A. Spitznagel (Ed.), *Geheimnis und Geheimhaltung* [secret and secrecy] (pp. 257-263). Göttingen: Hogrefe.

Steinberg L. & Silverberg S.B. (1986). The vicissitudes of autonomy in early adolescence. *Child Development, 57,* 841-851.

Stierlin, H. (1994). *Individuation und Familie: Studien zur Theorie und therapeutischen Praxis* [Individuation and family: studies on theory and practice of therapy]. F.a. M.: Suhrkamp.

Turiel, E. (1983). *The development of social knowledge: Morality and convention.* Cambridge, U.K.: Cambridge University Press.

Youniss, J. & Smollar, J. (1985). *Adolescent relations with mothers, fathers and friends.* Chicago: University of Chicago Press.

Zimmer-Gembeck, J.M. & Collins, W.A. (2003). Autonomy development during adolescence. In G.R. Adams & M.D. Berzonsky (Eds.), *Handbook of adolescence* (pp. 175-204). Oxford: Blackwell.

Brigitte Latzko
University of Leipzig, Germany

TINA MALTI, IRENE KRIESI & MARLIS BUCHMANN

ADOLESCENT'S PROSOCIAL BEHAVIOR, SYMPATHY, AND MORAL REASONING

In the present study, we will analyze the role of sympathy and moral reasoning as motivational prerequisites for pro-social action. Our analytic interest concentrates on the direct and indirect effects of these dimensions on pro-social action. We investigate this question for the developmental phase of adolescence. In this phase, considering the needs of others becomes an increasingly important motive for moral action (Keller, 1996). This process is closely linked with the development of a moral self (Keller & Edelstein 1993; Noam & Wren, 1993). It may (potentially) lead to an integration of moral principles and moral emotions in one's identity, thereby determining to which degree a person practices what he or she thinks and feels regarding moral obligations and principles (Blasi, 1995; Puka, 2004, p. 172).

Shared moral norms, and the willingness to act accordingly, are important prerequisites of integrated communities. Although a widely shared basis of moral values still exists even in individualized modern societies, individuals differ regarding their willingness to put known and recognized moral values into practice and act pro-socially (Nunner Winkler, 1999b). As people's motives are complex and contextualised, it is obvious that there are many reasons for these differences. In the philosophical and psychological literature, cognitive and affective dimensions have been discussed as motivational underpinnings of prosocial action (cf. Montada, 1993). Moral philosophers have evaluated the role of cognitions and emotions in the genesis of prosocial dispositions differently: While philosophers like Kant presuppose cognition as the *sine qua non* for moral action, Frankfurt's notion of a morally autonomous person, who develops second-order desires, additionally includes the role of affective-motivational aspects in the development of moral action (Frankfurt, 1971). In contrast, Hume's approach to ethics concentrates on emotions. According to his view, people have moral sentiments providing them with a spontaneous intuition or sense of what is right and wrong (cf. Haidt, 2001). This sense is at the core of moral and prosocial action (Hume, 1751/1957; Smith, 1759/1976; cf. Maxwell & Reichenbach, 2006).

In moral psychology, theoretical thinking about prosocial action has developed in a similar fashion. Cognitive-developmental theory has emphasized the role of moral judgment for moral and prosocial action (Kohlberg, 1984; Piaget, 1981). Cognitive decentration as well as differentiation and coordination of perspectives of self and other are necessary preconditions for moral stage level (Keller & Edelstein, 1991;

Piaget, 1965). The higher the stage level the greater the consistency between moral judgment and moral action (Kohlberg & Candee, 1984). Nonetheless, there appears to be a gap between moral judgment and moral action: Moral judgment seems to be a necessary but insufficient condition for moral action (Blasi, 1983). Potentially mediating mechanisms which have been discussed are for example personality and ego-development/ego-strength (Blasi, 1995; Narvaez & Rest, 1995), moral motivation (Nunner-Winkler, 1999a), and moral emotions (Hoffman, 2000). Although Piaget early recognized a cognitive-affective parallelism in moral development, the role of moral emotions for moral action has so far been more or less neglected by cognitive-developmental theory (Edelstein & Schröder, 2000). Moral emotions and their impact on moral and prosocial action have been emphasized within moral internalization theory (Hoffmann, 2000). Hoffman (1987) and Eisenberg (1986) assume that sympathy is a basic motive for prosocial action which may also stimulate altruistic moral reasoning. Haidt's intuitionist model goes one step further, stating that moral judgment is the result of automatic and quick evaluations, so-called moral intuitions. In contrast, moral reasoning is considered to be slow and only ex post (Haidt, 2001).

Gibbs (2003) has recently tempted to integrate the cognitive and intuitionist attempts to explain the motivational mechanisms involved in prosocial action. In Gibbs' view, interpreting justice as a mere empathy alloy is reductionist (2003, p. 113). Likewise, assuming primacy of cognition in the genesis of moral action is simplifying. Rather, he argues, a *coprimacy* of cognitive and affective aspects serves as a basic motivation of prosocial behavior. Gibbs and colleagues found some empirical evidence for this proposition, as moral type B reasoning and empathy were associated with prosocial behavior (Gibbs et al., 1986). Moral type B reasoning included in this study evaluations referring to reciprocal perspective taking, universal valuing and conscience; this type of reasoning was also related to the moral judgment stage (cf. Krettenauer & Edelstein, 1999). In the present study, we take up the notion of coprimacy by analyzing the role of sympathy and moral reasoning as motivational prerequisites for prosocial action.

Sympathy constitutes one of the most prototypical emotions in the moral domain. Its role for prosocial behavior has obtained tremendous attention in the psychological literature. Sympathy is defined as an understanding of another's situation and involves feelings of concern and involvement for the other, but it is not the same feeling which the other person may experience (Eisenberg, 2000, p. 672; Blum, 1980; Kienbaum, in press). Batson (1998) has shown that sympathy leads to a prosocial reaction that tries to alleviate another's negative emotion (the so-called empathy-altruism hypothesis). In contrast, personal distress is associated with self-oriented feelings, which lead to self-focused reactions (Eisenberg, 2000). Empirical research has lent support to the assumption that sympathy is an important motive for prosocial behavior (see Eisenberg & Fabes; 1998, and Eisenberg, Spinrad, & Sadovsky, 2006, for reviews; Zahn-Waxler, Radke-Yarrow, Wagner, & Chapman, 1992). Batsons' empathy-altruism hypothesis has been criticized as conceptually misleading, however (Puka, 2004). It conceptualized sympathy as a spontaneously evolving emotion resulting directly from a particular social situation. This view is one-dimensional and neglects that sympathy may, for example, also refer to individual values, which are integrated into a person's identity (Puka, 2004). Likewise, the expression of sympathy is closely connected to a complex history of socialization, and it is also related to the ability to coordinate and integrate perspectives of the self and of others (Hoffman, 2000; Keller, 1996; Keller & Edelstein, 1991). Empirically, the empathy-altruism hypothesis has been relativized by Cialdini and colleagues (1987). They found that altruistic behavior can be explained by many other than sympathetic motives. These issues point to the necessity to study different motives and moderators involved in the relationship between sympathy and prosocial behavior. Although researchers have suggested to investigate the moderating effects of moral reasoning (Eisenberg, 2000), rather few studies have investigated moral reasoning as a moderator in the relationship between sympathy and prosocial behavior in adolescence (but see Eisenberg, Miller, Shell, McNalley, & Shea, 1991). A study by Eisenberg, Zhou, and Koller (2001) found that sympathy was related to Brazilian adolescents' level of prosocial moral reasoning, which in turn motivated prosocial behavior. In our own previous study with kindergarten children, we found that children with high moral motivation (which was assessed by a combined score of emotion attributions and moral reasoning after moral rule transgressions, cf. Nunner-Winkler, Meyer-Nikele, & Wohlrab, 2007) displayed high prosocial behavior regardless of their level of sympathy. For children with low or moderate moral motivation, the level of prosocial behavior increased with the level of sympathy (Malti, Gummerum, & Buchmann, in press a; see also Miller, Eisenberg, Fabes, & Shell, 1996).

The present study aims at exploring adolescent's moral reasoning in relation to sympathy and prosocial behavior in the *domain of friendship*. We chose this approach for two reasons: On the one hand prosocial action occurs in interpersonal relationships. On the other hand the developmental significance of friendship for moral and prosocial development is unchallenged (Rubin, Bukoswski, & Parker, 1998). Prosocial behavior is closely related to constructive peer and friendship interactions, which may lead to opportunities for social perspective-taking and empathetic exchange, thereby fostering moral growth (Bukowski & Sippola, 1996, Krappmann, 1996; Piaget, 1965). Affective ties to friends may, through experiencing reciprocal empathy and care, help to create a sense of responsibility and a care-orientation in interpersonal relationships (see Edelstein, Keller, & Schröder, 1990; Keller & Edelstein, 1993; Keller, Edelstein, Schmid, Fang, & Fang, 1998). We therefore believe that reasoning about obligations and self-interest in the domain of friendship is particularly interesting with regard to an analysis of antecedents of prosocial behavior. Up to date, we are not aware of other empirical research focusing on adolescent's moral reasoning in close relationships and its relation with sympathy and prosocial behavior.

To sum up, the purpose of the present study is to examine the relations between sympathy, moral reasoning in close relationships, and prosocial behavior in adolescence. In line with previous research, we assume that sympathy will be positively related to prosocial behavior. Contrary to the majority of previous research making use of self-reported measures of sympathy susceptible to social desirability, our analyses are based on a combination of self reports and assessment by others. A combined measure will capture sympathy more reliably (Epstein, 1979). With regard to the relationship between moral reasoning and prosocial behavior, we expect that altruistic moral reasoning in a close friendship relationship will be related to sympathy and prosocial behavior. Vice versa, self-interested arguments will be negatively associated with prosocial behavior. This expectation is based on Hoffmans' (1987) and Eisenbergs' (1986) idea that altruistic moral reasoning can serve as a motive for prosocial action. Furthermore, we assume that adolescents with high altruistic reasoning will display high levels of prosocial behavior independent of sympathy, whereas adolescents with low levels of altruistic moral reasoning may need sympathy as a motive for prosocial action. This assumption is related to findings by Eisenberg and colleagues (2001) as well as to our own previous research (Malti et al., in press a; Malti, Bayard, & Buchmann, in press b). We will turn attention to gender differences in prosocial dispositions, which have been discussed controversially in the literature (cf. Gilligan, 1982; Walker, 2006).

METHOD

Participants

The analyses will be based on the first wave of the *Swiss Survey of Children and Youth COCON* (Buchmann & Fend, 2004). This representative longitudinal survey, which is currently being conducted in Switzerland, investigates the life course and competence development of three age cohorts (6 years, 15 years, 21 years) with a multi-informant approach. The age cohorts are prototypical for middle childhood, middle adolescence, and young adulthood. The present analysis is based on the data of the 15-year olds and their primary caregivers. A representative random sample from the German- and French-speaking parts of Switzerland was drawn by a two-stage-method. In the first step, 131 communities (broken down by community type and community size) were selected. In the second step, cohort members residing in the selected communities were randomly sampled on the basis of information provided by the official register of community residents (Schuler & Joye, 2004).

The final sample size is 1,255 adolescents with an average age of 15.3 years ($SD = 0.20$). There were 649 girls (52%) and 606 boys (48%). 1056 of the primary caregivers, who were predominantly mothers (87%), filled in a supplementary questionnaire. In sum, data from 1056 complete dyads (adolescents and primary caregivers) were available.

Analyses are based on a weighted sample which corrects for an over-sampling of particular community types and a moderate under-representation of lower educational strata, and adolescents with foreign nationality.

Procedure

First, all selected adolescents received a letter containing information about the study and the request for participation. Parents received a separate letter of information. Second, all potential participants were phoned by an interviewer who asked for participation in the survey. 63 percent of the contacted adolescents were willing to give an interview. They were individually interviewed at home via a computer-assisted personal interview (CAPI), lasting approximately 60 minutes. The primary caregivers filled in a supplementary written questionnaire.

Measures

Prosocial behavior   The primary caregivers evaluated the prosocial behavior of the adolescents on a four-point scale with three items from the prosocial behavior subscale of the Strength and Difficulties Questionnaire (SDQ) (e.g., *the child is helpful if someone is hurt, upset or feeling ill*). A mean score was computed. The reliability of the scale was $\alpha = .64$.

Sympathy   Adolescent's sympathy was assessed by self-reports and primary-caregiver ratings. Self-reported sympathy was measured with five revised items taken from Zhou, Valiente, and Eisenberg (2003). Primary caregivers' assessment of their child's sympathy was based on a six-point scale, with three items taken from Zhou et al. (2003) (e.g., *my child feels usually sorry for other children who are being teased*). Mean scores were derived. The reliability for the scales were $\alpha = .72$ for self-report, and $\alpha = .77$ for the primary-caregiver report, respectively.

Moral Reasoning   An interpersonal-moral dilemma was used to assess adolescents' moral reasoning (Keller, 1996; Selman, 1980). In the story, two adolescents are close friends. A third adolescent is new in class and does not yet have any friends. When the two close friends talk about the new classmate, one of them declares a dislike for him/her. The other one (protagonist) asks for understanding the new classmate's situation. The protagonist promises his/her best friend to meet him or her as usual on their special meeting day. The friend mentions some new records/clothes, but specifically wants to talk about an important problem. Later that day, the protagonist receives a phone call from the new classmate, who invites him or her to a pop concert at the very time of his or her meeting with the best friend. After listening to the story, the adolescents were asked the following questions:
1. *Action choice*: Imagine that you are the protagonist. What would you do? How would you decide in this situation?
2. *Reasons for action choice*: Why would you decide this way?
3. *Moral judgment*: Is your choice right?
4. *Reasons for moral judgment*: Why do you think it is right/wrong?

Coding: *Action choice* was classified according to its direction (i.e., new classmate, friend, or alternative options, i.e., some activity including all three). *Moral judgment* was classified as "right" or "wrong". The *reasons for action choice and moral judgment* were classified into seven content categories, including hedonistic reasons (interest for objects or for relationship), interpersonal reasons (altruism/empathy), moral reasons (obligation of promise), mixed interpersonal-moral reasons (obligation of friendship), consequences, balancing strategies/strategies of conflict resolution, and unscoreable reasons. The majority of categories for action choice refer to the friend or the new classmate. However, some comprise several options (e.g., promise and obligation of friendship for choice of friend) or refer to an alternative (e.g., activity including all three of them). Regarding reasons for moral judgment, the analyses are based on four dummy-coded categories only. According to Keller et al. (1998), they represent prototypical reasons in terms of egoistic concerns and moral duties or relationship responsibilities. The first two categories refer to the option "new classmate". They comprise *self-interest/hedonism* and *altruism/empathy*, indicating hedonistic interests or relationship concern, respectively. The third and fourth categories refer to the option "friend". They include *quality of friendship* and *promise*, indicating relationship or normative concerns.

RESULTS

Descriptive Statistics

Before presenting the interrelations between moral reasoning, sympathy, and prosocial behavior, we will briefly describe the three variables. Table 1 displays the means and standard deviations of prosocial behavior and self- and other-rated sympathy by gender.

Table 1 shows that primary caregivers rated girls as more prosocial and more sympathetic than boys with, $t(1013) = -5.68$, $p < .001$ and $t(1016) = -5.70$, $p < .001$, respectively. For sympathy, the values for the two types of rating correspond: Girls rated themselves as more sympathetic than boys $t(1253) = -7.67$, $p < .001$).

Table 1. Means and Standard Deviations of Continuous Study Variables by Gender

	Girls		Boys	
	M	SD	M	SD
Primary-caregiver-rated prosocial behavior	4.79	0.89	4.46	0.94
Primary-caregiver-rated sympathy	5.04	0.94	4.69	0.99
Self-rated sympathy	4.96	0.76	4.63	0.78

Table 2 displays the percentage frequencies of the action decision and moral judgment of the action decision.

Table 2. Percentage Frequencies of Action Decision and Moral Judgment

	Old friend	New classmate	Other
Action decision	60	30	10
Moral judgment of action decision: right	99	78	97

As for action decisions and their moral judgment, the results in table 2 show that 60 % of the adolescents opted for the old friend, whereas 30 % chose the new classmate. 10% preferred an alternative option, i.e., strategies of balancing (e.g., an alternative activity including all three of them). Almost all adolescents who chose either their old friend or another option judged their decision as right (99%). For those who would have met the new classmate, moral judement is less homogenous: Only 78% considered their decision to be right, whereas 22% thought it to be wrong. No substantial gender differences in action decision and moral judgment could be found.

The justification categories of the action decision and moral judgment are shown in figure 1.

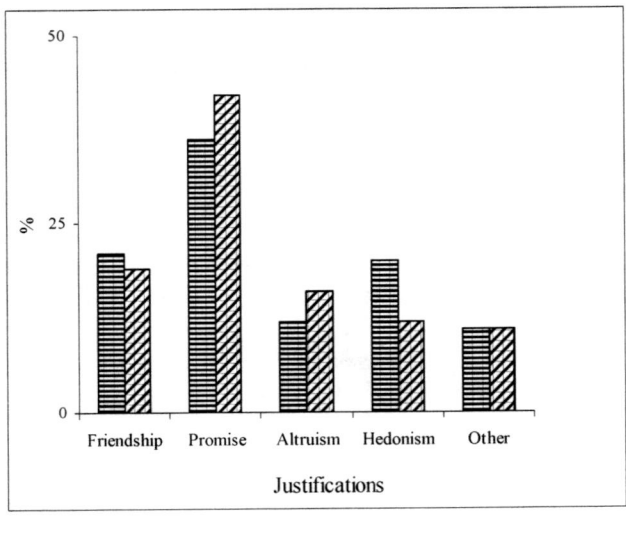

Figure 1. Percentage Frequencies of Justifications by Context.

In both contexts, adolescents referred most frequently to promise reasons (36% for action decision, and 42% for moral judgment). Reasons alluding to the quality of friendship were also mentioned frequently (21%, and 19%, respectively). Altruistic justifications and hedonistic reasons stressing self-interests were mentioned with a similar frequency (altruistic reasons: 12%, and 16%; hedonistic reasons: 20%, and 12%). Reasons related to other justifications occurred in 11% of the cases in both contexts.

Interrelations between Sympathy and Moral Reasoning

The interrelations between sympathy and the reasoning categories were analyzed by a correlation analysis. As primary-caregiver-rated sympathy and self-reported sympathy were significantly correlated, $r(1047) = .24$, $p < .001$, the two scores were aggregated into an overall score. This leads to a more reliable measure of sympathy (Epstein, 1979).

On a bivariate level, sympathy was positively associated with altruistic reasoning in the context of action decision, $r(1086) = .10$, $p < .01$ and in the context of moral judgment, $r(1051) = .08$, $p < .05$. Furthermore, sympathy was negatively associated with selfish interests in the context of the action decision, $r(1086) = -.06$, $p < .05$.

Prosocial Behavior, Sympathy, and Moral Reasoning

Hierarchical linear regression analysis was employed to analyze the role of sympathy and moral reasoning for adolescent's prosocial behavior. Two regression models were run for the primary caregivers' ratings of prosocial behavior as dependent variable. In the first model, we entered gender, sympathy, moral reasoning categories for action decision, and interaction terms as independent variables. In the second model, gender, sympathy, moral reasoning categories for moral judgments, and interaction terms were specified. All variables were standardised. The interaction terms consist of the product of the mean centred main effects of sympathy and moral reasoning. Gender was coded as 0.5 and -0.5. We tested the interaction terms in preliminary analyses. Only the significant interaction term between altruistic reasoning for action decision and sympathy was kept in the final model. The independent variables were entered in two steps: In the first step, gender, sympathy, and the moral reasoning categories in the corresponding context (i.e., action decision, moral judgment) were entered. The interaction term was entered in the second step.

The findings of the first model showed that prosocial behavior was significantly predicted by the independent variables, $R^2 = .22$, $F(8, 1036) = 36.19$, $p < .001$. Gender, $\beta = .06$, $p < .05$, sympathy, $\beta = .45$, $p < .001$, and the interaction between sympathy and altruistic reasoning of the action decision, $\beta = -.40$, $p = .05$, affect prosocial behavior substantially. The interaction was plotted using the procedure outlined by Aiken and West (1991). The slopes were calculated with the program ZumaStat. The corresponding slopes for low, moderate, and high altruistic moral reasoning

(- 1 *SD*, 0 *SD*, and +1 *SD*) were .60, .38, and .16, *ps* < .001, for the first two slopes and nonsignificant for the third (see figure 2): Girls display higher levels of prosocial behavior than boys. Furthermore, level of sympathy only affects the prosocial behavior of adolescents with low and moderate altruistic reasoning: their prosocial behavior increases with growing sympathy.

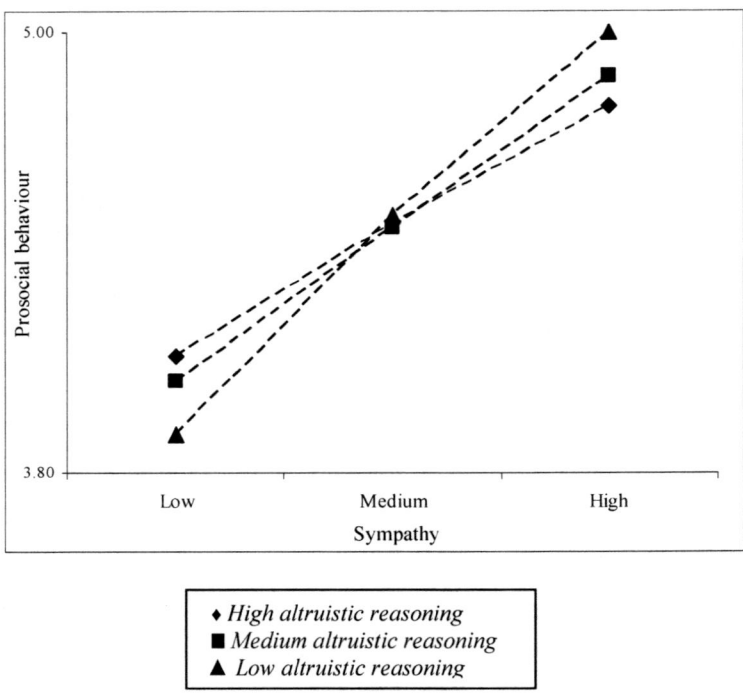

Figure 2. Interaction between sympathy and altruistic behavior in the prediction of prosocial behavior.

The second model also predicted prosocial behavior significantly, R^2 = .16, $F(8, 917)$ = 22.04, p < .001. Prosocial behavior was affected by sympathy, β = .37, p < .001, and hedonistic reasoning in the context of moral judgment, β = -.09, p < .05.

DISCUSSION

The purpose of our study was to investigate the relation between adolescent's prosocial behavior, their sympathy and moral reasoning. The analysis was based on the assumption that both affective and cognitive aspects of morality serve as motives for prosocial behavior (Gibbs, 2003), and that an integrative view on the antecedents of morally relevant behavior may be best suited to better understand the complex process of the development of moral commitment and moral self formation in adolescence. Based on previous research, we also hypothesized that altruistic moral reasoning may moderate the relationship between sympathy and prosocial behavior. The present study is among the few that use representative and large samples of adolescents to investigate the research questions. In contrast to other studies, we assessed adolescent's moral reasoning in a close friendship relationship. As friendships further the experience of reciprocal care and constructive discourse with a more ore less equal interaction partner (Youniss, 1980), we expected the friendship domain to be particularly well suited for examining our research question. Furthermore, sympathy was not only measured by self-reports, which may be prone to social desirability, but was based on a combined score of primary-caregiver and self-rating.

Our findings confirm that sympathy is an important motive for prosocial action: Adolescents with high levels of sympathy show more prosocial behavior. This result is in line with previous findings (Eisenberg et al., 1991, 2001). It extends previous research by demonstrating that the predicted interrelation between prosocial action and sympathy holds for adolescents at large and isn't restricted to specific social groups.

The hypothesis proposing an association between altruistic moral reasoning and prosocial behavior could only partially be confirmed with the present analysis: In particular, the results showed that adolescents with hedonistic reasons for their moral judgment displayed less prosocial behavior. In contrast, the justifications for action decisions did not predict prosocial behavior. On the one hand, this finding may indirectly reflect the context- and question dependency of moral reasoning (Keller et al., 1998; Nunner-Winkler, 1999a), which has been explicated within domain-theory by Turiel and colleagues (Turiel, 1983; Smetana, 2006). Empirical results of Malti and Keller (in press) confirmed a strong context dependency of moral reasoning for social behavior. On the other hand, the lack of a direct relation between moral reasoning in the context of action decision and prosocial behavior may indirectly resonate with research on moral exemplars. This line of research has shown that moral exemplars (i.e., people who display extraordinary high moral commitment and prosocial action) do not necessarily display higher moral reasoning levels (stages) compared to other individuals (Colby & Damon, 1992; Hart & Fegley, 1995). As this research focused on quality of moral reasoning rather than content of arguments, it's findings are not conclusive regarding the general relation between moral reasoning and prosocial action, however. To shed more light on the relation between prosocial behavior, action decisions and their justification, further research should analyse dilemmas about other types of relationships (i.e., close friendship versus parent-child-relationship). Likewise, it may also be important to differentiate between hypothetical and real-life dilemmas, because moral reasoning appears to be dependent on type of dilemma (cf. Skoe, Eisenberg, & Cumberland, 2002).

According to the bivariate analyses of sympathy and moral reasoning, altruistic adolescents express higher levels of sympathy compared to individuals with low values for altruism. Additionally, adolescents who reasoned hedonistically regarding their action decisions displayed lower levels of sympathy. Both results are theoretically plausible, as they express an orientation towards others: One refers to the cognitive side of morality, the other to the affective side. The finding is also in line with previous research conducted by Eisenberg and colleagues, which documents relations between sympathy and prosocial moral reasoning in other types of dilemmas (Eisenberg et al., 1991). It supports that there is – at least to some degree - consistency between adolescent's moral emotions and other-oriented moral reasoning, which is presumably related to the process of moral identity formation, and integration of these aspects into the self (cf. Damon, 1984; Hart, 2005).

Results pertaining to the interaction between sympathy and moral reasoning indicate that altruistic reasoning in the context of action decision moderated the association between sympathy and the primary-caregiver-rated prosocial behavior: Adolescents with high altruistic moral reasoning were high in primary-caregiver rated prosocial behavior, regardless of their level of sympathy. In contrast, for adolescents with low or moderate altruistic moral reasoning, the level of prosocial behavior increased with the level of sympathy. This moderating effect indicates that sympathy is a prerequisite for prosocial behavior of adolescents with low or moderate other-oriented moral reasoning, possibly acting as a substitute. This finding is in line with a previous study by Eisenberg et al. (2001) showing that sympathy predicted prosocial behavior in adolescence both directly and indirectly through moral judgment. Our own results on 6-year-old kindergarteners demonstrate a very similar moderating effect of altruistic reasoning for the relation between sympathy and prosocial behavior (Malti, et al., in press a). On a theoretical level, these findings support Eisenberg's (1986) thesis regarding sympathy as an important stimulus for prosocial moral reasoning (cf. Hoffman, 2000). They also imply that it is not a question of whether or not prosocial moral reasoning is associated with prosocial, moral action, but rather that the association depends on the strength of the altruistic motive and it's relevance to a person's values and self-concept. These findings contradict the assumption of intuitionist theory as proposed by Haidt (2001) that moral reasoning is always ex post and may not serve as a motivational underpinning for prosocial action.

In regard to gender differences, girls were rated as more sympathetic and prosocial by primary caregivers than boys. Girls also rated their own sympathy higher than boys. Gender differences in sympathy have been reported by other researchers as well (Eisenberg et al., 2006). As we did not find gender-differences in self-reported sympathy in a representative sample of 6-year-old Swiss kindergarteners (Malti et al., in press b), the pronounced gender differences in adolescence are likely to have been established through socialization influences within the most influential social contexts of family, school, and peer groups, and the community at large.

In sum, the present study emphasized the motivational function of sympathy and moral reasoning in a close friendship relationship on adolescent's prosocial behavior. Further research is needed to validate and extend these findings. On the one hand, it may be interesting to analyze moral reasoning in different contexts (e.g., parent-child versus peer relationships) in relation to reported and observed sympathy and prosocial behavior. On the other hand, the longitudinal investigation of sympathy and other-oriented moral reasoning from childhood to adolescence and their relations to prosocial, morally relevant behavior may shed further light on the process of moral self development (Lapsley & Narvaez, 2004).

ACKNOWLEDGEMENT

This research was funded by the Swiss National Science Foundation (SNF). We wish to thank all the children and parents for participation in the study. Likewise, we are very thankful to the interviewers and to the students for their help in data collecting and coding.

REFERENCES

Aiken, L. S., & West, S. G. (1991). *Multiple regression. Testing and interpreting interactions.* Newbury Park, CA: Sage.

Batson, C.D. (1998). Altruism and prosocial behavior. In D.T. Gilbert, S.T. Fiske, & G. Lindzey (Eds.), *The handbook of social psychology* (pp. 282-316). Boston: McGraw-Hill

Blasi, A. (1983). Moral cognition and moral action: A theoretical perspective. *Developmental Review, 3,* 178-210.

Blasi, A. (1995). Moral understanding and the moral personality: The process of moral integration. In W.M. Kurtines & J.L. Gewirtz (Eds.), *Moral development: An introduction* (pp. 229-253). Boston: Allyn & Bacon.

Blum, L.A. (1980). *Friendship, altruism and morality.* London: Routlege & Kegan Paul.

Buchmann, M. & Fend, H. (2004). *Context and competence: Swiss longitudinal survey of children and youth.* Research proposal, Swiss National Science Foundation.

Bukowski, W.M. & Sippola, L.K. (1996). Friendship and morality: (How) are they related? In W.M. Bukowski, A.F. Newcomb, & W.W. Hartup (Eds.), *The company they keep. Friendship in childhood and adolescence* (pp. 238-261). Cambridge: Cambridge University Press.

Cialdini, R.B., Schaller, M., Houlihan, D., Arps, K., Fultz, J. & Beaman, A.L. (1987). Empathy-based helping: Is it selflessly or selfishly motivated? *Journal of Personality and Social Psychology, 52* (4), 749-758.

Colby, A. & Damon, W. (1992). *Some do care.* New York: The Free Press.

Damon, W. (1984). Self-understanding and moral development from childhood to adolescence. In W.M. Kurtines & J.L. Gewirz (Eds.), *Morality, moral behavior, and moral development* (pp. 109-127). New York: Wiley.

Edelstein, W., Keller, M. & Schröder, E. (1990). Child development and social structure: A longitudinal study of individual differences. In P. B. Baltes, D. L. Featherman, & R. M. Lerner (Eds.), *Life-span development and behavior* (Vol. 10, pp. 152–185). Hillsdale, NJ: Erlbaum.

Edelstein, W. & Schröder, E. (2000). Full house or Pandora's box? The treatment of variability in post-Piagetian research. *Child Development, 71* (4), 840–842.

Epstein, S. (1979). The stability of behavior: 1. On predicting most of the people most of the time. *Journal of Personality and Social Psychology, 37,* 1097-1126.

Eisenberg, N. (1986). *Altruistic emotion, cognition, and behavior.* Hillsdale: Lawrence Erlbaum.

Eisenberg, N. (2000). Emotion, regulation, and moral development. *Annual Review of Psychology, 51,* 665-697.

Eisenberg, N. & Fabes, R.A. (1998). Prosocial development. In W. Damon (Series Ed.) & N. Eisenberg (Vol. Ed.), *Handbook of child psychology, Vol. 3: Social, emotional, and personality development* (pp. 701-778). New York: Wiley.

Eisenberg, N., Miller, P.A., Shell, R., McNalley, S. & Shea, C. (1991). Prosocial development in adolescence: A longitudinal study. *Developmental Psychology, 27*, 849-857.

Eisenberg, N., Spinrad, T.L. & Sadovsky, A. (2006). Empathy-related responding in children. In M. Killen & J. Smetana (Eds.), *Handbook of moral development* (pp. 517-549). Mahwah: Lawrence Erlbaum.

Eisenberg, N., Zhou, Q. & Koller, S. (2001). Brazilian adolescents' prosocial moral judgment and behavior: Relations to sympathy, perspective taking, gender-role orientation, and demographic characteristics. *Child Development, 72*, 518-534.

Frankfurt, H. (1971). Freedom of the will and the concept of a person. *Journal of Philosophy, 67* (1), 5-20.

Gibbs, J.C., Clark, P.M., Joseph, J.A., Green, J.L., Goodrick, T. & Makowski, D.G. (1986). Relations between moral judgment, moral courage, and field independence. *Child Development. 57*, 185-191.

Gibbs, J.C. (2003). *Moral development and reality. Beyond the theories of Kohlberg and Hoffman.* Thousand Oaks: Sage Publications.

Gilligan, C. (1982). *In a different voice.* Cambridge, MA: Harvard University Press.

Haidt, J. (2001). The emotional dog and its rational tail: A social intuitionist approach to moral judgment. *Psychological Review, 108*, 814-834.

Hart, D. (2005). The development of moral identity. In R.A. Dienstbier (Series Ed.) and G. Carlo & C. Pope Edwards (Vol.Ed.), *Nebraska symposium on motivation: Vol. 51. Moral motivation through the life span* (pp. 165-196). Lincoln: University of Nebraska Press.

Hart, D. & Fegley, S. (1995). Prosocial behavior and caring in adolescence: relations to self-understanding and social judgement. *Child Development, 22, 157-162.*

Hoffman, M.L. (1987). The contribution of empathy to justice and moral judgment. In N. Eisenberg & J. Strayer (Eds.), *Empathy and its development* (pp. 47-80). Cambridge: Cambridge University Press.

Hoffman, M.L. (2000). *Empathy and moral development. Implications for caring and justice.* Cambridge: Cambridge University Press.

Hume, D. (1957). *Inquiry concerning the principles of morals.* New York: Prentice Hall. (Original work published 1751).

Keller, M. (1996). *Moralische Sensibilität: Entwicklung in Freundschaft und Familie* (Moral sensibility: development in friendship and family). Weinheim: Psychologie Verlags Union.

Keller, M. & Edelstein, W. (1991). The development of socio-moral meaning making: Domains, categories, and perspective-taking. In W.M. Kurtines & J.L. Gewirtz (Hrsg.), *Handbook of moral behavior and development* (pp. 89-114). Hillsdale: Erlbaum.

Keller, M. & Edelstein, W. (1993) Die Entwicklung eines moralischen Selbst von der Kindheit zur Adoleszenz. In W. Edelstein, G. Nunner-Winkler & G.G. Noam (Hrsg.), *Moral und Person* (S. 307-334). Frankfurt a.M.: Suhrkamp.

Keller, M., Edelstein, W., Schmid, C., Fang, F.-X. & Fang, G. (1998). Reasoning about responsibilities and obligations in close relationships: A comparison across two cultures. *Developmental Psychology, 34* (4), 731-741.

Kienbaum, J. (in press). Entwicklungsbedingungen von Mitgefühl in der Kindheit. In T. Malti & S. Perren (Eds.), Soziale Kompetenzen entwickeln. Stuttgart: Kohlhammer

Kohlberg, L. (Ed.). (1984). The psychology of moral development. San Francisco: Harper & Row.

Kohlberg, L. & Candee, D. (1984). The relationship of moral judgment to moral action. In W.M. Kurtines & J.L. Gewirtz (Eds.), *Morality, moral behavior, and moral development* (pp. 52-73). New York: John Wiley & Sons.

143

Krappmann, L. (1996). Amicitia, drujba, shin-you, philia, Freundschaft, friendship: On the cultural diversity of a human relationship. In W. M. Bukowski, A. Newcomb, & W. W. Hartup (Eds.), *The company they keep: Friendship in childhood and adolescence* (pp. 19–40). New York: Cambridge University Press.

Krettenauer, T. & Edelstein, W. (1999). From substages to moral types and beyond: An analysis of core criteria for morally autonomous judgments. *International Journal of Behavioral Development, 23,* 899-920.

Lapsley, D. K. & Narváez, D. (Hrsg.) (2004) *Morality, self, and identity.* Mahwah, NJ: Erlbaum.

Malti, T., Bayard, S., & Buchmann, M. (in press b). Mitgefühl, soziales Verstehen und prosoziales Verhalten: Komponenten sozialer Handlungsfähigkeit in der Kindheit. In T. Malti & S. Perren (Eds.), *Soziale Kompetenzen entwickeln.* Stuttgart: Kohlhammer.

Malti, T., Gummerum, M. & Buchmann, M. (in press a). Contemporaneous and one-year longitudinal prediction of children's prosocial behavior from sympathy and moral motivation. *Journal of Genetic Psychology.*

Malti, T. & Keller, M. (in press). The relation of elementary-school children's externalizing behavior to emotion attributions, evaluation of consequences, and moral reasoning. *European Journal of Developmental Psychology.*

Maxwell, B. & Reichenbach, R. (2006). Educating moral emotions: a praxiological analysis. *Studies in Philosophy and Education, 7.* Early Online Publication.

Miller, P.A., Eisenberg, N., Fabes, R.A., & Shell, R. (1996). Relations of moral reasoning and vicarious emotion to young children's prosocial behavior toward peers and adults. *Developmental Psychology, 32,* 210-219.

Montada, L. (1993). Understanding oughts by assessing moral reasoning or moral emotions. In G. Noam & T. Wren (Eds.), *The moral self* (pp. 292-309). Cambridge: MIT Press.

Narvaez, D. & Rest, J. (1995). The four components of acting morally. In W.M. Kurtines & J.L. Gewirtz (Eds.), *Moral development: An introduction* (pp. 385-400). Needham Heights, MA: Allyn & Bacon.

Noam, G.G. & Wren, T. (Eds..) (1993). *The moral self.* Cambridge: MIT Press.

Nunner-Winkler, G. (1999a). Development of moral understanding and moral motivation. In F.E. Weinert & W. Schneider (Eds.), *Individual development from 3 to 12: Findings from the Munich longitudinal study* (pp. 253-290). New York: Cambridge University Press.

Nunner-Winkler, G. (1999b). Moralische Integration. In J. Friedrichs and W. Jagodzinski (Eds..), Soziale Integration. Sonderheft der Kölner Zeitschrift für Soziologie und Sozialpsychologie (pp. 293-319). Opladen/Wiesbaden: Westdeutscher Verlag.

Nunner-Winkler, G., Meyer-Nikele, M. & Wohlrab, D. (2007). Gender differences in moral motivation. *Merrill-Palmer Quarterly, 53* (1), 26-52.

Piaget, J. (1965). *The moral judgement of the child.* New York: Free Press.

Piaget, J. (1981). *Intelligence and affectivity: Their relationship during child development* (T.A. Brown & C.E. Kaegi, Trans. & Eds.). Palo Alto, CA: Annual Reviews.

Puka, B. (2004). Altruism and character. In D.K. Lapsley & D. Narvaez (Eds.), *Moral development, self, and identity* (p. 161-188). Mahwah: Lawrence Erlbaum.

Rubin, K.H., Bukowski, W. & Parker, J.G. (1998). Peer interactions, relationships, and groups. In W. Damon & R.M. Lerner (Eds.), *Handbook of Child Psychology: Vol. 1. Theoretical models of human development* (p. 619-700). New York: Wiley.

Schuler, M. & Joye, D. (2004). *Typologie der Gemeinden der Schweiz: 1980-2000.* Neuchâtel: Bundesamt für Statistik.

Selman, R.L. (1980). *The growth of interpersonal understanding: Developmental and clinical analyses.* New York: Academic Press.

Skoe, E., Eisenberg, N. & Cumberland, A. (2002). The role of reported emotion in real-life and hypothetical moral dilemmas. *Personality and Social Psychology Bulletin, 28,* 962-973.

Smetana, J. G. (2006). Social domain theory: Consistencies and variations in children's moral and social judgements. In M. Killen & J. G. Smetana (Eds.), *Handbook of Moral Development* (pp.119).

Smith, A. (1976). *The theory of moral sentiment.* Oxford: Oxford University Press (Original work published 1759).

Turiel, E. (1983). *The development of social knowledge: Morality and convention.* San Francisco: Jossey-Bass.

Walker, L. (2006). Gender and morality. In M. Killen & J. Smetana (Eds.), *Handbook of moral development* (pp. 93-115). Mahwah: Lawrence Erlbaum.

Youniss, J. (1980). *Parents and peers in social development.* Chicago: The University of Chicago Press.

Zahn-Waxler, C., Radke-Yarrow, M., Wagner, E. & Chapman, M. (1992). Development of concern for others. *Developmental Psychology, 28,* 126-136.

Zhou, Q., Valiente, C. & Eisenberg, N. (2003). Empathy and its measurement. In S.J. Lopez & R.C. Snyder (Eds), *Positive psychological assessment: A handbook of models and measures* (pp. 269-284). Washington: American Psychological Association.

Tina Malti, Irene Kriesi & Marlis Buchmann
University of Zurich, Switzerland

STEPHEN J. THOMA, MURIEL BEBEAU & ANNELIESE BOLLAND

THE ROLE OF MORAL JUDGMENT IN CONTEXT-SPECIFIC PROFESSIONAL DECISION MAKING

ABSTRACT

The Neo-Kohlbergian model of moral reasoning suggests three different levels of moral cognitions (i.e., bedrock schemas, intermediate concepts, and ethical codes). Following this view, we present a study that explores the link between moral schemas (estimated by the Defining Issues Test) and intermediate concepts. Using nine cohorts of dental students measured on the DIT in their freshman and again three-years later (n = 723), findings indicate that the small positive relationship between measures increases substantially when developmental phase is included in the analysis. These results are discussed in terms of how different moral cognitive systems are organized across development.

The Neo-Kohlbergian position outlined by Rest and his colleagues (e.g., Rest, Narvaez, Bebeau & Thoma, 1999) suggests that moral thinking is both multilayered and multi-determined. Building off of Rest's earlier Four Component Model, the expanded Neo-Kohlbergian model views moral decision-making (Component II) as influenced by a number of interpretive systems including, but not limited to justice reasoning, social norms, and religious prescription. This well-known view holds that it is an empirical question whether or not a particular interpretive system is used to generate the ideal moral choice. Further, it is strongly suspected that situational as well as developmental factors may influence which system is more or less favored by the individual (e.g., Thoma & Rest, 1999).

In addition to different interpretive systems, the Neo-Kohlbergian model adds the possibility that moral decision-making is layered as well. Specifically, the model describes three levels of moral cognition by which the individual may identify an optimal moral choice. These three levels differ in the degree of abstraction and connection to specific contexts. As described by the Neo-Kohlbergain model, Kohlberg's stages are an example of the most abstract level of moral thinking and serve as the foundational interpretive system or as a system of last resort. In contrast to Kohlbergian stages, moral codes are the most contextual and least abstract. In this view, moral codes are seen as triggering moral cognitions within clearly defined situations and require limited interpretation. Examples of these codes would include actions specified by professional organizations in response to client complaints, professional malfeasance and so on.

Residing between these two polls are intermediate concepts. First identified in the professions, intermediate concepts represent moral concerns that are described in terms of guiding ethical standards of the professional (Bebeau & Thoma, 1999). Common to these concepts is a targeted rationale for making ethical decisions about specific professional situations (e.g., informed consent) or for understanding particular ethical concepts (e.g., patient confidentiality). Unlike codes, these concepts cover a broader range of situations and require significant interpretation. Unlike moral stages, intermediate concepts are more content specific and narrow.

According to the Neo-Kohlbergian perspective, intermediate concepts are jointly formed through the application of an individual's moral understanding as described by moral judgment development and more generally through the process of discussion and deliberation with others (i.e., how the intermediate concept becomes generally understood in the profession or society). In this view, one's understanding of an intermediate concept is limited by the conceptual tools the individual can apply to the concepts as well as by one's exposure to these concepts such as through instruction. In support of this contention, Bebeau and Thoma (1999) have shown that in professional settings, moral judgment development as measured by the Defining Issues Test as well as exposure to these concepts within case studies, relates to the quality of reasoning about intermediate concepts.

In general, therefore, the Four Component Model suggests that there should be a relationship between moral judgment development and the quality of reasoning about intermediate concepts but one should not reduce to the other. Current data generally supports this view. Simple correlations between stage scores and intermediate concept scores fall within the moderate to small range for both young professionals assessed on profession-specific measures of intermediate concepts and adolescents assessed on the virtue-based generic intermediate concept measure (Bebeau & Thoma, 1999; Thoma, Hestevold & Crowson, under review). However, these analyses address only superficial links between the two layers of moral thinking and little is known about this relationship when other aspects of moral judgment development are included in the analysis such as developmental phase (i.e., phases of consolidation and transition).

Developmental phase is particularly interesting as an explanatory variable linking moral judgment development and intermediate concepts given that there is a growing body of data indicating that moral information is more central to the moral decision making process during periods of consolidation (e.g., Thoma & Rest, 1999; Thoma, 2006). That is, developmental phase information has been helpful in clarifying when justice reasoning is more likely to be prioritized in moral decision making. As such, these findings support the neo-Kohlbergain view that moral choices are multi-determined.

The current study is an attempt to assess whether developmental phase information also helps us understand the links between moral judgment development and the more contextualize reasoning about intermediate concepts. We suspect that during phases of consolidation, stronger links will be observed between moral judgment development and reasoning about intermediate concepts. Further, and based on the

Thoma and Rest (1999) findings that moral information is prioritized during periods of consolidation, we expect that the quality of reasoning about intermediate concepts will be higher during periods of consolidation – particularly at the higher developmental levels-than during periods of transition. This view is consistent with the notion promoted by the Thoma and Rest (1999, see also Thoma, 2006) that moral thinking, moral decisions and actions are more coordinated during periods of consolidation.

METHODS

Participants

Seven hundred, twenty-four dental students representing nine classes spanning the years from 1998-2006 were assessed on all measures as part of their dental ethics course requirements. Each class averaged 80 students (range 76-82) and was roughly balanced by gender. As a highly selective school of dentistry, students are consistently high performing undergraduates who survived a rigorous admission process. Demographics further suggest that the majority were raised in Minnesota and other adjoining states that comprise the northern plains. Most students were in their mid to late 20s while pursuing their degree.

Measures. Defining Issues Test (DIT)   The original DIT first constructed in the early 1970s consists of 6 stories or dilemmas; each followed by 12 items (as "issues" of the moral dilemma). Participants are first asked what should the protagonist in the story do, and are then asked to rate and rank the items in terms of their importance in solving the moral dilemma. For over 25 years the summary score of the DIT most frequently used has been the "P" score, which is calculated from ranking data and attends to items designed as Stages 5 and 6 in the Minnesota group's revision of Kohlberg's postconventional stages (e.g., Kohlberg, 1969). The P score is interpreted as the relative importance given to Postconventional (i.e., Stages 5 and 6) moral considerations. The N2 score used in this study is a recent improvement over the P score as an overall estimate of moral judgment development (Rest, Thoma, and Edwards, 1998). More recently, the construct measured by the DIT has been reinterpreted (Rest, Narvaez, Bebeau & Thoma, 1999). Based upon large-sample analyses, it appears that the DIT measures three developmentally ordered schemas: personal interest (incorporating aspects of Kohlberg's stages two and three), maintaining norms (closely aligned with Kohlberg's stage 4) and Post-conventional schema (the traditional P score mentioned above).The validity and reliability of the DIT is fully discussed in Rest, Narvaez, Bebeau, and Thoma (1999).

   In addition to the summary scores, the DIT provides information on developmental phase or the degree to which the individual's pattern of responses across schema-based items suggests a consolidated or transitional pattern (i.e., Thoma & Rest, 1999). The developmental phase information can be combined with the schema usage indicators to create the "Type" variable. This variable has seven levels.

Levels 1, 4 and 7 represent a consolidated pattern at each of the three moral schema measured by the DIT (1-personal interest, 4- maintaining norm and 7- post-conventional). The remaining levels reflect various transitional patterns based on the dominant and subdominant schema usage. Thus, Type 2 and 3 are both transitional patterns but Type 2 is associated with a dominant personal interest schema whereas Type 3 is defined by a dominant maintaining norms schema with personal interest schema as subdominant. Similarly, Type 5 and 6 vary by whether maintaining norms or personal interest is dominant or subdominant.

Intermediate Concepts Measures Intermediate concepts are assessed using the dental ICM. Participants are asked to read a story designed to illuminate a particular intermediate concept (e.g., informed consent) (Bebeau & Thoma, 1999). After reading the story, participants are provided with a number of statements that have been identified as acceptable or unacceptable action choices by expert judges. Expertise in this case was defined as established dentists with ethical training. In completing the measure, participants rate each item and then in a second pass through the items, rank the three most appropriate and two most inappropriate actions. This rating and ranking task is repeated for items written to reflect a range of appropriate and inappropriate justifications for action. Thus, for each story on the measure four major sources of information are provided: the participant's perception of good and bad action choices plus appropriate and inappropriate justifications. The dental ICM has five stories.

Individual ranking data is combined across stories and used to derive three summary indices: Totalgood, Totalbad and Totalicm. Totalgood is defined as the average of the good choices and justifications represented as a percentage of a perfect score (i.e., a Totalgood score of .50 indicates that the participant identified 50% of the experts acceptable items as good choices). Totalbad is defined similarly (i.e., a score of .50 reflects a correspondence between the participant's selection of bad choices and justification with the expert-defined key of bad items and justifications. The Totalicm score represents the average across all good and bad justifications taking into account the range differences of the good and bad scales (i.e., 42 vs. 21total points). It is also presented as a percentage. Therefore, a high Totalicm score indicates that the participant is identifying both acceptable and unacceptable items – across action choices and justification – as good and bad respectively.

The Dental ICM has demonstrated acceptable reliability estimates. Internal consistency estimates range in the 70s and low 80s (Bebeau & Thoma, 1999). The validity of the measure primarily has been supported by comparing known groups. For example, dental students beginning their program of study and who are presumably not well versed in the intermediate concepts within the profession score lower on the Dental ICM measure and scales than do senior dental students. Further, the Dental ICM has been shown to be sensitive to an ethics intervention (Bebeau & Thoma, 1999). Finally, correlations with the DIT indicate a significant but moderate correlation suggesting that the two scores represent similar domains yet the two measures do not subsume each other (Bebeau & Thoma, 1999).

Procedures   The DIT was administered twice: once during the freshman year and then four years later during the end of the senior year. Also assessed in the senior year was the Dental ICM. All assessments were administered in a classroom setting and all measures were taken as part of the dental ethics sequence.

FINDINGS

The results of this study are organized around two main questions. First, we assess whether the relationship between DIT and Dental ICM scores varies by developmental phase. This assessment is accomplished in two ways. After, replicating the simple correlation between scores we assess whether the strength of this relationship is moderated by consolidation or transitional status. In addition, we further explore whether change in developmental phase status (e.g., stable consolidation at both testings, or a change from transition to consolidation, and so on), is related to the strength in the relationship between DIT and dental ICM scores. Regarding the second question, we focus on the quality of reasoning on the Dental ICM and assess whether developmental phase is associated with higher or lower scores. In a final analysis we bring developmental level and phase information together using the Type variable in order to assess variation in Dental ICM means. Taken together, these analyses assess the moderating role of developmental phase on the strength of the relationship between Dental ICM scores as well as on the level-or quality- of Dental ICM responses. Prior to these analyses, we present a description of DIT and Dental ICM scores in this sample and then support our measurement of developmental phase by replicating the link between change in DIT scores as a function of developmental phase.

Changes in DIT scores by class   Change in DIT scores from freshman to senior year was assessed by a 2 X 8 repeated measures ANOVA with time as the two-level within subjects factor and class as the eight-level between subject factor. Findings indicate that seniors scored higher than freshman ($F_{(8, 714)} = 7.70$, $p < .05$, d =.11)) yet the difference is small. In addition, there was a significant class effect ($F, 8, 714$) = 8.21; $P < .05$) and a time by class interaction ($F_{(8, 714)} = 11.82$; $p < 05$) indicating that classes differ by DIT scores and the rate of change varies by grade. Inspection of the class differences indicates a declining trend of approximately 8 points on N2 Scores (see Figure 1). The Pre-post findings are similar to other previous descriptions of this population (e.g., Bebeau, 1994).however the declining trend in DIT scores is surprising.

Changes in Dental ICM scores by class   Dental ICM scores also differed by class ($F(8, 714 = 14.12$, $p < .01$). Further, inspection of the means indicated some evidence of a declining trend although there seems to be some recovery in scores. (see Figure 2). Specifically, Total ICM scores during the late 90s averaged around 55% whereas current classes obtain averages in the mid 40% range. This finding indicates that over time, student choices and justifications increasingly diverged from the expert-

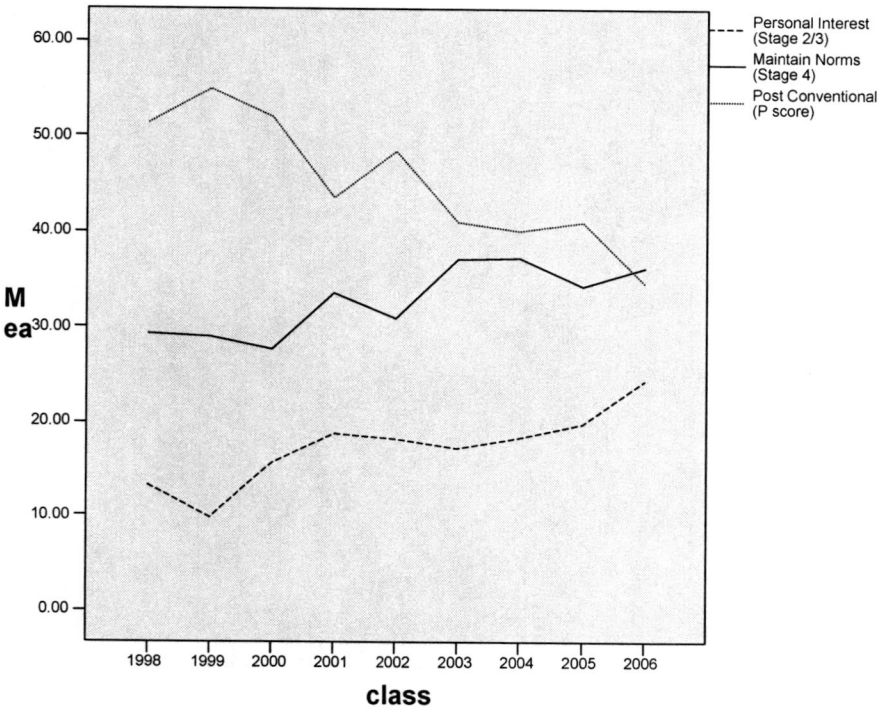

Figure 1. Changes in moral schema estimates by class

defined key such that by 2002 the Total ICM scores fell below 50%. Thus, and consistent with the expectation that the DIT and ICM scores are related both scores show evidence of decline over the time period assessed by this study.

Replicating the relationship between change in DIT scores by Developmental Phase   Also estimated from DIT responses was developmental phase information. As a group the majority of students were consolidated (60% as freshman, and 71% as seniors). Given that phase information was collected during both the freshman and senior year it was possible to assess change in developmental phase. Specifically, change in consolidation and transition was summarized by noting freshman and senior developmental phase status. One hundred and twenty-three (17%) students were categorized as transitional at both testings. Fifteen percent (n = 109) changed from a consolidation to transition status. Twenty-four percent (n = 174) shifted from transition to consolidation status. Finally, 318 students were identified as consolidated at both testing.

Following Thoma and Rest (1999), change in moral judgment summary scores was assessed by developmental phase shifts. This earlier work found that the highest rate of change was associated with the group moving from transition to consolidation. As Table

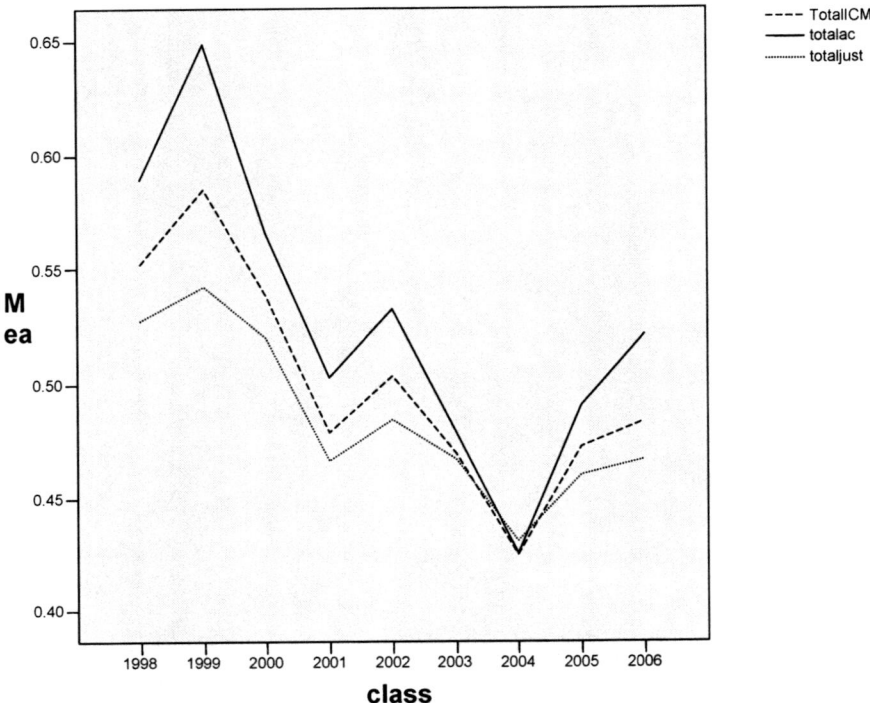

Figure 2. Changes in Dental ICM scores by class

Key: TotalICM = Total ICM score; TotalAC = Summary of good and bad Action choices; TotalJUST = Summary of good and bad justification choices.

1 indicates the expected relationship was observed as the group that shifted from transition to consolidation was associated with the greatest pre and post change. Again, the overall findings are consistent with pervious estimates (e.g., Thoma & Rest, 1999).

Table 1. Changes in DIT N2 scores by change in developmental phase

Change Group	Freshman		Senior		
	M	SD	M	SD	N
T-T	37.15	10.00	35.38	11.15	123
T-C	38.62	9.81	46.51	16.11	174
C-T	44.50	15.01	34.14	10.12	109
C-C	49.63	13.16	52.58	14.18	318
Total	44.82	13.45	46.40	15.66	724

Key: T-T: Transitional status at both testings; T-C a Transition to Consolidation shift; C-T a Consolidation to Transition shift; and C-C: Consolidated status at both testings.

Estimating the relationship between DIT and Dental ICM scores As expected, N2 and Total ICM scores were related (r(719) = .29, p < .05) suggesting that contextualized moral choices and justifications do relate to more general moral judgment schema. When the relationship between DIT N2 and Dental ICM scores are recalculated by developmental phase change group status, findings indicate that current transitional status is associated with smaller relationships between TotalICM and DIT N2 scores (See Table 2). Fisher's test of independent correlations indicated that the two transitional groups were significantly lower than that two consolidated groups. Taken together, therefore, we find that the relationship between DIT and Dental ICM scores are better understood when participants are divided by developmental phase. Specifically, and consistent with previous data on the moderating effect of developmental phase the relationships between moral judgment and criterion variables (Thoma, 2006), consolidated status is associated with stronger relationships between ICM and DIT scores.

Table 2. Correlations between DIT N2scores and Dental ICM Total scores

Change Group	r	N
T-T	.20	123
T-C	.34	174
C-T	.22	109
C-C	.33	318
Total	.29	724

Key: T-T: Transitional status at both testings; T-C a Transition to Consolidation shift; C-T a Consolidation to Transition shift; and C-C: Consolidated status at both testings. Fishers Z test of independent correlations suggests that T-T and C-T differs from T-C and C-C.

Mean difference on ICM scores by Developmental phase In addition to relationships between DIT and ICM scores, we also assessed mean differences in ICM scores by developmental phase estimated at senior year. These analyses address the question of whether the ability to formulate actions and suggest justification consistent with expert interpretations of the context is related to developmental phase information. Table 3 presents the means for the three main ICM indices (i.e., Total, justification and action choices) by consolidation and transition. In each case, participants identified as consolidated obtained higher scores than participants similarly identified as transitional. Additionally, Cohen's d statistic suggests that the difference is moderate to large.

154

Table 3. Mean Dental ICM scores buy Consolidation and Transition Status

| Dental ICM | Transition | | Consolidation | | |
	M	SD	M	SD	Cohen's d
TotalICM	.45	.13	.52	.11	.60
TotalJUS	.44	.14	.51	.12	.55
TotalAC	.48	.17	.55	.17	.41

Key: TotalICM = Total ICM score; TotalAC = Summary of good and bad action choices;
TotalJUST = Summary of good and bad justification choices.
Note:Transition N= 221; Consolidation N =500.

In addition to the overall comparison between consolidation and transition assessed during the senior year, we also compared ICM scores by the 4 developmental phase change groups. Table 4 provides the means and standard deviations associated with this analysis. A one-way ANOVA on ICM scores with planned comparisons indicated a significant overall effect ($F(3, 699) = 17.91$, $P<.05$). The planned comparisons tested mean differences between the stable transitional and consolidated group. As expected, the comparison was statistically significant with the higher mean associated with the consolidated group ($t(699) = 6.27$, $P < .05$). Additionally, the two change groups were compared with the group shifting to consolidation obtaining the higher ICM scores when compared to the group shifting away toward transition ($t(699)= 3.50$). In both comparisons, the consolidation status was related to higher ICM scores.

Table 4. Changes in DIT N2 scores by change in developmental phase

| Change Group | TotalICM | | 95% Confidence interval | |
	M	SD	Lower	Upper
T-T	.44	.14	.42	.47
T-C	.51	.16	.50	.53
C-T	.46	.12	.44	.48
C-C	.53	.12	.51	.54

Key: T-T: Transitional status at both testings; T-C a Transition to Consolidation shift;
C-T a Consolidation to Transition shift; and C-C: Consolidated status at both testings.

Differences in the relationship between Developmental phase and ICM scores by Type Differences in the quality of reasoning on the ICM measure by developmental level and phase were assessed using the Type variable (see Figure 3). As mentioned previously, Type is defined using developmental level (i.e., which of the three moral schema assessed by the DIT is prioritized) and developmental phase (i.e., consolidation and transition). Thus, Types 1, 4, and 7 are consolidated statuses at increasing developmental levels and 2, 3, 5 and 6 are the transitional steps in between.

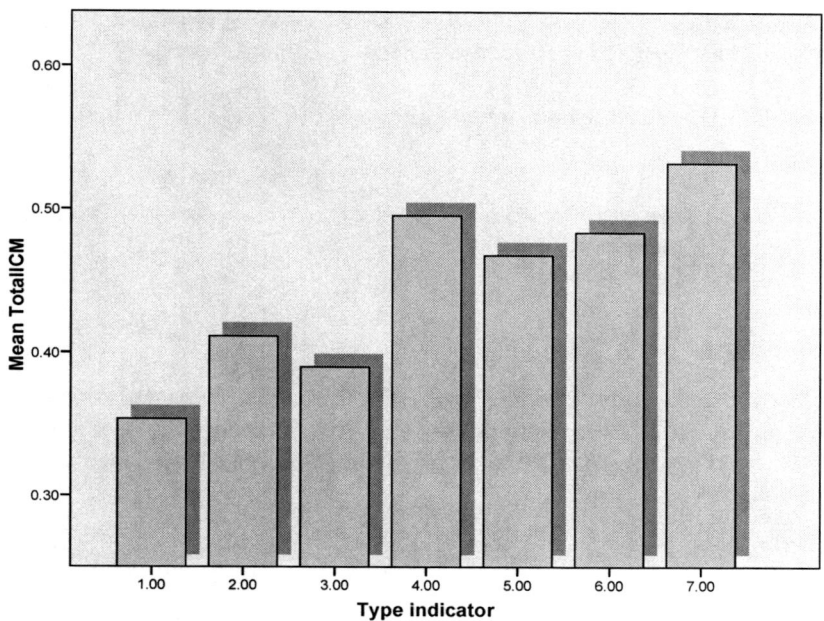

Figure 3. TotalICM scores by Moral Type

Two observations seem warranted. First, individuals scored as having a signifi-cant amount of personal interest reasoning (Types 1-3) are associated with lower ICM scores. Additionally, participants identified as consolidated in the maintaining norms and post-conventional levels score higher on the ICM measures than their transitional peers. To confirm these observations, one-way ANOVA with planned contrasts were used to assess ICM differences by Type. Contrast 1 directly com-pared participants who presented a significant amount of personal interest reason-ing (Types 1-3) with all other types (i.e., Types 4-7). Contrast 2 assessed differences between the consolidated phases within the maintaining norm and postconventional levels (i.e., Types 4 and 7 and the transitional levels of the same two schemas (e.g., Types 5 and 6). Finally, contrast 3 directly compared Type 4 (consolidated main-taining norms) with Type 7 (consolidated postconventional level).

Table 5 presents the results of the analyses. First, and as expected, the overall F test for the difference in ICM scores across Type classifications was statistically significant suggesting that ICM scores do vary by Type classifications ($F(6, 714) = 16.56$, $p < .05$). In addition, all of the planned comparisons were statistically signifi-cant. The most striking difference was associated with contrast 1. Here participants who evidence personal interest reasoning obtained substantially lower ICM scores than their peers. Contrasts focusing within the Type 4-7 range were all in the antici-pated direction although somewhat smaller in magnitude. Specifically, consolidated Types 4 and 7 were associated with higher ICM scores than the transitional Types

5 & 6. Similarly, ICM scores for the consolidated Type 7 group were higher than participants identified as Type 4 (consolidated maintaining norms).

Table 5. Effect sizes representing contrasts between moral types on ICM overall scores.

	TotalICM
Contrast 1 (T1, T2, T3 vs T4, T5, T6, T7)	.98*
Contrast 2 (T5, T6 vs. T4, T7)	.35*
Contrast 3 (T4 vs. T7)	.33*

*Key: * $p < 05$

Also listed in Table 5 are the effect sizes for each contrast. It is interesting to note that the magnitude of these relationships fall in the moderate to large range (using Cohen's rule of thumb). Thus, differences between levels and developmental phases are meaningful.

DISCUSSION

The findings of this study suggest that DIT and Dental ICM scores are related and developmental phase information helps us better understand the nature of this relationship. First, we found that Dental ICM scores correlated with DIT summary scores and when developmental phase was incorporated in the relationship, the patterns of correlations indicated that consolidation status was associated with stronger relationships between the two measures. Second, we found that performance on the Dental ICM measure varied by developmental phase such that the consolidated status was associated with higher Dental ICM scores. When developmental level and phase were considered together, personal interest reasoning was shown to be associated with lower Dental ICM performance. In the maintaining norms and post-conventional levels of moral reasoning, consolidated status was the most influential factor in ICM performance.

Taken together, these findings not only offer strong support for the view that moral judgment development and ICM measures are related in young professional students but provide support for Rest's Four Component model (e.g., Rest, Narvaez, Bebeau & Thoma, 1999). This model promotes the view that how one identifies the morally ideal choice (.e.g., Component II) can be the result of a number of systems that vary not only by the type of interpretive system (e.g., religious prescription, judgments of justice and fairness, social norms and so on) but also by their level of generalizability across issues and contexts. Driven by this view, the intermediate concepts are claimed to represent different levels of assessment from the more traditional DIT approach that builds into the measurement process a focus on a specific context and class of ethical issues. The model further assumes that the more fundamental judgments of justice and fairness based on different perceptions of social cooperation influence the formation of intermediate concepts thus there should be an overlap between them. In addition to the view that these interpretive levels ought to be related, the current study suggests that the relationship between levels of assessments is more subtle and complex.

Particularly interesting is the finding that individuals who evidence a significant amount of personal interest reasoning on the DIT (i.e., Types 1-3) obtain strikingly lower ICM scores than those participants who emphasize maintaining norms and postconventional reasoning. Consistent with this finding is the view that maintaining norms reasoning is a necessary but not sufficient condition for reasoning about ethical concepts in practical situations. That is, in the absence of a system-wide prospective first realized with a maintaining norms perspective, it is very difficult for an individual to determine choices and justifications that are recognized as most appropriate by experts in the field. This observation does not imply that postconventional reasoning is less central to an understanding of professional ethics. Indeed, the current study observed a statistically significant improvement in Dental ICM scores associated with the move to postconventional reasoning. However, the Dental ICM mean scores associated with the difference between maintaining norms and postconventional reasoning was clearly not as dramatic as the corresponding difference in scores related to the personal interest to maintaining norms contrast.

As others have noted, the primary goal of professional ethics courses is to establish a broad understanding of professional ethics and then to use this understanding in order to formulate solutions to ethical dilemmas in the profession (Bebeau, 2002). It seems central therefore, for educators to focus on the weakness of what the Neo-Kohlbergain perspective calls personal interest schema. In this view, personal interest reasoning is considered to have elements of Kohlberg's Stage 2 and 3 definitions (e.g., Colby and Kohlberg, 1987). That is, this schema emphasizes the self's perspective and/or a reliance on known relationships as the foundations of social cooperation. As noted here and elsewhere, personal interest reasoning occurs with some frequency in young adult populations (e.g., Bebeau, 2002). Thus, the target of reducing personal interest reasoning should be an important part in professional ethics curriculum and we can not assume that a focus on postconventional logic directly impacts personal interest reasoning. As this study suggests, a reduction of personal interest reasoning should result in an increase in ICM scores and presumably the quality of other choices and justification in professional situations.

A focus on personal interest reasoning is also important because, as noted in the preceding section, it appears that this conception is increasing. In the current study, we have evidence that dental students have been declining in their DIT summary scores and increasing in personal interest reasoning. This is a surprising finding especially when one considers that the population under study is very selective and academically highly able. In addition, the selection criteria used to admit students into dental school has only become more stringent (Bebeau, personal communication, 2007). Thus, it is troubling to note that dental students are increasing in the type of reasoning that has been shown in this study to be associated with poorer performance on the Dental ICM measure. One might ask why and to what degree the decline in moral judgment scores on the DIT is particular to entry-level dental students or is part of a more general trend in the population. Clearly, examining the extent of the decline in moral judgment development in the population is worthy of further study.

As mentioned previously, the favored view of the relationship between ICM and DIT scores suggests that an understanding of intermediate concepts is limited by moral judgment development and exposure to the target concepts. The current study supports this position by noting that not only is there a simple relationship between measures of moral judgment development and Dental ICMs but also a more complex association between levels when developmental phase information is included in the assessments. Specifically, the study found that consolidation status is associated with stronger relationships between the component 2 processes represented by the Dental ICM and DIT measures. Further and in addition to the finding that the relationship between moral judgment and Dental ICM scores is stronger during periods of consolidation, the current study found that Dental ICM scores are also more appropriate during periods of consolidation (i.e., are associated with higher scores). This finding further supports the view advanced by Thoma and Rest (1999) that developmental phases are associated with a more efficient and optimal processing of moral information. Indeed, there is a growing body of data that developmental phases help clarify moral thinking and strengthen the links between reasoning capacity as measured by the DIT, and commonly associated outcomes resulting from moral thinking such as moral actions and choices (e.g., Thoma, 2006). Thus, the findings of the current study are quite consistent with these overall findings incorporating developmental phase information as a moderator of the moral judgment and action or choices relationships. Further, these findings support the view of how phase shifts are linked to moral decision making (e.g., Thoma and Rest, 1999).

Finding that ICM scores are associated with developmental phases is particularly interesting when one considers that developmental phases are claimed to cycle as the individual develops (e.g., Snyder & Feldman, 1984; Walker & Taylor, 1991). In this view, developmental phases are epiphenomena of the developmental process. Individuals shift from consolidation to transition and back again, as new conceptions become understood and old views abandoned. Consistent with this view we should expect that scores on the intermediate concepts measure will increase under periods of consolidation and fall in transitional phases (particularly when personal interest schemas are no longer prioritized). That is, these findings suggest that during periods of consolidation, students are better able to reason about intermediate concepts and as such, these data support the view that the relationship between types of moral cognitions should predictably vary as individual's cycle through periods of consolidation and transition. Overall, therefore educators and others who interact with this population should be aware that developmental change is not simply a linear function in which intrapersonal change is associated with more defensible actions, choices and justifications. Indeed, development associated with movement into transitional statuses appears to lead to increased moral confusion (e.g., Thoma, 2006) and results in less optimal moral actions, justifications and choices.

REFERENCES

Bebeau, M. (2002). The Defining Issues Test and the Four Component Model: Contributions to professional education. *Journal of Moral Education, 31,* 271-298.

Bebeau, M. & Thoma, S.J. (1999). "Intermediate" concepts and the connection to moral education. *Educational Psychology Review,* 11, 343-360.

Colby A. & Kohlberg, L. (1987). *The measurement of moral Judgment.* Cambridge: Cambridge University Press.

Kohlberg, L. (1969). Stage and sequence. The cognitive- developmental approach to socialization. In Goslin (ed.) Handbook *of socialization theory and research.* Chicago: Rand McNally.

Rest, J.R., Narvaez, D., Bebeau, M., & Thoma, S.J. (1999). A neo-Kohlbergian Approach. *Educational Psychology Review,* 11, 291-324.

Snyder S.S. & Feldman, D.H. (1984). Phases of transition in cognitive development: Evidence from the domain of spatial representation. *Child Development, 55,* 981-989.

Thoma, S.J. & Rest, J.R. (1999). The relationship between moral decision-making and patterns of consolidation and transition in moral judgment development. *Developmental Psychology, 35,* 323-334.

Thoma, S.J., Hestevold, N. & Crowson, M. (2006). *Describing and testing a contextualized measure of adolescent moral thinking.* Under Review.

Thoma, S.J. (2006). *The developmental phase variable in moral judgment research.* Paper presented to the American Educational Research Association annual meeting, San Francisco.

Walker, L. J. & Taylor, J. H. (1991). Stage transitions in moral reasoning: A longitudinal study of developmental processes. *Developmental Psychology, 27,* 330-337.

Stephen J. Thoma
University of Alabama, USA
Muriel Bebeau & Annelieze Bolland
University of Minnesota, USA

JOHN C. GIBBS, KAREN S. BASINGER, REBECCA L. GRIME &
JOHN SNAREY

GLOBALIZATION AND CROSS-CULTURAL STUDIES OF MORAL JUDGMENT DEVELOPMENT[1]

In this chapter, we review cross-cultural studies of moral judgment development that have used a relatively new assessment method, the Sociomoral Reflection Measure-Short Form (SRM-SF), in 23 countries (Armenia, Australia, Bahrain, Belgium, Bosnia, Bulgaria, Canada, China, England, Germany, Ireland, Italy, Japan, Kenya, Malaysia, Netherlands, Nigeria, Russia, Saudi Arabia, Sweden, Scotland, Taiwan, and the United States). The very use of the SRM-SF across so many nations reflects globalization or the dramatic increase in cross-cultural contacts and dissemination. What have these studies found regarding moral development? Is moral judgment development basically the same across diverse cultural groups?

Perhaps no developmental psychologist has advanced the thesis of moral judgment development across cultures more boldly and extensively than did Lawrence Kohlberg. His "choice of topics" in the 1960s, namely, moral development, "made him something of an 'odd duck' within American psychology... No up-to-date social scientist, acquainted with [the relativism of] psychoanalysis, behaviorism, and cultural anthropology, used such words at all." Yet the development of moral judgment "is, after all, a very substantial aspect of human psychology" (Brown & Herrnstein, 1978, pp. 307). With his challenge to moral relativism, advancement of a cognitive developmental approach to morality, dilemma-based assessment method, six-stage model, and universality claims, Kohlberg eventually became one of the most frequently cited persons in the social and behavioral sciences (Haggbloom et al., 2000). Our aim in this chapter is to use SRM-SF studies to revisit Kohlberg's cognitive developmental claim of cross-cultural universality..

KOHLBERG'S COGNITIVE DEVELOPMENTAL APPROACH

Almost all individuals in all cultures use the same . . . basic moral categories, concepts, principles, [and values], and ... all individuals in all cultures go through the same order or sequence of gross stages of development, though they vary in rate and terminal point of development ... [given differential] opportunities for role-taking. (Kohlberg, 1971, pp. 176, 183)

Fritz Oser & Wiel Veugelers (eds.). Getting involved, 161–188.
© 2008 Sense Publishers. All rights reserved.

JOHN C. GIBBS, KAREN S. BASINGER, REBECCA L. GRIME & JOHN SNAREY

Moral Development as a Distinct, Unitary Domain of Development

For Kohlberg, moral judgment is not merely integral to social and nonsocial cognitive development, but rather is a distinct, unitary domain with a parallel trajectory in its own right. Kohlberg (1971) asserted that "moral development is its own sequential process, rather than the reflection of cognitive development in a slightly different content" (p. 187). Although moral judgment development should relate to intelligence and cognitive development, moral judgment should in any culture define its own distinct and homogeneous domain. An empirical implication—which we will review--is that moral reasons or justifications should yield a single factor in factor analyses across cultures. A final empirical implication to be reviewed is that the moral values to which the justifications refer should be relevant to diverse cultures.

Social Perspective-Taking Opportunities

Kohlberg argued that, although generic perspectival coordination and working memory may be relevant to moral development, the perspective-taking process facilitating moral growth is distinctly social (Gibbs, 2003). Taking and keeping in mind the perspectives of other persons is uniquely complex, not least because the social "object" can be a subject, i.e., may take its own perspective as well as the perspective of the perspective-taker (Damon, 1988; Flavell et al., 2002; Hoffman, 1981; Selman, 1980). Beyond Piaget's (1932/1965) emphasis on peer interaction, Kohlberg argued that opportunities to take the perspectives of other persons, roles, groups, and institutions in society should stimulate moral reflection and development.

Of particular relevance to this review will be the consequent expectation that moral judgment maturity should correlate with age, education, higher socioeconomic status, urban (versus rural) settings, and community participation, insofar as these variables index the affordance and accumulation of diverse social experiences and perspective-taking opportunities through social participation (Colby, Kohlberg, Gibbs, & Lieberman, 1983). In this connection, we will be particularly interested in correlations of moral judgment maturity with self-reported social perspective-taking opportunities and in cross-cultural studies of moral judgment developmental delay among delinquents.

Stage and Invariant Sequence

Kohlberg anticipated that, with the proper discernment of structure in content, a dominant pattern or framework would cohere in a person's moral judgment. Kohlberg based his expectation in Piagetian theory, although the extent to which Piagetian theory claims concurrence in the emergence of a stage is controversial (Carpendale, 2000; Chapman, 1988; Lourenco & Macado, 1996). In any event, Kohlberg anticipated that (with proper criteria) a new "stage" would signify not just a qualitatively new tendency of thought in a rough age trend, but a highly coherent frame-work that would "hang together" as such in an individual's moral judgment. Once the stage structures were precisely identified, not only would moral judgment be unitary, but each moral judgment stage would follow the next in a clearly invariant sequence. Findings bearing upon stage and invariant sequence are discussed in a subsequent section.

The testable implications of Kohlberg's domain-specific cognitive developmental approach to moral growth have attracted extensive research attention. This chapter examines this research in the two-decade aftermath of a landmark cross-cultural review of Kohlberg's work by John Snarey (1985). Was Kohlberg's generic claim correct, that moral understanding grows in systematic ways beyond the superficial across a diversity of cultural contexts? What of his universality claims for moral values and for facilitative social perspective-taking processes? What issues remain unresolved or underexplored? The data base for examining these questions consists of 75 cross-cultural moral judgment studies that used an assessment measure alternative to Kohlberg's (see Basinger, Gibbs, & Fuller, 1995; Gibbs, Basinger, & Fuller, 1992; Table 1).

REVISIONIST MODELS

Kohlberg's longitudinal and cross-cultural research on his three-level, six-stage model yielded empirical support but also anomalies and limitations, many of which were identified in Snarey's (1985) review. In response, Kohlberg made certain refinements (e.g., suspension of empirical claims for Stage 6; see Table 1) and qualifications with reference to his six-stage model. Among other responses were revisionist models proposed by Snarey (1985; Snarey & Keljo, 1991) and Gibbs (1977, 1979, 2003) (summarized in Table 2).

Snarey's Review

Snarey's 1985 review accepted in principle the viability of Kohlberg's search for universal morality as well as his cognitive developmental approach. In the main, Snarey's aim was to assess the evidence for or against the empirically testable assumptions implied by Kohlberg's universality claims. These claims, Snarey noted, implied that the dilemma-based moral interview adequately captures universal moral concerns and values across cultures. Also implied was that the stage sequence would be upheld and the full range of stages would be evident to some extent in every type of culture (e.g., folk versus urban; non-Western versus Western). Finally, all instances of genuine moral reasoning in all cultures should be classifiable in terms of Kohlberg's stages or stage transitions.

To assess the empirically testable implications of Kohlberg's universality stage claim, Snarey began by ascertaining and reporting the methodological details (regarding sample size, translation, dilemma adaptation, interview procedures, and

Table 1. Three Moral Judgment Assessment Techniques

A Story Pair Used by Piaget (1932/1965)	A Moral Dilemma Used by Kohlberg (1958)	Social Reflection Questionnaire (Gibbs, Basinger, & Fuller, 1992)
A. A little boy who is called John is in his room. He is called to dinner. He goes into the dining room. But behind the door there was a chair, and on the chair there was a tray with fifteen cups on it. John couldn't have known that there was all this behind the door. He goes in, the door knocks against the tray, bang go the fifteen cups and they all get broken! B. Once there was a little boy whose name was Henry. One day when his mother was out he tried to get some jam out of the cupboard. He climbed up on a chair and stretched out his arm. But the jam was too high up and he couldn't reach it and have any. But while he was trying to get it he knocked over a cup. The cup fell down and broke. 1. Are these children equally naughty? 2. Which of the two is naughtier, and why? [Interviewers are advised to begin by having the child repeat the stories. The opening two questions become "the occasion for a conversation more or less elaborate according to the child's reaction" (p.123).]	In Europe, a woman was near death from cancer. There was one drug the doctors thought might save her. A druggist in the same town had discovered it, but he was charging ten times what the drug cost him to make. The sick women's husband, Heinz, went to everyone he knew to borrow the money, but he could only get together half of what it cost. The druggist refused to sell it cheaper or let Heinz pay later. So Heinz got desperate and broke into the man's store to steal the drug for his wife. Should Heinz have done that? Why or why not? (paraphrased from Colby et al., 1983, p.77) <u>Sample Questions</u> 1. Should Heinz steal the drug? Why or why not? 2. If Heinz doesn't love his wife, should he steal the drug for her? Why or why not? 3. Suppose the person dying is not his wife but a stranger. Should Heinz steal the drug for the stranger? Why or why not? 4. Is it important for people to do everything they can to save another's life? Why or why not? 5. Should people try to do everything they can to obey the law? Why or why not? The Heinz Dilemma is the first of three dilemmas in Form A (the Moral Judgment Interview (MJI) Forms A, B, or C) Thinking in terms of society, should people who break the law be punished? [Sample questions following a dilemma concerning a father's promise to his son:] Is it important to keep a promise? Why or why not? Is it important to keep a promise to someone you don't know well and probably won't see again? Why or why not?	1. Think about when you've made a promise to a friend of yours. How important is it for people to keep promises, if they can, to friends? Circle one: very important important not important WHY IS THAT VERY IMPORTANT IMPORTANT NOT IMPORTANT (whichever one you circled)? [The same format is used for the remaining questions.] 2. What about keeping a promise to anyone? How important is it for people to keep promises, if they can, even to someone they hardly know? 3. How about keeping a promise to a child? How important is it for a parent to keep promises, if they can, to their children? 4. In general, how important is it for people to tell the truth? 5. Think about when you've helped your mother and father. How important is it for children to help their parents? 6. Let's say a friend of yours needs help and may even die, and you're the only person who can save him or her. How important is it for a person (without losing his or her own life) to save the life of a friend? 7. What about saving the life of anyone? How important is it for a person (without losing his or her own life) to save the life of a stranger? 8. How important is it for a person to live even if that person doesn't want to? 9. How important is it for people not to take things that belong to other people? 10. How important is it for people to obey the law? 11. How important is it for judges to send people who break the law to jail?

means and ranges of scores; Gielen, 1991) of Kohlberg's early small-scale cross-cultural studies. He included that information within a comprehensive survey of 45 studies (conducted within 27 countries or regions) of Kohlberg's moral judgment stage model. Snarey noted the particular scoring method used in each study and placed greater weight upon studies that used the relatively more recent method (Moral Judgment Interview [MJI] Standard Issue Scoring; Colby et al., 1987). He also noted ways in which the moral dilemmas and questions were adapted and translated for use in different cultures.

Snarey (1985) found partial support for Kohlberg's cognitive developmental approach and universality claims. Stages 1 to 4 were in evidence virtually universally when one took into consideration the age range and sample size of the population under study. Further, most cross-cultural studies reported positive associations between moral judgment stage and age, urban (versus folk) status, and upper (versus working) social class. Finally, the review found that "all folk [or village] cultural groups failed to exhibit any [Stage 5] post-conventional reasoning" (p. 226). Kohlberg interpreted these latter findings as simply supporting his cognitive developmental expectation of a relationship between social perspective-taking experiences and moral judgment development. Snarey, however, interpreted the findings as also indicating an association between moral judgment maturity (as defined by Kohlberg) and social privilege. This association, as well as the complete failure to find any postconventional reasoning (as defined by Kohlberg) in a particular type of cultural group, led Snarey to suggest a degree of cultural partiality.

Snarey reported that for studies in most of the non-English-speaking countries, the dilemmas and questions (and sometimes the manual) had been translated into the appropriate indigenous language. Many researchers also converted the dilemmas to functionally equivalent situations (e.g., converting the famous Heinz dilemma to a situation in which a husband would need to steal food, not a drug, to save his dying wife). Some researchers reported that respondents had little or no difficulty in understanding the dilemmas and questions. Most researchers, however, did not comment on issues of translation or ecological applicability (but cf. Dien, 1982). Snarey recommended that "future researchers pay closer attention to" the question of whether the dilemma method and associated moral values are broadly applicable (1985, p. 215).

Finally, the review's report included examples of arguably postconventional or principled reasoning among judgments in cross-cultural interviews that Kohlberg's scoring system had relegated to an "unscorable" or wastebasket category. The cumulative weight of these findings, for Snarey, implied a need for model revision.

Snarey's Revisionist Model: A Pluralist-Inclusionist Elaboration for Stage 5

Snarey (1985) did not agree with Kohlberg's (1971) social evolutionist claim that cultural groups in which some members used postconventional reasoning (Stage 5 or Stage 6) were necessarily more complex or advanced cultures. He pointed to anthropological evidence that economically and technologically simple cultures can be complex in many ways (e.g., in language and belief systems) and that members of these cultures can "reason about their customs and norms rather than blindly conforming to them" (p. 227). Accordingly, while a given society may differ in terms of the "proportion of its population reasoning at the higher stages, every culture is capable of supporting higher stage reasoning" (p. 228). The issue between Kohlberg and Snarey lay in the perception of the postconventional stages. Where Kohlberg saw the summit of social evolution, Snarey sees a particular philosophical tradition and a problem of monocultural bias.

To remedy the problem, Snarey called for greater cultural breadth in Kohlberg's stage typology and scoring manual, and proposed a philosophically pluralistic and culturally inclusive expanded model (see Table 2). In support of his proposal, Snarey (1985; cf. 1995) noted a certain pattern among instances in the cross-cultural research of genuine yet problematic moral judgment, that is, ethical justifications not readily classifiable in terms of any of the Kohlbergian stages. The Standard Issue Scoring system and manual had the greatest difficulty with the "collective or communalistic principled reasoning" of village or communitarian cultures (p. 226; cf. Baek, 2002). Had the manual included examples of non-Western philosophies or worldviews for postconventional reasoning, Snarey argues, postconventional or principled stage reasoning would have been more commonly recognized.

Kohlberg was persuaded, at least generally, of this point by the mid-1980s. He acknowledged that "general principles at Stage 6 may be one or several," including not only "universal human care or agape" but also other principles such as "maximum quality of life" (Kohlberg, 1986, p. 497). Nonetheless, Snarey's suggestion was not implemented by Kohlberg and colleagues. The Standard Issue Scoring Manual, already in press, was published in 1987 (Colby & Kohlberg, 1987; Colby, Kohlberg, Speicher, Hewer, Candee, Gibbs, & Power, 1987) without Snarey's proposed cross-cultural elaborations for Stage 5.

Gibbs's Revisionist Model: Two Phases of Life-Span Moral Judgment Development

Gibbs's (1977, 1979, 2003) response to the problem of non-universality of the highest stages can be compared (and contrasted) with the above perspectives. Like Snarey, Gibbs subscribes to a broad as well as (with qualifications) a domain-specific cognitive developmental approach to morality. Gibbs' perspective, however, is more revisionist than Snarey's in that Gibbs proposed a more fundamental, Piaget-based revamping of Kohlberg's stage model.

Gibbs (2006) argues that Kohlberg should not have retained his Dewey-based three-level (preconventional, conventional, postconventional) typology, especially in light of the challenges to that typology from Kohlberg's own longitudinal and cross-cultural data. Kohlberg (1985/1991) recollected that his work was based not only on Piaget's research but also on Dewey's writings (Dewey & Tufts, 1903) concerning three developmental levels. Although Dewey's association of reflection with maturity was helpful, his view of basic moral judgment stage maturity in terms of philosophical reflection (in Gibbs' view) was not. According to Gibbs, Kohlberg's longitudinal data fit Piaget's empirical work much better than it did Dewey's three-level typology. Indeed, Gibbs argues that Kohlberg should have discarded Dewey's preconventional-conventional-postconventional typology, not least because its emphasis on philosophical reflection encouraged a rarification of the construct of basic moral judgment maturity.

To replace the preconventional-conventional-postconventional typology, Gibbs proposed a model of lifespan moral judgment development consisting of overlapping standard and existential phases (see Table 2). Gibbs' emphasis was on the primary phase of standard or invariant stages. Although moral judgment in both phases entails growth beyond the superficial, development in the standard (mainly pre-adult) phase is more uniform and relates more consistently to general cognitive development. Although Gibbs largely shares Kohlberg's specific cognitive developmental expectations concerning the moral domain, social perspective-taking, and stage sequence, Gibbs argues that the stage mixture seen elsewhere in cognitive development is also evident in moral judgment development, clouding somewhat the picture of invariant sequence (Gibbs, 2003). Despite this stage mixture, moral judgment in the standard phase can generally be seen to progress with age from immature (Stage 1, centrations on or overattention to salient features; Stage 2, pragmatic or instrumental exchanges) to mature (Stage 3, mutualities or ideal moral reciprocity; and Stage 4, social systems) levels (see Table 2).

Within the mature level of standard stage development, Gibbs adopted Edwards' (1975, 1986) argument that Kohlberg was right in principle, if not in specifics, to associate moral judgment maturity with societal complexity. Stage 3 mutualities may represent moral judgment maturity sufficient for "the traditional and isolated peasant village." Although the village culture may be in certain respects complex and its members reflective (as Snarey argued), such a face-to-face, familiar community may not need the "formal and elaborate legal mechanisms" and standards required for dispute resolution and social equilibrium in a more heterogeneous or pluralistic "complex society such as a modern national state" (Edwards, 1975, p. 511, 525). For the latter societies, Edwards suggested, the mature level may entail reasoning at Stage 4 or higher (p. 511).

Despite the emphasis on standard development, moral maturity in the fullest sense in Gibbs' model is not only standard but also existential. Although Gibbs objected to Snarey's acceptance of Kohlberg's stage designation of moral philosophical principles, he agrees with Snarey that philosophical reflections or worldviews are cross-culturally pervasive. Beyond thinking about the deeper meaning of exchanges, "the mature thinker" in any culture "may think about all manner of abstract ideas and ideals in such areas as morality, religion, and politics" (Flavell, Miller, & Miller, 2002, p. 182), even about existential concerns such as the meaning of life. Life-span moral judgment development across cultures should encompass

Table 2. Moral Judgment Development Across Cultures: Three Revisionist Models

Revisionist Model	Kohlberg's Refined Stage Model	Snarey's Pluralist-Inclusionist Stage Model	Gibbs's Two-Phase Model
Revision	Empirical suspension of Stage 6[a]; Stage 5 as culturally specific product of social evolution	Acceptance of Stage 6 suspension; rejection of social evolutionism; elaboration of Stage 5 to include other cultural philosophies	Highest "stages" as part of existential phase; existential phase overlaps with standard phase of immature and mature stages
Implication for Assessment Method	Assimilation of possible Stage 6 responses into Stage 5 justifications in scoring manual; retention of dilemma method	Elaboration of Stage 5 justifications in scoring manual; provisional retention of dilemma method	Redesigned manual for scoring immature and mature standard stages; possible supplementation with moral philosophies[b]; new assessment method (non–dilemma)
Stage Typology	Three Levels I. Preconventional Level Stage 1. Punishment and obedience Stage 2. Instrumental purpose and exchange II. Conventional Level Stage 3. Interpersonal accord and conformity Stage 4. Societal accord and system maintenance III. Postconventional Level Stage 5 (and 6). Social contract, universal ethical principles	Three Levels I. Preconventional Level Stage 1. Punishment and obedience Stage 2. Instrumental purpose and exchange II. Conventional Level Stage 3. Interpersonal accord and conformity Stage 4. Societal accord and system maintenance III. Postconventional Level Stage 5 (and 6). Principled moral judgment encompassing a plurality of conceptions of justice and care, including non-Western philosophical systems.	Two Phases STANDARD DEVELOPMENT PHASE I. Immature Level Stage 1. Centrations on salient features such as size or power Stage 2. Pragmatic exchanges or concrete moral reciprocity II. Mature Level Stage 3. Mutualities or ideal moral reciprocity Stage 4. Systems. Expansion of mutualities into complex social systems EXISTENTIAL DEVELOPMENT PHASE Philosophical reflection on ethics, meaning of life.

[a]Subsequently recast and partially reinstated as ideal philosophical endstate (Kohlberg, Boyd, & Levine, 1990).
[b]Following from Snarey.

existential inquiry: "Adults who contemplate their morality and formulate ethical principles have not thereby constructed a new Piagetian stage. They have, however, engaged in a developmental process of existential inquiry with personal relevance for ethical living" (Gibbs, 2003, p. 7). Snarey sees the diverse ethical formulations within Gibbs's existential phase as stage-relevant philosophical voices, many of which are missing from Kohlberg's fifth stage.

AN ALTERNATIVE (DILEMMA-FREE) ASSESSMENT METHOD

In the early history of Kohlbergian research as it culminated in certain theoretical issues and revisionist models, a serious limitation can be noted: all of the moral judgment data were obtained through a single research instrument, namely, Kohlberg's dilemma-based assessment method. As noted, Snarey (1985) recommended that future researchers study more closely the cross-cultural validity of the conflicts and values entailed in Kohlberg's standard dilemma interview, the MJI. If Kohlberg's dilemma issues and values lack ecological validity for a given culture, then even adapted standard dilemmas might not elicit respondents' optimal competence, or for that matter, that culture's indigenous moral issues, judgments, and values. Dien (1982) argued that the Heinz dilemma in particular (whether drugs or food are at stake) was inappropriate to the collectivist culture of a Chinese village (see also Boyes & Walker, 1988). The alternative strategy of generating dilemmas idiosyncratic to a particular culture (e.g., White, 1983), although "admirable" in some respects, generates problems of nonstandardization (Snarey, 1985, p. 215).

Preempting the issue of whether to use adapted standard or non-standard indigenous dilemmas is the strategy of not using dilemmas at all. The use of any reliable and valid alternative assessment method can potentially bolster or diminish conclusions regarding the universality of a given model of moral judgment development and values. Although a non-dilemma assessment method may have its own limitations, they would differ at least in part from those of the dilemma method. In the multimethod approach (Brewer & Hunter, 2006) to the study of social phenomena, "the weakness of any one method can be, at least to some extent, compensated for by the strengths of another" (Miller, 2007, p. 113). Hence, "conclusions based upon a convergence of evidence from different methods can be held with a greater certainty than can conclusions based on one approach alone" (p. 113). In the present application of this point, a conclusion concerning moral judgment development, values, and social processes across cultures drawn from multiple methods (i.e., convergence from a multimethod extension) would be more definitive than a conclusion drawn exclusively from a single method.

This chapter focuses on the cross-cultural research literature pertaining to an alternative production measure, the Sociomoral Reflection Measure--Short Form (SRM-SF; Gibbs, Basinger, & Fuller, 1992). The SRM-SF has been used in at least 75 moral judgment studies in 23 countries (see below). In contrast to other assessment methods (recognition or production), the SRM-SF is unique in that it does not entail the use of moral dilemmas, stories, or other vignettes. Accordingly, research studies that use the SRM-SF may provide the basis for an alternative examination, across methods and cultures, of moral judgment development, values, and social processes. Description of the SRM-SF will provide an explanatory context necessary for the research review to follow.

Description of the SRM-SF

Derived from the MJI and a related dilemma-based method (the Sociomoral Reflection Method [SRM], Gibbs, Widaman, & Colby, 1982), the SRM--SF is a dilemma-free production measure consisting of a questionnaire, scoring manual, and self-training materials for achieving reliable and accurate stage scoring (Gibbs, Basinger, & Fuller, 1992). The SRM-SF questions were written at a fourth-grade reading level, and the questionnaire was designed for group administration (with instructions to the administrator to check for protocol completion and scorability). It has been group-administered to children as young as 8 or 9 (some researchers have orally administered the questions to individual children as young as 5 or 6; Gibbs et al., 1992; Snarey & Keljo, 1994). The questionnaire contains 11 items that elicit evaluations and justifications (see Table 1). Respondents evaluate the importance of the main "issues, values, or institutions" that (according to Kohlberg) comprise the core of morality and "are found in every society and culture," such as contract, truth, affiliation, life, property, law, and legal justice (cf. Kohlberg, 1984, pp. 189-190, 309; cf. Maccoby, 1980, pp. 297-299). In place of MJI dilemmas, concrete suggestions introduce the values those dilemmas encompass (e.g., to introduce contract and truth, question 1: "Think about when you've made a promise to a friend of yours;" to introduce affiliation and life, question 6: "Let's say a friend of yours needs help and may even die, and you're the only person who can save him or her"). The suggestions lead into general moral evaluation questions, e.g., "How important is it for a person (without losing his or her own life) to save the life of a friend? Circle one: Very Important / Important / Not Important." Respondents then explain or justify their evaluation (see Table 1).

This briefer, non-dilemma strategy for assessing moral judgment and values may offer certain advantages relative to the dilemma-based MJI. Snarey and Keljo (1994) noted that the lead-in statements serve to "stimulate reflective thought" (p. 184). Hart (1993) observed that "many of the more fruitful questions on the MJI are similar to those on the SRM-SF and do not pertain to the specifics of the dilemmas at all. Consequently, the decision to omit dilemmas from the SRM-SF appears to be wise" (p. 431). Although omitting the dilemmas preempts issues of dilemma translation, potential translation and relevance issues remain, of course, even with the briefer stimuli

The cultural relevance of Kohlbergian moral values at least in the United States (where most of the initial research concerning the SRM-SF was conducted) is suggested by the fact that the values are typically evaluated as either important or very important. In one USA study, at least 90 percent of both delinquents and nondelinquents evaluated most of the values as either important or very important (Gregg, Gibbs, & Basinger, 1994; cf. Palmer & Hollin, 1998). Another indicator that values are relevant to many cultural groups may be the low protocol attrition rate, as discussed later.

Moral judgment stage scoring pertains to participants' justifications for the importance of the values. Protocol justifications are matched with stage-indicative justifications (classified by stage aspect) in the SRM-SF scoring manual. The highest stage rating is entered for each item, and the average stage rating across the 11 items constitutes the overall protocol score (Gibbs et al., 1992). Protocol stage scores are sometimes reported in terms of global stage, which may involve either a differentiation of major and minor stages, e.g., 3(2) or 2(3), resulting in a 10-point scale, or a simpler transition designation, e.g., 2/3, resulting in a 7-point scale. Global stage is derived from Sociomoral Reflection Maturity Score (SRMS), a continuous variable ranging from 100 (a protocol yielding exclusively Stage 1 ratings) to 400 (a protocol yielding exclusively Stage 4 ratings).

For SRM-SF protocols to be usable, stage ratings must be obtained for justification responses to at least 7 of the 11 items. Group administrators of the SRM-SF are instructed to check protocols as they are collected for completion and scorability (to the extent feasible). A moral judgment can be defined as a justified or reasoned moral decision or value concerning just and/or benevolent social action (see Gibbs, 2003). Assuming the stage typology and scoring manual are adequately universal, any genuine and reasonably clear justification or reasoning should be scorable for stage or transition. The SRM-SF scoring manual describes categories of spurious or pseudo-justifications (e.g., repeat evaluations, tautologies, fragments, "word salads," and comments). Even a genuine justification may be problematic or unscorable if it is excessively ambiguous, defined in the scoring rules as matching at more than three adjacent levels (e.g., transition 1/2 to Stage 3). Very young and/or marginally literate participants are at risk for submitting unusable (incomplete and excessively ambiguous) protocols.

Attrition rates are indirectly relevant to the universality question concerning moral values and judgments. Attrition for SRM-SF protocols are generally 10 percent or lower (Basinger et al., 1995). Although a given sample may have a higher attrition rate for ordinary methodological reasons (poor test administration, participant literacy problems, etc.), consistently high attrition rates in samples from a given culture should be investigated.

Using the SRM-SF Outside the United States

The SRM-SF has been used to measure moral judgment development in at least 75 research studies. This data base may enable us to revisit, two decades after Snarey's review, Kohlberg's generic claim that cross-culturally general moral judgment stages, values, and social processes are identifiable as well as his specific claim for his particular stage model. SRM-SF instrumentation issues are less complex than those faced by Snarey. For example, whereas Snarey had to identify and evaluate distinct MJI scoring systems among the studies he reviewed, the SRM-SF entails a single scoring system (although several researchers did make certain adaptations, described later).

Using the SRM-SF as part of a multi-method reexamination of Kohlberg's universality claims presupposes the adequacy of the SRM-SF data base as well as the SRM-SF itself. The 2007 SRM-SF data base should be sufficiently large and diverse, and the SRM-SF should evidence adequate translatability, reliability, attrition rates, and validity in other countries.

Cultural Diversity of the Data Base. A cross-cultural data base should be adequate in terms of research volume as well as the diversity of cultures sampled. Snarey started his 1985 review by asking whether moral development research using the MJI dilemma method had "been conducted in a sufficiently wide range of sociocultural settings to jeopardize adequately the claim" of universality (p. 203). To assess the cultural diversity of his data base, Snarey classified the studies by the criteria of whether the populations sampled were: (a) Western or Westernized (vs. non-Western) and/or (b) urban (vs. tribal or village). Although the preponderance of his MJI data sets were from urban or Westernized societies (e.g., Canada, Germany, India), 10 of the 45 sampled populations were tribal or village and (arguably) non-Western (e.g., Alaskan Eskimos, Guatemalan villagers, rural Kenyan villagers).

The present SRM-SF data base (75 studies in 23 countries; see Gibbs, Basinger, Grime, & Snarey, 2007) is comparable to Snarey's MJI data base (45 studies in 27 countries) in research volume, although slightly less diverse in terms of variations in cultural complexity. Nevertheless, by Snarey's criteria, the present data base is still diverse. Although many of the SRM-SF samples are urban and Westernized, some are non-urban (rural communities in Armenia, Kenya, Nigeria), and others are outside Western Europe and North America (namely, Armenia, Bosnia, Bulgaria, and Russia in Eastern Europe; Sweden in Northwest Europe; China, Japan, Malaysia, and Taiwan in Asia; Kenya and Nigeria in Africa; and Bahrain and Saudi Arabia in the Middle East). Hence, the range of sociocultural settings in the present data base is sufficiently wide to allow a test of universality claims.

Suitability for Cross-Cultural Research. Cross-cultural suitability issues pertain to translatability, reliability, and validity. Each of these criteria will be addressed below (another criterion, protocol attrition, will be discussed in the next section).

Translatability. Because the SRM-SF questionnaire is briefer than the MJI interview (see Table 1), translation (needed in many of the studies) was less demanding. The questionnaire has been successfully translated into Arabic, Bahasa Malaysian, Bulgarian, Chinese, Dutch, Eastern Armenian, French, German, Italian, Japanese, Kikamba, Kiswahili, Russian, Serbo-Croatian, and Swedish. Researchers in Armenia, Germany, Italy, Japan, Russia, and Taiwan used a back-translation procedure to ensure accuracy. In Germany, Krettenauer and Becker (2001) chose to translate and administer only 8 of the 11 questionnaire items to streamline data collection (items

3, 5, and 8 were judged to be non-essential). In Belgium (Day & Naedts, 1995), the Netherlands (Zwart-Woudstra, Meijer, Fintelman, & Van IJzendoorn, 1993), and Taiwan (W.Y. Lin, 1995; Tang, 2004), not only the questionnaire but also the scoring manual were translated (into French, Dutch, and Chinese, respectively).

Reliability. Cross-cultural researchers contributing to the present data base addressed questions of instrument reliability. Snarey focused on reports of the MJI scoring system's interrater reliability, which were generally acceptable (interrater reliability was reported in 31 of the 47 studies comprising Snarey's data base). Similarly, the interrater reliability coefficients as reported in 53 of the 75 studies comprising the present data base were all at or above .80 (the minimum acceptable; Basinger et al., 1995).

A number of researchers also reported test-retest internal consistency reliability indices such as Cronbach's alpha. Magnitudes were comparable to those reported in the USA (.57 to.67; .93 for total sample; Basinger et al., 1995) and ranged from .64 (in Northern Ireland; Ferguson et al., 1994) to .90 (in Italy; Comunian & Gielen, 2000). In factor analyses, Basinger et al.'s (1995) USA finding of a single dominant factor was replicated (but with a small secondary factor) in England (Brusten, 2003) and Germany (Krettenauer & Becker, 2001). Test-retest reliability levels (using 2-3 week intervals) reported in Ireland and Italy were comparable to that reported by Basinger et al. (r = .88), although a level reported in Taiwan (r = .70, Chen & Hsieh, 2001) was somewhat lower. Finally, several international studies conducted factor analyses. Although factor analyses may also be considered relevant to questions of internal consistency, such results have particular relevance to theoretical tenets of Kohlberg's cognitive developmental approach and so are noted in the next section.

Validity. Other findings among the cross-cultural studies pertained to questions of concurrent, discriminant, and construct validity. The acceptable USA concurrent validity of the SRM-SF with the MJI was corroborated in Ireland (with the SROM), the Netherlands (marginally with the SROM-SF), and Taiwan (with the MJI and the DIT). Regarding discriminant validity, consistent with Basinger et al.'s (1995; cf. Schonfeld et al., 2005) USA results, SRM-SF stage scores were found not to correlate positively with social desirability measures in the Netherlands and Taiwan.

Several ad hoc findings among the cross-cultural studies are relevant to construct validity. Moral judgment maturity as measured by the SRM-SF was found to correlate with experiencing life as meaningful (Hauer, 2001), sense of spirituality (Woods & Jagers, 2003), attribution of prosocial intent (Palmer & Hollin, 2000), and positive parenting attitudes (Hubbs-Tait, Page, Huey, Starost, Culp, Culp, & Harper, 2006). Particularly intriguing – and worthy of systematic research – are findings of a relationship between moral judgment maturity and variables pertaining to self-regulation, self-control, or ego strength (cognitive inhibition, Schonfeld, Mattson, & Riley, 2005, and Stadler, Sterzer, Schmeck, Krebs, Kleinschmidt, & Poustka, 2007; emotional stability, Travis, Arenander, & DuBois, 2004; planning and problem-solving skills, Rose, 2005; goal orientation for females, Getty, 1996). Reported below, in connection with social participation and within-culture variation, are construct validity results pertaining to the relationship of moral judgment development to theoretical correlates such as delinquency, age, education, socio-economic status, urban versus rural environment, community volunteering, and self-reported social perspective-taking

RESULTS AND DISCUSSION

Given evidence for the adequacy of the SRM-SF and the 2007 SRM-SF data base, it should be worthwhile to revisit with this alternative assessment method Kohlberg's cognitive developmental approach and universality claims. Do the prior (MJI-based) and more recent (SRM-SF-based) results converge to yield a coherent cross-cultural picture of moral development?

Moral Values across Cultures

Kohlberg (1984) claimed that the conflicts and values entailed in his dilemma method were universal. Because the SRM-SF method does not use moral dilemmas, findings using the SRM-SF cannot address the question of applicability of the value conflicts depicted in the MJI dilemmas and probe questions. The SRM-SF method does, however, require ratings of the importance of the values entailed in those conflicts. Although Kohlberg (1984) simply referred to those values as the "issues, values, or moral institutions found in every culture" (p. 189), their universality is an empirical question. The SRM-SF values of contract, truth, affiliation, life, property, law, and legal justice were derived from the dilemmas and probe questions of the MJI. Respondent ratings of these values are obtained but not ordinarily reported. Where they have been reported (by Palmer & Hollin, 1998, in England; by Jeshmaridian & Babakhanyan, 2005, in Armenia; by Tang, 2004, in Taiwan; by Wasanga, 2004, in Kenya), the findings generally replicate Gregg et al.'s (1994) USA finding of high (above 90 percent selecting "important" or "very important") valuation. The main exceptions occurred for adolescent offenders and younger respondents, but even among these participants lower percentages were found only for certain items, e.g., keeping a promise to someone you hardly know.

Also relevant to evaluating value universality is attrition rate. High protocol attrition rates in a study could indirectly reflect a number of factors, including low value ratings by the respondents. Attrition rate was reported by some but not all of the researchers in the 2007 SRM-SF data base. In some cases, we were able to contact the researcher and obtain this information. Ultimately, attrition rate information was obtained for 23 of the 72 studies in the data base. Protocol attrition rates were acceptably low, i.e., around or below 10 percent, in Armenia, Bosnia, Canada, England (most studies), Germany, Ireland, Italy, Nigeria, Scotland, Taiwan, and most of the USA studies. Exceptions were attributed to marginal literacy (Leenders & Brugman, 2005), insufficient time for protocol completion (Getty, 1996; Hauer, personal communication, June 10, 2005), and use of an unorthodox, across-item scoring procedure (Brusten, 2003). Most important for the present purpose, none of the researchers linked cases of protocol attrition to low value ratings (or, for that matter, to unclassifiably novel moral judgments, a point which relates to the next section).

Our 2007 data base, then, permits us to visit anew Kohlberg's universality claim concerning moral values. Snarey noted some researchers' comments that the Kohlbergian value conflicts or (adapted) dilemmas seemed to be considered relevant by the respondents in their sample, and the general absence of reports to the contrary (but cf. Dien, 1982). Many researchers did not comment on the issue one way or the other. Our data are similarly partial but also consistent with Kohlberg's claim of value universality. Value ratings where reported are high, and procotol attrition where reported is not attributed to low value ratings. Although partial, the anecdotal and evaluation information that we do have from researchers is consistent with the value universality claim. Given the incomplete nature of these data, more systematic attention should be accorded the question of value universality in future research (cf. Siddle-Walker & Snarey, 2004).

Moral Judgment Stage Development across Cultures

Kohlberg's main universality claim pertained to basic moral judgment development. Are stages of moral judgment commonly identifiable across different assessment methods and diverse cultures? Below we will describe the basic moral judgment development across cultures in terms of the general age periods of childhood, adolescence, and the adult years. Our results stem from a multimethod extension (Brewer & Hunter, 2006), that is, they represent commonalities in the results from the differing methods used in the 1985 and the present data bases. (For a tabular summary of the of the 75 SRM-SF cross-cultural studies in terms of moral stage and mean maturity scores by age-groups and age, see Gibbs, Basinger, Grime, and Snarey (2007, pp. 478-480).

Moral Judgment in Childhood

According to the developmental expectations of original Piagetian as well as revisionist models (Table 2), much moral reasoning produced in late childhood (approximately ages 9-11 years) is still characterized by pragmatic considerations or quid pro quo exchanges that serve the individual (Stage 2). Kohlberg's theory predicts, as a secondary tendency, (declining from early childhood) appeals to salient features such as size, power, immediate status, unilateral relations, physical damage, and punitive consequences (Stage 1). Gibbs (2003) stressed that the level of moral judgment associated with childhood is immature and superficial insofar as that which is moral in a mature sense tends to be confused with the pragmatic and instrumental (Stage 2) or the physical or momentary (Stage 1). Often not grasped in childhood are the mutualistic and other intangible bases for relationships and society. In Kohlberg's and Snarey's models, this level is termed preconventional.

The data bases support the developmental expectations. The 1985 MJI and 2007 SRM-SF studies of 9-11 year-olds both included the USA, where Stage 2 predominated (207 MJI mean, 215 SRM-SF mean). Stage 2 also predominated among children in Turkey (MJI) as well as Japan, Italy, and Ireland (SRM-SF). Stage 1 reasoning was more prominent among village or lower class children in Turkey, Bahamas, or India (MJI), and in Bosnia, Kenya, and Nigeria (SRM-SF). Stage 1 characterized the mean protocol reasoning in only one of the MJI samples (Tibetan village children in India) and in none of the SRM-SF samples.

It is likely that generic standard measures such as the MJI or SRM-SF, although useful for identifying broad, basic cross-cultural age trends, fall short of what is needed for more intensive exploration of reasoning at particular age periods or in particular cultural contexts. Some of the child-oriented research (such as that generated by Selman's [1980; cf. 2003] social perspective-taking stories) corroborate Kohlberg's basic four stages. Aligning "tolerably well" with Kohlberg's "general progression" (Lapsley, 2006, p. 53) are the developmental levels suggested by data from Damon's (1977) distributive justice tasks featuring tangible goods such as bracelets or candy bars, and Eisenberg's (e.g., Eisenberg, 1986; Eisenberg, Fabes, & Spinrad, 2006) child-friendly stories concerning prosocial behavior. Nonetheless, these research literatures also identify precocities in childhood moral reasoning not suggested by Stage 1. The social domain research of Turiel and colleagues (e.g., Nucci, 2006; Smetana, 2006; Turiel, 2006a, 2006b; Turiel & Smetana, 1998) has identified an apparent sophistication in young children's understanding of moral matters as distinct from conventional and personal matters (but cf. Fowler, 1998, 2007; Glassman & Zan, 1995; Lourenco, 2003; J. Miller, 2006; Rest et al., 1999). In general, however, "vulnerability to salient features of the here-and-now" is broadly evident in young children's social and nonsocial cognition (Flavell et al., 2002, p. 181), including their moral reasoning.

Moral Judgment in Adolescence

In the years from late childhood into early adolescence, a crucial qualitative advance seems to take place in many young persons' moral judgment. As we have seen, this qualitative transition has been variously characterized as a shift from concrete to ideal moral reciprocity (Piaget), from preconventional-level Stage 2 instrumental purpose to conventional-level, Stage 3 interpersonal accord (Kohlberg or Snarey), or from immature-level Stage 2 pragmatic exchanges to mature-level Stage 3 mutualities and equities (Piaget or Gibbs). Gibbs stresses that the emergence of mutualistic moral understanding, although sometimes embedded in social conventions (Kohlberg's Moral Type A, Colby & Kohlberg, 1987), nonetheless represents a basic achievement of moral maturity in its own right for interpersonal relationships. It is an achievement that, given adequate social perspective-taking experiences (Comunian & Gielen, 2006; Grime, 2005) and cognitive advances such as formal operations (Moshman, 1998), should become clearly evident by early adolescence.

Again, our review corroborates this expectation. Stage 3 already makes an appearance in the stage ranges of some late-childhood samples, but generally gains prominence (sometimes even full-stage prominence) during early adolescence. In the 1985 MJI data base, Stage 3 was prominent in the moral reasoning of young adolescents in the Kibbutz, Taiwan, and the USA (upper middle-class). In the 2007 SRM-SF data base (Table 3), Stage 3 is prominent as at least a major global stage, 2/3 or 3, among early adolescents in Canada, China, Ireland (Northern, Republic of), Italy, Japan, the Netherlands, Scotland, Taiwan, and in one USA study (Schonfeld et al., 2005).

By late adolescence, Stage 3 normally becomes the mean global moral judgment stage. In the 1985 MJI data base, this was the case in India (upper middle class), Israel, Taiwan, and USA. In the 2007 SRM-SF data base as shown (Table 3), Stage 3 is the mean for older mainstream adolescents in Bahrain, Belgium, England (Palmer & Hollin, 1998, 2000, 2001), Ireland, Italy (most samples), Japan, Russia, Sweden, and the USA. The main exceptions are delinquent or adjudicated late adolescents, discussed below.

Older adolescents (at least in national states) may also be beginning to extend their Stage 3 mutualistic understanding to grasp the importance of agreed-upon standards and institutions for the common good. In a USA study of developmental transitions in the concept of law, Adelson, Green, and O'Neil (1969) used semi-structured interviews based on a "desert island" situation ("Imagine that a thousand people move to an island in the Pacific, and set about building a community de novo …," p. 327) to compare the understandings of early adolescents (ages 11-13) and late adolescents (ages 15-18). As with the MJI or SRM-SF moral judgment results, the preadolescents' or early adolescents' reasoning concerning the purpose of laws tended to be more concrete and pragmatic. For example, an 11-year-old responded: "Well, [they'd have laws] so everybody won't fight and they have certain laws so they won't go around breaking windows and stuff and getting away with it." In contrast, reasoning in late adolescence tended to be more abstract and ideal, e.g., an 18-year-old's response: "Well, the main purpose [of the laws] would be just to set up a standard of behavior for people, for society living together so that they can live peacefully and in harmony with each other" (p. 328). With reference to effects of the absence of law, older adolescents appealed not only to outer misconduct but also to more subtle or intangible effects upon inner feelings and character (e.g., personal confusion, anomie, and a dwindling of moral sense and capacity).

This beginning movement from interpersonal to societal frames of reference in late adolescence is represented theoretically in moral judgment models as movement from Stage 3 to Stage 4. In Kohlberg's and Snarey's models, this movement is from "interpersonal accord and conformity" (Kohlbergian Stage 3) to "societal accord in system maintenance" (Kohlbergian Stage 4) within the conventional level. Gibbs recasts Stages 3 and Stage 4 as already mature in their appreciation of the

Table 3. Cross-Cultural Samples in Rank Order by Mean Sociomoral Reflection Maturity Score, Grouped by Age

Sample/age range (mean) in years	n	Global Stage Range	M
MIDDLE ADULTHOOD (approx. 40-50 years old)			
USA, adults with Transcendental Meditation (TM) experience/ (44.5)	20	NR	357
USA, university parents/ (50.1)	58	3/4	350
USA, adults without TM experience/ (39.7)	9	3	310
USA, offenders/ (41.7)	29	2/3-3	289
YOUNG ADULTHOOD (approx. 20-35 years old)			
USA, university students/ (34.5)	20	3/4-4	372
Italy, adult volunteers/ (33.9)	154	NR	359
USA, university students/ 18-22 (19.5)	47	3-3/4	344
Australia, university students/ (26.9)	94	3-3/4	340
USA, university students/ 17-54 (26.6)	91	3-3/4	337
USA, university students/ 17-39 (20.8)	153	3-3/4	335
Saudi Arabia, upper-division university students/ 20-26 (22.5)	60	3-4	333
Italy, university students/ (22.6)	133	NR	331
Italy, male adults (non-drug abusers)/ 27-33 (29.2)	60	3-3/4	330
England, university students/ 18-25 (19.5)	64	3-3/4	327
Bulgaria, adults in romantic relationships/ (19-73 (29.8)	163[c]	3-3/4	325
Italy, graduate students/ 22-26 (24.2)	120	3-3/4	322
Belgium, university and vocational students/ 21-24	57	NR	311
Italy, male adults (drug abusers)/ 26-32 (30.1)	60	3-3/4	309
Australia, male and female offenders/ (31.2)	99	3-3/4	307
Japan, university students/ (19.8)	80	2/3-3/4	300
USA, Head Start mothers/ 19-46 (29.1)	199	2/3-3/4	300
Italy, adult non-volunteers/ (34.6)	63	NR	299
USA, male and female offenders/ 18-24 (20.1)	90	2/3-3	276
Italy, adults (8th grade max.)/ (22.5)	38	NR	269
England, young offenders/ 18-21 (19.5)	59	2-2/3	235
LATE ADOLESCENCE (approx. 16-19 years old)			
Italy, volunteers/ (16.)	70	NR	329
Italy, volunteers/ 15-21 (17.9)	49	3-3/4	328
Japan, high school students/16-18 (17.1)	22	NR	320
Bahrain, male high school students/ 17-18 (17.7)	30	3-3/4	313
USA, university students/ (19.2)	72	3-3/4	312
Russia, high school students/ (15.6)	419	NR	311
USA, university students/ 16-19 (18.2)	181	3-3/4	305
England, female secondary and university students/ 13-22 (17.9)	210	2/3-3/4	304
Italy, non-volunteers / 15-21 (17.5)	60	3	303
Italy, 10th graders/ (15.4)	38	NR	298
USA, high school students/ (17.3)	89	2/3-3	296
Belgium, secondary school students/ 18-20	37	NR	292
Sweden, female non-delinquents/ 13-18 (16.0)	29	2/3-3/4	291
Japan, 11th graders/ (16.8)	95	2/3-3	289
USA, female high school students/ 13-19 (16.1)	77	2/3-3	289
England, male secondary and university students/ 13-22 (17.6)	122	2/3-3/4	286
USA, high school students/ 15-17 (16.2)	77	2/3-3	285

England, middle and high school students/ 12-18 (15.7)	94	2/3-3	281
Ireland, secondary school students/ 16-19 (17.3)	61	2/3-3	281
England, male high school students/ 12-24 (17.4)	77	2/3-3	279
USA, male high school students/ 13-19 (15.7)	86	2/3	272
Sweden, non-delinquents (matched)/ 13-18 (15.6)	29	2/3-3	266
Germany, participants without CD (matched)/9-15 (12.8)	14	2-3	265
England, male high school students/ 14-16 (15.5)	149	2-3	264
England, female high school students/ 14-16 (15.1)	117	2/3-3	262
Germany, high school students/ 14-16 (15.6)	309	2/3-3	261
Sweden, female delinquents/ 13-18 (16.0)	29	2-3	256
Bahrain, delinquents/ 14-19 (16.8)	30	2/3-3	254
USA, female delinquents/ 13-18 (16.6)	71	2-3	254
Kenya, high school students/ 17-19	94	2-3	250
England, delinquents/ 13-21 (18.2)	97	2-2/3	249
Netherlands, nondelinquents/ (15.1)	81	2-3	249
Italy, non-volunteers/ (16.0)	131	NR	247
England, delinquents/ 13-21 (17.4)	126	2-3	247
Belgium, secondary school students/ 15-17	52	NR	244
England, delinquents/ 13-17 (16.0)	42	2-3	243
Germany, delinquents/ 14-17 (15.6)	39	2-3	243
Netherlands, delinquents/ 12-21 (16.8)	108	2-3	243
USA, delinquents/ 13-18 (15.9)	89	2-2/3	243
USA, delinquents/ 15-18 (16.0)	57	2-3	243
Netherlands, delinquents/ (16.5)	64	2-2/3	241
Netherlands, delinquents/ 12-21 (16.8)	108	2-2/3	241
Sweden, delinquents/ 13-18 (15.5)	29	2-2/3	228
Germany, participants with CD/ 9-15 (12.7)	13	2-2/3	226
England, delinquents/ 14-17 (15.9)	147	2-2/3	223
Australia, delinquents (1 female)/ 14-18 (16.5)	38	1/2-2/3	211
EARLY/MIDDLE ADOLESCENCE (approx.12-15 years)			
Taiwan, 7th and 8th grade students/13-14	45	NR	292
Italy, 9th grade students/ (14.4)	52	NR	291
Japan, 6th grade students/ (12.4)	46	2/3-3	279
Ireland, secondary school students/ 14-15	325	2/3-3	278
Taiwan, 5th and 6th grade students/11-12	45	NR	272
Ireland, adolescents/ 14-15	219	2/3-3	269
Ireland, secondary school students/ 14-15	85	NR	269
Canada, 6th and 7th grade students/10-13 (11.7)	47	NR	268
USA, middle school students (62 problem-referred)/ 12-15 (13.7)	258	2/3-3	268
Ireland, adolescents/ 14-15	239	2/3-3	267
USA, middle school students/ 12-14 (13.2)	260	2/3-3	267
USA, 6th through 12th grade students/ 12-19 (15.2)	180	2/3-3	265
Japan, 8th grade students/ (14.3)	62	2-3	264
USA, 8th grade students/(14.1)	74	2/3-3	260
Canada, urban middle school students/10-13 (11.6)	49	NR	257
USA, 7th and 8th grade students/12-14	146	NR	256
Scotland, middle school students/ 14-15	157	2/3-3	255
USA, juveniles (no prenatal alcohol exposure)/ 10-18 (13.2)	29	2-3	255
China, non-delinquents/ 13-15	10	NR	251
USA, 8th grade African-American students/ 13-14 (13.4)	50	2-3	245

179

England, middle school students/ 12-15/13.0)	789	2-3	242
USA, 6th graders/ 11-14 (11.8)	276	2-3	240
Netherlands, secondary school students/ 12-17 (14.3)	216	2-2/3	237
USA, 6th graders/ (12.1)	43	2-2/3	237
USA, 4th to 8th grade students/ 10-18 (11.6)	211	2-2/3	235
Ireland, primary school students/ 14-15 (14.7)	58	2-2/3	235
Canada, at-risk 5th and 6th grade students/ 10-13 (11.5)	53	2-2/3	233
Bosnia, primary school students/ 11-12 (11.8)	23	2-2/3	230
Ireland, primary school students/ NR	28	2-2/3	230
USA, 7th grade students/ NR	221	2-2/3	228
USA, juveniles with prenatal alcohol exposure/ 10-18 (13.8)	27	2-2/3	228
Belgium, primary school students/ 12-14	48	NR	223
USA, 5th and 8th grade African-American students/ (12.0)	90	1/2-2/3	207
Kenya, middle school students/ 14-16	67	1/2-2/3	191
Kenya, middle school students/ 11-13	83	1/2-2	185
China, delinquents/ 13-15	10	NR	182
LATE CHILDHOOD (approx. 9-11 years old)			
USA, primary school students/ 11-12 (11.4)	17	2-2/3	243
Japan, 4th graders/ (10.3)	37	2-3	239
Taiwan, primary school students/ 9-12	450	2-2/3	225
Ireland, primary school students/ 10-11	84	NR	223
Italy, 6th graders/ (11.2)	52	NR	223
Ireland, primary school students/ 10-11	48	2-2/3	222
Ireland, primary school students/ 10-11	96	2-2/3	221
USA, 4th graders/ (10.1)	48	2-2/3	215
Canada, 5th graders/ 10-12 (11.0)	45	NR	209
USA, 5th grade students/ NR	61	2-2/3	209[b]
USA, primary school students/ 7-9 (7.8)	20	1/2-2/3	196
Nigeria, primary school students/ 10-11	37	1/2-2	181
Kenya, primary school students/ 8-10	69	1/2-2	179
Bosnia, primary school students/ 7-9 (8.1)	18	1/2	164

Notes: NR indicates information not reported. Students include both genders unless otherwise indicated. Delinquents or offenders are male unless otherwise specified. Stage scores are presented using the 7-point global scale. Global stage range is estimated on the basis of +/- 1 SD (SDs provided in the majority of the studies unless otherwise indicated. For a bibliography of the cross-cultural studies cited in this table, see Gibbs, et al., 2007.

intangible bases of relationships and society. The Stage 3 and Stage 4 reasoning may not be conformity- or maintenance-oriented when the orientation is field-independent (Gibbs, Clark, Joseph, Green, Goodrick, & Makowski, 1986).

The data bases generally corroborate the cognitive developmental expectation for moral judgment development in adolescence. In the MJI data base, although most late adolescents' reasoning was predominantly Stage 3, transition 3/4 made a strong secondary showing (it was the mean stage for 66.5 percent of 18-year-olds in Taiwan). In the SRM-SF data base, transition 3/4 marked at least the upper range of late adolescents' moral judgment in Bahrain, England (Palmer & Hollin, 1998), and Italy (community service volunteers). Indeed, transition 3/4 was the mean moral judgment stage vicinity evidenced by the Italian volunteer sample. The volunteers provided help through charitable Catholic institutions to needy individuals such as

Bosnian refugees as well as the elderly, ill, and/or handicapped (Comunian & Gielen, 1995, 2000). That community service is associated with greater use of transition 3/4 and Stage 4 is consistent with cognitive developmental hypotheses regarding the developmental impact of such "enlarged" social perspective-taking opportunities (Comunian & Gielen, 2006; Edwards, 1986; Kohlberg, 1981, 1984; cf. Hart, Atkins, & Donnelly, 2006), as will be discussed below.

Moral Judgment in Adulthood

If Stage 3 gains in prominence during adolescence, the same may be said for transition 3/4 or Stage 4 during the adult years. In the MJI data base, transition 3/4 is the most frequent level used among adults in India (upper middle class), Israel, Taiwan, and the USA, although it is not seen among adults in rural Kenya or Turkey. Stage 4 also makes a strong showing, and in fact is the modal stage in a USA upper middle class sample. Stages 3 and 4 remain mixed in the SRM-SF data base, but transition 3/4 or Stage 4 defined the upper (+1 SD) range for 15 of the adult samples where range was reported (the two exceptions were both adult offender samples: Palmer & Begum, 2006; and Peterson, 2001).

Higher education appears to be particularly important for moral judgment development in the adult years, perhaps because of the opportunity it typically affords for expanded social perspective-taking. The mean stage of adults in Italy having no more than an 8th grade education was transition 2/3 (SRMS = 269) and of USA Head Start mothers (23 percent of whom had not completed secondary school and only 4 percent of whom had attended or completed college) was Stage 3 (SRMS = 300). In contrast, adult university students in Australia, Italy, Saudi Arabia, and the USA evidenced mean SRMS scores in the transition 3/4 range (university students in Japan and a mixed sample in Belgium were the only exceptions) (see Table 3). Mason and Gibbs (1993a, 1993b) as well as Comunian and Gielen (2006) found that the extent of university students' moral judgment maturity beyond Stage 3 was correlated with their agreement on social perspective-taking items such as "I have encountered and become friends with other students or co-workers of different ethnic or cultural backgrounds (for example, a student from another country)," "I have been involved in a group or organization where it was necessary for me to deal with various points of view," and "I have learned just how culturally varied the world is since coming to college." (cf. Edwards, 1975; Harkness, Edwards, & Super, 1981). Comunian and Gielen (2006) found that a sociomoral intervention promoted both expanded social perspective-taking and moral judgment beyond Stage 3, but they did not investigate whether social perspective-taking mediated the gains in moral judgment. Research is needed to address this question.

As adolescents or adults in university or complex work settings increasingly experience and seek to coordinate diverse viewpoints, they may not only increasingly appreciate the need for agreed-upon standards (Stage 4), but may also move beyond Stage 4 to reflect upon the customs and norms of their society, indeed, of morality or life itself. In Needleman's (1982) overstatement, "man cannot live without philosophy" (p. 3). In ethics, meta-ethical reflection may lead for a time to an "unbridled relativism" (Boyes & Chandler, 1992, p. 285) that Kohlberg and Kramer (1969) referred to as a transitional 4 1/2. In Kohlberg's theory, adults (especially those with philosophical training) may achieve a postconventional or principled philosophical level of theoretical discourse on the bases for moral values, a Stage 5 and perhaps a Stage 6. In Snarey's pluralist-inclusionist stage model, this level in the theory and scoring manual must be broadened beyond Western philosophical traditions. In Gibbs' two-phase model, this level pertains to a fundamentally new phase of human development, an existential inquiry that reflects moral judgment maturity in the fullest sense and transcends stages and stage scoring manuals (morally relevant existential reflection could be profitably included in the manual, albeit as examples of post-standard quests for existential insight rather than as a stage).

Moral Judgment Stage Development within Cultures

We can now summarize the within-culture evidence, which is generally consistent with Kohlberg's view that social interaction, social participation, and, in particular, social perspective-taking opportunities facilitate moral judgment development. Noted earlier were Italian studies (Comunian & Gielen, 1995, 2000, 2006) that found relations between community service volunteering or related communitarian experiences and greater use of transition 3/4 and Stage 4. USA (e.g., Colby et al., 1983) findings relating moral judgment maturity to index variables such as age, education, socioeconomic status, urban settings, and community service volunteering were corroborated in Snarey's cross-cultural MJI review as well as in the present data base. For example, positive correlations with chronological age were generally reported in studies in which the samples included participants representing a wide range of ages. The relationship of moral judgment stage with SES level was replicated in an Armenian study (Jeshmaridian & Babakhanyan, 2005). Urban samples evidenced more mature moral judgment compared with rural samples in Armenia (Jeshmaridian & Babakhanyan, 2005) as well as Ireland and Scotland (Ferguson & Cairns, 2002). Studies in Belgium, England, Italy, Japan, Kenya, Malaysia, Taiwan and USA that compared students at different educational levels all found significant differences favoring higher education. Researchers in Canada (Krivel-Zacks, 1995), Malaysia (Chu, 1999), the Netherlands (Brugman & Aleva, 2004), Taiwan (Chen & Hsieh, 2001) and USA (Van Someren, 2000) reported positive correlations with academic achievement. Also relevant are studies that relate moral judgment maturity directly to self-reports of social participation and perspective-taking. Studies (Comunian & Gielen, 2006; Mason & Gibbs, 1993a, 1993b) that related transition 3/4 and Stage 4 to self-reported experiences of exposure to and interaction with culturally diverse individuals or groups in university or complex work settings were described above. Grime (2005; cf. Sedikides, 1989) found that adolescents' self-reported general and friendship perspective-taking correlated with their use of interpersonally mature (Stage 3) moral judgment even after controlling for verbal intelligence. Furthermore, moral judgment developmental delay among delinquents relative to their comparison groups was evident in all countries where it was studied, namely, Australia, Bahrain, China, England, Germany, the Netherlands5, Sweden, Taiwan, and the USA (cf. Stams, Brugman, Dekovic, Rosmalen, van der Laan, & Gibbs, 2006) A Kohlbergian interpretation of these numerous associations is still speculative, of course, because correlations cannot establish the direction or even the existence causality.

CONCLUSION

Kohlberg's cognitive developmental approach and stage model were used in this review to study, across different assessment methods, moral judgment development across cultures. Although Kohlberg died in 1987, cognitive developmental research and theory continue to grow as assessment methods continue to be disseminated by researchers around the globe. Areas of consensus indicate progress in the cognitive developmental contribution to our understanding of moral judgment development and behavior across cultures; evidently, moral development is not entirely relative to particular cultures and socialization practices. Areas of controversy reflect continued vitality as well as the opportunity for advances through systematic research. As Kohlberg recognized, beyond the broad cognitive developmental approach of age-related trends, his specific stage model and claim for moral judgment development across cultures require qualification and revision. Nonetheless, as Snarey (1985) concluded, "the significant shortcomings of Kohlberg's work should not overshadow its remarkable achievements" (p. 229). The review's findings are, in principle, consistent with Kohlberg's views regarding the universality of basic moral judgment development, moral values, and related social perspective-taking processes across cultures.

NOTE

1   This chapter, which was originally presented at the 2007 annual conference of the Association for Moral Education held in Fribourg, is an abridged and revised version of a paper appearing in Developmental Review, 27(4), 443-500.

REFERENCES

Adelson, J., Green, B. & O'Neil, R. P. (1969). Growth of the idea of law in adolescence. *Developmental Psychology, 1*, 327-332.

Baek, H. J. (2002). A comparative study of moral development of Korean and British children. *Journal of Moral Education, 31*, 373-391.

Basinger, K. S., Gibbs, J. C. & Fuller, D. (1995). Context and the measurement of moral judgment. *International Journal of Behavioral Development, 18*, 537-556.

Boyes, M. C. & Walker, L. J. (1988). Implications of cultural diversity for the universality claims of Kohlberg's theory of moral reasoning. *Human Development, 31*, 44-59.

Boyes, M. C. & Chandler, M. (1992). Cognitive development, epistemic doubt, and identity formation in adolescence. *Journal of Youth and Adolescence, 21*, 277-304.

Brewer, J. & Hunter, A. (2006). *Foundations of Multimethod Research: Synthesizing styles.* Thousand Oaks, CA: Sage.

Brown, R. & Herrnstein, R. J. (1978). *Psychology.* Boston: Little, Brown.

Brugman, D. & Aleva, A. E. (2004). Developmental delay or regression in moral reasoning by juvenile delinquents? *Journal of Moral Education, 33*, 321-338.

Brusten, C. M. (2003). *Investigation of the moral reasoning of offending and non-offending adolescents using the Sociomoral Reflection Measure--Short Form.* Unpublished doctoral dissertation, Oxford Brookes University, UK.

Carpendale, J. I. M. (2000). Kohlberg and Piaget on stages and moral reasoning. *Developmental Review, 20*, 181-205.

Chapman, M. (1988). *Constructive evolution: Origins and development of Piaget's thought.* Cambridge, UK: Cambridge University Press.

Chen, C-A. & Hsieh, C-C. (2001). An investigation comparing moral cognitive development between delinquent and nondelinquent adolescents [Mandarin Chinese]. *Chinese Journal of Criminology, 8*, 127-176

Chu, T. B. (1999). *Effects of the factors of teaching and learning of moral education on the moral reasoning and empathy of secondary school students.* Unpublished doctoral dissertation, National University of Malaysia.

Colby, A. & Kohlberg, L. (1987). *The measurement of moral judgment: Vol. 1. Theoretical foundations and research validation.* Cambridge, UK: Cambridge University Press.

Colby, A., Kohlberg, L., Gibbs, J. C. & Lieberman, M. (1983). A longitudinal study of moral judgment. *Monographs of the Society for Research in Child Development, 48* (1-2, Serial No. 200).

Colby, A., Kohlberg, L., Speicher, B., Hewer, A., Candee, D., Gibbs, J. C. & Power, C. (1987). *The measurement of moral judgment (Vol. 2).* Cambridge, UK: Cambridge University Press.

Comunian, A. L. & Gielen, U. P. (1995). A study of moral reasoning and prosocial action in Italian culture. *Journal of Social Psychology, 135*, 699-705.

Comunian, A. L. & Gielen, U. P. (2000). Sociomoral reflection and antisocial behavior: Two Italian studies. *Journal of Social Psychology, 135*, 699-705.

Comunian, A. L. & Gielen, U. P. (2006). Promotion of moral judgment maturity through stimulation of social role-taking and social reflection: An Italian intervention study. *Journal of Moral Education, 35*, 51-69.

Damon, W. (1977). *The social world of the child.* San Francisco: Jossey-Bass.

Damon, W. (1988). *The moral child: Nurturing children's natural moral growth.* New York: Free Press.

Day, J. & Naedts, M. (1995). Convergence and conflict in the development of moral judgment and religious judgment. *Journal of Education, 177*, 1-29

Dewey, J. & Tufts, J. H. (1908). *Ethics.* New York: Holt.

Dien, D. S. (1982). A Chinese perspective on Kohlberg's theory of moral development. *Developmental Review, 2*, 331-341.

Edwards, C. P. (1975). Social complexity and moral development: A Kenyan study. *Ethos, 3*, 505-527.

Edwards, C. P. (1985). Rationality, culture, and the construction of "ethical discourse": A comparative perspective. *Ethos: The Journal of Psychological Anthropology, 13*, 318-339.

Eisenberg, N. (1986). *Altruistic emotion, cognition, and behavior.* Hillsdale, NJ: Lawrence Erlbaum Associates.

Eisenberg, N., Fabes, R. A. & Spinrad, T. L. (2006). Prosocial development. In W. Damon & R. M. Lerner (Series Eds.) & N. Eisenberg (Vol. Ed.), *Handbook of child psychology: Vol. 3. Social, emotional, and personality development* (6th ed., pp. 646-718). New York: John Wiley.

Ferguson, N. & Cairns, E. (2002). The impact of political conflict on moral maturity: A cross-national perspective. *Journal of Adolescence, 25*, 441-451.

Ferguson, N., McLernon, F. & Cairns, E. (1994). The Sociomoral Reflection Measure-Short Form: An examination of its reliability and validity in a Northern Irish setting. *British Journal of Educational Psychology, 64*, 483-489.

Flavell, J. H., Miller, P. H. & Miller, S. A. (2002). *Cognitive development* (4th ed.). Upper Saddle River, NJ: Prentice-Hall.

Fowler, R. C. (1998). *Limiting the domain account of early moral judgment by challenging its critique of Piaget.* Merrill-Palmer Quarterly, 44, 263-292.

Fowler, R. C. (2007). *Reestablishing the limits: A response to Turiel and Smetana's commentary* (1998). Unpublished manuscript, Salem State College.

Getty, D. (1996). The relationship of goal orientation to perceived sport competence, social interdependence, sociomoral reasoning, and sport participation for sixth-grade girls and boys. *Dissertation Abstracts International Section A: Humanities and Social Sciences, 57*(4-A), 1539 (UMI no. 9627436)

Gibbs, J. C. (1977). Kohlberg's stages of moral judgment: A constructive critique. *Harvard Educational Review, 47*, 43-61.

Gibbs, J. C. (1979). Kohlberg's moral stage theory: A Piagetian revision. *Human Development, 22*, 89-112.

Gibbs, J. C. (2003). *Moral development and reality: Beyond the theories of Kohlberg and Hoffman.* Thousand Oaks, CA: Sage.

Gibbs, J. C. (2006). Reply [to R. Bergman's "Gibbs on Kohlberg on Dewey: An essay review of John C. Gibbs' Moral Development & Reality"]. *European Journal of Developmental Psychology, 3*, 312-315.

Gibbs, J. C., Basinger, K. S. & Fuller, D. (1992). *Moral maturity: Measuring the development of sociomoral reflection.* Hillsdale, NJ: Erlbaum.

Gibbs, J. C., Basinger, K. S., Grime, R. L.,& Snarey, J. R. (2007). Moral judgment development across cultures: Revisiting Kohlberg's universality claims. *Developmental Review, 27*(4), 443-500.

Gibbs, J. C., Clark, P. M., Joseph, J. A., Green, J. L., Goodrick, T. S. & Makowski, D. G. (1986). Relations between moral judgment, moral courage, and field independence. *Child Development, 57*, 185-191.

Gibbs, J. C., Widaman, K. F. & Colby, A. (1982). Construction and validation of a simplified, group-administrable equivalent to the Moral Judgment Interview. *Child Development, 53*, 895-910.

Gielen, U. P. (1991). Research on moral reasoning. In L. Kuhmerker (Ed.), *The Kohlberg legacy for the helping professions.* Birmingham, AL: R. E. P. Books.

Glassman, M. & Zan, B. (1995). Moral activity and domain theory: An alternative interpretation of research with young children. *Developmental Review, 15*, 434-457.

Gregg, V. R., Gibbs, J. C., & Basinger, K. S. (1994). Patterns of developmental delay in moral judgment by male and female delinquents. *Merrill-Palmer Quarterly, 40*, 538-553.

Grime. R. L. (2005). *Social perspective-taking, intimate friendship, and the adolescent transition to mutualistic moral judgment.* Unpublished doctoral dissertation, The Ohio State University.

Haggbloom, S. J., Warnick, R., Warnick, J. E., Jones, V. K., Yarbrough, G. L., Russell, T. M., et al., (2000). The 100 most eminent psychologists of the twentieth century. *Review of General Psychology, 6*, 139-152.

Harkness, S., Edwards, C. P. & Super, C. (1981). Social roles and moral reasoning: A case study in a rural African community. *Developmental Psychology, 17*, 595-603.

Hart, D. (1993). [Review of Moral maturity: Measuring the development of sociomoral reflection.] *Merrill-Palmer Quarterly, 37*, 429-437.

Hart, D., Atkins, R. & Donnelly, T. M. (2006). Community service and moral development. In M. Killen & J. G. Smetana (Eds.), *Handbook of moral development* (pp. 933-656). Mahwah, NJ: Erlbaum.

Hauer, J. (2001). *Innovation in Russian moral education: A study of the impact of a new program on the sociomoral judgment and meaning in life of Russian adolescents.* Unpublished doctoral dissertation, University of Bridgeport.

Hoffman, M. L. (1981). Perspectives on the difference between understanding people and understanding things: The role of affect. In J. H. Flavell & L. Ross (Eds.), *Social cognitive development: Frontiers and possible futures* (pp. 67-81). Cambridge, UK: Cambridge University Press.

Hubbs-Tait, L., Page, M. C., Huey, E. L., Starost, H.-J., Culpt, A. M., Culp, R. E. & Harper, M. E. (2006). Parenting quality: Confirmation of a higher-order latent construct with mothers of Head Start children. *Early Childhood Research Quarterly, 21,* 491-206.

Jeshmaridian, S. & Babakhanyan, A. (2005). *Psychological, social, and economic dimensions of Armenian youths' mental health.* Paper presented at the meeting of the World Congress of Psychiatry, Cairo.

Kohlberg, L. (1958). *The development of modes of moral thinking and choice in the years ten to sixteen.* Unpublished doctoral dissertation, University of Chicago.

Kohlberg, L. (1971). From is to ought: How to commit the naturalistic fallacy and get away with it in the study of moral development. In T. Mischel (Ed.), *Cognitive development and epistemology* (pp. 151-235). New York: Academic Press.

Kohlberg, L. (1981). *The philosophy of moral development: Moral stages and the idea of justice: Vol. 1. Essays on moral development.* San Francisco: Harper & Row.

Kohlberg, L. (1984). *Essays on moral development: Vol. 2. The psychology of moral development.* San Francisco: Harper & Row.

Kohlberg, L. (1986). A current statement on some theoretical issues. In Modgil, S., Modgil, C. (Eds.), *Lawrence Kohlberg. Consensus and controversy* (pp. 485-546). Philadelphia, PA: Falmer Press.

Kohlberg, L. (1991). My personal search for universal morality. In L. Kuhmerker (Ed.), *The Kohlberg legacy for the helping professions* (pp. 11-17). Birmingham, AL: R. E. P. books. (Original work published in 1985).

Kohlberg, L., Boyd, D. R. & Levine, C. (1990). The return of Stage 6: Its principle and moral point of view. In T. Wren (Ed.), *The moral domain: Essays in the ongoing discussion between philosophy and the social sciences* (pp. 151-181). Cambridge: MIT Press.

Kohlberg, L. & Kramer, R. (1969). Continuities and discontinuities in childhood and adult moral development. *Human Development, 12,* 93-120.

Krettenauer, T. & Becker, G. (2001). Developmental levels of sociomoral reasoning: German version of the Sociomoral Reflection Measure-Short Form [German]. *Diagnostica, 47,* 188-195.

Krivel-Zacks, G. (1995). *Effects of an intervention for facilitating social reasoning and prosocial behavior in preadolescents.* Unpublished master's thesis, University of British Columbia.

Lapsley, D. K. (2006). Moral stage theory. In M. Killen & J. G. Smetana (Eds.), *Handbook of moral development* (pp. 37-66). Mahwah, NJ: Erlbaum.

Leenders, I. & Brugman, D. (2005). Moral/non-moral domain shift in young adolescents in relation to delinquent behaviour. *British Journal of Developmental Psychology, 23,* 1-16.

Lin, W. Y. (1995). *Reliability and validity analysis of the Sociomoral Reflection Measure-Short Form (SRM-SF)* [Mandarin Chinese]. Unpublished master's thesis. Chinese Culture University, Taipei, R.O.C.

Lourenco, O. (2003). Making sense of Turiel's dispute with Kohlberg: The case of child's moral competence. *New Ideas in Psychology, 21,* 43-68.

Lourenco, O., & Macado, A., (1996). In defense of Piaget's theory: A reply to 10 common criticisms. *Psychological Review, 103,* 143-154.

Maccoby, E. E. (1980). *Social development: Psychological growth and the parent-child relationship.* New York: Harcourt Brace.

Mason, M. & Gibbs, J. C. (1993a). Role-taking opportunities and the transition to advanced moral judgment. *Moral Education Forum, 18,* 1-12.

Mason, M. & Gibbs, J. C. (1993b). Social perspective-taking and moral judgment among college students. *Journal of Adolescent Research, 8,* 109-113.

Miller, J. G. (2006). Insights into moral development from cultural psychology. In M. Killen & J. G. Smetana (Eds.), *Handbook of moral development* (pp. 375-398). Mahwah, NJ: Erlbaum.

Miller, S. A. (2007). *Developmental research methods* (3rd ed.). Thousand Oaks, CA: Sage Publications.

Moshman, D. (1998). Cognitive development beyond childhood. In W. Damon (Series Ed.) & D. Kuhn & R. S. Siegler (Vol. Eds.), *Handbook of child psychology: Vol. 2. Cognition, perception, and language* (5th ed., pp. 947-978). New York: John Wiley.

Needleman, J. (1982). *The heart of philosophy.* New York: Knopf.

Nucci, L. (2006). Education for moral development. In M. Killen & J. G. Smetana (Eds.), *Handbook of moral development* (pp. 657-683). Mahwah, NJ: Erlbaum.

Palmer, E. J. & Begum, A. (2006). The relationship between moral reasoning, provictim attitudes, and interpersonal aggression among imprisoned young offenders. *International Journal of Offender Therapy and Comparative Criminology, 50,* 446-457.

Palmer, E. J. & Hollin, C. R. (1998). A comparison of patterns of moral development in young offenders and non-offenders. *Legal and Criminological Psychology, 3,* 225-235.

Palmer, E. J. & Hollin, C. R. (2000). The inter-relations of sociomoral reasoning, perceptions of own parenting, attributions of intent, and self-reported delinquency. *Legal and Criminological Psychology, 5,* 201-218.

Palmer, E. J. & Hollin, C. R. (2001). Sociomoral reasoning, perceptions of parenting, and self-reported delinquency in young non-offenders. *Applied Cognitive Psychology, 15,* 85-100.

Peterson, A. T. (2001). The moral reasoning of child molesters: The social cognitions of sex offenders. *Dissertation Abstracts International: Section B: The Sciences and Engineering, 62*(4-B), 2073. (UMI no. 7289206)

Piaget, J. (1965). *The moral judgment of the child* (M. Gabain, Trans.). New York: Free Press. (Original work published 1932)

Rest, J., Narvaez, D., Bebeau, M. J. & Thoma, S. J. (1999). *Postconventional moral thinking: A neo-Kohlbergian approach.* Hillsdale, NJ: Lawrence Erlbaum.

Rose, M. S. (2005). A comparison of students with and without Attention-Deficit/Hyperactivity Disorder on measures of moral reasoning and executive functions. *Dissertation Abstracts International. 67*(02),

Rutter, M. (1989). Age as an ambiguous variable in developmental research: Some epidemiological considerations from developmental psychopathology. *International Journal of Behavioral Development, 12,* 1-34.

Schonfeld, A. M., Mattson, S. N. & Riley, E. P. (2005). Moral maturity and delinquency after prenatal alcohol exposure. *Journal of Studies on Alcohol, 66,* 545-555.

Sedikides, A. (1989). *Relations between role-taking opportunities and moral judgment development.* Unpublished doctoral dissertation, The Ohio State University, Columbus.

Selman, R. L. (1980). *The growth of interpersonal understanding.* New York: Academic Press.

Selman, R. L. (2003). *The promotion of social awareness: Powerful lessons from the partnership of developmental theory and classroom practice.* New York: Russell Sage Foundation.

Siddle-Walker, V. & Snarey, J. R. (2004). Race-ing moral formation. New York: Teachers College Press.

Smetana, J. G. (2006). Social-cognitive domain theory: Consistencies and variations in children's moral and social judgments. In M. Killen & J. G. Smetana (Eds.), *Handbook of moral development* (pp. 119-154). Mahwah, NJ: Erlbaum.

Snarey, J. (1985). The cross-cultural universality of social-moral development: A critical review of Kohlbergian research. *Psychological Bulletin, 97,* 202-232.

Snarey, J. (1995). In a communitarian voice: The cross-cultural expansion of Kohlbergian theory, research, and practice. In W. Kurtines & J. Gewirtz (Eds.), *Moral development: An introduction* (pp. 109-133). Boston, MA: Allyn & Bacon.

Snarey, J. & Keljo, K. (1991).*The cross-cultural expansion of moral development theory. Handbook of moral behavior and development* (Vol. 1, pp. 395-424). Hillsdale, NJ: Earlbaum.

Snarey, J. & Keljo, K. (1994). Revitalizing the meaning and measurement of moral development [essay review of Moral maturity: Measuring the development of sociomoral reflection]. *Human Development, 37,* 181-186.

Stadler, C., Sterzer, P., Schmeck, K., Krebs, A., Kleinschmidt, A. & Poustka, F. (2007). Reduced anterior cingulated activation in aggressive children and adolescents during affective stimulation: Association with temperamental traits. *Journal of Psychiatric Research, 41,* 410-417.

Stams, G. J., Brugman, D., Dekovic, M., van Rosmalen, L., van der Laan, P. & Gibbs, J. C. (2006). The moral judgment of juvenile delinquents: A meta-analysis. *Journal of Abnormal Child Psychology, 34,* 697-713.

Tang, K. (2004). *Comparison by gender of elementary school students' moral development* [Mandarin Chinese]. Unpublished master's thesis, Chinese Culture University, Taipei, R.O.C.

Travis, F., Arenander, A. & DuBois, D. (2004). Psychological and physiological characteristics of a proposed object-referral/self-referral continuum of self-awareness. *Consciousness and cognition, 13,* 401-420.

Turiel, E. (2006a). The development of morality. In W. Damon & R. M. Lerner (Series Eds.) & N. Eisenberg (Vol. Ed.), *Handbook of child psychology: Vol. 3. Social, emotional, and personality development* (6th ed., pp. 789-857). New York: John Wiley.

Turiel, E. (2006b). Thoughts, emotions, and social interactional processes in moral development. In M. Killen & J. G. Smetana (Eds.), *Handbook of moral development* (pp. 7-36). Mahwah, NJ: Erlbaum.

Turiel, E. & Smetana, J. (1998). *Limiting the limits on domains: A commentary on Fowler and Heteronomy.* Merrill-Palmer Quarterly, 44, 293-312.

Van Someren, D. A. (2000). The relationship between religiousness and moral development: A critique and refinement of the Sociomoral Reflection Measure – Short Form of Gibbs, Basinger, and Fuller. *Dissertation Abstracts International, 61*(03), 887B.

Wasanga, C. M. (2004). *An investigation of the development of moral reasoning of school children in Nairobi and Makueni District.* Unpublished doctoral dissertation, Kenyatta University.

White, C. (1983, February). *Moral reasoning in Bahamian and United States adults and children.* Paper presented at the annual meeting of the Society for Cross-Cultural Research, Washington, D.C.

Woods, L. N. & Jagers, R. J. (2003). Are cultural values predictors of moral reasoning in African American adolescents? *Journal of Black Psychology, 29,* 102-118.

Zwart-Woudstra, H. A., Meijer, T., Fintelman, M. & Van IJzendoorn, M. H. (1993) *Vragenlijst sociale relaties* [Dutch translation of the Sociomoral Reflection Measure-Short Form]. Unpublished manuscript, Center for Child and Family Studies, Leiden University.

John C. Gibbs
Ohio State University, Columbus, USA
Karen S. Basinger
Urbana University, USA
Rebecca L. Grime
Washington & Jefferson College, Washington, USA
John R. Snarey
Emory University, Atlanta, USA

MARVIN W. BERKOWITZ, WOLFGANG ALTHOF, VAL D. TURNER
& DANIEL BLOCH

DISCOURSE, DEVELOPMENT, AND EDUCATION

Educators, especially those focusing on the socio-moral development of students, have long emphasized the role of classroom discourse. Fritz Oser, for example, has emphasized the notion of discourse in moral problem solving since the 1970s (e.g., Oser, 1981, 1984). He emphasized that moral discourse is "the common denominator that should encompass different elements of moral learning" (Oser, 1986, 919).

Oser further expanded the application of discourse to teachers' professional discourse (e.g., Oser & Althof, 1993). Discourse also was central in the work of Lawrence Kohlberg, who inspired much of Oser's work. Kohlberg's theory of moral reasoning development led to two major educational models. The moral dilemma discussion approach focused on teacher facilitated classroom discussions of open-ended moral problems (Berkowitz, 1985). In the "Just Community" approach to democratic schooling, the "moral dilemma discussion" becomes a school wide institution (Power, Higgins, & Kohlberg, 1989). Small group discussions, school-wide democratic "town meetings", and student/faculty judiciary committees all take the hypothetical moral discourse of moral dilemma discussions to a school-wide and real world level. It emphasizes the procedural and discourse related aspects of democratic decision-making and moral learning more strongly (Oser & Althof, 2001).

In the late 1970s and early 1980s, Kohlberg's work was informed by Jürgen Habermas' theory of communicative action (Althof, 2003; Habermas, 1981) and his discourse ethics. In this process, claims and propositions have to be justified in a way that can be "accepted by free and equal persons seeking fair terms of cooperation" (Gutmann & Thompson, 2004, 3). Actors are expected to give reasons, and reasons of other parties must be explicitly considered. This, again, requires that reasons in the process must be accessible and understandable to everyone involved. "It would not be acceptable, for example, to appeal only to the authority of revelation, whether divine or secular in nature" (ibid., p. 4). Cohen (1996) discusses which considerations count as reasons in this context and he strongly points to the argumentative nature of the exchange:

"In an idealized deliberative setting, it will not do simply to advance reasons that one takes to be true or compelling: such considerations may be rejected by others who are themselves reasonable. One must instead find reasons that are compelling to others, (...) aware that they have alternative reasonable commitments, and knowing something about the kinds of commitments that

Fritz Oser & Wiel Veugelers (eds.), Getting involved, 189–201.

they are likely to have – for example, that they may have moral or religious commitments that impose what they take to be overriding obligations. If a consideration does not meet these tests, that will suffice for rejecting it as a reason. If it does, then it counts as an acceptable political reason" (p. 100).

In other words, the quality of reasoning is critical. Deliberative reasoning "operates on the reasoning of another" (Berkowitz & Gibbs, 1983) – it is, in our terms, transactive. We will spend the rest of this chapter examining this particular line of theory and research about developmental discourse.

TRANSACTIVE DISCUSSION

Origin and Overview

Although it aligns with the more philosophically justified discourse work of Oser, the model of transactive discussion actually comes out of basic psychological theory and research. Based heavily on the work of Piaget and Kohlberg, it has become clear to both social scientists and educators that students encounter the world through the lens that is their current system for making meaning of the world, in this case the socio-moral world. This lens is their stage of socio-moral cognition, for Kohlberg their stage of moral reasoning. The stages themselves, whether Piagetian stages of logico-mathematical understanding, Oser's stages of religious thinking, Selman's stages of interpersonal reasoning, or Kohlberg's stages of moral reasoning, develop in an invariant and universal sequence from less differentiation and integration of cognitive elements to greater differentiation and integration. Much is now known about this developmental process. The structures (stages) evolve into more adequate ways of knowing as a product of the interaction between one's direct grappling with the world (either alone or with others) and the world that one is trying to comprehend. One key feature of the process of development is the "stretching" and challenging of one's current meaning-making structure through social discourse, most typically peer discourse in the classroom setting. It is this feature that leads to an interest in the discursive structures of classroom practice and student interaction. In education, this discursive developmental process can be manifested as formal moral dilemma discussions (Berkowitz, 1985) or more generally through pedagogical strategies such as cooperative learning or the inquiry method in science education (Berkowitz & Simmons, 2003).

As Berkowitz and Simmons (2003) pointed out in their discussion of the role of peer moral discourse in science education, "The core of this process for structural development (i.e., the development of more effective ways of thinking about the world) is social interaction about cognitive problems, whether logical, physical, or social. ...The basic tenets of such an educational approach are the same: implementing developmentally stimulating programs of peer discussion in the classroom that serve both the goals of science education and the goals of character and citizenship education" (p. 129).

This focus on peer discussion arose in the 1970s in a set of parallel but independent ways. A group of colleagues of Piaget in Switzerland, from the perspective of social psychology, used peer discussion, less as a phenomenon of interest in itself but rather more as a method to promote the development of Piagetian logico-mathematical stages of reasoning (e.g., Doise, Mugny & Perret-Clermont, 1975; Mugny, Perret-Clermont & Doise, 1981). Nonetheless, despite their focus on the discursive nature of their pedagogical and laboratory interventions, this group was pioneering the use of peer discourse in a cognitive-developmental framework. At the same time in the US, Scott Miller and Celia Brownell (1975) were engaged in a very similar project, still without the focal interest in the interactive methods used to promote structural development.

At about the same time, working not within the logico-mathematical development domain but rather within the moral development field, Berkowitz, Gibbs, and Broughton (1980) studied the same social processes from the perspective of uncovering Piagetian disequilibration processes. They had noted that all of the effective intervention strategies were centrally focused on peer moral dilemma discussion methods. The assumption was that such interactions (whether in pairs in the laboratory or in whole classroom discussions in schools) produced cognitive conflict in the discussants from the interpenetration of their different meaning structures and that this experience led to the stimulation of structural development within the individual. The goal was to observe and measure the overt social aspects of this developmental process, but this initial work merely inferred it from the individual effects of participation in the discussions. This initial project failed, as individuals did not seem to overtly express measurable signs of internal disequilibrium. So the project shifted to identifying the discursive conditions that were theoretically anticipated to promote internal experiences of disequilibrium, and hence individual cognitive-structural development.

This work was in synchrony, at times intentionally and at times coincidentally, with other researchers who had begun to turn their attention to the direct study of this interactive process by examining the social interactions and creating models for coding and analyzing them. In the US, Damon and Killen (1982), Bearison (1982), and Berkowitz and Gibbs (1983) and, in Germany, Max Miller (1980a,b; 1984) all began to codify the features of peer discussion that could be related to the structural development that had been observed to result from peer discussions.

The most detailed and developed model of peer discursive processes undergirding structural development was the work on transactive discussion by Berkowitz and Gibbs (1983). The term "transactive" was inspired by the work of Dewey and Bentley (1949) in which they philosophically contrast "interaction" with "transaction." The former is defined, using a physical model, as "presentation of particles or other objects organized as operating upon one another" and transaction as "functional observation of full system" (p. 75). The emphasis was on understanding the world through interdependent and interpenetrative systems, rather than as mechanical directional interactions. Transactive discussion was defined as peer discussion where one discussant manifests discursive reasoning about another discussant's reasoning. They identified 18 different discursive behaviors that represented a range of transaction (see Table 1). The highest forms were called Operational as they represented a transformation of the other's reasoning (e.g., by logically critiquing it, by integrating it with one's own reasoning, by extending it). The lower form was called Representational as it was more a re-presentation of the other's reasoning (e.g., a paraphrase or a juxtaposition with one's own reasoning).

Table 1. Table of Transacts

A. Representational Transacts
    1. *Feedback Request (R):* Do you understand or agree with my position?
    2. *Paraphrase(R)*
       (a) I can understand and paraphrase your position or reasoning.
       (b) Is my paraphrase of your reasoning accurate?
    3. *Justification Request (R)* Why do you say that?
    4. *Juxtaposition (R):* Your position is X and my position is Y.
    5. *Dyad Paraphrase (R):* Here is a paraphrase of a shared position.
    6. *Competitive Juxtaposition (R):* I will make a concession to your position, but also reaffirm part of my position.

B. Hybrid Transacts
    7. *Completion (R/O):* I can complete or continue your unfinished reasoning.
    8. *Competitive Paraphrase (R/O):* Here is a paraphrase of your reasoning that highlights its weakness.

C. Operational Transacts
    9. *Clarification (O):*
       (a) No, what I am trying to say is the following.
       (b) Here is the clarification of my position to aid in your understanding.
   10. *Competitive Clarification (O):* My position is not necessarily what you take it to be.
   11. *Refinement (O):*
       (a) I must refine my position or point as a concession to your position or point (subordinative mode).
       (b) I can elaborate or qualify my position to defend against your critique (superordinative mode).
   12. *Extension (O):*
       (a) Here is a further thought or an elaboration offered in the spirit of your position.
       (b) Are you implying the following by your reasoning?
   13. *Contradiction (O):* There is a logical inconsistency in your reasoning.
   14. *Reasoning Critique (O):*
       (a) Your reasoning misses an important distinction, or involves a superfluous distinction.
       (b) Your position implicitly involves an assumption that is questionable (premise attack).
       (c) Your reasoning does not necessarily lead to your conclusion/opinion, or your opinion has not been sufficiently justified.
       (d) Your reasoning applies equally well to the opposite opinion.
   15. *Competitive Extension (O):*

(a) Would you go to this implausible extreme with your reasoning?

(b) Your reasoning can be extended to the following extreme, with which neither of us would agree.

16. *Counter Consideration (O):* Here is a thought or element that cannot be incorporated into your position.

17. *Common Ground/Integration (O):*

(a) We can combine our positions into a common view.

(b) Here is a general premise common to both of our positions.

18. *Comparative Critique (O):*

(a) Your reasoning is less adequate than mine because it is incompatible with the important consideration here.

(b) Your position makes a distinction that is seen as superfluous in light of my position, or misses an important distinction that my position makes.

(c) I can analyze your example to show that it does not pose a challenge to my position.

Berkowitz and Gibbs (1983) first introduced this concept and the model in a study of undergraduate dyads who engaged in a series of moral dilemma discussions (Berkowitz, Gibbs, & Broughton, 1980). The dialogues were transcribed and analyzed and from a sub-set the transactive coding scheme was generated. When applied to the rest of the dialogues, it was found that dyads manifesting more transactive discussion, especially operational transaction, showed more pre-test to post-test development of Kohlbergian moral reasoning.

Two subsequent studies examined the development of transactive discourse competencies themselves. Berkowitz and Gibbs (1985) report a study (Gibbs, Schnell, Berkowitz, & Goldstein, 1983) of the relation of formal operational reasoning (Inhelder & Piaget, 1958) to higher order transaction in 40 undergraduate dyads. It was found that higher order transaction was rarely evident in dyads where members were not fully formal operational, and were present in most dyads were both members were fully formal operational.

In a later cross-sectional study of the presence and types of transactive discussion, Berkowitz, Oser, and Althof (1987) first examined the developmental data from the current research on transaction finding some evidence of a developmental pattern in the frequency of transaction across subjects from seven to 24 years of age. The reviewed studies were quite varied, but the suggestive summative findings prompted a cross-sectional study of dyads from six to twenty years of age. Furthermore, the sample was cross-sectional with half of each age group in Switzerland and half in the US. There was a clearly significant increase in total transaction with increasing age, and the pattern held similarly across both cultures. Finally, this pattern was also found separately for operational and representational transaction. These studies suggest that transaction not only fosters development, but is developmental itself.

Over the quarter century since Berkowitz and Gibbs (1983) introduced the concept of transitive discussion, research has accumulated demonstrating (1) the conditions that promote the use of transactive discussion and (2) that the presence of transactive discussion in peer interactions is related to the development of cognitive structures, especially moral reasoning structures. This body of research will be briefly reviewed here.

Research on the Effects of Transactive Discussion

Research on the relation of transactive discussion to development and learning began with Berkowitz and Gibbs' (1983) report that more transactive discussion in adolescent peer moral discussions resulted in greater moral reasoning development. This finding of the relation of transactive discussion to moral reasoning development was replicated by Kruger (1992) in girls' discussions with either peers or mothers, by Pratt et al. (1999) in adolescent discussions with parents, and by Walker and Taylor (1991) in children's and adolescents' discussions with their parents. Kruger reported that the effect held for both peer and mother-daughter discussions, but the change was greater for peer dyads as they engaged in more active transactive discussions. Pratt et al., only found the effect for discussions with fathers and not for discussions with mothers. Overall, these four studies suggest that peer and/or parent-child discussions of moral issues can promote moral reasoning development in both children and adolescents when the discussions are rich in transactive discourse behaviors. In a complex and creative study of the role of classroom group discussion on the development of the capacity to coordinate perspectives, Mischo (2005) reports results that support these findings about moral reasoning. Although Mischo combines transaction with other variables, he reports that "the interaction process promoting perspective coordination may be characterized by the combination of an explanation-oriented discussion style and trait-like subject-related consensus-motive" (p. 58). When peer discussion was focused on the interpenetration of reasons and justifications (competitive operational transaction) and discussants were motivated to reach consensus (consensus instructions often foster more discussion and transaction), subjects showed more development in social perspective coordination competency.

The findings in the socio-moral domain have led other researchers to study the effects of transactive discussion on other aspects of development and on learning. Four studies examined the impact of transaction on the development of scientific reasoning and one on the development of mathematical reasoning. In the first study applying transaction in the science education sphere, Azmitia and Montgomery (1993) reported that children who used more transaction in peer science discussions showed better scientific problem-solving skills. In two studies of children's peer collaborative discussion of science topics, Teasley (1997) reported that dyads who engaged in more transactive discussion showed more improvement in peer collaborative scientific problem solving than dyads that did not use much transaction. More recently, Russell (2006), working with high school students reported that peer transactive discussion correlated with the development of reasoning about genetics. Similarly, in working with college students' and their abilities to understand mathematical proofs, Blanton, Stylianou, & David (2003) reported that whole-class discussions rich in transaction resulted in greater gains in students' ability to construct mathematical proofs than discussion with less transaction.

A study by Miell and MacDonald (2000) expanded the content sphere further. Same gender pairs of 11 and 12 year old boys and girls were observed working on a collaborative musical composition. Teachers rated the ultimate composition and their ratings were significantly related to the amount of transaction in the dyads, with higher ratings related to more transaction.

Taken together, these studies suggest that transactive discussion is a robust developmental stimulant for a range of cognitive outcomes (moral reasoning, scientific reasoning, mathematical reasoning, musical composition), in a range of contexts (peer dialogues, parent-child discussions, whole-class discussions), and for a range of age groups (children through college students).

Conditions for Transactive Discussion

As no models exist for the training of transactive discussion, all relevant research capitalizes on its spontaneous usage. It is therefore helpful to understand the conditions under which transactive discussion is more or less likely to occur. Relationship between discussants appears to be an important variable in the likelihood of transactive discussion. Kruger and Tomasello (1986) report that young girls use more transaction, especially operational higher order transaction (which Berkowitz and Gibbs, 1983, revealed as the more developmentally powerful form of transaction) with peers than with mothers, but that they used more reactive (responsive) transacts with mothers because mothers asked for clarification more than peers did. Parents seem to adjust their levels and kind of transaction when talking to children. Walker and Taylor (1991) noted that parents used less operational transaction and more representational transaction when discussing the child's real life dilemma than when discussing hypothetical dilemmas. Santolupo and Pratt (1994) found that mothers used higher level transaction with sons than with daughters in discussion of political issues.

Relationships in peer discussions also were relevant to levels and types of transaction. Azmitia and Montgomery (1993) found that children used more transaction in moral discussions with friends than with acquaintances. Miell and MacDonald (2000) similarly found that children used more transaction with friends than with non-friends, in this case when working on a collaborative musical composition. Bloch (2002) found more transaction in social dilemma discussions with different age child dyads than in same age dyads. Leadbeater (1988), in adolescent and adult peer dialogues, found different types of transacts used in same gender female, same gender male, and mixed gender dialogues. Female dyads tended to focus on the partner and be non-competitive, male dyads tended to focus on self and partner and be competitive, and mixed gender dyads tended to focus on the partner both competitively and non-competitively. Faulkner et al. (2000) reported that similarity in ability impacted transaction. Working with 9 and 10 year olds on scientific reasoning tasks, they reported that mixed ability pairs used more transaction than did same ability pairs.

Developmental level and age are also related, not surprisingly, to the amount and type of transaction one produces. Berkowitz and Gibbs (1985) reported that high levels of Piagetian logical development were related to higher levels of transaction. Santolupo and Pratt (1994) found older adolescent girls using more transaction than younger adolescent girls, but did not find this difference for boys.

Other conditions for transactive discussion were studied as well. Teasley (1997) examined the amount of transaction generated when working with a partner or working alone (self talk). Faulkner et al. (2000) compared child dyads working with a computer simulation or with physical apparatus on scientific problems, and found more transaction in the groups working with computers. Similarly, Anderson et al. (2000) reported more transaction in undergraduate psychology major group project work when the groups worked with a computer program designed to assist group process. Finally, Blanton, Stylianou, and David (2003) found that teachers could effectively scaffold undergraduate whole-class discussion of mathematical issues to facilitate more transactive discussion.

While more research is needed, these studies suggest that conditions can be manipulated to increase the amount of transactive discussion in children and adolescents, and in dyads and larger groups. These findings are encouraging for educators who wish to reap the developmental benefits of discussion based pedagogies such as cooperative learning, class meetings, and moral dilemma discussions.

Transaction and Family Dynamics

It has already been noted above that research on the role and nature of transaction in parent-child discourse is different than in peer discourse. The first such investigation was done by Sally Powers (1982; Powers et al., 1983) with a non-psychiatric and a psychiatric sample of high school-aged adolescents and their parent(s). Using an adapted version of the transact model and combining it with measures of affective interactive behaviors (e.g., rejection, support), Powers created the Developmental Environments Coding Scheme (DECS). Parent child discussions of moral issues were related to child ego development. A key finding is that the competitive style of peer transactive discussion does not seem to be as developmentally rich when manifested between adolescent and parent. It is only when there is a high level of emotional support from the parents that competitive cognitive transaction is related to higher levels of ego development. Using the DECS, Walker and his colleagues engaged in two similar longitudinal studies of the relation of parent-child moral discussions to child moral reasoning development. Walker and Taylor (1991), in a two year longitudinal study of mother-father-child triads with children aged 6-16 (Time 1), reported that moral development was greatest for interactions where the topic was a real child-focused dilemma (not a hypothetical one) and where family interactions were characterized by high moral stage disparity and more supportive parents and representational transaction. Unfortunately the sample size was small in this cluster of families (n=4). Nonetheless the pattern partially replicates Powers' and Krugers' findings. In a later four year longitudinal study of children (ages 9-17), a parent and a friend, Walker, Hennig and Krettenauer (2000), again using the DECS, found that development over the four year period was related to aspects of the parent-child discussions of the child real moral dilemma (but neither the hypothetical nor the real parent moral dilemmas) and aspects of the peer hypothetical and child-focused real dilemmas. The pattern most strongly related to child moral reasoning development was for high representational transaction, high moral stage disparity between parent and child, and low informative discourse. This was somewhat different from the peer discussions where development. For hypothetical dilemma discussion, development was predicted by high representational transaction, low informative discourse, and high interfering behavior. For the peer child-focused real dilemma discussions, development was predicted by high representational transaction and low informational discourse. In essence, it is clear that the power of peer discourse comes from a more conflictual style than does the power of parent-child discourse. Children seem to be able to benefit from cognitive tussling with peers, but need a supportive parental context to reap similar developmental benefits.

Positioning and Justifying Developmental Discussion in Education

There are clearly numerous justifications for the study and implementation of developmentally rich forms of peer discussion, such as transactive discussion, in educational settings. Oser has highlighted ethical concerns of procedural justice in classrooms and schools, as well as pedagogical pragmatics. In doing so, he has partly positioned school discourse in a philosophical perspective of communicative ethics. Berkowitz and Gibbs, and their followers, have focused largely on the developmental power of such forms of school discourse and have positioned transactive discussion in a cognitive-structural theoretical framework.

Such forms of discourse can be positioned and justified in other ways as well. Prior to the genesis of the terminology and the conceptualization of transactive discussion, Russian psychological theorists such as Lev Vygotsky were exploring conceptual frames that also can accommodate some or all of the research on transactive discussion (cf. Turner & Berkowitz, 2005). Using Vygotsky's work, Wood, Bruner, and Ross (1976) developed the metaphor of "scaffolding" to better understand the learning process occurring in tutorial settings. Bruner would go on to expand upon the concept of scaffolding by associating it with cognitive development and advancement within the "zone of proximal development" (ZPD). With the Vygotskian emphasis on language as the primary mediational tool involved in cognitive development, it is not surprising that the growing socio-cultural paradigm would resonate with the construct of transactive discussion.

Following Bruner's example of observing tutorial settings, King (1989, 1994) developed Guided Peer Questioning, where learners are taught to ask and answer each other's questions. This work, with its obvious linkage to scaffolding and the ZPD, would evolve and expand into what King (1997), in a strange and seemingly unrelated coincidence, called Transactive Peer Tutoring. King (1998) speaks of language based "transactive cognitive partnerships" (p. 59) that support and encourage scaffolding as well as the learner's ability to begin controlling and regulating their own learning process. King positioned this outcome in Vygotsky's view of initially other-directed learning that can be appropriated and internalized by the learner. While King is coincidentally using the transaction term, it is being used in a way that is highly consistent with that of Berkowitz and Gibbs (1983).

Others, some already mentioned above, have used the Berkowitz and Gibbs concept of transaction from a socio-cultural perspective. Santolupo and Pratt (1994) found levels of transactive discussion correlated to the adolescent's age, gender, and family parenting style, within a Vygotskian framework. Faulkner, Joiner, Littleton, Meill, and Thompson (2000) investigated the effect of different learning task formats on children's collaborative activity. Faulkner et al. found that specific task formats substantially increased levels of transactive discussion between the students as well as their improvement in scientific reasoning. The discussion of these findings was supportive of the socio-cultural importance attached to tools for mediating collaborative learning.

Goos (1999) has worked to apply socio-cultural theory to the specific task of mathematics education. In Goos, Galbraith, and Renshaw (2002), the conceptualization of the ZPD is expanded through the introduction of "collaborative ZPD" (p. 196) terminology. According to this way of thinking, zones of proximal development are always two-way in character, with all participants appropriating ideas and actions of others. Goos et al. found that level of transactive discussion was key to creating a collaborative ZPD and inversely, metacognitive failure was primarily due to the inability of students to engage with each other's ideas. For the Goos et al. study of higher level secondary mathematics students, it was the "challenge" created by transactive discussion which created a collaborative ZPD that permitted students to rise to the level of thinking like mathematicians.

Operating from a socio-cultural perspective, Blanton and Stylianou (2002) looked to determine how students appropriate strategies for advanced mathematical reasoning. They determined that transactive discussions were a critical factor but also suggested that the ability to enter into such discourse could substantially be increased by teacher scaffolding through the use of transactive prompts encouraging dialogue. Such an assessment is interesting in raising the idea that transactive discussion is effective in raising reasoning levels, but to be effective in the classroom, teaching, practicing, and modeling this type of discourse may be required. Again, transactive discussion was seen as a key facilitator to cognitive development within the ZPD.

It may well be accurate to state that the constructivist paradigm emphasizes the processes involved in the construction of knowledge and that the socio-cultural paradigm stresses the transmission of knowledge. It is also true that Piaget saw the issues of conflict and disequilibrium as central to cognitive growth where Vygotsky centered upon the cooperative outcome of discourse. To claim that these factors, however, are the defining differences between these paradigms is probably a gross oversimplification. Both paradigms are broad enough to integrate all of these factors even though there may be differences in emphasis. The truly remarkable factor is that both the constructivist paradigm and the socio-cultural paradigm found within transactive discussion an educational practice capable of enlightening and expanding our understanding of cognitive processes both theoretical and practical. And, as Oser reminds us, such discourse is also the basis of ethical and effective schools and classrooms.

REFERENCES

Althof, W. (2003). Implementing „just and caring communities" in elementary schools: A Deweyan perspective. In W. Veugelers & F.K. Oser (Eds.), *Teaching in moral and democratic education* (pp. 153-172). Bern: Peter Lang.

Anderson, A., Cheyne, W., Foot, H., Howe, C., Low, J. & Tolmie, A. (2000). Computer support for peer-based methodology tutorials. *Journal of Computer Assisted Learning, 16*, 41-53.

Azmitia, M. & Montgomery, R. (1993). Friendship, transactive dialogues, and the development of scientific reasoning. *Social Development, 2*, 202-221.

Bearison, D.J. (1982). New directions in studies of social interactions and cognitive growth. In F.C. Serafica (Ed.), *Social-cognitive development in context* (pp. 199-221). New York: Guilford.

Berkowitz, M. (1985). The role of discussion in moral education. In M.W. Berkowitz and F. Oser (Eds.), *Moral education: Theory and application* (pp. 197-218*)*. Hillsdale, N.J.: Lawrence Erlbaum.

Berkowitz, M.W. & Gibbs, J.C. (1983). Measuring the developmental features of moral discussion. *Merrill-Palmer Quarterly, 29* (4), 399-410.

Berkowitz, M. & Gibbs, J. (1985). The process of moral conflict resolution and moral development. In M. Berkowitz (Ed.), *Peer conflict and psychological growth. New directions for child development, no. 29* (pp. 71-84). San Francisco: Jossey-Bass.

Berkowitz, M.W., Gibbs, J.C. & Broughton, J.M. (1980). The relation of moral judgment stage disparity to developmental effects of peer dialogues. *Merrill-Palmer Quarterly, 26*, 341-357.

Berkowitz, M.W., Oser, F. & Althof, W. (1987). The development of sociomoral discourse. In W.M. Kurtines & J.L. Gewirtz (Eds.), *Moral development through social interaction* (pp. 322-352). New York: John Wiley.

Berkowitz, M.W. & Simmons, P. (2003). Integrating science education and character education. The role of peer discussion. In D. L. Zeidler (Ed.), *The role of moral reasoning on socioscientific issues and discourse in science education* (pp. 117–138). Dordrecht, The Netherlands: Kluwer.

Blanton, M. L. & Stylianou, D. A. (2002). Exploring sociocultural aspects of undergraduate students' transition to mathematical proof. In *Proceedings of the 24th Meeting for PME-NA* (Vol. 4, pp. 1673-1680). Athens, GA.

Blanton, M.L., Stylianou, D.A. & David, M. (2003). The nature of scaffolding in undergraduate students' transition to mathematical proof. In N. Pateman, B. Dougherty, & J. Zilliox (Eds.), *Proceedings of the 2003 Joint Meeting of PME and PMENA*, (vol.2, pp. 113-120), Honolulu, Hawaii: Center for Research and Development Group, University of Hawaii.

Bloch, D. (2002). *Transaktive Diskussion zwischen altersheterogenen Peers. Empirische Untersuchung zum Einfluss von Altersunterschieden auf die Transaktivität in dyadischen Diskussionen zwischen Grundschulkindern.* Unveröffentlichte Lizentiatsarbeit, Philosophische Fakultät der Universität Freiburg, Schweiz.

Cohen, J. (1996). Procedure and substance in deliberative democracy. In S. Benhabib (Ed.), *Democracy and difference. Contesting the boundaries of the political (pp. 95-119).* Princeton, N.J.: Princeton University Press.

Damon, W. & Killen, M. (1982). Peer interaction and the process of change in children's moral reasoning. *Merrill-Palmer Quarterly, 28*, 347-367.

Dewey, J. & Bentley, A. F. (1949). *Knowing and the known*. Boston: Beacon Press.

Doise, W., Mugny, G. & Perret-Clermont, A.N. (1975). Social interaction and the development of cognitive operations. *European Journal of Social Psychology, 5*, 367-383.

Faulkner, D., Joiner, R., Littleton, K., Miell, D., & Thompson, L. (2000). The mediating effect of task presentation on collaboration and children's acquisition of scientific reasoning. *European Journal of Psychology of Education, 15* (4), 417-430.

Gibbs, J. C., Schnell, S., Goldstein, D. & Berkowitz, M. W. (1983). *Formal reasoning as a necessary condition for transactive socio-moral discourse*. Paper presented at the Biennial Conference of the Society for Research in Child Development, Detroit.

Goos, M. (1999). Scaffolds for learning: A sociocultural approach to reforming mathematics teaching and teacher education. *Mathematics Teacher Education and Development, 1*, 4-21.

Goos, M., Galbraith, P., & Renshaw, P. (2002). Socially mediated metacognition: Creating collaborative zones of proximal development in small group problem solving. *Educational Studies in Mathematics, 49*(2), 193-223.

Gutmann, A. & Thompson, D. (2004). *Why deliberative democracy?* Princeton and Oxford: Princeton University Press.

Habermas, J. (1981). *Theorie des kommunikativen Handelns*. 2 Bände. Frankfurt/M.: Suhrkamp.

Inhelder, B. & Piaget, J. (1958). *The growth of logical thinking from childhood to adolescence*. New York: Basic Books.

King, A. (1989). Effects of self-questioning training on college students' comprehension lectures. *Contemporary Educational Psychology, 14*, 1-16.

King, A. (1994). Guiding knowledge construction in the classroom: Effects of teaching children how to question and how to explain. *American Educational Research Journal, 30*, 338-368.

King, A. (1997). ASK to THINK – TEL WHY: A model of transactive peer tutoring for scaffolding higher-level complex learning. *Educational Psychology, 32*, 221-235.

King, A. (1998). Transactive peer tutoring: Distributing cognition and metacognition. *Educational Psychology Review, 10* (1), 57-74.

Kruger, A.C. (1992). The effect of peer and adult-child transactive discussions on moral reasoning. *Merrill-Palmer Quarterly, 38* (2), 191-211.

Kruger, A.C. & Tomasello, M. (1986). Transactive discussions with peers and adults. *Developmental Psychology, 22* (5), 681-685.

Leadbeater, B.J. (1988). Relational processes in adolescent and adult dialogues: Assessing the intersubjective context of conversation. *Human Development, 31*, 313-326.

Miell, D. & MacDonald, R. (2000). Children's creative collaborations: The importance of friendship when working together on a musical composition. *Social Development, 9*, 348-369.

Miller, M. (1980a). *Learning how to contradict and still pursue a common end – The ontogenesis of moral argumentation*. Unpublished manuscript, Max Planck Institute, Starnberg, Germany.

Miller, M. (1980b) Zur Ontogenese moralischer Argumentationen. *Zeitschrift für Literaturwissenschaft und Linguistik, 38/39*, 58-97.

Miller, M. (1984). Kollektive Lernprozesse. Studien zur Grundlegung einer soziologischen Lerntheorie. Frankfurt/M.: Suhrkamp.

Miller, S.A. & Brownell, C.A. (1975). Peers, persuasion, and Piaget: Dyadic interaction between conservers and non-conservers. *Child Development, 46*, 992-997.

Mischo, C. (2005). Promoting perspective coordination by dilemma discussion. The effectiveness of classroom group discussion on interpersonal negotiation strategies of 12-year-old students. *Social Psychology of Education, 8*, 41-63.

Mugny, G., Perret-Clermont, A.N. & Doise, W. (1981). Interpersonal coordinations and sociological differences in the construction of the intellect. In G.M. Stephenson & J.M. Davis (Eds.), *Progress in applied social psychology* (Volume 1, pp. 315-343). New York: John Wiley & Sons.

Oser, F. (1981). *Moralisches Urteil in Gruppen – Soziales Handeln – Verteilungsgerechtigkeit. Stufen der interaktiven Entwicklung und ihre erzieherische Stimulation.* Frankfurt/M.: Suhrkamp.

Oser, F. (1984). Cognitive stages of interaction in moral discourse. In W. M. Kurtines & J. L. Gewirtz (Eds.), *Morality, moral behaviour and moral development* (pp. 159-174). New York: John Wiley and Sons.

Oser, F. (1986). Moral education and values education: The discourse perspective. In M.C. Wittrock (Ed.), *Handbook of research on teaching, 3rd edition (pp. 917-941).* Chicago: Rand McNally.

Oser, F. & Althof, W. (1993). Trust in advance: on the professional morality of teachers. *Journal of Moral Education, 22.* 253-275.

Oser, F. & Althof, W. (2001). Die Gerechte Schulgemeinschaft: Lernen durch Gestaltung des Schullebens. In W. Edelstein, F. Oser & P. Schuster (Eds.), *Moralische Erziehung in der Schule. Entwicklungspsychologie und pädagogische Praxis (pp. 233-268).* Weinheim and Basel: Beltz.

Power, C., Higgins, A. & Kohlberg, L. (1989). *Lawrence Kohlberg's approach to moral education: A study of justice and community in the high school.* New York: Columbia University Press.

Powers, S.I. (1982). *Family interaction and parental moral development as a context for adolescent moral development.* Unpublished doctoral dissertation, Harvard University.

Powers, S.I., Hauser, S.T., Schwartz, J.M., Noam, G.G.,& Jacobson, A.M. (1983). Adolescent ego development and family interaction: A structural-developmental perspective. In H.D. Grotevant, & C.R. Cooper (Eds.), *New directions for child development: Adolescent development in the family* (No.22, pp. 5-25). San Francisco: Jossey-Bass.

Pratt, M.W., Arnold, M.L., Pratt, A.T. & Diessner, R. (1999). Predicting adolescent moral reasoning from family climate: A longitudinal study. *Journal of Early Adolescence. 19* (2), 148-175.

Russell, H.A. (2006). Transactive discourse during assessment conversations on science learning. *Dissertation Abstracts International. 66* (9-A), p. 3214.

Santolupo, S. & Pratt, M.W. (1994). Age, gender, and parenting style variations in mother-adolescent dialogues and adolescent reasoning about political issues. *Journal of Adolescent Research. 9* (2), 241-261.

Teasley, S.D. (1997). Talking about reasoning: How important is the peer in peer collaboration? In L.B. Resnick, R. Saljo, C. Pontecorvo, & R. Burge (Eds.), *Discourse, tools, and reasoning: Essays on situated cognition* (NATO ASI Series F, Vol. 160, pp. 361-384). Berlin: Springer.

Turner, V.D. & Berkowitz, M.V. (2005). Scaffolding morality: Positioning a socio-cultural construct. *New Ideas in Psychology, 23,* 174-184.

Walker, L.J., Henning, K.H. & Krettenauer, T. (2000). Parent and Peer Contexts for Children's Moral Reasoning Development. *Child Development, 74* (4), 1033-1048.

Walker, L.J. & Taylor, J.H. (1991). Family interactions and the development of moral reasoning. *Child Development, 62,* 264-283.

Wood, D.J., Bruner, J. & Ross, G. (1976). The role of tutoring in problem solving. *Journal of Child Psychology and Psychiatry, 17,* 89-100.

Marvin W. Berkowitz, Wolfgang Althof, Val D. Turner & Daniel Bloch
University of Missouri-St. Louis, USA
Daniel Bloch
University of Fribourg, Switzerland

PART 3

**TEACHERS ENGAGEMENT
FOR DEMOCRATIC SCHOOL**

ELIZABETH C. VOZZOLA & KENNETH J. LONG

TEACHING THE POLITICAL PSYCHOLOGY OF GENOCIDE:

Aiming for Activists and Ending up with Cynics

To explore whether honors students would demonstrate significant increases in political activity and interest after taking a team-taught political psychology course, we replicated portions of Isbell's (2003) study of her course's effect on undergraduates' political knowledge, behavior and interest. Isbell had noted the growth in programs and courses in political psychology (Sears & Funk, 1991) and hoped her article would encourage more psychology departments to offer the course. As a political scientist and a psychologist teaching in an honors program with a capstone interdisciplinary seminar, we saw great potential for team teaching a course that integrated theory and research from our respective disciplines. We hypothesized that upper division honors students, a select sample encouraged throughout their schooling to think "in more global, flexible and creative ways" (Isbell, p. 149), would show even stronger gains in political knowledge, behavior, and interest than did Isbell's sample. This paper compares the goals, content, and format of the two courses as well as the pretest and posttest scores for political knowledge, behavior and interest.

Our initial simple replication study led to additional research questions when, after an intensive study of past ethno-political conflicts, we offered our honors students the chance to suggest a class response to the ongoing genocide in Darfur. During class discussions of past ethno-political conflicts and genocides, students had frequently asked "How could the world allow that to happen?" Thus, we were startled when students responded that there was really nothing they could do about the genocide in the Sudan that would make a difference.

Westheimer and Kahne's (2004) conception of three kinds of citizens provides a lens for an analysis of the gaps between our goal of encouraging justice-oriented citizens (who critically assess structures and seek out and address areas of injustice), the students' interest in being personally responsible citizens (who act responsibly in their communities, obey the law and volunteer) and the pretest/posttest measure's grounding in the concept of participatory citizens (active members of community organizations who know how government works).

Westheimer and Kahne (2004) conceptualize citizenship as a call to personal responsibility, participation, or, best of all, a justice-orientation. The personal respon-

Fritz Oser & Wiel Veugelers (eds.), Getting involved, 205–213.

sibility model of citizenship, they argued, assumes that to solve social problems requires merely that citizens be of good character, honest, law-abiding, and responsible. Citizens contribute to society through actions such as obeying laws, working, paying taxes, and making contributions. The participatory model requires more. It assumes that, to solve social problem, citizens must actively participate and assume leadership positions within established community systems and structures. Participatory citizenship requires activism in the sense of knowing how things work and assuming the initiative to organize strategies and efforts to get things done within the current political structures.

By contrast, the justice-orientation model of citizenship assumes that, to solve social problems, citizens must question and change the current political systems and structures assumed to be the root causes of injustices (Westheimer & Kahne, 2004). The essence of this concept of citizenship is critical analysis of social, political, and economic structures that encourages the possibility of working outside of these structures or, more radically still, working to change or even overturn these structures. This model contains the prospect of everything from reformist initiatives to revolutionary ones.

After describing our course and the results of measures of student learning and satisfaction, we discuss differences between students' and professors' conceptualizations of political action. We end with ideas for ways to revise course assignments and bring in activist speaker role models who might motivate students to move beyond the academic approach to politics modeled by their professors and actually get involved.

COURSE GOALS AND STRUCTURE

This course examined contemporary topics in political psychology. Broad topic areas included the politics of personality, the psychology of national politics, and the psychology of international politics. We designed assignments to promote reflection on how politics, with all its flaws, attempts to craft solutions to societal moral dilemmas. By the end of the course, students had to demonstrate their ability to apply theories and research from the discipline of political psychology to topics such as political leadership, campaign strategies, genocide, and international conflict.

The course had an enrollment of 24 female honors students. As did Isbell, we conducted the course as an advanced undergraduate seminar that met for 75 minutes twice a week for 15 weeks. We did not require the two prerequisites to Isbell's class, social psychology and research methods.

Course Outline

Like Isbell, we reviewed the few texts in print specifically devoted to political psychology (e.g., Kressel, 1993; Sears, Huddy & Jervis, 2003) and used the International Society for Political Psychology (ISPP) Web site (http://ispp.org/ppsyl.html) to collect ideas from other political psychology syllabi. We decided to give students an overview of the field using several articles from an older political psychology text (Kressel, 1993) and chose Chirot and Seligman's text on ethno political warfare (2001) and Molly Ivin's and Lew Dubose's collection of political essays (2001), *Shrub*, to cover the major course themes of political leadership, campaign strategies, genocide, and international conflict. Students also subscribed on line to the *New York Times* (www.nytimes.com) to follow current news about the U.S. elections and ongoing ethno political conflicts. Although Isbell's (2003) course focused primarily on the political process (e.g, voter's personalities, political socialization, political information processing and political attitudes, persuasion and propaganda), our team-taught effort devoted only five classes to those topics. After several introductory readings about the field of political psychology, we spent the next four classes discussing readings about Milgram's experiment (Blass, 1999), right wing authoritarianism (Altemeyer, 1996), the Stanford Prison Experiment (Zimbardo, Maslach, & Hanley, 1999) and the psychology of evil (Zimbardo, 2000). Students also spent three classes reading about the politics of madness (e.g., Foucault,1973) before moving into 13 classes devoted to the psychology of ethno political conflict and genocide (Chirot & Seligman, 2001).

Course Activities and Requirements

Both Isbell's non honors course and our honors course emphasized active learning techniques (e.g., Johnson & Ware, 2000; McKeachie, 2002). Both also required students to read and integrate literature from psychology and political science, to analyze and evaluate a presidential campaign, to write critical reflections (short papers for Isbell, journal reactions to *New York Times* material and a final integrative paper in the honors course), to watch videos that illustrated political psychology concepts, and to take written measures (quizzes in Isbell's course and a midterm exam in ours). A major difference between the two courses was that Isbell brought in politicians and guest speakers whereas the honors course required students to form groups to conduct further research on ethno political conflicts covered in the Chirot and Seligman (2001) text and present their findings to the class. Class requirements were listed in the syllabus as follows: 20% Journals, 20% Midterm Exam, 20% Group Presentation (selected ethno political conflict), 20% Final Integrative Paper (4-6 pages), and 20% Class participation (Attendance, participation in class conversations and contributions of relevant articles influenced this component).

METHOD

The course had an enrollment of 24 female honors students (Isbell taught 8 men and 14 women) with a mean age of 20.8 years (compared to Isbell's mean of 22.05 years) and mean grade point average of 3.7. The majority of the students were White (88% as compared to 91% in Isbell's class) and most were graduating seniors (63%,

207

as compared to 82% in Isbell's). Unlike Isbell's students, who were all psychology majors, the students came from a broad range of majors including math, English, sociology, psychology and nursing. Thirty-eight percent, compared to 30% of Isbell's sample, had taken a previous course in political science.

All 24 students completed pretests and 17 completed posttests that collected demographic data and asked about their voting behavior; political activism; and attention to television news, newspapers and local and national politics. Twenty-two students completed a midterm evaluation giving open-ended feedback about aspects of the course that were working well for them and about what we could be doing better. Twenty of the students completed a teacher-designed final course evaluation rating the effectiveness of class assignments and activities and the effectiveness of the teachers. They also completed a course evaluation form administered by the Honors program that repeated the midterm questions and asked students to rate the level of challenge, professors' fairness and organization and the most important learning they took away from the class. All measures were anonymous.

RESULTS

Changes in Students' Political Knowledge, Behaviors and Intentions, and Interest in Politics

Despite 38% of the students having taken a previous class in political science, they were similar to Isbell's sample in having "minimal political knowledge, and little or no background in American government" (p. 150). Most indicated that they took this course to meet the honors capstone requirement rather than out of an interest in the topic. Isbell measured growth in political knowledge with a specific pretest/posttest measure. Our evaluation of the growth in knowledge used open-ended course evaluations of significant learning. Numerous comments noted that the course was "eye-opening" and "makes you think a lot about things that aren't necessarily offered in other classes." One student noted "I felt I learned more about politics and current events than I ever did before. I do not feel so 'clueless' about our world and government." Another wrote that her most important learning was that "I have been perceiving [sic] the world differently than it actually works." In their initial class, the majority of students admitted to little interest in politics but by the final evaluation, comments such as "Pay attention to politics—it's so important to our lives!" captured the growth in interest and knowledge.

As shown in Table 1, after taking the course, students were more likely to report engaging in, or intending to engage in political behaviors. The largest gains occurred in student reports of registering to vote (100% v. 72%), signing a political petition (64.7% v. 33.3%) and trying to convince someone to vote for a particular candidate (70.6% v. 50%), $t(7) = 2.45$, $p < .05$, Cohen's $d = . 4.12$.

Table 1. Percentages of Students Reporting Political Behaviors and Intentions in January and May 2004

	January	May
1. Are you registered to vote?	79%	100%
2. Are you eligible to vote?	88%	82%
3. Did you vote in the last election?	42%	50%
4. Have you ever worn a button or put a bumper sticker on your car in support of a political candidate?	13%	24%
5. Have you ever worked in a local organization to solve some community problems?	46%	47%
6. Have you ever signed a political petition?	33%	65%
7. Have you ever tried to convince someone to vote for a a particular political candidate?	50%	71%

Table 2 shows increases in students' reported mean level of political interest. The largest gain surfaced in terms of devoting more attention to national politics. On scale from 0 (*not at all*) to10 (*a great deal*), the class means for attention to items such as attending to national politics moved from 4.63 (SD = 2.53) to 7.25 (SD = 1.52). Answers to the four political interest questions evidenced significant gains in student attention to news and politics by the end of the course, $t(3) = -10.06$, $p <$ .005, Cohen's $d = .97$.

Table 2. Students' Mean Level of Political Interest in January and May 2004

	January	May
	M SD	M SD
How much attention do you pay to political news when:		
You watch the evening news?	4.13 2.88	6.35 2.96
You read the newspaper?	4.08 2.86	6.59 2.58
Overall, how much do you follow:		
National politics?	4.63 2.53	7.24 1.52
Local politics?	3.38 2.37	5.00 2.69

Note: Students rated items from 0-10 where 0 = not at all and 10 = a great deal

Students Evaluations of the Course

Students evaluated the course positively. Their mean global evaluation, using 1 as the lowest possible rating and 10 as the highest, gave the course a rating of 8.9 and the teachers a rating of 9.2. Both categories had a mode of 10. Isbell used global ratings of how much students enjoyed the course and how important a learning experience they found it to be. She reported a means of 9.89 (SD = .46) and 9.84 (SD = .50) respectively. Among the specific students ratings of teaching effectiveness in our honors class, mean scores ranged from 8.7 (effective communication) to 9.7 (enthusiasm). Honors professors design capstone courses to challenge students and student ratings of the effort they put into the course suggest that the level was indeed challenging. Nineteen of the 20 students who filled out the two final evaluation measures (95%) reported putting "quite a bit" or "a great deal" of effort into the class. In contrast, 58% of Isbell's students found the workload "moderate—just about right," a "goodness of fit" that may have contributed to the high global ratings of her course.

Table 3 shows that our students identified class lectures and discussions as the most useful course aspects with 100% and 95% respectively endorsing these activities as quite helpful or extremely helpful. The group presentations on ethno political conflict and genocide had the lowest ratings with 50% of the students finding them either *not very helpful* or *only somewhat helpful*. Isbell measured both the usefulness and enjoyment of class assignments and activities (thought papers, speaker reaction papers, class discussions, quizzes, assigned readings, final class paper and videos). On a scale of 1-10, her students' ratings ranged from a low of 6.37 (SD = 3.00) for "thinking about and writing the final class paper" to a high of 9.58 (SD = 0.84) for the usefulness of class discussions.

Table 3. Students' Evaluations of Usefulness of Specific Course Aspects

Assignment/activity	Not Very Helpful	Somewhat Helpful	Quite Helpful	Extremely Helpful
Reading: a. *Shrub*	5%	15%	35%	40%
b. *Ethnopolitical Conflict*	10%	25%	45%	20%
New York Times Journals	10%	20%	55%	15%
Lectures	-	-	10%	90%
Class Discussions	-	5%	25%	70%
Group Presentations	5%	45%	25%	20%

N = 20

CONCLUSION

Results from the pretest/posttest measures, along with course evaluation data, demonstrated that, like Isbell's non honors group of psychology majors, our honors women "learned a great deal, enjoyed the course and became more . . . politically interested." (Isbell, p. 148) Both groups of students gave particularly high ratings to class discussions, which suggests that this teaching technique is one of the most effective and enjoyable ways to help students better understand topics in political psychology.

Like Isbell's students, the honors students in the current study became more politically active in terms of political participation markers such as registering to vote or signing a petition. We interpreted these findings with caution given that only 17 of the 24 students handed in the posttest measure. In an attempt to encourage honest feedback, we had kept the surveys anonymous and compiled mean data. In the future, we would code measures and analyze data only from students who completed both surveys. Although it is possible that the data were skewed by only the most politically active and interested students returning surveys, it was more likely that it simply reflects a drop in attendance on the day we collected the last survey. Moreover, the two course evaluations suggest that the movement towards greater interest and taking politically responsible actions like registering to vote were indeed widespread.

However, despite apparent progress in political interest and minimal forms of political participation, the students' inability to take significant social change action suggests little to no growth in terms of becoming justice-oriented citizens. It seems likely that the professors' implicit rather than explicit conception of a justice-oriented conception of citizenship (Westheimer & Kahne, 2004) undermined their efforts to motivate students to change root causes of injustice. Students, whose comments throughout the course suggested that most held an implicit personal responsibility model of citizenship, were satisfied to be the honest, responsible; law abiding citizens required by this model and thus felt little motivation to work outside social, political, and economic structures to effect radical change. To muddy the analysis further, we had replicated measures from a study of a course whose content is best described under Westheimer and Kahne's third conception of citizenship, the participatory model. Isbell structured a course and assignments which encouraged the active participation within established community and political structures that are the hallmark of this citizenship model.

Our course clearly was conceptualized from the perspective of Westheimer and Kahne's (2004) justice-oriented model. Although admirable in the broad scope of activism envisioned (we believe that this is the most robust of the three models of citizenship), our endorsement of this model posed a unique potential pitfall: by stressing the importance of critical assessment we may have inadvertently fostered *more* criticism and *less* activism. The "less robust" models of citizenship, without the emphasis on working outside or against the prevailing systems, at least do not have to suffer the distractions of critical analysis. Courses from less radical perspectives can focus on encouraging personal contributions and organizational efforts within established social and political structures without having to take so much time away to question these structures themselves. In the final analysis, we believe such approaches are less fruitful in large part because our current political environment is so constraining, prone as it is to gridlock or, at best, merely incremental changes. Still, we must admit that we spent far more time criticizing the world than undertaking efforts to change it. We also must admit that trying to change the world is a far more daunting endeavor than just trying to understand it; it is easy to doubt that much can be done to change things in significant ways. However, we could have done more to argue that although efforts at changing the world rarely come with any certainty of, or even likelihood of, success, the ethical person makes the effort anyway simply because it is the right thing to do.

Perhaps it is not surprising that, in the final analysis, our students emulated what we modeled (abstract criticism of injustices in our country and in the world) rather than what we merely voiced (and at times only subtly at that): the need for them to take the initiative to become actively engaged in an effort to promote social justice in some sustained and thoughtful way. Maybe it is too much to expect undergraduates to become much more than mere armchair activists. Maybe this result is especially likely if we as instructors spend the bulk of our time in front of them engaged in the purely academic pursuits of argument, analysis, lecture, and discussion, despite the topic at hand being the ubiquitous nature of social injustice and the need for change. Given the lack of any actual practice or models of activism, it is no wonder that when we asked them what they could do personally to take some steps (however modest) aimed at the ultimate goal of trying to encourage a halt to the genocide in Darfur, all we received were blank stares and a presumed disbelief that they could do anything of any consequence.

Our analysis suggests to us that despite the barriers involved, we may have better success in fostering activism if we revise two structural details of the course design. First, one major difference between our course and Isbell's was her use of outside speakers. It is possible that exposure to politicians and activists who have succeeded as change agents could have provided powerful role models for our students. Kohlberg (1984) held that cognitive complexity and role-taking ability were necessary but not sufficient prerequisites for moral development. Our students had two academics modeling moral critique rather than moral actions—role models for cynicism rather than activism. Second, the strong course focus on genocide may have inadvertently left the students with a sense of despair rather than possibility. Even the relatively successful cases we studied (e.g. South Africa's peace and reconciliation efforts) stressed the fragility of the situation and the on-going possibility of future violence. Bandura's concept of selective moral disengagement (Bandura, 2002) and Lifton's concept of psychic numbing (1982) remind us that people frequently need to psychically distance themselves from the horrific details of human evil. One student wrote that her primary learning from the course was that "The world is a terrible place. . . ."

We are considering changing the primary focus of the class from ethno-political conflict to political leadership as a way to stress our goal of promoting agency. When we do deal with issues of genocide, it will be important to complement our political analysis with stories of human engagement (e.g. showing the film *Hotel Rwanda*, 2004, or assigning readings from Oliner and Oliner's 1992 study of Holocaust rescuers).

In the final analysis, our students were probably like most college students. They seemed to come to the course with little knowledge of, or experience with, politics. They seemed to think more highly of the importance of being kind than of being politically conscious, critical, and even, perhaps, confrontational. They seemed quick to see the problems with politicians and vested interests but a good bit more reticent about realizing how their own inactivity could be part of the problem. We designed the course with many objectives but among them was a desire to encourage our students to take the first few baby steps in trying to change the world. Sadly, in the end, as a class, perhaps all we achieved was questioning the world and perhaps, hopefully, the first few baby steps in trying to change ourselves into people who someday will not only criticize injustice but also confront it as well.

REFERENCES

Altemeyer, R. (1996). *The authoritarian specter.* Cambridge, Harvard University Press.

Bandura, A. (2002). Selective moral disengagement in the exercise of moral agency. *Journal of Moral Education 31,* 101-119.

Blass, T. (1999). The Milgram paradigm after 35 years: Some things we now know about obedience to authority. In T. Blass (Ed.), *Obedience to authority: Current perspectives on the Milgram paradigm* (pp. 35-59). Mahwah, NJ: Erlbaum.

Chirot, D. & Seligman, M. (Eds.). (2001). *Ethnopolitical warfare: Causes, consequences, and possible solutions.* Washington, DC: American Psychological Association.

Foucault, M. (1973). *Madness and civilization: A history of insanity in the age of reason.* (Richard Howard, trans.) New York City: Vintage Books.

Isbell, L. M. (2003). Teaching an undergraduate course in political psychology. *Teaching of Psychology 30,* 148-153.

Ivins, M. & Dubose, L. (2000). *Shrub: The short but happy political life of George W. Bush.* New York City: Vintage Books.

Johnson, D. & Ware, M.E. (Eds.) (2000). *Handbook of demonstrations and activities in the teaching of psychology, Vol. II.* New Jersey: Lawrence Erlbaum.

Kohlberg, L. (1984). *Essays on moral development: Vol. 2. The psychology of moral development.* San Francisco: Harper & Row.

Kressel, N. J. (Ed.). (1993). *Political psychology: Classic and contemporary readings.* New York: Paragon.

Lifton, R. J. (1982). Beyond psychic numbing: A call to awareness. *American Journal of Orthopsychiatry 52,* 619-629.

McKeachie, W. J. (2002). *McKeachie's teaching tips: Strategies, research, and theory for university teachers.* Boston: Houghton Mifflin Company.

Oliner, S. P. & Oliner, P. M. (1992). *The altruistic personality: Rescuers of Jews in Nazi Europe.* New York: The Free Press.

Sears, D. O. & Funk, C. L. (1991). Graduate education in political psychology. *Political Psychology, 12,* 345-362.

Sears, D. O., Huddy, L. & Jervis, R. (Eds.). (2003). *The Oxford handbook of political psychology.* New York: Oxford University Press.

Westheimer, J. & Kahne, J. (2004). What kind of citizen? The politics of educating for democracy. *American Educational Research Journal 4,* 237-269.

Zimbardo, P. (2000). The psychology of evil. *Eye on Psi Chi, 5,* 16-19.

Zimbardo, P.G., Maslach, C. & Hanley, C. (1999). Reflections on the Stanford prison experiment: Genesis, transformations, and consequences. In T. Blass (Ed.), *Obedience to authority: Current perspectives on the Milgram paradigm* (pp. 193-297). Mahwah, NJ: Erlbaum.

Elizabeth C. Vozzola & Kenneth J. Long
Saint Joseph College, West Hartford, Connecticut, USA

CHI-MING (ANGELA) LEE

STUDENT AND TEACHER PERCEPTION OF MORAL ATMOSPHERE IN TAIWAN SCHOOLS

ABSTRACT

The purpose of this quantitative study was to explore student and teacher perception of school moral atmosphere in Taiwan's elementary and junior high schools. Students and teachers from 48 schools filled in a questionnaire entitled "School as Caring Community Profile II". The key findings were: 1. SCCP scores of both students and teachers were above the median. Students and teachers displayed a positive attitude toward their schools. 2. Students and teachers had significantly different sense of school moral atmosphere in sub-scales for "perceptions of student respect for one another" (IA) and "Students' perceptions of student friendship and belonging" (IB). However, there was no significant difference between students' and teachers' scores in "perceptions of students' shaping of their environment" (IC). 3. Teachers' scores in "Perceptions of Support and Care By and For Faculty/ Staff" (IIA) and "Perceptions of Support and Care By and For Parents" (IIB) were higher than in sub-scales IA, IB and IC. 4. There was significantly different sense of "perceptions of school caring community for students" (sub-scales IA, IB and IC) between students and teachers on the following points: female, elementary schools, junior high schools, schools in northern Taiwan and in central Taiwan respectively. 5. Factors which most significantly affected both student and teacher perception of school moral atmosphere were their educational level, school district and school size. 6. Factors which significantly affected teachers' perceptions of school environment (SCCP total) were their gender, club leader experience in college/university, educational level of teaching, participation in administrative jobs in teaching school, teaching school type, area and sizes, and their teaching experience. Accordingly, the author offered some recommendations on how to improve students' and teachers' mutual understanding, and enhance their school moral atmosphere.

PURPOSES

Formal moral curricula had existed in Taiwan's compulsory educational system (ages 6-14) and played a central role in moral education for the past several decades. In 1997, Taiwan's government instituted a revolutionary educational reform, which had a tremendous impact on elementary and junior high schools. The "*Guidelines*

Fritz Oser & Wiel Veugelers (eds.), Getting involved, 215–226.

for a 9-Year Joint Curricula Plan" was promulgated in 1998 and scheduled to be fully implemented by the end of 2004. It recognized the absence of formal moral curricula in Taiwan's schools. Therefore, how to make up the loss and provide other strategies (such as school moral life and atmosphere) are challenges to educational systems. Several educational policies were set up by Ministry of Education, e.g. *"Character Education Improvement Project"* and *"Human Rights and Friendly Campus"*. In addition, the concepts of school-based curricula, community building and modern civil society have been formally adopted in recent educational reforms.

To build school as a moral community, which is democratic, plural and intimate, is desirable. The moral atmosphere of the school becomes a key factor influencing the moral development of young people in Taiwan's present educational system. Consequently, this study focused on exploring student and teacher perception of school moral atmosphere in Taiwan's elementary and junior high schools. The purposes were as follows: to conduct a thorough analysis of the theoretical basis of school moral atmosphere, to examine the similarities and differences in perception of school moral atmosphere between students and teachers, to understand whether students and teachers have different perceptions in their school moral atmosphere due to their gender, learning/ teaching educational level (elementary school and junior high school), or school location (northern, central, southern and eastern Taiwan), to understand what factors influence student and teacher perception of school moral atmosphere; and to make recommendations for the improvement of teacher education and moral education, both in theory and in practice.

THEORETICAL FRAMEWORK AND PRIOR RESEARCH

One of educational goals in Taiwan's school system is to cultivate students as morally educated people. The school moral life and atmosphere is a powerful and effective influence on students' moral aspect. From the 1970s, several dissertations, e.g. Scharf, 1973; Reimer, 1977; Wasserman, 1977; and Jennings, 1979 postulated a relationship between institutional climate and individual moral development. (Power et al, 1989) And further, F.C. Power, A. Higgins and L. Kohlberg in 1989 compiled their past research results about moral culture and published a book, *"Lawrence Kohlberg's Approach to Moral Education."* In the introduction of that book, the authors showed clearly that their approach to moral education was simple and direct. They attempted to establish schools, which did more than teach about democratic citizenship, were establishing themselves as democratic societies. (Power et al, 1989) Thus, they began to foster the sense of community throughout the entire school day.

In 1993, P.W. Jackson and his fellows published a book entitled, *"The Moral Life of Schools"*, which gave a more concrete dimension to moral life and atmosphere. They described their moral life project as seeking to investigate the ways in which moral considerations have permeated the everyday life of schools and classrooms. (Jackson, 1993, xiv) In the book, the author arrayed a set of eight categories along a continuum ranging from the more readily visible to the less visible. They were in descending order: moral instruction as a formal part of the curriculum; moral instruction within the regular curriculum; rituals and ceremonies; visual displays with moral content; spontaneous interjection of moral commentary into ongoing activity; classroom rituals and regulations; the morality of the curricular substructure; and expressive morality within the classroom. (Jackson, 1993, 4-29) That proved moral education had broad meaning, including direct and indirect, apparent and concealed methods.

In contrast to Kohlberg's moral development and just community, caring-oriented atmosphere was originally borrowed from C. Gilligan's female "voice" and morality of caring. The publication in 1982 of Gilligan's book, "*In a Different Voice: Psychological Theory and Women's Development*", marked the emergence of a discussion of gender difference which had become the basis for re-examination of the assumptions of psychological theory generally. In her view, the morality of caring and responsibility was premised in nonviolence, while the morality of justice and rights was based on equality. The morality of caring emphasized interconnectedness and emerged to a greater degree in girls owing to their early connection in identity formation with their mothers.

Broadly speaking, caring was extended beyond personal relationships to a general recognition of the interdependence of self and other, accompanied by a universal condemnation of exploitation and hurt. "Voice" was a metaphor and it was a powerful psychological instrument and channel, connecting inner and outer worlds. Voice was also a key for understanding the psychological, social and cultural order. (Gilligan, 1993) Three characteristics of voices were noteworthy: First, voices combined both emotion and content. Voices were embodied in a way that theories were not. Second, voices were described assessed in a wide range of terms, most of which had little to do with true and false or right and wrong. Third, voices might be different without excluding one another. Their voices might blend in a choir and interact with one another. (Hinman,1994, 329) Voice of caring not only represents female or individual morality, but is also a central tenet in school moral life and atmosphere.

Additionally, N. Noddings published a series of major works regarding ethics of care, for examples, "*Caring: A Feminine Approach to Ethics and Moral Education*" (1984), " *The Challenge to Care in Schools*" (1992) and " *Educating Moral People*" (2002). She emphasized caring is a kind of encounter not only in a restricted community. She also indicated caring is a mutually satisfying relation between caregiver and cared-for persons, including both girls and boys. (Noddings, 2002) However, she distinguished two-folds of caring sources, which are natural caring and ethical caring. She mentioned "*Because we (lucky ones) have been immersed in relations of care since birth, we often naturally respond as careers to others... Further, ethical caring requires reflection and self-understanding. We need to understand our own capacities and how we are likely to react in various situations.*" (Noddings, 2002, 15) Therefore, she pointed out moral education is an essential part of an ethic of care. The four components of moral education as Noddings' theory are modeling, dialogue, practice and confirmation. (Noddings, 2002)

Furthermore, several centers and organizations have been implementing programs of caring community in the US. For example, Character Education Partnership (CEP) addressed "*Eleven Principles of Effective Character Education*". One of the principles was "to create a caring school community." What that meant was that "*all school members form caring attachments to one another, and involves developing caring relationships among students (within and across grade levels), among staff, between students and staff, and between staff and families. These caring relationships foster both the desire to learn and the desire to be a good person.*" (http://www.character.org/principles/)

Besides, the Caring School Community (CSC) program, which has been set into action by Developmental Studies Center (DSC) for more than fifteen years, is a nationally recognized, research-based K–6 program that builds classroom and school-wide community. This program emphasized that "*students have basic psychological needs for autonomy, belonging, and competence. When children are in a school that fulfills these three needs, they will be intrinsically motivated to learn. Likewise, children's motivation is undermined to the degree to which any of these conditions is not met.*" (http://www.devstu.org/csc/scientific.html)

In short, the importance of positive social context/culture, including justice and caring, of the school to effective educational practice and students' moral development from both in theory and practice has been revealed. Consequently, school moral atmosphere is a central factor of moral education.

METHOD

Participants and procedure

The main method of this inquiry was through questionnaire. The questionnaire was translated and derived from "School as Caring Community Profile II" (SCCPII, 2001 version), which represent perceptions of school moral atmosphere. 2701 (valid questionnaire) students (5th graders in elementary schools and 2nd graders in junior high schools) and 313 (valid questionnaire) teachers of the same 48 schools around Taiwan participated in this study in the periods from February to April 2002 and from April to May 2004 respectively. The author carried out the statistical results using SPSS-PC 12.0 software, including analyses of t-test and one-way ANOVA.

Iinstrument

The *School as a Caring Community Profile—II (SCCPII)* is an instrument developed by Professor T. Lickona and Dr. M. Davidson at the Center for the 4th and 5th Rs (Respect and Responsibility), SUNY Cortland, USA to help schools assess themselves as caring communities. (http://www.cortland.edu/character/sccp-ii.htm) It is a 43-question survey in a 5-point Likert format, which may be taken by both children and adults. Confirmatory factor analysis supports the hypothesized breakdown into five sub-scales. Sub-IA, IB and IC are for both students and teachers, while sub-IIA and IIB are only for teachers. Sub-IA and IC are more justice-oriented and the others are more caring-oriented content. Reliability alphas in the USA samples range from .73 to .86 for youth and from .73 to .88 for adults. In this study, consistency reliability alphas were from .72 to .79 for Taiwan's students and from .862 to .951 for Taiwan's teachers. Some examples of SCCP-II survey and its subscale are as follows (see table1):

Table 1. Some Examples of SCCP-II survey and its sub-scale

Sub-scale IA. Perceptions of Student Respect (9 items)
 e.g. Students treat classmates with respect.
 e.g Students are disrespectful toward their schoolmates. (Reverse)
 e.g. Students respect the personal property of others.
Sub-scale IB. Perceptions of Student Friendship and Belonging (9 items)
 e.g. Students share what they have with others.
 e.g. Students help each other, even if they are not friends.
 e.g. Students work well together.
Sub-scale IC.Perceptions of Students' Shaping of Their Environment (8 items)
 e.g. Students resolve conflicts with fighting, insults, or threats. (Reverse)
 e.g. When students do something hurtful, they try to make up for it
 e.g. When students see another student being picked on, they try to stop it.
Sub-scale IIA: Perceptions of Support and Care by and for Faculty/Staff (10 items)
 e.g. Students can talk to their teachers about problems that are bothering them.
 e.g. Teachers go out of their way to help students who need extra help.
 e.g. In this school you can count on adults to try to make sure students are safe.
Sub-scale IIB. Perceptions of Support and Care By and For Parents (7 items)
 e.g. Parents show that they care about their child's education and school behaviour.
 e.g. Students are disrespectful toward their parents in the school environment. (Reverse)
 e.g. Teachers treat parents with respect.

RESULT

The important findings of this study were as follows:

1. SCCP (IAIBIC) scores of students (mean=3.23), SCCP (IAIBIC) scores of teachers (mean=3.07) and SCCP (total) scores of teachers(mean=3.48) were all above median score. Although both students and teachers displayed a positive attitude toward their schools, there was significant difference between students' and teachers' scores in SCCP (IAIBIC). (see table 2) Students' scores were higher than teachers' scores in SCCP (IAIBIC). SCCP (IAIBIC) scores of teachers were lower than SCCP (total) scores of teachers.

2. Students and teachers had significantly different scores in sub-scales for "perceptions of student respect for one another" (IA) (student mean=3.27, teacher mean=2.89, students scored higher than teachers) .There was no statistical significance between students' and teachers' scores in "Students' perceptions of student friendship and belonging" (IB) (student mean=3.21, teacher mean=3.15) and "perceptions of students' shaping of their environment" (IC) (student mean=3.22, teacher mean=3.19). (see table 2)

Table 2. The SCCP scale and sub-scale scores of students (s) and teachers (t)

Scale		Mean	SD	Sig
SubIA. Perceptions of student respect				
	s:	3.27	0.624	p[xxx] .001
	t:	2.89	0.284	
SubIB. Perceptions of student friendship and belonging				
	s:	3.21	0.644	n.s.
	t:	3.15	0.393	
SubIC. Perceptions of students' shaping of their environment				
	s:	3.22	0.715	n.s.
	t:	3.19	0.504	
SCCP IAIBIC score				
	s:	3.23	0.600	p[xxx] .001
	t:	3.07	0.290	
SCCP total score	t:	3.48	0.460	

3. Teachers' scores in "perceptions of support and care by and for faculty/staff" (IIA) (mean=3.77, SD=0.528) and "perceptions of support and care by and for parents" (IIB) (mean=3.74, SD=0.545)were higher than in sub-scales IA (mean=2.89, SD=0.284), IB (mean=3.15, SD=0.393) and IC (mean=3.19, SD=0.504). The score of "perceptions of support and care by and for faculty/staff"(IIA) by teachers was the highest among them.

4. There was significantly different sense of "perceptions of school caring community for students" (sub-scales IA, IB and IC) between students and teachers on the following points: female, elementary schools, junior high schools, schools in northern Taiwan and in central Taiwan respectively. Students scored higher than teachers in all of above points. In particular, female students scored highest in gender variable both students and teachers, as well as elementary students in educational level variable, northern Taiwan students in school location variable and small school students in school size variable. (see table 3-6)

Table 3. The difference of SCCP (IAIBIC) scores in gender between students and teachers

variable		N	Mean	SD	Sig
male					
	s:	1388	3.18	0.601	n.s.
	t:	86	3.07	0.293	
female					
	s:	1313	3.29	0.584	p^{xxx} .001
	t:	197	3.06	0.294	

Table 4 the difference of SCCP (IAIBIC) scores in educational level between students and teachers

variable		N	Mean	SD	Sig
elementary school					
	s:	1285	3.31	0.610	p^{xx} .01
	t:	136	3.17	0.265	
junior high school					
	s:	1416	3.17	0.572	p^{xxx} .001
	t:	148	2.97	0.290	

Table 5 the difference of SCCP (IAIBIC) scores in school location between students and teachers

variable		N	Mean	SD	Sig
northern Taiwan (metropolis)					
	s:	1240	3.31	0.597	p^{xxx} .001
	t:	120 3	.07	0.314	
central Taiwan					
	s:	557	3.27	0.562	p^{xx} .01
	t:	73	3.06		0.280
southern Taiwan					
	s:	727	3.10	0.597	n.s.
	t:	70	3.01	0.258	
eastern Taiwan (rural district)					
	s:	177	3.12	0.567	n.s
	t:	19	3.26	0.274	

Table 6. The difference of SCCP (IAIBIC) scores in school size between students and teachers

variable		N	Mean	SD	Sig
small (less than 13 homeroom classes)					
	s:	94	3.40	0.500	n.s.
	t:	17	3.25	0.277	
middle (13-36 homeroom classes)					
	s:	1144	3.23	0.589	p^{xx} .01
	t:	96	3.05	0.288	
large (more than 36 homeroom classes)					
	s:	1463	3.23	0.606	p^{xxx} .001
	t:	171	3.05	0.295	

5. Factors which most significantly affected both student and teacher perceptions of school moral atmosphere (SCCP-IAIBIC) were their educational level (p^{xxx} .001, elementary > junior high), school location (p^{xxx} .001, northern & central > southern & eastern) and school size (p^{x} .05, small > middle & large). In other words, Elementary school students and teachers perceived their school atmosphere more positively than junior high school students and teachers did. Northern and Central Taiwan school students and teachers perceived their school atmosphere more positively than their counterparts in southern and eastern Taiwan schools. Small school students and teachers perceived their school atmosphere more positively than in middle or large schools did. In addition, students' gender significantly affected their perceptions of school moral atmosphere (p^{xxx} .001, female > male). Female students perceived their school atmosphere more positively than male students. There was no significant difference for teachers' scores of school moral atmosphere when referenced by gender.

6. Factors which significantly affected teachers' perceptions of school environment (SCCP total) were their gender, educational level of teaching, participation in administrative jobs in teaching school, teaching school type, area and size, and their teaching experience. More specifically, male teachers' SCCP score (mean=3.55, SD=0.433) was higher than female's (mean=3.42, SD=0.478); elementary school teachers' score (mean=3.6,SD=0.410) was higher than junior high school's (mean=3.34,SD=0.483); score of teachers with administrative jobs (mean=3.63, SD=0.460) was higher than those without (mean=3.39, SD=0.456); score of teachers teaching in private schools (mean=3.82, SD=0.307) was higher than those in

public schools (mean=3.43, SD=0.466). In addition, score of teachers teaching in small schools was higher than those teaching in middle and large schools; and score of teachers who had more than 16 year teaching experience was higher than those whose teaching experience was less than 5 years. In particular, SCCP total scores of teachers teaching in eastern and central Taiwan were higher than those teaching in northern and southern Taiwan. This result was different from SCCP-IAIBIC scores mentioned above. There were no significant difference among several factors, including learning moral curricula in college/university, club leader experience in college/university, interaction between professor and student in college/university experience, educational background, in-service educational training and teaching subjects.

DISCUSSION

1. Students and teachers perceived above median score about school moral atmosphere Statistical analyses in this study indicated SCCP II scores of students and teachers were above median score. M. Davidson's original research on SCCP in 1998 showed that elementary school teachers' average score was 2.44 while students' average score was 3.04 (Davidson, 1998). Accordingly, Taiwan's student and teacher perception of school moral atmosphere scored higher than that of the USA. In other words, both Taiwan's students and teachers displayed a positive attitude toward their schools. This finding fits well in Taiwan's educational context. Students from elementary to high schools have their own homeroom classes in which 30-40 fixed classmates study and play together all school day. Consequently, most students have strong sense of belonging to their homeroom class and close relationship with other classmates. Elementary and high school teachers in Taiwan have moderate salaries and prestige, so they often devote themselves to teaching over a long period of time, usually until retirement. They usually have close attachment and deep identification with their schools, too. Hence, the score of their perceptions of school environment was above median score. Particularly, the scores of sub-scale IIA (Perceptions of Support and Care By and For Faculty/Staff) and IIB (Perceptions of Support and Care By and For Parents) were high. This is similar to Roberts et. al (1995) paper which was shown *"For teachers, sense of community is largely determined by relationships with other teachers and participation in activities outside of the classroom (e.g. faculty meetings)."*

2. Similarity and difference between students' and teachers' scores in SCCP (IAI-BIC) Statistical analyses in this study revealed SCCPII –IAIBIC scores of students and teachers were significantly different, particularly in sub-scale for "perceptions of student respect for one another" (IA). Students scored higher than teachers in both SCCP-IAIBIC and sub-scale IA. This is like Davidson (1998) research result, too. In other words, teachers and students usually have their own "voices". Besides, this study discovered that female students scored highest in gender variable both students and teachers, as well as elementary students in educational level variable, northern Taiwan (metropolitan) students in school location variable and small school students in school size variable. This is similar to Roberts et. al (1995) research results which showed female students scored higher than male and sense of community among students declined significantly with increasing grade. However, there was no significant difference in sub-scales IB and IC scores between students and teachers.

3. Factors related to SCCP scores of students and teachers   Factors which significantly affected both student and teacher perception of school moral atmosphere (SCCP-IAIBIC) were their educational level, school location and school size. That is, elementary students and teachers perceived more just and caring atmosphere than junior high school students and teachers did because of different student development. Metropolitan school students and teachers perceived more just and caring atmosphere than their counterparts in rural schools due to different resources. Small school students and teachers perceived more just and caring atmosphere than middle or large school students and teachers did because of intense contact. In addition, students' gender significantly affected their perception of school moral atmosphere. There was no significant difference between male and female teachers' SCCP-IAIBIC score, while the former scored higher than the latter in SCCP (total). Teachers' result was opposite to students'. Besides, the statistical result in school location of SCCP total score of teachers was different from SCCP-IAIBIC score of teachers. This revealed that teachers in eastern Taiwan (rural district) displayed less positive attitude toward their students and more positive attitude toward the support and care from their staff and parents than other districts' teachers did, while teachers in northern Taiwan (metropolis district)was the opposite. Furthermore, most college /university characteristics and experience for teachers had no relation to their scores. However, teaching school characteristics and teaching school experience had significant influence on teacher perception of school moral atmosphere. This indicates the importance of teachers' socialization in their teaching schools and their school characteristics to elementary and junior high school teacher perception of moral atmosphere.

CONCLUSION

This paper sought to provide an objective analysis and comparison between student and teacher perception of school moral atmosphere in Taiwan schools. It also examined several factors which influenced student and teacher perception of school moral atmosphere respectively. Finally this paper offered some recommendations on how to improve students' and teachers' mutual understanding, and their school moral atmosphere which may foster both students' character formation and quality education for schools. However, in reviewing the findings from this study, readers may become aware of several limitations. First, the author didn't specifically define several terms used in this study, e.g., school environment, school culture, school moral atmosphere and school as caring community. Moreover, the author couldn't obviously differentiate "actual" school moral atmosphere and "perception" of school environment. Thirdly, several factors impacted in perceptions of school moral atmosphere by students or teachers still need to be testified through more scientific researches.

In Taiwan's case, although the scores of both students and teachers in perception of school moral atmosphere were above median score, students and teachers had different perception within several items. There were some factors in this study affected students and teacher perception of school environment. Hence, there are four recommendations for Taiwan's or other countries' academia and government. Firstly, they should concern and promote stronger identity or participation of those students ,who are male, junior high, studying in middle or large schools, and in southern or eastern (more rural district) Taiwan's schools. Secondly, they should also pay attention and encourage stronger sense of identity or participation of those teachers, who are female, teaching in junior high, middle or large, public and metropolitan schools (northern Taiwan), and who don't take part in school administrations now, and whose teaching experience are totaled less than 5 years. Thirdly, government and schools themselves may actively reshape school moral atmosphere/ culture for both students and teachers and enforce their mutual understanding, e.g., offering more opportunities for school members to participate and intensely interact with one another in their schools and in order to form a strong sense of justice and caring community. Finally, government should concern itself with how to relate moral education and teacher education, particularly in-service professional development, in order to promote teachers' competence of understanding students and cultivate better school moral atmosphere in classes and schools.

REFERENCES

Chien, C.H. (1987). Care ethics and education: A feminine approach by C.Gilligan and N.Noddings. *Bulletin of BingDong Teachers College.* Vol.10,133-164. (in Chinese)

Davidson,M. (1998). Towards the development of an instrument for measuring the school as a caring community. Cornell University. (unpublished)

Gilligan, C. (1982) (1993). *In a different voice: Psychological theory and women's development.* Massachusetts: Harvard University Press.

Himan, L. M. (1994). *Ethics.* Florida: Harcourt Brace Jovanovich.

Jackson, P.W. (et al.) (1993). *The moral life of schools.* California: Jossey-Bass.

Kohlberg, L.(1983). The moral atmosphere of the school. In H. Giroux and D.Purpel(Eds.). *The hidden curriculum and moral education.* California: McCutchan. pp.61-81.

Lee, Chi-Ming. (2002). Examining moral community: Ethnography research on moral life and atmosphere in one junior high school. *Journal of Taiwan Normal University: Education.* Vol.47 No.1, pp.83-106. (in Chinese)

Lee, Chi-Ming. (2003). Justice, caring and discipline—A case study on moral life of elementary school. *Bulletin of Civic and Moral Education.* Vol.13, pp.21-46. (in Chinese)

Lee, Chi-Ming (2004). A survey of the moral atmosphere of elementary and junior high schools in Taiwan. *Journal of Taiwan Normal University: Education.* Vol.49 No.1, pp1-20 (in Chinese)

Noddings, N. (1984). *Caring, a feminine approach to ethics & moral education*. Berkeley: University of California Press.

Noddings, N. (1992). *The challenge to care in schools: an alternative approach to education*. New York: Teachers College Press.

Noddings, N. (2002). *Educating moral people—a caring alternative to character education*. New York: Teachers College, Columbia University.

Power, C. (1981). Moral education through the development of the moral atmosphere of the school. *Journal of Educational Thought*. Vol.15, No1, pp.4-19.

Power, C. (1987). School climate and character development. in K. Ryan and G..F. McLean (Eds). *Character development in schools and beyond*. New York: Praeger. pp.145-171.

Power, C. (1988). The just community approach to moral education . *Journal of Moral Education*. Vol.17, No.3, pp.195-208.

Power, C., Higgins, A. & Kohlberg, L. (1989). *Lawrence Kohlberg's approach to moral education*. New York: Columbia University.

Power, C. & Reimer, J. (1978). Moral atmosphere :An educational bridge between moral judgment and action. in W. Damon (Ed.). *Moral development: New directions for child development*. California: Jossey-Bass.

Power, C. & Makogon, T.A. (1995). The just community approach to care. *Journal for a Just and Caring Education*. Vol.2 pp.9-24.

Roberts, W., Hom, A. & Battistich, V. (1995). *Assessing students' and teachers' sense of the school as a caring community*. Presented at the meeting of the American Educational Research Association. San Francisco.

Reimer, J. (1989). A week in the life of cluster. in C. Power, A. Higgins, L. Kohlberg et al (Eds). *Lawrence Kohlberg's approach to moral education*. New York: Columbia University Press. pp63-98.

Chi-Ming (Angela) Lee
National Taiwan Normal University, Taipei, Taiwan

DAWN E. SCHRADER

TEACHING MORAL LEADERSHIP:

Becoming Moral Leaders and Being Moral Leadership

"Leaders are born, not made." Many people believe this old adage. Yet business schools, departments of educational leadership, ethics commissions, and countless authors, publishers, and would-be leaders spend millions of dollars each year developing books, programs, consultation enterprises, and self-help manuals that develop the leadership "potential" they see in their students, in professionals, and in themselves. If leaders are born, not made, this is not only a tremendous waste of resources, but also, the practice would also be ethically in violation of *moral* leadership: specifically, leading people who could never become leaders down a "garden path" toward an unattainable goal. Leadership coaches, mentors, and educators make their living developing leaders. They claim significant success, and thus further their enterprise. When they fail, they recognize the significant contributions of such things as innate traits and inborn dispositions.

Perhaps the adage should be "leaders are made, not born." Leaders are human selves, with personal qualities and characteristics, values, a social history, a personal history, and live within a context. As a positive inspiration for ordinary people to become moral, "soulful" leaders, Bolman & Deal (2001) note that "History is full of stories of common people who do extraordinary things" (p. 66). Yet history is also full of great leaders who have done extraordinary horrific things – charismatic and brimming with leadership traits and skills that exemplify the prevailing model of "transformative leadership" and motivate many to follow them. The challenge before society is to educate people to be *moral* leaders, to bring out those characteristics, skills, and moral principles that inspire others to work for a common moral good, while simultaneously upholding and affirming through moral means the dignity of all humans in social interaction and discourse.

Teaching moral leadership is not an easy process. Leadership involves more than traits, character, skills, problem solving ability, and reflection. It involves more than social and economic intelligence. It involves understanding the self, the nature of others, learning and teaching as a process, and the importance of means and ends. Teaching leadership is about the mind and the heart and the soul (Maak & Pless, 2006; Burke & Cooper, 2006; Bolman & Deal, 2001), of the self-other-context relationship, and how that relationship moves through time. Moral leadership is a process of evolution: evolution of the self and of the other, and of that ever-changing relationship, and how all those evolutionary movements are situated in ever chang-

Fritz Oser & Wiel Veugelers (eds.), Getting involved, 227–248.

ing contexts and amidst challenges. It is about how we come to know ourselves, how people develop, and what Lerner (2002) refers to as the "dynamic interaction developmental contextualism." This concept refers to the interactive nature and bi-directional influences between people and various contexts, indicating how all are changed by such interaction. It takes into account nature and nurture, individual development and the role of history and culture-in essence, the very same stuff of which leadership theories consist. Leadership, and consequently moral leadership, then, is grounded fundamentally in moral, self, and social psychology and the dynamic developmental qualities therein. Therefore teaching moral leadership involves understanding both leadership and moral leadership, how it is learned and practiced. The teaching of moral leadership benefits from drawing from developmental psychology in those domains, and as such, mirrors the human process of learning.

This chapter analyzes these aspects of leadership. Beginning with theories of leadership, it examines the stuff of which leadership is thought to be made, and how leadership is thought to develop. Next, leadership is distinguished from moral leadership, examining the moral components that exist in current leadership models, and how these models reflect moral components. Thirdly, I examine aspects of psychological developmental theories that may contribute to theories of moral leadership and how it is developed or taught.

LEADERSHIP

If leadership is learned and can be taught, we need to know what leadership is, how it is learned, how it is practiced, what the opportunities are for learning or developing leadership potential, and what the obstacles are that must be faced and overcome in the process. Much of the leadership development literature falls short of analyzing the dynamic interactions of psychological influences and development that potentiates moral leadership. But first it is relevant to overview categories of how leadership is conceptualized in current leadership theories.

Traditionally, leadership theories have fallen into several general categories, reflecting not only the field of leadership itself, but also the changing times of society and advances in psychology. These categories are trait and character theories, transactional theories, transformational (or transforming) theories, and holistic theories. While this chapter will not provide a complete review of leadership theories, since others have done so (Chemers, 1997), it will highlight important aspects of definitions and approaches to leadership. Unfortunately, some old theories never die, but they just fade away or lurk like ghosts in the background of promising new movements, and occasionally resurface in both helpful as well as haunting ways. However, there is much to be learned by looking at the historical frameworks, and acknowledging their contributions to the new inhabitants of the leadership theory world.

TRAIT LEADERSHIP THEORIES

Chemers (1997) states that traits of leadership have been sought for the last several centuries, and that the ideal traits leaders possess reflect the values of society at the time. For example, during the first half of the 1900's, psychologists focused on measuring skills such as IQ and individual differences of characteristics and personality traits. Thus, the trait psychology approach was applied to leadership as a way of finding what personalities are best suited for leading people and organizations.

Trait theory states that there are certain traits or characteristics within a person that define leadership. These include traits of personality as well as acquired traits such a patience, courage, tenacity, and charisma. Looking historically and through fiction, through systematic research and anecdotal data, characteristics of leaders have been identified (Chemers, 1997) and cites Sarachek's (1968) examination of literature and leadership traits evidenced in Homer's Iliad, finding four traits important to leadership: 1) justice and judgment, 2) wisdom and counsel, 3) shrewdness and cunning, and 4) valor and action. Stogdill (1948) reviewed the leadership literature of his time, analyzing 124 separate studies of traits ranging from physical characteristics such as height and appearance, to personal traits such as adaptability, originality, dominance, and persistence, and to skills of social interaction, social knowledge and judgment. Chemers concludes (p. 21-22) that traits reflect that historical moment and culture, and that different traits of leadership and character may be desired in different eras and societies. Thus, the foundation is laid to continually discern the current ideal of leadership traits, suggesting perhaps some kind of moral relativism to what is valuable and desired in a leader. Alternatively, a search for traits that persist across time and place which are common to all leaders, indicating a kind of "principle" in the nature of what leadership has been and ought to be, that can persist across time, space, and culture; a kind of moral prescriptive of leadership. It is this potential for principles of character leadership that contributes to the idea of moral leadership.

In attempting to distill the principle character traits for leadership, leaders have been studied scientifically and anecdotally (Bennis & Nanus, 1985). This trend continues today by leadership scholars, and by leaders themselves who reflect autobiographically on the traits that have made them great leaders (e.g. Lee Iacocca, Jack Welch, Warren Bennett, and John Pepper). In identifying the principles of leadership from personal narratives, there is a sense of hope that the qualities (or traits) of leadership can be learned.

Although the trait approach to leadership did not result in a parsimonious constellation of traits which all leaders possess or ought to possess, though this approach to studying desirable and effective leadership traits continues. The idea that individuals have a "moral compass" (Lickona, 1991) or have certain "moral pillars" of character is the character education approach to developing moral leaders. However, trait approaches, while of value, fail to encompass the full spectrum of what it takes to be a leader. Leaders fail to lead despite their innate resources, indicating that there is more to leadership than the possession of traits. A leader must have the knowledge of when to employ these traits in appropriate ways in appropriate situations, for appropriate goals, to inspire or motivate others. Thus, although many books and articles support or trait and character approaches to leadership, also known historically as the "great man theory" (Carlyle, 1841, 1907) or the "nature" side of leadership (Stogdill, 1948), others purport the "nurture" side of leadership, indicating that leaders are made and not born. This latter approach includes behavioral theories such as contingency theories (cf., Fiedler, 1971, 1978) which become popular as the behaviorist view in psychology achieved dominance over personality trait psychology. Transactional leadership (cf., Homans, 1974; Kelley & Thibaut, 1978), situational leadership (e.g., Hershey & Blanchard, 1977), and normative model leadership (Vroom & Yetton, 1973) built on the psychological processes involved in behavioral and contingency theories to look at such things as management by objectives, rewards, modeling, perceptions of equity of rewards, perception of leaders, and similar psychological constructs that underlie human motivation and behavior. These approaches are discussed next, yet are also subject to the same critique of not being "enough" for the teaching of moral leadership.

TRANSACTIONAL LEADERSHIP THEORIES

As discussed above, leaders vary in traits, character, and values, but share many in common. Personal dimensions bring forward different motives for leading, and not all leaders have the best motives and goals, and if they do, they do not evidence themselves in behavior. Some use their leadership traits and character for personal ends of greater personal wealth or recognition, while others use them to further the company, the social good, or to promote the leadership abilities and potential contributions of other people. For example, in trait and character approaches, indeed moral traits can be developed, and are an indication of "the good." In transactional theories there is a distributive justice process of fair exchange. These theories examine the transactions that take place so that people feel like they are getting rewards or just compensation for their efforts and contributions to the goals and visions of the leader. Given that individuals value different rewards differently, transactional theories examine what rewards motivate whom, an dhow, so that the contingencies can be manipulated or regulated to get desired results.

Variants may exist in terms of who is controlling the contingencies, whether individual preferences are considered, if there is an exploitation of power issues and the like, as well as who is judging the traits and outcomes that are of value. In good leadership, there would ideally be an atmosphere where "individual and collective goals are compatible and mutually reinforcing" and where leaders may "arouse collectivist motives in group members that would encourage them to subdue their individual goals and interests in favor of group goals" (Chemers, 1997, p. 62). Kelley and Thibaut (1978) articulated the dynamism that exists when the rewards are manipulated by the use of power, resulting in sense of comparison and possible exploitation. Hollander (1993) likewise recognized the importance of exchanges in his "idiosyncrasy credit" theory, where the leader earns legitimacy from followers via positive interpersonal evaluations that allow the leader to be innovative and even push the limits of traditional strategies of operations – that is, as long as the leader proves competent and trustworthy. The more success the leader has, the more influence and status they earn, and the more freedom they are given to deviate from institutional or group norms. This, however, sets up the opportunity for moral abuse, if the leader is or becomes disrespectful or abusive of the credit given by the followers, and if the leader takes then the opportunity for personal or selfish gain.

Transactional leadership theories fall under the psychological rubric of social learning and behavioral learning theories (for example, Bandura, Vroom, Skinner). In all of the theories of that kind, contingencies in the physical and social environment influence behavior, consciously or not. As transactions, leaders could be manipulated by, and can manipulate, the environment or others, via social psychological phenomena such as conformity (e.g., Milgram, 2004), dispositional and situational attributions (Weiner, et. al., 1972; Kelley & Thibaut, 1978; Brown, 1984), social facilitation (Zajonc, 1965) and cognitive dissonance between thought and action (Seligman, 1991).

Kurt Lewin's psychological field theory contributes another layer of complexity to the transactional theory of leadership. Specifically, he states that there are a variety of social relationships whose interactions influence perceptions of how equitable transactions and exchanges are, and thus influence leaders and followers' actions. Lewin demonstrated that leadership "style" is important because it has a profound influence on how contingencies such as rewards are perceived and pursued in context (Lewin, Lippit, & White, 1939). These types of psychological phenomena complicate the issue of moral leadership, making transactional leadership, while effective in many ways, open to a slip between intent and motivation to act as a moral leader, and acting immorally or as an immoral leader.

TRANSFORMATIONAL (TRANSFORMING) LEADERSHIP THEORIES

Another, more blended, approach utilizes leaders' traits, character, context, and psychological expertise in knowing others to motivate. Indeed, as early as 1948, Stogdill recognized that "leadership must be conceived in terms of the interaction of variables which are in constant flux and change" (p. 63-64) and that it is important for leaders not only to have traits and characteristics of leadership, but also be aware of the relationship between the leader and the led. This claim set the groundwork for some of the complex leadership theories prevalent today, particularly those known as transformative, or as Bass now prefers the term "transforming" leadership theories (Chemers, 2006). Bass (1985) found "a reasonably stable factor structure" of seven leadership factors; four for transformational leadership, namely charisma, inspirational motivation, intellectual stimulation of followers, individualized consideration of followers, and two for transactional leadership, namely contingent reward, management by exception (taking action only when something goes wrong) and one non-leadership factor, namely laissez faire or the absence of leadership. In transformational leadership, while it has factors of other leadership styles such as the common goal of helping subordinates to develop and to be effective, it is unique in that the leader has a "transcendent vision" that is the motivational force to develop or transform others so that there can be a high degree of personal identification to the vision (Chemers, 2006). Thus, there is a high degree of importance for the leader in making that vision a moral vision, and making the means of transformation of followers moral as well, since there is tremendous power in their status as leaders in creating change in others. Because of such power over others' transformation, it is also easy for transformational leaders to go awry and become charismatic leaders whose ends and means are immoral (Bass, 1985; 1990).

Even with reference to moral foundations, some leadership theories see transformational leadership as fundamentally linked with moral principles and objectives (Burns, 1978). For this reason, it is important to conceptually deconstruct leadership characteristics, traits, and skills and examine their relationship to the person doing the leading, their moral constructions – that is the meaning they construct from their socio-moral experiences, and the contexts that facilitate and inhibit moral leadership.

It is the general consensus that leaders ought to lead to the higher good for individuals and their organizations, and thus it is our responsibility as educators to teach moral leadership, to all, and not the few, and to transcend the traits, behaviors and skills approaches, think about the moral obligations of transformational leadership, and link them together to encourage leaders to embody ethical principles of thought and action. That is, to link to the inner dimensions of the moral psychology of individual leaders.

INNER, SOULFUL AND SPIRITUAL LEADERSHIP THEORIES

The current phase in leadership theory is a more holistic approach. The concept of "inner leadership" (Fairholm, 2001) is one that may illuminate more fully the moral components of leadership theory. Inner leadership connotes two things: the inner characteristics of the leader, and also the inner or middle leadership that occurs among subordinates as they work together in work groups or in their daily jobs. The latter of these meanings is referred to as "Number Two" (Fairholm, 2001) leadership. These leaders lead by their personal values, acted on in everyday relationships. They inspire others as an equal, rather than motivate from a formal leadership role. Inner leaders' leadership comes from trust from others and not authority to influence others and gain support and thus, they represent the two meanings of "inner leadership." Their leadership is personal, not from the position of power, and they lead from "a foundation of a whole-souled spirit" (Fairholm, 2001, p. xix) that aids in reaching common goals. It could be said that this whole person approach to leadership is the essence of the qualities of *moral* leadership since interactions are more egalitarian, and the leading and following is done through mutual respect and cooperation rather than manipulated contingencies, rewards, and other transactions. In inner leadership, one's moral character ultimately "counts."

In many ways, these inner, soulful or spiritual leaders possess a unique blend of the various aspects of leadership discussed thus far: traits, behaviors, and skills at transforming others. Kouzes & Posner (2007) outline skills for successful leadership that combine trait, behavioral skills and contingencies, and are transformational. They identify five actions for successful leadership: modeling, inspiring, challenging, enabling, and encouraging. Modeling means living the behaviors you want others to adopt. People tend to attend to actions more than words. Inspiring a vision that can be shared captures people's imagination and in that way inspires them to make the leader's vision their own. Leaders need also to thrive on challenging the old ways of doing things to find new innovations and ways to change the process. Leaders lead best by enabling others to act independently and feel valued for their contributions. And lastly, leaders who lead best encourage passion and "heart" in themselves and their followers. Within these five skills are components of behavioral and transactional theories (modeling), charismatic leadership trait theory (being inspiring and thriving on challenge), and transforming and transformational theories (challenging, enabling, encouraging good work and feel valuing the dignity of others). Kouzes and Poser's skill set articulates a blending of leadership approaches into a psychological model of leadership, even if they do not name it as such. What is implicit in Kouzes & Posner's work is that the leader utilizes these skills from a moral point of view, by modeling moral action, inspiring moral values and visions, enabling without undercutting or undermining the dignity of others, and innovating and encouraging passion that is not self serving but rather is other-directed and for the greater good. Without the moral component to their theory, immoral means and ends to transformation and leadership can be inflicted on followers as well as the organization.

In sum, leadership theories contain decidedly moral foundations, whether explicitly acknowledged as such or not. While simultaneously citing traits and characteristics of the leader, such as charisma, transformative theories take into account moral considerations of the follower and the dynamic relationship between leader and others. Other theories look at the role context plays on perceptions, expectations, and contingencies. Other theories look at the self as a leader, and the individual characteristics that gain the respect of others, and often that respect is gained by treating others with dignity, care, and equality. The movement of leadership theories is more and more toward the inner leader characteristics, and an examination of the interior of the self who is to become the leader. It is about self development, about reflection on the self and how one thinks – makes decisions and judgments in business and personal domains, how one acts in relation to others, how one creates and is dynamically effected by a context for mutual moral growth, development, and respect. In so doing, leadership is moral leadership, and includes the person, context, and social interactions as fundamental considerations in defining what a leader is, and what leadership is. It is my conclusion, along with Bass who prefers the term "transforming" to transformational" leadership (Chemers, 2006), that leadership is an action; a verb and not a noun. People, Number Ones and Number Twos, that is--all people, are in the process of *being leadership* and due to what counts as good leadership, they are *being moral leadership.*

TEACHING LEADERSHIP AND MORAL LEADERSHIP

In reviewing the theories of leadership discussed above, it is clear that there are several ways that morality is embedded in the history of leadership theories. I demonstrated that leadership theories have psychological components to understanding human behavior, social interaction, and the development of cognitive and emotional competencies. Newer leadership models such as soulful, spiritual, inspiring models, are ever more psychologically grounded, complex, and integrative of self, others, and context than earlier theories. I also demonstrated that one can be a leader while being immoral in that leadership, as witnessed in situations such as Enron Corporation, WorldCom and the like. These cases simply provide the evidence that connects leadership to morality.

What remains to be explored is how one "acquires" or develops moral leadership, how it is taught, how it is expressed in practice, and what the implications of moral leadership are for both the leaders and followers, as well as the organization. Just as leadership theories were summarized above, it is important to look at the "moral" side of moral leadership apart from the leadership side for a moment. This section will therefore examine how morality develops within the individual self and in context and social interaction such that the person herself becomes the kind of leader who is moral in her leadership. In part, that calls the question, how does one become moral? And then further, how does one become a moral leader, demonstrating moral leadership?

Bolman & Deal (2001) recognize that leadership, and I will add *moral* leadership, is about "human imperfection and human transcendence" (p. 67). They relate a story by Kurtz and Ketcham, in their book, *The spirituality of imperfection*:

A preacher once asked a group of children, "If all the good people in the world were red and all the bad people were green, what color would you be?" One girl thought for a long time, looking very serious. Then her face brightened, and she said, "Reverend, I'd be streaky." (Kurtz & Ketcham, 1992, p. 56)

Bolman and Deal go on to say that we are all streaky (p. 68). Thus in recognizing that there is human imperfection in all--there are no "great men" (or women). However, there is the possibility of transformation and transcendence. To be a moral leader, one must be self reflectively aware of the self, of morality and moral principles, and one's actions and the importance of relationship with others as moral beings who by their very nature demand respect. One must act in such as way as to earn and display trust and respect, demonstrate integrity, lead with fidelity to moral principles and with "spirit" (Fairholm, 2001) or "soul" (Bolman & Deal, 2001; Csikszentmihalyi, 2003). But the question is, how do we teach people, who are by nature streaky, to be moral leaders? Because moral leaders are both born *and* made; we need to know how people as leaders develop, and how leadership is taught.

To begin, I make the following claims and assumptions, grounded in decades of psychological research, which are necessary to consider when contemplating teaching moral leadership.

– All people develop morally, and all people are born leaders – leaders in the sense that others will follow them in what they do, how they think and how they interact with the world.
– By virtue of being human, we develop from childhood through adulthood.
– People have innate dispositions and traits that may make them more sensitive to phenomena, more intellectually or socially or emotionally oriented and skilled, more empathic, and the like, than others.
– Some people will emerge as leaders in a formal sense, rising to the head of the social group or organization, and some will be "inner" leaders (Fairholm) – leading both from within the social group and/or from within their own sense of the moral self. Other leaders will be followers – that particular form of leadership that is often ignored but veritably existent. For truly followers lead, and social psychology is replete with examples of social facilitation and conformity studies that illustrate this.
– Some leaders, within all of the various types of leaders, will not develop to as high a degree as others. Development includes cognitive, emotional, social, moral, perspective taking, self-awareness, and skill levels. These components are things which all people learn, to some degree, as living beings through maturation, experience, and social interaction.

CONSTRUCTIVE DEVELOPMENTAL AND CONTEXTUAL THEORIES OF LEADERSHIP AND MORAL LEADERSHIP

The assumptions above imply that leaders develop via the same processes that everyone else does, and further, that everyone is a moral leader of sorts. If this is the case, then moral leadership is within the potentiality of all people, regardless of the level of leadership to which they aspire and to which they ascend in formal social organizations. The idea of traits (which I will refer to as qualities) are important in leadership, as seen in the leadership theories mentioned above, and they play no less a role in moral leadership. Extending beyond that approach are leadership models of behaviors and skills, and when these components of leadership are combined with leadership qualities, can be "taught." By "taught" I mean that the meaning of leadership is learned, and that there are "teachers" who provide the fodder for fueling the flame of leadership development. Those "teachers" are the self, others, the context, and experience. Thus, teaching moral leadership is not a much different process than teaching one's language, thought, behavior, or any other social or intellectual phenomenon (Rogoff, 1990; Vygotsky, 1978; Piaget, 1952; Colby & Kohlberg, 1987). Like learning any subject or skill or behavior or way of being, it is fundamentally what one does with their experience in social interaction, in context, that makes one a leader or not; that makes one moral or not; and that makes one a moral leader, or not. The one component that makes for moral leadership, however, is that it essentially involves integrity, which in my definition, includes self-awareness and self-reflectivity combined with principled and complex moral reasoning and moral action that upholds the good, the right, and the dignity of all. In the famous sentiment regarding character, ethics, principles, and action: in the old adage "it is what you do even when no one is looking." That requires self-conscious awareness of the living of one's principles and the effect on others.

Since self-consciousness is a characteristic of leadership that makes the leader more likely to be consistent with his or her values, it likewise is the same for followers, who may be led by immoral or charismatic leaders. Self-consciousness or reflective awareness is a "golden ticket" to winning control of one's self and freedom from subjugation of immoral power or leadership. So, not only does self-consciousness create the opportunity for moral leadership, but also for moral followership, and the subsequent development of moral leadership in those followers as they experience the negative outcome of what immoral leadership does to erode their personal dignity, sense of trust, and respect.

Referring back to qualities in leadership theories, some leaders use (consciously or unconsciously) their leadership traits and skills immorally. They use their inflated sense of self-importance, their expansive goals, their limitless self-confidence, and their high communication skills to lead (Chemers, 1997). Followers get "caught up" in joining the vision and in so doing, lose their own best judgment and blind themselves to what they would otherwise see as reality. Thus, one of the first most important goals in teaching moral leadership is in teaching moral followership. If we take the assumption that leaders are made, not born, then it takes followers to make a leader – at least in part (Colby & Damon, 1992). What is critically important is to discourage self-importance in favor of the moral good, and to encourage self reflective awareness in all people to see when moral principles are being violated, ensuring that all the people in social interaction are treated with respect, dignity and caring. If they are not, such leadership is not moral, and the leader fails to have moral integrity. Blasi (2005) states that integrity is "always a result of a conscious concern about, and intentional care to avoid, the contradictions between what we say or do and those commitments on which the sense of self of who we are was constructed" (Blasi, 2005, p. 90). Moral leaders have a strong awareness of their own integrity—and they seek to encourage integrity-awareness in others (e.g., Maak & Pless, 2006; Chemers, 1997). Moral leaders must act responsibly toward themselves and others—their motivation to act (and their struggle with themselves) comes partially from the tension between the ideal and the real selves—who we want to become in light of who we are now (Higgins-D'Alessandro & Power, 2005). It is the awareness of one's moral relationship to the world and responsibility to that, which is moral leadership.

TEACHING MORAL LEADERSHIP: WHAT AND HOW

The importance of teaching moral leadership is that our social life, our society, counts upon those in positions of power and influence to set the tone for others to act; to create an ethical culture of behaviors in which others are encouraged to learn to act morally and in accordance with the best ideals of what it means to be in society. By society, I mean not only a group of people with shared norms and values (acknowledging that the simple sharing of norms and values may not in itself be moral or principled), but the definition of society as "the totality of social relationships among human beings." Ethical leadership must be taught to those in positions of power so that their influence is moral, and the results of their decisions, choices, and actions are moral.

The reason for ethical breaches that so often lead to the demise of the leader in an organization or the organization itself is multidimensional. Lack of moral character or the moral self is one. Poor moral decision-making is another. Lack of ethical knowledge is yet another, but so is having ethical knowledge that is ignored, denied, or trumped by personal self-interest, self-indulgence – consciously or unconsciously. Zimbardo (2006) sites influences that lead ordinary people to do things previously believed they would not do, including offering them an "excuse" that would justify the means to an end, setting up a contract or obligation, giving meaningful roles to play, presenting rules that "must" be followed, replacing reality with rhetoric of a desired end, creating situations of diffusion of responsibility, gradually increasing opportunities that lead to abuse, changing a seemingly "just" authority's influence to unjust, and increasing the stakes for dissent or noncompliance with authority. These influences do not excuse abuse of moral action and leadership, but provide psychological explanations as to the potential disconnect between moral judgment and moral action, and leadership and moral leadership.

The traditional approach to teaching moral leadership is to look to professional schools to educate the next generation of leaders. In the best case scenario, professional preparation programs will include ways to find those who possess leadership traits, moral character and integrity, and teach components of moral thought, decision making and action, and to hope for the best. Yet still very few professional education programs implement comprehensive deliberate ethical education to a significant degree, and when they do, it is in similar ways. How moral leadership is taught tends to rely on a course or set of cases discussed within academic courses to address philosophical ethics or decision-making strategies (Mahoney, 2006). Beck & Murphy (1994) report that many programs use a problem-solving or decision-making approach with cases and examples. Focus on professional codes of ethics and occasionally the development of personal ethical codes. They identified three types of courses: those that stress knowledge about ethics, issue-oriented courses, and a combination of the two (Beck & Murphy, 1994). Strike (2006) and others are increasingly focusing on the development of ethical climates that are "competent, caring and collegial" to increase professional ethical behavior and accountability.

Aspects of leadership and morality are continually being examined to help elucidate the complex components that can contribute to the teaching of moral leadership. Yet the human being – the self – who is making the decisions, and is becoming a moral leader, is important to include in the development of skills for ethical behavior. The question becomes, how is moral leadership taught to the individual self, remembering that leadership is thought to be a combination of traits that one possesses inherently, as well as those characteristics, skills, and behaviors learned, acquired, and practiced over the course of individual experiences in their own social world? That is, there social, psychological, and developmental issues that are a part of the teaching of moral skills and components of action. The next section addresses the process of how one attains or constructs the characteristics, dispositions, virtues, perspectives, attitudes, thought processes, decision-making abilities, and sensitivity, courage, compassion, and people- and policy-orientation that leadership theories describe as being essential to becoming a leader, and more specifically to become a moral leader. The most important of these processes of developing moral leaders are the process of development itself, the role of experience and social interaction, the role of self in context, and the role of active self-reflection. These processes dynamically influence one another to create changes in each process. Developing moral leaders may be not much different from developing moral people in general, and developing leaders in particular, but with the added "bonus" of developing people who are in leadership roles who have the opportunity to set an example of moral thought in action.

The process development

Constructive developmental theories posit that development is a process of interaction between the person, their environment, and maturation. Maturation includes physical (including brain) maturation as well as the results of transformations due to lived experiences. The roots of moral leadership can, and ought to, be found in everyday life.

How does cognitive constructive development of leaders occur? How is there a match between judgment and action? Development requires being open to, and taking advantage of, opportunities in life and work. More complex demands provide greater opportunities for increasingly complex thought (Commons & Bresette, 2006; Commons & Richards, 2002; Kegan, 1994), and leaders face complex decisions frequently and are responsible for the welfare of many people and organizational decisions. Development requires lived experience, reflection on that experience, and integration of self and knowledge on lived experience. Piagetian and neo-Piagetian (Kegan, 1982; Case, 2000), as well as social constructivist psychologists (such as Rogoff, 1990; Vygotsky, 1978; Lave and Wenger, 1991) insist that any change or development requires some sort of opportunity for shifting out of the current, and often comfortable, way of looking at and interacting with the world, and taking psychological advantage – consciously or unconsciously – of opportunities for changing one's lens or way of seeing the world (Kegan, 1994). With that, there is a change in our way of knowing, reflecting, experiencing, and acting on the world.

The explanations for these changes or developments share commonalities, yet there are theoretical differences. These theoretical debates of the processes of development will not be differentiated here, since they are widely debated in the field, yet it is important for teaching moral leadership to highlight some of the ways in which it is thought that people can be taught and can learn moral leadership. Cognitive development is not sufficient for a model of moral leadership development, however. Moral action must also be considered.

James Rest's 4 component model of moral action has been applied extensively in moral education of professionals (Rest & Narvaez, 1994). The way in which individuals make sense of knowledge, or their cognitive moral development, influences their decisions and actions. Leadership and moral leadership require thought *and* action. In each component, a cognitive appraisal is involved: first, perceiving and interpreting a situation as moral, second, deliberating about social and moral norms, principles and obligations – albeit filtered through cognitive and sociomoral structures of thought, third, deciding amongst courses of action, influenced by motivations and values as well as social cognitive perspective as in component 2, and fourth implementing an action choice that moral leadership exemplifies by being the moral action choice. However, not all cognitive deliberation results in moral action, and leaders are not immune to falling victim to self-interest, social psychological factors, or character flaws, as discussed earlier, that can override cognitive judgment. Colby and Kohlberg (1987) demonstrated a monotonic relationship between moral judgment and moral action, and between moral type B and moral action, even though other studies demonstrate that situational, motivational and other social psychological phenomena, including conceptualization of the self (eg, Blasi, 2004) frequently interfere with the consonance between thought and action (e.g. Zimbardo, 2006). In contrast, moral leaders, regardless of moral stage, demonstrate a moral action despite social obstacles, because they think "it is the right thing to do" (Colby & Damon, 1992; Walker, 2002). Thus, moral leadership development might best be constructed to consider a wide range opportunities to experience and reflect on social, personal, and situational challenges in the context of leadership domains in which a person is involved.

In sum, cognitive development is not a singular construct or panacea for developing moral leaders; it must be one part of a constellation of components of moral psychology in leadership contexts. It is important to foster in leaders because it had demonstrated significant associations with moral action, and because it is the frame through which moral decisions are made, is one of the most fundamental aspects of personal development to promote in developing leaders to be moral leaders. The development of moral reasoning, and principled reasoning in particular, is vital to moral leadership.

The role of experience and social interaction

Through experiencing living, Piaget states (e.g. Piaget, 1952) that people have a natural propensity to make sense of information and encounters in their daily life. They seek to find how what they observe and act upon fits into their current formulations of meaning about the world, and seek equilibration of their thought processes and the new experiences. Through the process of assimilation and accommodation, individuals reach a form of equilibration or balance where there is consonance between their meaning system and theirs actions in context. Everyday provides experience to construct cognitive, emotional and moral meaning, as described above. Through mismatches between a current knowing system and new experience, the individual reconstructs meaning and thought operations which result in more complex, hierarchically integrated operations which the individual then uses in the next iterations of experience (Kegan, 1982, 1998; Piaget, 1965; Beilin & Pufall, 1992). Social constructivists' views of this meaning making evolution involve less emphasis on the individual reconstruction of thought through reflexive and reflective abstraction, and focus more on the nature of the social interactions that constitute individuals' meaning making. Rogoff (1990), Vygotsky (1962, 1978), and Lave & Wegner (1991), for example, explain this sociocultural theoretical perspective which demonstrates how all people can and will develop, how people learn, and is especially relevant to the concept of all people being moral leaders in terms of being able to learn moral leadership via social interaction and reflection on it, as well as all people being teachers of moral leadership. Using concepts such as proleptic learning, zone of proximal development, guided participation, and participatory appropriation, the individual participates in daily experiences with novice and expert others who facilitate or create opportunities both consciously and unconsciously for individual to learn the actions, norms, mores, signs, symbols, and meanings of the context and culture and to apply that learning in similar and subsequent experiences in their lives. Turiel (1983) and Nucci (2001) specify the cultural considerations involved in development.

The essence of the process of development is that people are learning leadership every day in every interaction. They observe and experience and practice the characteristics, qualities, behaviors and skills that more expert others use in leading others, making moral choices, and acting morally. Attention must be paid to what is learned, what is taught by adults and perceived expert others, such as leaders, so that what is moral and good has a chance to triumph over immoral actions by leaders who fall prey to negative situational influences and learning.

The role of self in context

An important yet often overlooked aspect of leadership in all but the latest theories is to recognize self in leadership contexts. In moral leadership, one must consider a multitude of aspects of learning good leadership: the person or self, the self as a leader, the profession, the self as a professional – in all, the self in a leadership context both personally and organizationally. But mostly, the integration of all of these components is essential.

Context can refer to many things; the cultural milieu, the specific situation that arises, a sense of continuity over time, and the location of the self in relation to others and moral principles. Creating climates that are supportive, caring, just, and open to transformation is important to moral leadership, since climates of injustice, self-centeredness and indulgence, egocentric, distant, and those where the mindset is maximizing personal wealth (in its various forms) predominates blocks moral leadership (Strike, 2006; Pruzan & Miller, 2006).

Location of the self asks, in part, in what capacity is one a leader? One ought not accept a formal position of a leader if one is not a morally principled person, that is, one who can coordinate their personal responsibilities for others and society with their role as a leader to look beyond self-interest to uphold the trust that others put in them, and to treat others with dignity in the means and ends of their relationships. Moral leaders are moral exemplars, and have integrity. People look to them to learn to be leaders themselves, in formal or informal leadership roles, to act in such as way as to earn the trust and respect of others, and to uplift and promote the dignity of others. An important component of that trust is for leaders to recognize that not only are they leading the organization toward fiscal success and the implementation of institutional goals, but that as leaders, they are responsible for the professional and personal development of those with whom they work and share the world – in other words, with whom they are "in society."

Of course, there is a problem such that unethical people will not recognize their immorality, or if they do, may act immorally in overlooking this moral obligation to serve others and society by engaging in the accumulation of personal wealth that supports their ego by taking leadership roles and leading others, though immorally, and without integrity (Brenkert, 2006; Pruzan & Miller, 200). Brenkert (2006) maintains there is an "axiological dimension" to integrity (p. 99), with moral components of self and social relations central dimensions to it, and additionally, that integrity is temporal, or a characteristic of a person – an ongoing cohesiveness and attachment to core values and principles and actions over time. As such, the context of self in time and space (social and physical) is essential to moral leadership. In teaching moral leadership, a critical component is to teach self-reflection on one's relationship to self, others, core values and principles, and a self-reflective practice to ensure integrity of self as a moral leader over time.

DAWN E. SCHRADER

The role of self-reflection

"We are only human" is a justification or rationalization of immoral behavior, used explain why good people are inadequate and/or immoral leaders, succumbing to temptation, acquiescence, conformity, or subjugation of one's will or desires in a given context – all possibly without self-conscious reflection on why, or the recognition of, moral failure as a leader. But that is not the excuse of moral leaders. Moral leaders have an integrity of self that self-consciously recognizes contextual influences and works through cognitive, metacognitive, and self-regulatory actions to mediate those influences and find the moral course of action. What is sought it the idea of "authentic" moral leadership that occurs when one is aware of one's own power, cognitions, social influences, and actions.

George (2003) in his book, Authentic Leadership, states that values and character are essential to leadership, and these qualities are formed through experiences that are continually challenged through study and introspection and consultation with others. Further, that being authentic, namely, "leading with integrity," is possible only if principles and practice match. This is one claim around which new theories of leadership agree (cf., Bolman & Deal, 2001; Burke & Cooper, 2006; Fairborn, 2001). Teaching self reflection, or metacognitive awareness and metacognitive strategies is one additional step toward developing integrity of self, thought, and action that leads to moral leadership.

BEING MORAL LEADERS, AND BEING MORAL LEADERSHIP

The position presented here is that leaders are made and not simply born. "The first and most basic domain of ethical responsibility is as a human being. In this domain, an educational leader considers the humanly ethical thing to do, taking into account the intrinsic dignity and inviolability of the other person." Starratt (2005, p. 125). I maintain that being born creates the possibility to become a moral leader if given the moral disposition, increasingly complex opportunities for moral engagement and action, and self-conscious reflection on thought and action – including reflection on self, context, and social interaction--that helps transform one's thinking and action.

The following are suggestions for developing leaders as moral leaders, and for encouraging moral leaders to evidence moral leadership in their everyday actions.

Recognize self and others, and the leader's role in development Regardless of the type of leadership theory one might embrace, whether trait, transactional, transformational or inspirational, leaders are taught lead, generally without regard to context, or the psychology of the persons being led; without understanding the moral psychology of individuals. The focus in leadership tends to be motivation and inspiration and management of resources (including human capital), and meeting institutional goals/standards. Moral leadership exudes the interpersonal: elevating the role of formal and informal communication and learning to the status it should be accorded, and leading with the intention of critical and self-reflective awareness of the influence of one's role as a leader on one's interactions with others, with a conceptualization and intention of fairness, goodness, respect for persons and what is morally right. Moral leadership is recognizing and embracing the special obligations for the growth and development of others, and the self, in social interaction.

Acknowledge special obligations of leaders for the development of others   Many leadership theories of the last half century have recognized leaders as more expert than their followers, including recognizing the leadership qualities of "informal" leaders who are in follower roles – referred to as "inner leaders." Leaders teach and inspire others to develop, but doing so requires an awareness of how others are making meaning and interpreting the world. Moral leadership involves sensitivity to the possibility of potential mismatches between leader and follower cognitive, moral, social, personal and interpersonal development. Leaders must become aware of a potential gap in understanding of the demands they are making and the ability for followers to understand what is expected of them. Kegan (1994) refers to this as followers being "in over their heads." Understanding mismatches requires a degree of sensitivity to developmental issues such as the claims the institution is making on the person (what is the school requiring a person to do or think that they find "too risky" to do/think about?), the claims the leader is making on the person, or the claims the person is making on him or herself. Teaching leaders developmental theories and contextual influences could be the beginning of a dialogue to help leaders construct developmentally appropriate learning and contextual situations to support growth and change for all people involved.

Develop self-reflective awareness   Moral leadership also requires sensitivity to the moral quality of leadership, and how one is living with moral integrity. People vary in their degree of self-reflective awareness of their own thought processes, as well as the thought processes of others. Moral leadership additionally requires a high degree of ethical self awareness and reflection on one's own moral and personal development, and how that influences, and is influenced by, the context – including the historical moment in which we are living.

Moral leadership involves being a self-conscious role model or guide, one who is expert who is teaching others, who is leading. Csikszentmihalyi (2003) states that people ought to develop a habit of paying attention--paying attention to others, to details, to the self and one's actions. Moral leadership is mastering your consciousness of your self, values, and principles, mastering self control over actions. If one is able to be self-consciously aware, they are then able to engage in conversation with others that is authentic, caring and responsive. It is, in Fairholm's (2001) words, mastering inner leadership – leadership of the interior of the self as well as one's leadership context.

Lead by moral example   Business leadership literature is replete with examples of leaders who have successfully integrated moral and professional ethics into the core of their personal identity and act accordingly. Like exemplars in the moral domain (Colby & Damon), moral leaders do not act alone but with a supportive following, they have a vision and awareness beyond oneself that they cultivate within oneself and in co-workers that the people and the institution are part of something bigger than themselves. They act with humility and selflessness. Walker's (2002) research finds that moral exemplars have different and varied personality traits, but "share some common core traits: honesty, dependability, and self-control; as well as many traits of an interpersonal nature that reflect an other-oriented orientation. Other themes included personal agency, positivity, emotional stability, and openness (p. 3)." These themes and traits seem to harken back to theories of trait or character theories of leadership, yet have the dimension of moral purpose. Teaching moral leadership will necessarily involve moral action. If one leads by moral example, the cognitive developmental and socioconstructivist theories of learning have a chance to work, since the moral "experts" will be interacting morally, creating opportunities for cognitive restructuring, appropriation, and participation, and allow for "plus one" or proleptic learning. Social learning theory tells us that not all examples or models will be followed, but interacting with moral exemplary leaders may obviate the processes conducive to social, self, and moral development and action.

Lead with your (moral) self and spirit   The movement in leadership theories is to toward leadership of, or with the heart, often called spiritual leadership. In this perspective, the self is intricately intertwined with their role as leader. Famous for his concept of "flow" Csikszentmihalyi applies this concept to leadership in his 2003 book "Good Business: Leadership, Flow, and the Making of Meaning." He talks about five things that appear to be most important to leaders' attitude toward life and may be responsible for their success: optimism about human beings in general and about the future, strong belief in integrity to principles and trust, ambition coupled with perseverance, curiosity and the desire to learn, and empathy for others coupled with mutual respect (p. 156). These five things are tied closely to a self-consciously reflective life, in a vocation-like interest in serving others and having a broader vision for the betterment of the world. Likewise, spiritual leadership theories focus on several elements that are at once personal and moral (Fairholm, 2001): searching for creating and making shared meaning, inspiring by modeling ethical conduct, respecting their power and influence to lead and be followed, intuiting ingrained values held by the self and group, taking risks when needed, having an attitude of service, and commitment to transformation of self, others and the organization. There is also a sense of common ethical values where the leader sets the moral climate for the group, but respects and understands that people have freedom to choose to participate. Additionally, overall there are three characteristics that are embedded in the previous ones: integrity, willingness to tell the truth, and loyalty and commitment. These numerous characteristics illustrate the concepts discussed in this paper: making moral meaning, interacting morally with those sharing a cultural context, and being self-aware of the moral impacts of self on others and the environment.

CONCLUSION

Moral leadership should be consciously taught, since it is naturally learned, appropriated, and internalized as a natural part of social life. Making moral leadership part of the explicit rather than the hidden curriculum of life is essential to what I am calling "being moral leadership." All people must learn to live in society with understanding of the inherent dignity and worth of others, and be intimately involved in creating a respectful, caring, and just moral climate. People learn moral leadership through respectful peer interactions; through modeling, plus-one methods, through appropriation of values and processes of social discourse, and through experiencing positive moral interactions. Whether the process of learning and teaching of moral leadership is explained via constructivist notions such equilibration processes, zone of proximal development, expert-novice interaction, cognitive reconstruction, guided participation or any other psychological construction of the process of development, it can be nonetheless stated that people learn. And they learn through experience, so it is imperative to create situations of moral learning. The responsibility all citizens have is to become consciously aware of what they are teaching, and *that* they are teaching moral leadership. Leaders and followers are in dynamic interaction, and the reciprocal influence of persons in context fosters or inhibits moral development. My concept of "being moral leadership" requires that those in formal and informal positions of power exercise moral responsibility in both the means and ends of that dynamic interaction to facilitate and promote the growth of all participants in the interaction.

In conclusion, teaching moral leadership is not only possible, but it is everyone's responsibility. Formal leaders, informal leaders, and followers alike, ought to engage in self-reflective awareness of their role in being moral leaders who engage one another in everyday life, in their full human-ness. All people might be encouraged to come to understand the role of their influence, and their responsibility to be a moral mentor, to convey the values of the larger society, and to not perpetuate stereotypes and subjugation. That is being moral leadership. In this chapter I suggested that it is essential to understand how community, civic participation, and the "interpersonal basis" of character come together to affect moral understandings and behavior (Power & Lapsley, 2005, p. 337). Graduate schools and professional education programs could purposively develop ways to enhance the moral leadership as process in all members of their communities – leaders, managers, teachers, students, citizens. As such, all people provide catalysts and opportunities for change and development through their own expertise and experience. As we interact in our social worlds and contexts, moral leadership develops. Moral leadership is setting an example for others, in which shared meaning can be made, and all of society benefits from the dynamic interaction.

DAWN E. SCHRADER

ACKNOWLEDGEMENT

Jess Matthews Duval is gratefully acknowledged for her review of earlier drafts of this paper. John Pijanowski is acknowledged for his past participation in presentations of parts of this work.

REFERENCES

Bass, B. M. (1985). *Leadership and performance beyond expectation.* New York: Free Press.

Bass, B. M. (1990). From transactional to transformational leadership: Learning to share the vision. *Organizational Dynamics, (Winter):* 19-31.

Beilin, H. & Pufall, P. B. (1992). *Piaget's theory: Prospects and possibilities.* Mahwah, NJ: Lawrence Erlbaum Associates.

Bennis, W. & Nanus, B. (1985). *Leaders: The strategies for taking charge.* New York: Harper & Row.

Blasi, A. (2005). Moral character: A psychological approach. In D. Lapsley & F.C. Power (Eds.), *Character psychology and character education* (pp. 67-100). Notre Dame, IN: University of Notre Dame Press.

Blasi, A. (2004). Moral functioning: Moral understanding and personality. In Daniel K. Lapsley & Darcia Narvaez (Eds.) *Moral development, self, and identity* (pp.335-348). Mahwah, NJ: Lawrence Erlbaum Associates, Publishers.

Bolman, L. G. & Deal, T. E. (2001). *Leading with soul: An uncommon journey of spirit.* San Francisco, CA: Jossey Bass.

Brenkert, G. G. (2006). Integrity, responsible leaders, and accountability (pp. 95-107). In Maak, T. & Pless, N. M. (Eds.), *Responsible leadership.* New York: Routledge.

Brown, K. A. (1984). Explaining group poor performance: An attributional analysis. *Academy of Management Review, 9,* 54-63.

Burns, J. M. (1978). *Leadership.* New York: Harper & Row

Burke, R. J. & Cooper, C. L. (2006). *Inspiring leaders.* New York: Routledge.

Carlyle, T. (1907/1841). *Heros and hero worship.* Boston: Adams.

Case, R. (2000). *How people learn: Brain, mind, experience, and school: Expanded Edition.*

Chemers, M. M. (1997). *An integrative theory of leadership.* Mahwah, NJ: Lawrence Erlbaum Associates.

Colby, A. & Damon, W. (1992). *Some do care.* New York: Free Press.

Colby, A. & Kohlberg, L. (1987). *The measurement of moral judgment.* New York: Cambridge University Press.

Commons, M. L. & Bresette, L. M. (2006). Illuminating major creative innovators with the model of hierarchical complexity. In C. Hoare (Ed.). *Oxford handbook of development and learning.* (pp. 255-280). New York: Oxford.

Commons, M. L. & Richards, F. A. (2002). Organizing components into combinations: How stage transition works. *Journal of Adult Development, 9* (3), 159-177.

Csikszentmihalyi, M. (2003). *Good business: Leadership, flow and the making of meaning.* New York: Viking.

Dewey, J. (1922). *Human nature and conduct.* New York: Random House.

Fairholm, G. W. (2001). *Mastering inner leadership.* Westport, CT: Quorum Books.

Fieldler, F. E. (1971). Validation and extension of the contingency model of leadership effectiveness: A review of empirical findings. *Psychological Bulletin, 76,* 128-148.

Fiedler, F. E. (1978). The contingency model and the dynamics of the leadership process. In L. Berkowitz (Ed.), *Advances in experimental social psychology, Vol 11* (pp. 59-112). New York: Academic Press.

Habermas, J. (1990). *Moral Consciousness and Communicative Action.* Cambridge, MA: MIT Press.

246

Hershey, P. & Blanchard, K. H. (1977). *Management of organizational behavior.* Englewood Cliffs, NJ: Prentice Hall.

Higgins-D'Alessandro, A. & Power, F.C. (2005). Character, responsibility, and the moral self. In D. Lapsley & F.C. Power (Eds.), *Character psychology and character education* (pp. 101-120). Notre Dame, IN: University of Notre Dame Press.

Iacocca, L. (2007). *Where have all the leaders gone?* New York: Scribner.

Kegan, R. (1998). *In over our heads: The mental demands of modern life.* Cambridge, MA: Harvard University Press.

Kegan, R. (1982). *The evolving self: Problem and process in human development.* Cambridge, MA: Harvard University Press.

Kelley, H. H. & Thibaut, J. W. (1978). *Interpersonal relations: A theory of independence.* New York: Wiley.

Kouzes, J. M. & Posner, B. Z. (2007). *The leadership challenge* (4th Edition). San Francisco: Jossey Bass.

Kutrz, E. & Ketcham, K. (1992). *The spirituality of imperfection: Modern wisdom from classic stories.* New York: Bantam.

Lave, J., and Wegner, E. (1991). *Situated learning: Legitimate peripheral participation.* New York: Cambridge University Press.

Lerner, R. M. (Ed.). (2002). *Concepts and theories of human development* (3rd ed.). Mahwah, NJ: Erlbaum.

Lewin, K., Lippitt, R. & White, R. K. (1939). Patterns of aggressive behavior in experimentally created social climates. *Journal of Social Psychology, 10,* 271-301.

Lickona, T. (1991). *Educating for character: How our schools can teach respect and responsibility.* New York: Bantam.

Mahoney, D. (2006). *Ethics and the school administrator: Balancing today's complex issues.* Rowan & Littlefield Education

Maak, T. & Pless, N. M. (2006). *Responsible leadership.* New York: Routledge.

Meindl, J. R. (1990). On leadership: An alternative to the conventional wisdom. In B. A. Staw (Ed.), *Research in organizational behavior. Vol. 12,* pp. 159-203. New York: JAI Press.

Mewton, L. (2002, December 15). Leaders are made, not born: Strategies for self-leadership. *MassWIT Spectrums Newsletter-Broaden horizons, enlighten, share wisdom & exchange ideas.* http://www.imakenews.com/masswit/e_article000115018.cfm

Milgram, S. (2004). *Obedience to authority: An experimental view.* New York: HarperCollins.

Nucci, L. (2001). *Education in the moral domain.* New York: Cambridge University Press.

Piaget, J. (1952). *The origins of intelligence in children.* M.Cook, trans. New York: International Universities Press.

Power, F.C. & Lapsley, D. (2005). Concluding themes and issues for the future. In D. Lapsley & F.C. Power (Eds.), *Character psychology and character education* (pp. 335-338). Notre Dame, IN: University of Notre Dame Press.

Pruzan, P. & Miller, W. C. (2007). Spirituality as the basis of responsible leaders and responsible companies (pp. 68-92). In Maak, T. & Pless, N. M. (2006). *Responsible leadership.* New York: Routledge.

Rest, J. & Narvaez, D. (1994). *Moral development in the professions: Psychology and applied ethics.* Mahwah, NJ: Lawrence Erlbaum Associates.

Rogoff, B. (1990). *Apprenticeship in thinking: Cognitive development in social context.* New York: Oxford University Press.

Sarachek, B. (1968). Greek concepts of leadership. *Academy of Management Journal, 11,* 39-48.

Schrader, D. E. (1990, November). *Judgment-Action-Awareness: A model for consistency and change.* Presented at the annual meeting of the Association for Moral Education, South Bend, Indiana.

Seligman, M. (1991). *Learned optimism.* New York: Knopf.

Staratt, R. J. (2005). Responsible leadership. *The Educational Forum, Vol. 69,* 124-133.

Stogdill, R.M. (1974). *Handbook of leadership: A survey of the literature.* New York: Free Press.

Strike, K. (2006). *Ethical leadership in schools: Creating community in an environment of accountability.* Leadership for Learning Series. Thousand Oaks, CA: Corwin Press.

Vroom, V. H. & Yetton, P. W. (1973). *Leadership and decision-making.* Pittsburgh: University of Pittsburgh Press.

Turiel, E. (1983). *The development of social knowledge: Morality and convention.* New York: Cambridge University Press.

Vygotsky, L.S. (1962). *Thought and Language.* Cambridge, MA: MIT Press.

Vygotsky, L. S. (1978*). Mind in society: The development of the higher psychological processes.* Cambridge, MA: The Harvard University Press. (Originally published 1930, New York: Oxford University Press.)

Walker, L. (2002). *The character of moral exemplars.* White House Conference on Character and Community. June 19, 2002. http://www.ed.gov/admins/lead/safety/character/walker.doc

Weiner, B., Frieze, I., Kukla, A., Reed, L., Rest, S. & Rosenbaum, R. M. (1972). Perceiving the causes of success and failure. In E. E. Jones, D. E. Kanouse, H. H. Kelley, R. E. Nisbett, S. Valins, & B. Weiner (Eds.), *Attribution: Perceiving he causes of behavior.* Morristown, NJ: General Learning Press.

Zajonc, R. B. (1965). Social faciliation. *Science, 149,* 269-274.

Dawn E. Schrader
Cornell University, USA

PART 4

METHODS AND STRATEGIES FOR FOSTERING ENGAGEMENT IN CONFLICTING FIELDS

LEO MONTADA

MORAL EDUCATION BY CONFLICT MEDIATION

Moral education may pursue various aims: the internalization of norms, the development of faculties to behave according to the norms accepted as valid, self control of desires or addictions, strengthening assertiveness to maintain one's normative convictions in a social context where they are not shared, the development of faculties to dispute norms, furthering insights needed to implement normative maxims in concrete situations and cases according to their basic meanings, encouraging autonomy, enhancing the development of moral reasoning, etc.

In this chapter, one further object of moral education will be discussed: enhancing readiness and abilities to preserve and to make peace by settling social conflicts. Autonomous actors have the possibility and the privilege to prevent and to settle conflicts by contracts. Fair contracts are a distinguished option to make or to assure peace. This is the basic idea in social contract theories of state constitutions. And it is the basic idea in conflict mediation at all levels of social life.

In order to achieve fair and sustainable agreements normative prerequisites have to be observed. And observing the reciprocal rights and obligations agreed upon is a binding ought of all contracting parties.

To form free and autonomous personalities qualified to conclude fair contracts is a preeminent aim of moral education. Cultivating conflict resolution by mediation is a promising way of life long moral education.

THESIS 1: EVERY SOCIAL CONFLICT IS AT ITS CORE A NORMATIVE CONFLICT

People expect that everybody will observe the generally valid normative standards and will respect their justified entitlements. Social conflicts result from perceived violations of normative standards or the disregard of own justified claims by others. In conflicts, people may claim justice for themselves or for others with whom they feel solidly united.

People react with resentment when they view norm-violating actors as responsible without having a convincing justification for their behavior. Conflicts will become manifest, when "victims" or observers reproach "the perpetrators" for their behavior, but "the perpetrators" ignore the reproaches and neither change their behavior nor justify it convincingly nor beg pardon.

"The perpetrators" will ignore or refuse the reproaches when they feel being justified. Maybe, they are convinced that their behavior is legitimized by self interest, by legal, moral, or social norms, or that it is a just retaliation of an antecedent

Fritz Oser & Wiel Veugelers (eds.), Getting involved, 251–264.
© 2008 Sense Publishers. All rights reserved.

misbehavior of the claimant "victim." In manifest conflicts, the opponents justify their own behavior and reproach their adversaries for their behavior.

It should be emphasized that social conflicts result from perceived injustices, not from incompatibilities. Incompatible goals, plans, and opinions may bear the risk of conflicts, but only if normative expectations are violated. Diverging views may be appreciated as creative and worthy of consideration or, else, they may be viewed, for instance, as disrespectful or insulting. Diverging goals may be considered as legitimate or, else, as an offence. Diverging religious beliefs may be tolerated as matter of personal freedom or, else, they may be condemned as a sin, a betrayal, or a threat to the community.

Fair competition is not a social conflict. If all actors in competitive markets or in sports are considered to behave legitimately, frustrations and losses are possible but they do not evoke resentment. There are winners and losers but not victimizers and victims. The losers may have performed poorly, they may have been unfortunate, but they have no reason for any reproach, unless they believe that the competition has not been fair. Being treated unjustly is quite another experience than having lost a game.

However, competition as such is not always considered to be legitimate by everybody. Instead, solidarity and mutual support, not competition, are normatively expected in some social contexts, e.g., within a close friendship or when a social group is striving for a common goal.

Resentment is the key symptom of conflicts. Perceived injustice instigates resentment, reproaches, wishes for retaliation, claims for compensation, or punishment. A look at aggression research reveals that it is not mere frustration that is instigating aggressive tendencies, but illegitimate frustration which is not justified by some good reason (Moore, 1978, Pastore 1952). Similarly, relative deprivation instigates aggression, but only if it is considered unjust. Aggression theories which emphasize anger as emotional antecedent of aggression share this basic assumption (Berkowitz, 1993). Aggression may have other motives, e.g., selfishness, envy, or striving for power, but, no doubt, resentment is one of the frequent motives of aggression (Montada, in press).

THESIS 2: WHILE THE JUSTICE MOTIVE IS UNIVERSAL, THE VIEWS OF WHAT IS JUST AND WHAT IS UNJUST ARE HIGHLY DIVERGING

The concern for justice as an anthropological universal. Claims for justice and protests against injustice are ubiquitous in social life:
- Political movements, revolutions, and wars are initiated under the banner of justice.
- Justice is a prominent issue in all fields of politics.
- The courts are swamped with law suits, and many of their judgments arouse protest or bitterness by those who consider them as unjust.
- Perceived injustices are at the core of everyday conflicts in private life.

- Close relationships are put at risk by experienced injustice.
- Victims of misfortune have to cope with the perceived injustice of their fate and, moreover, with being derogated and blamed by observers who try to preserve their belief in a just world by insinuating that the misfortune had been self-inflicted.

Humans are averse to injustice. They have a justice motive (cf. Ross & Miller, 2002). The concern for justice seems to be an anthropological universal.

Divergent Views about Justice

Beliefs about what is just and what is unjust are not at all universally shared. Consequently, conflicts about justice are universal Looking at all the various and diverging sources of normative standards which may shape and implement persons' sense of justice, this becomes obvious.

It is worthwhile to become aware of the long list of sources for the emergence of justice beliefs: human rights, constitutions, social roles, interaction scripts, game rules, bylaws, contracts, promises, etc. Many of the innumerable norms and normative maxims within these categories are highly diverging and contradict each other:

- The legal codes of different states are diverging.
- Each single law can be criticized on the basis of some justice principle.
- Many legal codes world wide violate human rights or violate the rules of some religion.
- Highly diverging principles of distributive justice are applied.
- Different religions have diverging normative rules.

Moreover, most normative maxims are open to interpretation, e.g., human rights, principles of justice and constitutional rules. Nevertheless, all these sources may have impact on the shaping of the sense of justice – at the individual level, the collective level, and the cultural level. Within pluralistic societies many diverging sources have influence on the formation of normative beliefs and expectations of subpopulations and individual persons. Diverging views and expectations are "epidemic" and, often, result in social conflicts.

Everybody is speaking of justice in the singular as if for every case one single view of justice would be the valid one and had to be acknowledged and shared by everybody (Rüthers, 1991). The use of the singular "the justice" is a mistake which bears the risk of conflicts. It may be used as a strategy to put through one's claim as the solely just one.

THESIS 3: THE SETTLEMENT OF CONFLICTS REQUIRES A CONVERGENCE OF NORMATIVE VIEWS AND BELIEFS

The conception of social conflicts outlined so far has implications for their settlement, for the making of peace and the healing of social relationships.

What does it mean to settle a conflict? Conflicts may be brought to an end without reconciliation. That means that the quarrels, disputes, or fights are not continued, but that the relationship between the adversaries remains poisoned, that the conflict remains to be a mortgage for future exchanges, or that social exchanges are terminated.

One option to settle a conflict is a rapprochement of normative views. That is illustrated by the appeasing effects of apologies. Honest apologies are a remarkably efficient way to avoid or to settle a conflict. Why? As Goffman (1971) has emphasized, by remorse and apologies perpetrators express that they share the victims' views of the case. By the apology perpetrators express
- that they, too, consider the violated norm as a valid ought,
- they concede that they have offended the norm,
- that they are responsible and
- blameworthy, because their offence was not justified.

Moreover, they concede that it is up to the victim to accept or to reject their apologies. That means, the normative views of the victim and the perpetrator are congruent. It is empirically proven that sincere apologies appease victims (judges and observers, as well) and reduce their desire for retribution (Ohbuchi et al., 1989). A perpetrator's attempt at reparation has similar effects, when it implies all the components of a sincere apology (Darley & Shultz, 1990).

Can conflicts be settled by trial? One of the standard ways of conflict resolution in the Western world is to bring the case to trial, if the case is liable for trial, at all. If litigants accept the authority of courts, the decisions of judges will terminate the conflict. This does not necessarily mean that the conflict is settled. Conflicts are settled only if all parties, especially the losers, are convinced that the judgment is a just one.

Judges can try to convince the losers that their judgment is just. To that end they have to give voice to all parties, to make sure that they have understood all conflicting views and positions, and to take time and effort to justify their views of the law, their view of the case, and their judgment with convincing arguments. If that is done in a respectful way, judges have a good chance that the losers get the impression of being treated in a fair manner.

This impression induces the just procedure effect (cf., Lind & Tyler, 1988) meaning that even unfavorable judgments are accepted without resentment, when the procedure is considered fair.

The conflict is settled, when the views of the parties are brought more into line, when feelings of injustice get resolved or are prevented. However, judges have to obey the law. And the law may not adequately fit the essential features and contents of an actual conflict. The laws may be criticized as unjust with some good reason. And the losers may not share the views of the judges and the reasons they give for their judgement. Consequently, the conflict will not be settled.

THESIS 4: CONFLICT-MEDIATION OFFERS A RICH AND EFFICIENT REPERTOIRE OF PROCEDURES AND STRATEGIES TO SETTLE CONFLICTS

In conflict mediation the legal code is not given particular weight in relation to the opponents' subjective sense of justice – at least as long as "compulsory laws" are not violated. The parties have the opportunity to advocate their personal views of the conflict and their personal normative beliefs, and they have the opportunity to negotiate a "social contract" for their future exchanges on the basis of their personal senses of justice.

Conflicts may be settled by mediation in two different ways: (1) by getting more convergence of the opponents' normative views, or (2) by qualifying the subjective importance attributed to the conflicting normative views and positions.

Bringing Normative Views To More Convergence

According to the outlined model of social conflicts, perceived injustice is resulting from the following views: The adversaries are blameworthy because they have violated a valid normative claim without remorse and apologies and without having an acceptable justification. Moreover, they are held responsible for their behavior. All these views can be questioned and put in a new perspective.

Qualifying attributions of responsibility Attributions of responsibility can be qualified or recognized as erroneous (cf. Hamilton & Hagiwara, 1992; Montada, 2001). If a person did not have volitional control over his or her behavior because of lacking competences, fatigue, external forces, etc., he or she is not responsible. If the consequences of an action have not been foreseeable, nobody is responsible, either.

Less responsibility will be attributed when malevolent intentions are no longer presumed, when, instead, the behavior is qualified as sufficiently careful or as well intended but failing, or when co-responsibility of other actors is assumed. Co-responsibility can be assumed, when the "victim" had consented to participate in a risky activity having a bad end (e.g., losses at the stock markets).

Qualifying blameworthiness by justifications The blameworthiness of an actor can be qualified by convincing justifications: by offering good reasons for the resented behavior, e.g., making reference to legitimate self interest, to professional or social obligations, by claiming the right to defend one's freedom or one's reputation (Montada, 2001). Quite often, own behavior is justified as retaliation for a prior misdeed of the adversary.

Justifications may be convincing and accepted. In that case they calm down resentment (Bernhardt, 2001). They may also be resentfully rejected. For instance, reproaches of having behaved selfishly may not be calmed down by the argument that selfishness is legitimate (pretending that maximizing own profit is the cardinal human motive), when the victim does not share the economic theory of behavior.

Qualifying normative convictions by discourses In conflicts, the opponents are convinced to be in the right with their own views and claims and the adversaries being wrong. It is a facet of normative beliefs that their validity is taken for granted and, consequently, that they have to be respected by everybody.

Conflicts about diverging normative beliefs cannot be settled by simple compromises. One possible solution might be that the opponents consent to appeal to a commonly respected authority for a decision. The approach in mediation is to reflect the conflicting beliefs and positions in normative discourses.

The function of discourses in mediations is not the search for general ethical truths, but to generate the insight that good reasons can be put forward not only for one's own normative views and claims but, equally, for the opponent's views and claims.

Mediators try to generate a culture of communication similar to the one designed for ideal ethical discourses (Apel, 1976): A rhetoric of persuasions and manipulations is banned, mutual understanding and unbiased free deliberation are actively supported. The aim is to reconstruct the conflicting views and positions as normative dilemmas, meaning that sole ethical truth cannot be claimed for the own view or position alone.

Imparting comprehension of existing normative dilemmas Settling conflicts is made easier when the opponents acknowledge that divergent norms or normative maxims may be advocated with good reasons, i.e., that a normative dilemma exists and, consequently, that neither party is solely right or wrong. If the opponents recognize that their conflict reflects a normative dilemma, they no longer view the position of the other side as completely illegitimate and their own position as the solely legitimate one. Normative dilemmas exist at several levels. Some examples may serve as an illustration. Normative maxims, e.g., justice principles, may be conflicting:

- Should the inheritance of parents be divided equally among their children or equitably according to their merits (e.g., to the amount of care they have provided for their parents or to their contributions to the social status of the family by their professional achievements) or according to their neediness (e.g., their income or the number of dependant children), or should non-kin persons, who have been very close to the parents, receive a share? There are good reasons for all options.
- Which employees should be dismissed first, when business is running low? Several justice principles may be considered: seniority, merits by previous perfor-

mances, current performance level, neediness (e.g., defined by the number of dependent children), gender, age, nationality etc.? Which one is right? There are good reasons for all.

A second category of dilemmas underlying social conflicts shall be mentioned. It is a matter of fact that attempts to remove one injustice frequently cause other injustices. Some examples on the level of legislation are given (cf. Montada, 2003):

- Is it just that young women are privileged by affirmative action programs in competition with young men in the labor market as a compensation for the unquestionable historical discrimination of women in the labor market? Or else, are only those young women to be privileged who have individually suffered discrimination, and are they to be privileged only when they compete with young men who have been unjustly privileged before? In other words: May we apply the justice principle of compensation for suffered disadvantages and undeserved advantages at the level of social categories (women and men) or only at the level of individuals and perhaps social groups.
- Is the raising of taxes for pollution a just measure? Pollution causes risks and costs for others who do not have profit or fun by the polluting activities (e.g., industrial productions, air-conditioning, car-driving). Raising taxes for pollution prevents or reduces the unjust externalization of costs, and the tax revenues may be used to compensate for suffered impairments by pollution, to reduce risks etc. However, raising of taxes may also cause new injustices because rich people can pay the taxes and, nevertheless, continue their polluting activities, whereas poorer ones may have to give up or restrict them (cf., Montada & Kals, 2000).

Unjust side effects of measures to prevent or to reduce injustices are quite common, from social welfare policies to the containment of terrorism. Laws are made to avoid injustices, bat every law can create other injustices. All these cases are normative dilemmas.

Strategies of discourses in conflicts mediation   In normative discourses conflicting claims for justice are advocated. When good arguments are put forward in the mediation of conflicts, the opponents may qualify their views and claims. They recognize that none of the conflicting claims is solely valid. This is not a normative relativism meaning "No norm or normative maxim is really valid!" In contrast, it is the insight that a normative dilemma exists, meaning "No normative maxim has exclusive, sole validity. Many maxims may be applied with good reason in a specific case." Applying, for instance, one single principle of distributive justice would violate all other principles that might be also taken into consideration. When the opponents come to realize, that a dilemma is underlying their conflict, the conflict will be defused which might, in turn, be a good precondition for future cooperation.

It is the wisdom of institutions to consider various principles of justice in their regulations and decisions. The social market economy, for instance, is an attempt to harmonize the right of all citizens to free economic activities with maxims of the social welfare state. Rawls' famous "maximin - principle" is also a suggestion how to harmonize economic freedom which is necessary for productivity and common wealth with the entitlement of every citizen to participate in the general prosperity (Rawls, 1971). This holds equally true for the basic maxims of the French Revolution: freedom, equality, and fraternity: Applying only one of the three maxims excluding the other two would result in quite diverging constitutions of the state.

Habermas (1993) has argued, that the justification of the validity of a moral maxim or principle is to be distinguished from the justification of decisions in concrete cases where competing maxims and principles are considered relevant with good reason.

In many institutional orders for the allocation of scarce resources several principles of distributive justice are considered. This is evidenced by comparative research on the allocation of university positions, subsidized lodgings, transplants in medicine, legal regulations for the layoff of employees, etc. (Elster, 1992). Making reference to these facts as well as to observations that various norms of justice are used in different spheres of justice (Walzer, 1983) may help to qualify rigid insisting on one single maxim.

A strategy in mediation may be to make the opponents aware that they are used to apply different normative maxims, e.g., principles of justice, in different situations and context. In order to transcend the actual conflict between the opponents, mediators may offer further normative standards that are or could be applied in similar cases. Becoming aware that their conflicting claims are not the only ones that can be reasonably advocated contributes to a different perspective.

When the parties recognize that a normative dilemma exists, they no longer view the position of the opponents as completely illegitimate and their own position as the single legitimate one.

STRATEGIES FOR QUALIFYING THE SUBJECTIVE IMPORTANCE OF THE CONFLICTING POSITIONS

Heavy conflicts frequently produce a mental constriction. The opponents are "out of their mind" insofar as they are no longer aware of the whole spectrum of their important concerns, value-orientations, and self-concept. The blameworthiness of the opponents, winning or retaliation became the dominant mental topics.

In conflicts both the blameworthiness of the adversaries and the impairments caused by them are frequently exaggerated. An injury caused by a biker on a footpath will be dramatized compared to a similar injury resulting from an own failure. Therefore, reducing the subjective importance attributed to the conflict may open the mind to think about constructive solutions.

Transcending the Actual Conflict

Transcending the conflict is the general advice for qualifying the importance of conflicts. Several strategies may be used in mediation. Some of them will be briefly mentioned.

Reminding the opponents of the whole spectrum of their concerns This strategy might be illustrated by an example. A couple, both spouses in the fifties, had a serious conflict about the question whether they should take the mother of the husband into their family because she needs care. The husband felt himself obligated to do this. His wife rejected this idea strictly and confronted her husband with the question: "Do you take care for her or for me?" The husband's response was: "Do you really wish me to violate my moral responsibility." Both feel betrayed by the partner.

The actual conflict could be transcended by making the opponents aware of the whole spectrum of their important concerns and their self concepts. In this specific case, this procedure has revealed a lot of shared concerns: Both partners loved each other; they shared moral concerns; both were concerned about the views of their children who loved their grandmother; they wanted to set a good example for their children. Moreover, they also shared economic concerns and worried that the income and property of the mother would get used up when the family would not be included in her care.

Having all these concerns in mind, the couple was ready to generate options how the needed care could be organized within or outside their home and to check which ones fit best to all their various concerns.

Exploring opportunities for positive exchanges In conflicts, the exchanges are negative: criticisms, blame, hindrances, harm, exclusion, slandering, mistrust, hostility etc. The exchange of mutual retaliations is costly for all, a looser – looser outcome for the sake of retributive justice. Refraining from retaliations is not costly but avoids anger and harm of the opponents. One of the important changes of perspective in mediation is that from negative exchanges to the opportunities of positive exchanges, positive with respect to important concerns of the parties.

The opponents have to become aware which positive exchanges are feasible ones – from material goods, information, and practical support to friendliness, consideration, sympathy, and emotional support. It is easy to create win – win outcomes when the opportunities of positive exchange are used.

Neighbors may exchange services like care for kids, pets or plants, manifold supports and favors, and they can save money by sharing equipment and tools, etc. What is offered and invested may be easily accomplished and inexpensive, it may be very valuable for the recipient. That is why both parties may win (subjectively) much more than they invest.

One common recommendation for negotiations and mediations is "to enlarge the cake" to be distributed. However, not every conflict is about distributions, and it is not always possible to increase the cake. However, it is always possible to look at additional concerns of the parties than merely the ones at stake in the actual conflict. In doing so, the number of options for positive exchanges will certainly grow.

Including unsettled previous conflicts in an overall solution   In long lasting social relationships, an actual conflict may be preceded by a series of conflicts that are not settled so long.. A neighborhood conflict for illustration. Neighbor A has intervened when B wanted to put up a basket for his sons to play basketball at the side of a dead end street. B's reaction was to refuse A's request to build a carport on the borderline of his property. As a counter move, A rejected B's request to fell a tree throwing shadow on his kitchen garden. And so forth. Supposing that most of these mutual impairments have been retaliations, one may assume that complying with the neighbor's requests would not have been costly for every side. Therefore a win – win agreement is possible when both comply with each other's requests that, in turn, would be a starting point for mutually productive exchanges in the future.

Considering the concerns of third parties   Many conflicts affect and impair third parties who are not directly involved. Conflicts between parents have effects on their children, on the grandparents and others. Conflicts at the workplace may have impact on colleagues, on the whole organization, on the families etc. The same is true for resolutions of conflicts: though not directly involved, third parties are affected. This fact may be used to transcend the conflict by stipulating the opponents to take the concerns of others into consideration, at least of those they feel close to. Reflecting the concerns of others constitutes a change of perspective and may qualify the subjective perception and importance of the conflicting positions.

Making internal conflicts aware   Not seldom do opponents in a social conflict hold vigorously a claim repressing own doubts and internal conflicts regarding this position. E.g., a young couple had given a lot of thoughts to the problems how to make compatible their professional careers and their desire to have children. It now happened that the young wife got a very attractive offer for an academic position. This position would, however, need her full commitment requiring her to postpone the desire to have a child. Her spouse strongly pleaded to reject this offer. Thereby, he caused heavy reactance on the part of his wife. The result was a serious conflict between the spouses. She was emphasizing all positive aspects of an academic career, reproached her husband for hindering her career, and claimed that it is her free personal decision whether and when she wants a child. The social conflict suppressed their internal conflicts. Making these again aware calmed down the social conflict and facilitated a discourse about the complex issues of personal freedom in close relationships and about the shared responsibilities of both parents for their children.

All these strategies to transcend the conflict open new perspectives that may allow the opponents to qualify the views and claims they hold in the conflict and encourage them to explore new options for social exchanges.

THESIS 5: SOCIAL CONFLICTS ARE BEST RECONCILED BY CONTRACTS

The specific features of conflict resolution by contracts can be emphasized in contrast to conflict resolutions by courts or other authorities? Contracts are concluded by self-dependant actors deciding at their own responsibility. They do not delegate their conflict to an authority or to an instance like a court for making a decision. They are not subjecting themselves to existing the existing law. They are in the position of "law-makers" with respect to their relationship. They preserve the control and the autonomy to settle their conflict themselves by a contract, aiming at the same time to prevent conflicts in the future.

In social contract theories of the state and its institutions the citizens are conceived of as legislators, as self-dependent, autonomously but cooperatively deciding actors who at their own free will subordinate themselves to the rules and mutual obligations they have agreed upon.

While the scenarios of the founding of a state within social contract models are fictitious, conflict resolution by a consensual agreement is a real opportunity. The conflicting parties search for an agreement the contents and rules of their future relationship. It is to assume that autonomously concluded contracts will be obeyed on the free will of the contracting parties.

Whether contracts will be observed on the own free will of the contracting parties depends of their perceived justice.

The Justice of Contracts

Contracts are regarded as just when the partners are equally informed and equally free to consent (Nozick, 1974). In conflict mediation, the ultimate criterion for the appraisal of a solution as just is the free agreement of the parties according to the famous principle in Roman law: "Consenti not fit iniuria." A contract that the parties have agreed upon freely and informed cannot be unjust. However, justice is violated if relevant information was withheld, if pressure was exerted, or if one party was not free to refuse the contract on account of a predicament, e.g., neediness.

Because contracts are of eminent importance in social life, many legal norms have been established which specify the obligations of the contracting parties. Above all, specific legal rules have been established to protect the supposedly less powerful or less informed parties.

Though mediators cannot guarantee equal freedom and information, they may take care that these conditions of fairness are realized. To be able to do this, mediators should be informed about possible restrictions of freedom, from material neediness to social and emotional dependency. And they should be informed about the manifold inequalities of power in social interactions, from differences in status, in rhetoric abilities and communication strategies, etc. Such knowledge will help them to prevent imbalances.

Mediators have also to take care that the relevant information are available and grasped by every body. They have also to prevent that one party makes one-sided concessions for the sake of peace, when the other party assertively tries to put through the own position. Sustainable contracts must be considered just by each contracting party.

The Justice of Contracts with Regard to Third Parties

The preconditions for justice within the internal exchange between the contracting parties- equal freedom and information – is not sufficient to guarantee that a contract would be just also for the exchange with third parties.

Assessing the justice of contracts would be incomplete without having a look at their impact on third parties. Adverse effects on third parties raise new justice problems and new conflicts. Contracts may be fair with respect to the exchanges between the contracting parties but may be seriously unfair with respect to third parties or the larger community. For instance, cartel contracts may be fair for the contracting parties, but they are made at the expense of others.

Labor contracts between employers' organizations and unions may be viewed as a fair distribution of profits, but they may also be impairments for others or the public if they result in layoffs or prevent an expansion of the workforce. In case of divorce the financially dependent partner is not allowed to renounce continuous material support by the divorced partner to avoid the risk of becoming dependant on public welfare.

It is an ought and it is prudent to expand the view from the contracting parties to the impact of an agreement on third parties and the public. Contract at the cost of third parties are externally unjust and a cause for new conflicts.

Limitations of Conflict Mediation

Limitations to achieve agreements cannot be disclaimed. Besides deep rooted hostility or mistrust between the parties the most difficult problem are fundamentalist convictions that the own normative beliefs are the sole truth. Diverging normative fundamentalisms are a serious obstacle to come to an agreement.

Dealing with subjective normative truths in conflict mediation. How to deal with ethical truths, which one of the opponents considers to be "eternally" and "universally" valid and not negotiable at all, for instance, religious oughts or human rights or what else?

Everybody has normative convictions which are subjectively not negotiable. The possibilities to conclude a contract are to be explored creatively also in these cases. Becoming aware of unbridgeable incompatibilities, conflicts are not unavoidable. To come to contracts, the parties must not share every normative belief. It may well be contracted that incompatibilities are mutually respected but excluded from the common social life and to explore options for mutually productive exchanges leaving aside the conflicting positions. That means a segmentation or restriction in the scope of the relationship. Divorce may be a way to find peace in partnerships. Borderlines, walls, and hedges may be the (second-) best solutions to prevent, to confine, or even to reconcile a conflict.

To give an example at the societal level: In the Western World the public social order is conceived of as a social contract between the citizens. To prevent religious wars, the social contract guarantees religious freedom to everybody, and demands to respect everybody's religious freedom. The social contract conception of the legal order is incompatible with the concept of theocracy, where the public social order is prescribed by a divine revelation of eternal truth. To keep peace, a separation agreement may be the single option: either the separation of a public and a private sector of life and to restrict the religious beliefs strictly to the private sector or to separate the populations according to their irreconcilable normative convictions.

What, when agreements are not achievable?

- If the case is justifiable, it can be brought to trial.
- Sometimes, the opponents agree to ask a commonly accepted authority for a decision.
- In other cases the relationship is given up with more or less losses for either party.

What is remaining beyond these options is the large spectrum of aggression from violent enforcement or retaliation to discrimination and exclusion.

CONCLUSION

The contract is the prototypical instrument to create and to keep peace between social actors. Making contracts is the instrument of Man as autonomous, self-governed being to organize social life by creating and establishing social norms.

The social contract theories of the state presuppose the idea of man as a free and autonomously acting being who reasonably organizes social exchanges by social norms. The validity of social norms is derived from the free and informed agreement in social contracts, implying a self- binding at the contract. Moral education is the education to free and autonomously deciding persons able to make contracts and ready to keep the responsibilities they have agreed upon.

Cultivating conflict resolution by mediation is a promising way of life long moral education.

REFERENCES

Apel, K.O. (1976). *Transformation der Philosophie. Das Apriori der Kommunikationsgemeinschaft.* Bd. 2. Frankfurt/M.: Suhrkamp.

Bernhardt, K. (2001). *Ein kognitives Trainingsprogramm zur Steuerung von Empörung.* Universitäts-bibliothek Trier {< http://ub-dok.uni-trier.de/diss/diss11/2001>}.

Berkowitz, L. (1993). *Aggression. Its causes, consequences, and control.* New York: Mac Graw Hill.

Bierhoff, H.W. (1998). Ärger, Aggression und Gerechtigkeit. In H.W. Bierhoff & U. Wagner (Eds.), *Aggression und Gewalt: Phänomene, Ursachen und Interventionen* (pp 26-47). Stuttgart: Kohlhammer.

Darley, J. & Shultz, T. (1990). Moral rules: Their content and acquisition. *Annual Review of Psychology, 41,* 525-556.

Elster, J. (1992). *Local Justice.* Russel Sage Foundation. New York.

Goffman, E. (1971). *Relations in public: Microstudies of the public order.* Harmondsworth: Penguin.

Habermas, J. (1993). *Justification and application.* Cambridge, MA: MIT Press.

Hamilton, V. L. & Hagiwara, S. (1992). Roles, responsibility, and accounts across cultures. *International Journal of Psychology, 27,* 157-179.

Lind, E. A, & Tyler, T. R. (1988). *The social psychology of procedural justice.* New York: Plenum Press.

Mikula, G. & Wenzel, M. (2000). Justice and social conflicts. *International Journal of Psychology, 35*(2), 126-135.

Montada, L. (2001). Denial of responsibility. In A. E. Auhagen & H. W. Bierhoff, *Responsibility – The many faces of a social phenomenon*(pp. 79-92). London: Routledge.

Montada, L. (2003). Justice, equity, and fairness in human relations. In J. Weiner (Ed.). *Handbook of Psychology, Vol. 5* (Volume Editors: Th. Millon & M.J. Lerner)(pp. 537 – 568). Hoboken, NJ: Wiley.

Montada, L. & Kals, E. (2000). Political implications of psychological research on ecological justice and pro-environmental behaviors. *International Journal of Psychology, 35,* 168 – 176.

Montada, L. & Kals, E. (2007). *Mediation. Ein Lehrbuch auf psychologischer Grundlage..* Weinheim: Beltz PVU.

Moore, B. (1978). *Injustice: The social bases of obedience and revolt.* London: Macmillan..

Nozick, R. (1974). *Anarchy, state and utopia.* New York: Basic Books.

Ohbuchi, K,. Agarie, N. & Kameda, M. (1989). Apology as aggression control: Its role in mediation appraisal of and response to harm. *Journal of Personality and Social Psychology,* 56(2), 219-227.

Pastore, N. (1952). The role of arbitrariness in the frustration - aggression hypothesis. *Journal of Abnormal and Social Psychology, 47,* 728-731.

Rawls, J. (1971*). A theory of justice.* Cambridge: Harvard University Press.

Montada, L. (in press). Emotions based aggression motives. In Steffgen, G. & Gollwitzer, M. (Ed.), *Emotions and Aggressive Behavior.* Göttingen: Hogrefe.

Ross, M. & Miller, D.T. (Eds.) (2002), *The justice motive in everyday life.* New York: Cambridge University Press.

Rüthers, B. (1991). *Das Ungerechte an der Gerechtigkeit: Defizite eines Begriffs.* Zürich: Edition Interfrom.

Vidmar, N. (2000). Retribution and revenge. In J. Sanders & V.L. Hamilton (Eds.), Handbook of justice research in law (pp. 31-69). New York: Kluwer.

Walzer, M. 1983. *Spheres of justice: A defense of pluralism and equality.* Basic Books. New York.

Leo Montada
University of Trier, Germany

JAMES M. LIES & TONIA BOCK

WHAT DOES IT TAKE TO GIVE?

Moral Identity, Moral Reasoning and Religiosity as Predictors of Civic Engagement

INTRODUCTION

One of the great challenges that moral development theorists face is explaining the disparity between judgment and action. It is apparent that there are those who can well *reason* to the good, but that doesn't historically mean they'll actually *do* the good. What motivates the moral person to act? This study examines three possible predictors of moral action: moral identity, moral reasoning, and religiosity. The moral action is operationalized here as civic engagement, i.e., participation in a service-learning program. A pre-post quasi-experimental design was employed with two groups (one service-learning and one comparison group) of traditionally-aged college students from a large Midwestern religiously-affiliated university. The Service-learning group participated in a summer service project, coupled with a reflection/learning component that took place over the semester following the summer service project. Though a pre-post design, it is the pre-service data that is employed in this analysis. The theoretical underpinnings of this study lie in the Four Component Model of Morality, a process theory of moral behavior developed by James Rest (1983) and his colleagues. While there are a number of investigations of the potential effects of service-learning on college students (e.g., Borzak, 1981; Burwell, Butman, & Van Wicklin, 1992; McNeel, 1994), there appear to be very few which examine the motivators, or predictors, of such service within the broader context of the Four Component Model of moral behavior.

REVIEW OF PERTINENT LITERATURE

A discussion of service-learning and its possible predictors requires attention first to the theoretical framework within which this examination takes place and, additionally, a clarification of the definition of each of the examined constructs as they are understood here.

Theoretical Underpinnings

Four Component Model of Moral Behavior   The Four Component Model (FCM)

Fritz Oser & Wiel Veugelers (eds.), Getting involved, 265–277.

of Morality was first articulated by James Rest (1983) and his colleagues (Rest, Bebeau, & Volker, 1986; Rest, Narvaez, Bebeau, & Thoma, 1999) and addresses the limitations of Kohlberg's (and others') single-variable theories in favor of one that provides a more balanced, coherent, and comprehensive account of moral behavior (Walker, 2004). This expanded model grew out of the increasing concern that a singular focus on moral judgment, without linking it to motivation and action, was in large part futile (Bergman, 2004; Blasi, 1980). Rest and colleagues became convinced that the concern was not methodological, but conceptual. A complete model of moral functioning, according to Rest (1983), includes not only judgment, but other processes as well. Concurrent with Blasi's work (1980, 1984) focusing on the transition from moral cognition through moral motivation to moral action, the FCM provides the superstructure within which to understand the relationships among these processes; and provides a framework for understanding the distinct components that lead to moral behavior.

It is for this reason, that the FCM is employed in this study. It provides a fitting theoretical framework within which to understand any examination of the possible predictors of service-learning among college students (Bergman, 2004). The FCM broadens the widely held view that Kohlberg's (1969) work in moral development remained largely in the realm of moral reasoning. The FCM outlines four distinct components or functional processes which help to broaden moral development beyond the realm of moral reasoning. Along with moral judgment, the model includes moral sensitivity, moral motivation, and implementation, or moral action (see Table 1 for a description of each). Rest's FCM started with the question: How does moral behavior come about? From this question, Rest and colleagues suggested that the literature points to at least these four functional processes that are required in order for moral behavior to occur (Bebeau, 2001). It is worth noting that the model is not conceived as a linear, problem-solving model. The components are interactive and thus can impact each other, with each component having its own cognitive and affective dimensions.

Table 1. The Four Component Model of Moral Behavior

Component	Description
Moral Sensitivity	Moral behavior requires that the situation be interpreted as moral
Moral Judgment	A judgment is made between available actions about which is most ethically justified
Moral Motivation	Requires a prioritising of the moral over other significant and potentially competing concerns
Moral Action	Requires the ability to construct and implement actions that allow for competent and effective action in the moral situation

This model is particularly useful as a framework for understanding the nature of the intervention in this study, as well as the motivations and judgment that lead to civic engagement. In a study that begins with Component 4, moral action (e.g. service-learning), a post hoc assessment is made of the moral happening. The study begins with the assumption that by entering into service, students reveal an appreciation for the moral realm (Component 1: Sensitivity); even as they may not know the specifics of their service project, they are aware in a general sense of human need and are moved to address it. In the study, an assessment was made of the moral reasoning of each student participant (Component 2: Judgment); and an examination was made of three possible pre-intervention motivators (Component 3: Motivation): religiosity, moral identity, and moral reasoning itself.

Definitions

Service Learning   For the purposes of operationalizing the concept, we have deemed participation in an 8-week summer service-learning program the measure of civic engagement. Service-learning is the term used to describe the efforts of the undergraduate sample examined in this study. The term attempts to couple two complex concepts: "community action, the 'service,' and efforts to learn from that action, and connect what is learned to existing knowledge, the 'learning'" (Stanton, Giles, & Cruz, 1999, p. 2). Structured opportunities that link the service with self-reflection and self-discovery, beyond the service itself, facilitate and enhance both the experience and the learning. Service-learning advocates consider a well-rounded education as including the very important notions of social and civic responsibility, leadership development, moral and ethical development, as well as career development (Kendall et al., 1990). The reciprocality of service-learning is rooted in the structured reflection that takes place during and after the experience.

Moral Reasoning   Lawrence Kohlberg outlined a six-stage theory of moral reasoning, adopting Piaget's focus on justice and asserting that the development of justice reasoning is the very essence of moral reasoning, and of moral development itself (Kohlberg, 1969; 1981; 1983). Although criticized by some for its apparent recognition of only one moral virtue, that of justice (Nucci, 2004), Kohlberg's seminal work in outlining his stages of moral reasoning significantly altered our contemporary understanding of the reasoning with which one engages the moral context. Building upon Kohlberg's work, Rest and colleagues have constructed new measures of moral reasoning and refined how moral reasoning development is conceptualized. Kohlberg characterized moral reasoning development as progressing from preconventional reasoning (stages 1 and 2, with an egocentric focus) to conventional reasoning (stages 3 and 4, emphasizing broader perspective taking on issues of justice) to postconventional reasoning (stages 5 and 6, focusing on the importance of social contracts and moral principles). Rest and colleagues have been able to better capture and conceptualize postconventional reasoning with the use of the Defining Issues Test and Defining Issues Test-2 (DIT and DIT-2, respectively), which are paper-pencil measures of moral reasoning development that have impressive evidence of reliability and validity. Moral Development, Self, and Identity (pp. 1-20). Mahwah, NJ: Lawrence Erlbaum. nctioning. In D.K. Lapsley & D. Narvaez (Eds.),Similar to Kohlberg's moral judgment interview method, the first part of the DIT presents moral dilemmas, but rather than articulate arguments for a particular course of action in each case, the respondent is asked to rate twelve items per story on a five-point importance scale in terms of what the protagonist in the story ought to consider in making a decision (Rest & Narvaez, 1994; Thoma, 2002). Each item on the DIT represents a certain developmental level of moral reasoning with the assumption that the respective items will only make sense to the respondent who has attained the associated stage of moral development (as defined by Kohlberg in the early 70s). During the second part of the DIT, "items and ratings are again considered in order to select the four issues that best represent the respondent's rationale for a solution to the dilemma" (Thoma, 2002, p. 226). The N2 score of the DIT has emerged as the index of choice (Bebeau & Thoma, 1994; Rest, Narvaez, Bebeau, & Thoma, 1999) in measuring postconventional moral reasoning.

Moral Identity   Moral identity is an amorphous concept that seemingly has as many meanings as there are those who consider the concept. One might be tempted to refer to those who can delineate "right" from "wrong," or who appear able to articulate what he or she "ought" to do in a moral situation, as having a strong moral identity. Unfortunately, there is considerable evidence in the world of individuals who reason well morally and can speak to the right and wrong of human behavior but who routinely transgress the very moral "imperatives" about which they are so articulate. Thus, the moral person is something more than one who "knows" but is also one who "prioritises" and ultimately "does" the moral good. Moral identity can be seen to exist within the third component of the FCM. A strong moral identity should enhance the motivational impetus to see the self as responsible in the moral situation, rather than to dismiss or avoid it.

According to Marvin Berkowitz (2001), moral identity is a person's sense of his or her own morality. "It is the part of one's self-concept that has to do with how good or moral one is and wants to be. It describes the centrality of morality to one's self-concept" (p. 4). This understanding echoes the work of Erik Erikson (1969) who understood identity to be one's core or essential self. Similarly, Augusto Blasi (1995) uses self-identity as the central explanatory concept in moral functioning (Walker, 2004). According to Bergman (2002), and addressing the links between judgment, motivation and action in the FCM, only when moral understanding is integrated into the structures of the self does it acquire any motivational power and lead, ultimately, to moral action. This motivational power, according to Blasi (1995), is present to the degree that moral understanding is integrated into one's moral identity.

Religiosity   Historically, in psychology, religion has been viewed as both an individual and an institutional construct (Hill & Pargament, 2003). There has been considerable debate in the literature about the difference (or similarity) of the terms "spirituality" and "religion" and how they might be measured (Zinnbauer, Pargament, Cole, Rye, Butter, & Belavich, 1997). As early as William James (1902), direct and immediate "firsthand" experiential religion was distinguished from "secondhand" institutional religion. In contemporary parlance, the distinction is more pronounced. The concept of religion verges on the derogatory in the social sciences and is more closely associated with the latter of James' definitions, that of the influence of the dogmatic teachings that "fail to represent the dynamic personal element in human piety" (Wulff, 1996, p. 46). The term spirituality has come to be more often applied to the personal, subjective aspect of religious experience. In the United States, particularly, there appears a polarization of religiousness and spirituality, with the former representing "an institutional, formal, outward, doctrinal, authoritarian, inhibiting expression and the latter representing an individual, subjective, emotional, inward, unsystematic, freeing expression" (Hill & Pargament, p. 64). Beyond any discussion of religion, the term spirituality can, and has, taken on very disparate uses, including engagement in witchcraft, the occult, or other realms entirely unrelated to institutional religion, and which will not be examined here.

Even with that, we do not hold strongly to the notion that religion and spirituality are two entirely distinct domains, since it is evident that most forms of spiritual expression unfold in a social context. The personal (i.e., spirituality) informs the institutional (i.e., religion) and vice versa. Religion and spirituality represent related rather than independent constructs (Hill et al., 2000). Nonetheless, the amorphous and subjective nature of spirituality and the remarkable breadth of spiritual experience render it a difficult construct to adequately define and measure. Religiosity, on the other hand, has been operationalized in a variety of ways. In most studies, the religion/spirituality measure consists of a sort of global index of religious involvement; most notably, denominational affiliation and/or frequency of church attendance.

METHOD

Research Design

This study was intended to examine whether self-reported pre-intervention assessments of moral identity, religiosity, and moral reasoning prove predictive of student engagement in service-learning activities. The extant data upon which the analyses are based were obtained from a pre-post, quasi-experimental design involving two groups of undergraduates. The first group of students ($\underline{n}$=77) participated in an 8-week summer service-learning program; the second group ($\underline{n}$=80) did not.

Context and Student Profile

The university from which participants were recruited has approximately 7,800 undergraduates, about 85% of whom are Roman Catholic. Rooted in the Catholic social justice tradition, the university's mission statement articulates a concern for social justice: "[The university] seeks to cultivate in its students not only an appreciation for the great achievements of human beings but also a disciplined sensibility to the poverty, injustice, and oppression that burden the lives of so many. The aim is to create a sense of human solidarity and concern for the common good that will bear fruit as learning becomes service to justice" (Colby, Ehrlich, Beaumont, & Stephens, 2003). The university's commitment to justice is evident in programmatic ways throughout the institution, though perhaps most prominent in its service-learning center, which is both a research center and an institutional clearinghouse for service-learning opportunities for faculty, staff, and students. This center also acts as an institutional liaison between the university and numerous local, national, and international volunteer and service organizations.

Participants

The participants were 157 undergraduate first year students ($\underline{n}$=12), sophomores ($\underline{n}$=58), juniors ($\underline{n}$=55), and seniors ($\underline{n}$=28). Their demographic characteristics are comparable to those of the general student population at the University, the majority of whom are traditional age (18-22) for their undergraduate year of study. Seventy-seven service-learning participants agreed to complete the measures in this study. Participants in the comparison group (n=80), who were randomly selected with the help of the university's registrar's office, agreed to participate in the study.

Instrumentation

All participants were asked to complete a large survey and a separate measure of moral reasoning. The survey consisted of 276 items developed by a research team at the university's service-learning center. It included a large section of demographic information, including sex, predominant ethnic background, academic year, and major. The survey also included general questions related to moral identity and development, and to religion and faith involvement (Trozzolo & Brandenberger, 2001).

Moral Identity A moral identity scale was constructed from the large survey. Moral identity was operationalized as the prioritization of issues of morality and the immediacy of attending to them. This Moral Identity Scale (MIS) consisted of eight four-point Likert-type items (1=Strongly Disagree, 4=Strongly Agree). The respondents were asked about their own convictions with regard to civic and social responsibility and levels of personal conviction and motivation, without use of any direct mention of the moral. Examples of questions include "it is my responsibility to share with those who have less," "I feel personally committed to getting involved in the civic affairs of my community," "I feel that I have a personal role to play in efforts aimed at the betterment of humankind," and "My purpose in life is to make the world a better place to live." The Cronbach alpha for the MIS revealed a reliability coefficient of .83, indicating good internal consistency.

The MIS points to identity as motivation toward the moral good in what might be described as a "communitarian context" (Durkheim, 1973). The MIS items were weighted toward an assessment of the moral good as it is accomplished in a social context and as a measure of personal responsibility (Blasi, 1980). The nature of the scale assumed that the moral good is accomplished in an inherent civic and societal context wherein the individual needs to participate in voluntary associations to experience the benefits of social solidarity (Durkheim, 1973). The scale attempted to assess the degree to which the social good is near to the core of the self.

Religiosity Like moral identity, a scale of religiosity was constructed from the large survey. For the purposes of this study, religiosity was operationalized as the extent to which participants engaged in religious practices, including frequency of prayer, bible reading, and church attendance, and the amount of guidance religion provides the respondent. This Religiosity Scale (RS) consisted of nine, four-point Likert-type items that, similar to the MIS, asked for levels of agreement on two items, and levels of importance on three items; the other four items contained a four-point scale asking the respondent about the frequency of specific events. The content of the RS items examined several religiously related constructs/concepts: the role of religious teaching in shaping their social views; whether their church provided clear ethical guidance on social and political issues; the frequency of attendance at religious services and/or reading the Bible; and finally, whether religious beliefs and convictions are best expressed in performing good deeds rather than in attending religious services (Trozzolo & Brandenberger, 2001). The Cronbach alpha of the RS was .86, indicating good internal consistency. This scale was similar to a number of scales that were developed in a series of studies assessing the role of religiosity in health outcomes, with some of the items virtually identical (Miller & Thoreson, 2003).

Moral Reasoning The moral reasoning variable in this study was the N2 score from the Defining Issues Test-2 (DIT-2). Developed by Rest and Narvaez (1998), the purpose of the DIT-2 is to determine the complexity of reasoning that the participant uses in resolving moral dilemmas, specifically that of postconventional reasoning. The N2 score is an index of their reasoning complexity, with higher scores representing more postconventional reasoning.

RESULTS

A multivariate backward logistic regression analysis was used to determine the extent to which three morally-related variables predicted service-learning participation. Significant positive correlations were found between moral identity and religiosity and between moral identity and group (Service-learning or Comparison).

The logistic regression analysis included the Service/Comparison (non-service)

271

group as the dichotomous dependent variable and three continuous independent variables: moral identity, religiosity, and moral reasoning. A total of 157 participants from both the service-learning and the comparison groups were entered into the logistic regression analysis. Missing data caused a purging of 48 participants, resulting in 109 cases for the analysis, 36 for the service-learning group and 73 for the comparison group. A test of the full model with all three predictors was found to be statistically reliable, X^2 (3, $\underline{n}$ = 109) = 17.05, $p < .001$. A second step was performed in the backward logistic regression that included two of the three predictors. The model in the second step was also significant, X^2 (2, $\underline{n}$ = 109) = 17.05, $p < .001$. Prediction success was mixed. As Table 3 shows, 39% of the service-learning group and 92% of the comparison group were correctly predicted in the second step, for an overall success rate of 74%.

Table 4 shows the results of the predictors for each step of the backward logistic regression. As seen in Step 2, two of the three predictors reliably distinguished between the Service-learning and the Comparison group participants: moral identity (b = .24, Exp(b) = 1.27) and moral reasoning (b = .05, Exp(b) = 1.05). Thus, participants with high moral identity scores were 1.27 times more likely to participate in a service-learning experience, and participants with high moral reasoning scores were 1.05 times more likely to engage in service-learning. Religiosity was not found a reliable predictor of service-learning participation.

Table 2. Correlation Table

Pre-Intervention Data	Group Moral Identity		Religiosity	Moral Reasoning
Group	-	.28**	.09	.10
Moral Identity		-	.34**	.06
Religiosity			-	-.08
Moral Reasoning				-

**$p < .01$; $\underline{n}$=109

Table 3. Classification Table from Step 2 of the Backward Logistic Regression

	Predicted Group	
Actual Group	Service-Learning	Comparison
Service-Learning	67	6
Comparison	22	14

Table 4. Logistic Regression Models Predicting Service-Learning Regression

Variable	b	SE Wald (z)				Exp (b)	CI (odds)
STEP 1							
Moral Identity	.23	.08	8.09**	1.26	1.07-1.49		
Religiosity	.00	.04	.01	1.00	.92-1.09		
Moral Reasoning	.05	.02	5.88*	1.05	1.01-1.09		
STEP 2							
Moral Identity	.24	08	9.43**	1.27	1.09-1.48		
Moral Reasoning	.05	.02	5.88*	1.05	1.01-1.09		

**n=109

DISCUSSION

Moral Identity

This study attempted to determine if moral identity predicts participation in service-learning activities. The findings of the logistic regression indicate that moral identity is a reliable predictor of service in this study. This finding gives credence to the Four Component Model (FCM) of Morality in which this study is framed. It logically follows that the participants in the service-learning group should show both higher levels of Component 2, moral judgment, and of Component 3, moral motivation. Like religiosity, which will be discussed later, levels of moral identity were assumed to enhance the motivational impetus to view the self as responsible in the moral situation, rather than to dismiss or avoid it. It appears clear that higher levels of motivation, as measured here by moral identity, predict moral action. Indeed, the empirical evidence supports the assumption that those who show higher levels of moral identity are more likely to engage in service-learning opportunities.

Religiosity

The second of the three variables of interest in this study was religiosity. The present study attempted to determine if religiosity is a predictor of engagement in service-learning activities. The findings of the logistic regression indicate that religiosity, as measured here, was not a reliable predictor of service, even as moral identity and moral reasoning were found to be.

In explaining this finding, it should be noted that both the service-learning and the comparison groups scored quite high on the religiosity scale (of the highest possible score of 36, the mean score for the service-learning group was 27, with the comparison group having a mean score of 26). High levels of religiosity for both groups would be largely expected given the context of the university from which the participants came: as a university committed to the Catholic tradition, and with approximately 85% of its 7,800 undergraduates Catholic, the institution puts a pervasive emphasis on spirituality, religion, and religious participation. As a result, it is not surprising that the two student groups did not report radically varying levels of religiosity (i.e., attendance at weekly services, frequency of prayer and/or Bible reading, etc.). Variance in religious practice would typically be quite common for this age group. Given, however, the significant likelihood that a vast majority of undergraduates from this university experienced a similar religious upbringing, it is not unexpected that religiosity would not sort out as a predictor of service in this environment. The history of Catholic social teaching and the likelihood of significantly high levels of participation in obligatory Sunday Mass, at which this and other Catholic doctrine and dogma were undoubtedly exhorted, lessens considerably the likelihood of finding any differences between the service-learning and the comparison groups on religiosity.

Moral Reasoning

For this study, an analysis of the two groups on the predictive nature of moral reasoning was performed. The results showed that moral reasoning was a reliable predictor of service-learning participation. It should be noted that moral reasoning was not as strong a predictor of participation as was moral identity.

An abundance of anecdotal evidence would support this finding in that not all who show impressive levels of moral reasoning are actually motivated enough to act on their heightened appreciation for the moral good. In this study, those with higher levels of motivation, as measured here by moral reasoning, were likely to participate in service-learning. These findings support the assumption built into the Four Component Model (FCM) that moral reasoning is a necessary but not sufficient component for moral behavior. In conclusion, the motivational variable of moral identity proved to be a stronger predictor of service than did moral reasoning, even as moral reasoning was indeed a predictor of service-learning participation.

Limitations

The nature of the university setting as private and religiously affiliated limited the sample population to largely upper-middle to upper class, mostly Caucasian Catholic students attending a very competitive Midwestern university. The generally high levels of religiosity in this context may have prevented the variable from distinguishing between the service-learning and the comparison groups. A secular university context, or a more diverse religiously affiliated university context, would make an examination of the impact of religiosity a far more interesting proposition.

A further limitation became evident during the analysis of the data; some missing data, particularly for the service group on the extended student survey, caused a substantial purging of the data set (from 77 to 36 for the service-learning group), thus limiting the types of statistical analyses that could be conducted, and compromising the power of the analyses that were performed. The difference in the number of those who completed the DIT-2 and the survey at pre-intervention is a function of the design in that they were actually administered at two different times. As a consequence, while there were a large number of the service-learning group who filled out the DIT-2 at pre-intervention, the smaller sample size for the service-learning group on the student survey lead ultimately to a failure in meeting the assumptions for logistic regression analysis, which recommends a minimum of 50 cases per predictor to achieve accurate results. Under this recommendation, we came somewhat under our minimum sample size (109 out of 150). Finally, while the Cronbach's alpha revealed high internal consistency for two of the variables that were examined for their predictive value, religiosity and moral identity, further verification of the variables' reliability and validity is in order.

Conclusion

This study's intention was to examine if, prior to a service-learning intervention, any of three factors, moral identity, religiosity, and moral reasoning, might prove possible predictors of service learning participation. The finding that moral identity and moral reasoning are reliable predictors of participation in service-learning, even as religiosity was not, further supports the need to examine a whole array of variables that might motivate young people to moral action. The burgeoning prevalence of service-learning opportunities, as a complement to traditional institutional learning environments, makes the empirical investigation of both predictors and impact all the more important. Determining the direction of the educational enterprise within and beyond the classroom, particularly as it promotes citizenship and moral development, requires careful attention to these and related issues.

REFERENCES

Bailis, L.N. & Melchior, A. (2003). Practical issues in the conduct of large-scale, multisite research and evaluation. In S.H. Billig & A.S. Waterman, (Eds.). *Studying service-learning: Innovations in educational research methodology.* Mahwah, NJ: Lawrence Erlbaum Associates, Publishers.

Bebeau, M.J. (2001). Influencing the moral dimensions of professional practice: Implications for teaching and assessing for research integrity. *Proceedings: Investigating research & integrity.*

Bebeau, M.J. & Thoma, S.J. (1994). The impact of a dental ethics curriculum on moral reasoning. *Journal of Dental Education, 58.* 684-693.

Bebeau, M.J. & Thoma, S.J. (2003). *Guide for DIT-2: A guide for using the defining issues test, version 2 and the scoring service of the Center for the Study of Ethical Development*. Minneapolis, MN: University of Minnesota.

Bergman, R. (2002). Why be moral? A conceptual model from developmental psychology. *Human Development, 45*, 104-124.

Bergman, R. (2004). Identity as motivation: Toward a theory of the moral self. In D.K. Lapsley, & D. Narvaez, (Eds.). *Moral development, self, and identity*. Mahwah, NJ: Lawrence Erlbaum Associates, Publishers.

Berkowitz, M.W. (2001). In S. Sherblom (Chair), *Living with yourself: The role of moral identity in character*. Symposium presented at the annual meeting of the Association for Moral Education, Vancouver, Canada.

Blasi, A. (1980). Bridging moral cognition and moral action: A critical review of the literature. *Psychological Bulletin, 88*, 1-45.

Blasi, A. (1984). Moral identity: Its role in moral functioning. In W.M. Kurtines & J.L. Gewirtz (Eds.), *Morality, moral behavior, and moral development* (pp. 128-139). New York: Wiley.

Blasi, A. (1995). Moral understanding and the moral personality: The process of moral integration. In W.M. Kurtines & J.L. Gewirtz (Eds.), *Moral development: An introduction* (pp. 229-253). Boston: Allyn & Bacon.

Borzak, L. (Ed.). (1981). *Field study: A sourcebook for experiential learning*. Beverly Hills, CA: Sage.

Burwell, R., Butman, R. & Van Wicklin, J. (1992). *Values assessment at three consortium colleges: A longitudinal follow-up study*. Houghton, NY: Houghton College.

Colby, A., Ehrlich, T., Beaumont, E., & Stephens, J. (2003). *Educating citizens: Perparing America's undergraduates for lives of moral and civic responsibility*. San Francisco, CA: Jossey-Bass.

Durkheim, E. (1973). Moral education: A study in the theory and application of the sociology of education. New York: Free Press.

Erikson, E. (1969). Gandhi's truth: On the origins of militant non-violence. New York: Norton.

Evens, J. (1995). *Indexing moral judgment using multidimensional scaling*, unpublished doctoral dissertation, University of Minnesota. Cited in Thoma, S.J. (2002). An overview of the Minnesota approach to research in moral development. *Journal of Moral Education, 31*, 225-246.

Gunnoe, M. L. & Moore, K. A. (2002). Predictors of religiosity among youth aged 17-22: A longitudinal study of the National Survey of Children. Journal for the Scientific Study of Religion, 41(4), 613-622.

Hill, P. C. & Pargament, K.I. (2003). Advances in the conceptualization and measurement of religion and spirituality: Implications for physical and mental health research. *American Psychologist, 58*, 64-74.

James, W. (1902). *The varieties of religious experience*. New York: Random House.

Kendall, J.C. et al (Eds.) (1990). *Combining service and learning: A resource book for community and public service* (Vols. 1-3). Raleigh, NC: National Society for Experiential Education.

Kohlberg, L. (1969). Stage and sequence: The cognitive-developmental approach to socialization. In D.A. Goslin (Ed.), *Handbook of socialization theory and research* (pp. 347-480). Chicago: Rand-McNally.

Kohlberg, L. (1981). *The meaning and measurement of moral development*. Worcester, MA: Clark University Press.

Kohlberg, L., Levine, C. & Hewer, A. (1983). *Moral stages: A current formulation and a response to critics: Contributions to human development, Vol. 10*. Basel, Switzerland: Karger.

McNeel, S.P. (1995). College teaching and student moral development. In J. Rest & D. Narvaez (Eds.), *Moral development in the professions* (pp. 27-49). Mahwah, NJ: Lawrence Erlbaum Associates, Publishers.

Nucci, L. (2004). Reflections on the moral self construct. In D. Lapsley & D. Narvaez (Eds.), *Moral development, self, and identity*. (pp. 111-132). Mahwah, NJ: Lawrence Erlbaum Associates, Publishers.

Rest, J. (1974). Manual for the Defining Issues Test of moral judgment development, available from the Center for the Study of Ethical Development, University of Minnesota.

Rest, J. (1979). *Development in judging moral issues.* Minneapolis: University of Minnesota Press.

Rest, J. (1983). Morality. In: Mussen, P.H., series ed., Flavell, J., Markman, E., volume eds. *Handbook of child psychology: Vol. 3. Cognitive development.* 4th ed. (pp. 556-629). New York: Wiley.

Rest, J., Bebeau, M. & Volker, J. (1986). In Rest, J. (Ed.) *Moral development: Advances in research and theory* (pp. 1-39). Boston: Praeger Publishers.

Rest, J., Narvaez, D., Bebeau, M. & Thoma S. (1999). *Postconventional moral thinking: A neo-Kohlbergian approach.* Mahwah, NJ: Lawrence Erlbaum Associates, Inc.

Rest, J., Narvaez, D., Thoma S. & Bebeau, M. (1999). DIT-2: Devising and testing a revised instrument of moral judgment. *Journal of Educational Psychology, 91,* 644-658.

Rest, J., Thoma, S.J., Narvaez, D. & Bebeau, M. (1997). Alchemy and beyond: Indexing the Defining Issues Test. *Journal of Educational Psychology, 89,* 498-507.

Stanton, T.K., Giles, D.E. & Cruz, N.I. (1999). *Service-learning: A movement's pioneers reflect on its origins, practice and future.* San Francisco: Jossey Bass.

Thoma, S.J. (2002). An overview of the Minnesota approach to research in moral development. *The Journal of Moral Education, 31,* 225-246.

Trozzolo, T.A. & Brandenberger, J.W. (2001). Religious commitment and prosocial behavior: A study of undergraduates at the University of Notre Dame. *Studies in Social Responsibility, Report #2: Notre Dame Center for Social Concerns* (http://centerforsocialconcerns.nd.edu/sub_research.html).

Walker, L.J. (2004). Progress and prospects in the psychology of moral development. *Merrill-Palmer Quarterly, 50,* 546-557.

Walker, L.J. (2004). Gus in the gap: Bridging the judgment-action gap in moral functioning. In D.K. Lapsley & D. Narvaez (Eds.), *Moral development, self, and identity* (pp. 1-20). Mahwah, NJ: Lawrence Erlbaum.

Wright, R.E. (1995). Logistic regression (Chapter 7) in L.G. Grimm & P.R. Yarnold (Eds.), *Reading and understanding multivariate statistics.* Washington, DC: American Psychological Association.

Wulff, D.M. (1996). The psychology of religion: An overview. In E.P. Shafranske (Ed.), *Religion and the clinical practice of psychology* (pp. 43-70). Washington, DC: American Psychological Association.

Zinnbauer, B.J., Pargament, K.I., Cole, B., Rye, M.S., Butter, E.M. & Belavich, T.G. (1997). Religion and spirituality: Unfuzzying the fuzzy. *Journal for the Scientific Study of Religion, 36,* 549-564.

James M. Lies
University of Portland, USA
Tonia S. Bock
University of St. Thomas, Minnesota, USA

DANIEL K LAPSLEY & DARCIA NARVAEZ

"PSYCHOLOGIZED MORALITY"
AND ETHICAL THEORY, OR,
DO GOOD FENCES MAKE GOOD NEIGHBORS?

INTRODUCTION: FENCES AND NEIGHBORS

In this chapter we reconsider the boundary between ethics and moral development theory, and respond to recent challenges to our call for a "psychologized morality." The boundary issue has a discernible historical arc. When much of American psychology was in the grips of behaviorism – during the first six or seven decades of the twentieth-century – its stance towards ethical terms was entirely in keeping with the epistemology of logical positivism. On this score ordinary moral language ("good", "ought" "values") was useless for scientific investigation without "operational" translation into the constructs of behavioral science ("positive reinforcement"). Behavioral psychology thus staked out its claims against metaphysics, erecting a fence and extending a boundary against it.

But the autonomy of (behavioral) psychology from ethics was challenged by the rise of Kohlberg's moral stage theory. Indeed, Kohlberg's stage theory was a much better neighbor to ethical theory than was behavioral theory. Kohlberg's embrace of the formalist ethical tradition as the starting point of his investigation essentially lowered the fence between ethical theory and moral development and effaced the boundary between them. This affirmed the autonomy of morality, but at the expense (we argue) of the autonomy of psychology. Our call for a psychologized morality is an attempt to revisit the boundary between ethical theory and developmental studies of moral functioning.

The boundary we have in mind calls for a greater sense of partnership across both sides of the fence, rather than the one-sided, unilateral respect of developmental studies for ethical theory. We take aim at the autonomy of morality by our embrace of ethical naturalism, and affirm the independence of psychological research, but we do so convinced that a new understanding of the boundary will encourage mutual respect and partnership and, indeed, make good neighbors of us all.

A Poetic Metaphor: The Mending Wall

A poetic metaphor best captures our understanding of the partnership between ethics and developmental psychology. We have in mind the famous line from Robert

Fritz Oser & Wiel Veugelers (eds.), Getting involved, 279–291.
279

Frost's great iconic poem, *The Mending Wall* – "*good fences make good neighbors*."
This expression is familiar to most Americans, even if they don't always remember
its source. Unfortunately, the expression is often misunderstood. The line usually is
interpreted to mean that a good neighbor is one that we keep at arm's length, behind
a fence. The good neighbor is one we never see, who does not intrude on us and
minds his own business. The good neighbor leaves us alone. However, the actual
poem comes to a completely opposite conclusion.

The poem begins:

> "*Something there is that doesn't love a wall*
> *That sends the frozen ground swell under it*
> *And spills the upper boulders in the sun*
> *And makes gaps even two can pass abreast*."

The poem explains that no one has seen or heard the gaps being made, but there they
are "at spring mending time." The narrator informs his neighbor ("beyond the hill")
about the gaps in the wall. The neighbor comes down and together they walk the line
"and set the wall between us once again." They go about repairing the wall, wearing
their fingers rough handling the boulders. And it amazes the narrator because all of
this wall-building is quite unnecessary because when it comes down to it:

> "*We do not need the wall*
> *He is all pine and I am all apple orchard*
> *My apple trees will never get across*
> *And eat the cones under the pines, I tell him.*
> *He only says: 'Good fences make good neighbors.'*"

The poem reminds us that we need occasions to be and feel like neighbors, to work
together on a common project, to walk the line together handling the rough stones
mending the wall. A fence is "good" not because it keeps neighbors apart and distant but because the occasion of repairing it gives them reason to work together in
partnership. A good fence does not keep people separated but brings them together
in collaboration and fellowship, which in fact makes us ìgoodî neighbors, and probably in some moral sense of good.

The point of the wall, then, is that it brings us together and does not separate us;
it needs mending and we must cooperate in a common project. It is in this spirit that
developmental psychologists walk the mending wall with ethicists, as we handle the
rough stones repairing the gaps that have emerged in the boundary between ethics
and psychology. Although the disciplines enjoy relative autonomy ("He is all pine
and I am all apple orchard"), there are occasions for ethicists and psychologists to
walk the line together for mutual benefit.

In the next section we provide the background argument that motivated our call
for a psychologized morality, and then note its key claims. We claim, for example,
that a psychologized morality and naturalized ethics are "fellow travelers," bound
by a similar understanding of the mending wall between ethics and the social and

cognitive sciences. Insofar as we embrace naturalism in ethics, we clarify our intentions in this respect, and respond to recent criticism of our approach. Our concluding post-script brings us back to Kohlberg. Here we will argue that the naturalizing tendencies endorsed by our perspective have deep roots in Kohlberg's own project.

AT A CROSSROAD

Recently we argued that moral development research is at a crossroad (Lapsley & Narvaez, 2005). For nearly forty years Kohlberg's paradigm defined the terms of reference for the study of moral reasoning, yet there are unmistakable signs that it now sits on the margins of cognitive and social developmental research. The debates and issues that once swirled around the moral stage theory, and which provided an exciting momentum to research, now seem to hold little interest, and not because all the questions have been answered (Lapsley, 2006).

Certainly part of the story of the declining influence of Kohlberg's moral stage theory can be traced to the general decline of Piaget's approach in developmental psychology (Lapsley, 2006). Kohlberg's (1969) "cognitive developmental approach to socialization" traded on the prestige of the Piagetian paradigm, so that when Piaget's theory waned in influence, or was eclipsed by alternative conceptualizations of intellectual development, Kohlberg's theory became deprived of much of its paradigmatic support.

In retrospect the preoccupations of Kohlberg's research program seemed far removed from what is the overriding concern of parents and educators, which is how to raise children of a certain kind, that is, children who possess important moral dispositions, who possess traits that are desirable and praiseworthy and whose personalities are imbued with a strong ethical compass (Lapsley, in press). On these matters moral stage theory surprisingly is silent. It has relatively little to say about how to raise moral children. It provides little guidance for parents, let alone educators, for how morally-crucial dispositions are to be encouraged in young children, and, indeed, provides only a slight framework for understanding moral behavior in young children more generally (Lapsley & Narvaez, 2006).

Of course, this was not Kohlberg's project. He actively rejected any claim to address issues of character. Instead, his was an attempt to chart ontogenetic variation in how individuals resolve hard-case moral dilemmas. With increasing development individuals will call upon increasingly complex sets of sociomoral operations to sort out questions of fairness, adjudicate conflict, and justify decisions. They come to appreciate with increasing transparency and articulacy the moral point of view as it is understood by formalist ethics.

These are not unimportant developmental achievements, yet it seems to pass by the ordinary moral experience of children and the overriding concerns of their parents. Moral stages do not, after all, classify individuals but rather the structural properties of reasoning. They permit no aretaic evaluation nor prompt reflection about the moral qualities of personhood. They say nothing about virtue or character. They do not even describe moral stage development in *childhood*. Indeed, children rarely encounter the sort of moral dilemmas used in the typical assessments; and parents would find it odd to learn that the reasonable goal of moral socialization held out by moral stage theory is for adolescents to think about dilemmas (they would hardly encounter) in conventional ways.

This is not in any way to diminish the extraordinary significance of Kohlberg's theory. As we will note below, Kohlberg's remarkable contribution first raised the visibility of the moral domain, indeed, made it possible, in an era that was hostile to notions of cognitive structure and stage development. What's more, Kohlberg's research team scored significant empirical successes in its pursuit of moral stages in its restrictive domain of application (e.g., Colby, Kohlberg, Gibbs & Lieberman, 1983). Rest (1987) termed the validation results "spectacular" (p. 466) and noted that "for no other measurement procedure in the field have such strong confirmatory trends been reported" (p. 464). Moreover, the addition of moral discussion and just communities to the arsenal of the moral education is an enduring contribution of the Kohlberg team (e.g., Power, Higgins & Kohlberg, 1989).

Yet even on its own terms the moral stage theory seemed to turn in on itself as it wrestled with recalcitrant data. On Kohlberg's account the construct validity of moral stages rested on positive evidence regarding the holistic consistency of moral reasoning (*structure d'ensemble*) and its "invariant sequence" of development. But early evidence was not encouraging. Indeed, data generated by early scoring systems presented Kohlberg with a prima facie refutation of the moral stage theory. The research program did regroup and evolve new scoring systems to resolve the anomalous data, but at the price of purging Stage 6 as the endpoint, larding the sequence with sub-stages, and restricting the range of extension of a moral structure to something narrow and cramped – to only those data obtained from spontaneous interviews and not in any other way; and only on hypothetical justice dilemmas and not those that pull for other types of moral issues (Lapsley, 2006)..

Of course, every research program must proceed in the face of anomalies, and there is always recalcitrant data with which to contend. "All theories are born refuted and die refuted," as (Lakatos, 1978, p. 5) put it. But progressive research programs deal with anomalies in content-increasing ways. Degenerating research programs do not. Degenerating research programs assume a strictly defensive posture by adopting a series of ad hoc stratagems that do more to protect its core claims than to anticipate novel facts (Lakatos, 1978). By these criteria it seems clear that we are met here at the crossroad with a degenerating research program in moral stage theory.

MORALIZED PSYCHOLOGY AND PSYCHOLOGIZED MORALITY

Progressive research programs that struggle with unruly evidence often look to other theories, constructs and traditions to explore the resources that meaningful integration might afford. But this option was not easily available to the Kohlberg paradigm, largely because its core assumptions and philosophical commitments resisted easy commerce with contemporary psychological research. To see this consider what is arguably Kohlberg's greatest accomplishment: Kohlberg quite simply *moralized* psychology with his stage theory. He brought ethics to psychology, creating a field of study in the process. He used ethical theory to set the terms of reference for his investigations. Indeed, Kohlberg argued that the study of moral development must begin with certain metaethical assumptions that define a moral judgment (Kohlberg, Levine & Hewer, 1983). Kohlberg's embrace of Kantian formalism allowed him to carve out a domain of study against the backdrop of psychoanalysis and behaviorism; and it provided a way to articulate and define the emerging cognitive developmental alternative (Kohlberg et al., 1983)

And from Kohlberg we learned a lesson about the division of labor between ethics and psychology: First, make certain ethical assumptions; use ethical theory to define the terms of reference, to define the domain of inquiry; and then, once this is done, get on with your psychological work. Kohlberg's instruction on this was so successful that it is now part of the received view that philosophical analysis must precede psychological work. Psychological explanations must be grounded by philosophical explanations (see e.g., Turiel, 1998). Put tendentiously, while ethics is autonomous psychology is not. Psychological research on moral functioning is to be constrained by ethical theory.

This cognitive developmental *rapprochement* with ethics raised many suspicions on both sides of the disciplinary boundary. Although philosophers seemed pleased that Kohlberg at least got his priorities straight – first come to terms with ethical theory then do psychology – they nonetheless wondered if he was committing the naturalistic fallacy or else got his formalist ethics wrong. Psychologists worried that by accepting a particular philosophical definition of morality as a starting point, one might be tempted 1) to narrow the scope of inquiry, 2) resolve philosophical problems with empirical data; or 3) use strictly philosophical criticism to trump the empirical claims of a theory (e.g., Blasi, 1990; Lapsley & Narvaez, 2005).

We think the Kohlberg paradigm succumbed to the temptations of (1) and (2), but was largely the victim of (3). The scope of inquiry certainly was narrowly fixed on justice alone. It did attempt to resolve philosophical problems with empirical data, in this case the problem of ethical relativism (see below). And there were many who seemed to think that Kohlberg's developmental theory was wrong solely because of doubts about the adequacy of his philosophical commitments – a move we think illegitimate but perhaps inevitable given Kohlberg's moralization of psychology.

Kohlberg moralized psychology, then, in a double sense, not just by using formalist ethical theory to set the terms of reference, but to establish the very purpose of investigation. The purpose of Kohlberg's work was to provide the psychological resources to defeat ethical relativism. Ethical relativism is defeated at the highest stages of development, where the moral point of view commits us to seek moral consensus around rationally-grounded universal imperatives.

But it was the commitment to the anti-relativism project that led ultimately to the marginalization of moral stage theory, in our view. Kohlberg's attempt to transform the study of moral behavior by appealing to a set of philosophical assumptions and definitions imported from ethics, along with his pursuit of an empirical basis to defeat relativism, had the unintended consequence of isolating moral psychological research from advances in other domains of psychology, effectively pushing it to the margins of contemporary psychological research. Entire lines of research were ruled out of bounds not for the usual scientific reasons but on the grounds that they might, in some way, give aid or comfort to ethical relativism. Hence research on selfhood and personality, the study of traits and dispositions, the language of virtues and character, and moral emotions, – all were deemed suspect, tangential or irrelevant to what was wanted most, which was a way to resolve the question of ethical relativism on empirical grounds.

We have complained, too, about other moral philosophic starting points, such as Kohlberg's insistence on a principle of phenomenalism for defining moral phenomena (Lapsley & Narvaez, 2005). This principle asserts that "moral reasoning is the conscious process of using ordinary moral language" (Kohlberg, Levine & Hewer, 1983, p. 69). On this view the moral quality of behavior hinges solely on the subjective perspective, judgment and intention of the agent. A behavior has no particular moral status unless is it motivated by an explicit moral judgment. It implies "reference to conscious processes" (Kohlberg et al., 1983, p. 8). Phenomenalism is so deeply rooted in the cognitive developmental tradition that Blasi (1990) could assert that morality "*by definition*, depends on the agent's subjective perspective" (p. 59, our emphasis).

But the principle of phenomenalism is a mixed blessing. Kohlberg used it as a cudgel against behaviorism (which denied cognitivism) and psychoanalysis (which asserted the primacy of emotions and the unconscious). Moreover, it seems the guarantor of radical moral freedom to the extent that it frees behavior from "stimulus control" and places it instead under the command of rational calculation. Yet the principle of phenomenalism also closed off recourse to rich veins of contemporary research in social cognition – ruling out the legitimacy, for example, of recent research on tacit, automatic and implicit cognition for the moral domain. These philosophical roadblocks have essentially isolated moral development from the resources of other domains of psychology. As a result the study of moral development has been unaffected by developments in cognitive psychology, neuroscience and personality, although there are encouraging signs that this is now changing (e.g., Killen & Smetana, 2006; Narvaez, in press; Narvaez & Lapsley, 2005; Walker & Hennig, 1998).

Our remedy for the marginalization of moral development is for *more psychology* (Lapsley & Narvaez, 2005). That is, we suggested that the next generation of research would do well to *psychologize* morality, rather than pursue the moralized psychology advocated by the cognitive developmental tradition. By "psychologized morality" we mean an approach to inquiry that avails itself of the full range of psychological literatures, including personality and cognitive psychology, social cognition and motivation, evolutionary psychology and the neurosciences, among others. A psychologized morality asserts the autonomy of psychology in the study of moral functioning. It jettisons a priori philosophical constraints and seeks integrative possibilities between moral psychology and other human sciences, including the neurosciences.

Moreover, we argued that the movement towards a psychologized morality converges with the "naturalized ethics" perspective that attempts to stake normative ethics to a defensible account of human nature. Indeed, psychologised morality and naturalized ethics are "fellow travelers" well-met at the crossroad of our disciplines, and pointing towards a common problematic, which is how to account for moral personality, selfhood and agency.

ETHICAL NATURALISM

We invoked the notion of a "psychologized morality" in the context of an historical reconstruction of the Kohlberg paradigm. We did so to call attention to the problem of boundaries between ethics and psychology. The Kohlberg team accepted a division of labor that not only respected the autonomy of morality but gave it certain prerogatives to constrain the psychological agenda – to establish its boundary, define its starting points, and rein in its explanations. Our call for a psychologized morality was a way to register our objection to this extraordinary arrangement. It was a way to assert the autonomy of psychology (*"We keep the wall between us as we go"*) as we walk the mending wall with ethical theory.

What is new, however, is the very notion that ethical theorists ever need to walk the mending wall with psychologists in the first place. The autonomy of morality, which is a presumption of the ethical tradition from Kant to Moore to Hare, renders such effort pointless. Morality is sui generis, it is asserted, and there is nothing about it that depends upon natural or social scientific knowledge. Ethical naturalism challenges this view. It asserts that the human sciences are not irrelevant for ethics. At its core ethical naturalism asserts that we live in a single natural world (Wong, 2006). Consequently normative ethics can make no appeal to non-natural entities or phenomena – no appeal to gods, to noumenal metaphysics, souls, free wills, rational moral agents, epistemic subjects, Platonic forms, and so on.

Of course, apart from its commitment to a "single natural world" ethical naturalism is not univocal, and different positions are possible with respect to it (e.g., Forrest, 2000; Garfield, 2000; Railton, 1989). Moreover, there are a number of ways of categorizing the different approaches to naturalized ethics. Indeed, a recent paper by Maxwell (2007) has criticized us for not specifying the sort of ethical naturalism that is most congenial to a psychologized morality, so getting this right is a matter of some importance to us.

Varieties of Ethical Naturalism

Casebeer (2003) sketches out three possible positions with respect to the relation between ethics and science. There are first of all "Separatists" who advocate ab-

285

stinence – no intercourse is possible between the findings of science and the articulation of ethical norms. What ìisî is irrelevant to what ìoughtî to be, from the perspective of Separatists. Here the boundary between ethics and science is fortified, and the fence is high and guarded. Then there are ìConfederatesî who are "mildly promiscuous". Confederates allow the findings of science to place limits on the demands that norms can place upon us; or else rule out some moral theories as inconsistent with our best natural knowledge. Put differently, Confederates insist that ethical theory satisfy strong (William, 1981) or weak (Flanagan, 1991) criteria of psychological realism. Confederates are mindful of the naturalistic fallacy but claim to evade it; and they are likely to make good neighbors insofar as they acknowledge the existence of a boundary wall that needs mending.

Finally there are Unionists. Unionists demand not simply that ethical theory be consistent with natural knowledge but that it reduces to more fundamental naturalized theories. They assert that the methodological and epistemological assumptions of the natural sciences should serve as the standard of ethical inquiry. Unionists are dismissive of the ("so-called") naturalistic fallacy; and see no need for a wall just because there are not two sides – there are not all pines on the one side and apples on the other– itís just one big orchard of natural science.

Wong (2006) is a good Confederate. He argues that there are multiple true moralities, although there are natural limits on what can count as a true morality, given the realities of human needs, desires and purposes. His methodological naturalism is committed to an integration of morality "with the most relevant empirical theories about human beings and society, such as evolutionary theory and developmental psychology" (Wong, 2006, p. xiv). Indeed, psychology's role looms large in many accounts of ethical naturalism. As Flanagan put it, "...scientific psychology has the potential for destabilizing, as well as for developing and refining certain assumptions underlying traditional moral theoryî (1991, p. 21).

Wong (2006) emphasizes two methodological themes. One is that philosophy "should not employ a distinctive a priori method for yielding substantive truth shielded from empirical testing" (p. 30). Another is that "there is no sharp boundary between epistemology and the science of psychology" (p. 30). His methodological naturalism does not rule out claims asserted on the basis of non-natural analytical, logical or conceptual analysis, or by non-empirical methods, just that "the deliverances of such methods cannot be taken as self-evident or permanent" (p. 30).

Maxwell (2007) identifies three varieties of ethical naturalism: normative, neo-Aristotelian and evidential. Naturalized normative ethics, following Flanagan (1991), is one that satisfies criteria of psychological realism. The norms and standards that ethics holds out must be a possibility for ordinary human beings. Neo-Aristotelian naturalism, following Hursthouse, (1999, 2003) and McKinnon (2005), justifies ethical prescriptions from the standpoint of the essential features of human nature. Evidential naturalism, following Doris (2002; Doris & Strich, 2005), is a methodological naturalism (like Wong's) that constrains ethical theory by the empirical findings of the social sciences.

286

Which variety of ethical naturalism is a fellow traveler with psychologized morality? Maxwell (2007) is correct to note that our psychologized morality draws inspiration from all three of his varieties, but that it is evidential naturalism that is the best fit. Indeed, we admit to being Confederates (but with Unionist sympathies) and find Wong's (2006) methodological naturalism congenial with our own perspective about boundary issues.

In our view the findings of the human sciences already cast grave doubt on the plausibility of certain ethical notions. We nominate the "unity of the virtues" and Aristotle's conception of an ideal virtuous agent as two notions that run counter to the requirement of psychological realism. Flanagan (1991) nominated the putative distinction between character and moral character and the accuracy of first-person reports as philosophical notions (among others) made implausible by psychological realism. But we hasten to add that psychological research lends empirical support to several aspects of classical ethical theory, too. For example, that moral sensibility must be cultivated in context; that moral education requires the guidance of mentors until self-guidance takes over; that virtue cannot be taught like history but must emerge from lived experience, among others, these claims are well-grounded by developmental and educational psychology.

Is "Psychologized Morality" Based on a Fallacy?

But does psychologized morality run afoul of the "is-ought problem" (in violation of "Hume's Law")? Does it commit the "naturalistic fallacy" (Moore, 1903/1993)? The is-ought problem is traced to a section of Hume's (1740/2000) Treatise (Book 3, Part 1, Section 1) that cautions against moving from descriptive statements ("is" or "is not") to prescriptive statements ("ought" or "ought not'); or, alternatively, from non-moral premises to moral conclusions – "...for what seems altogether inconceivable, how this new relation can be a deduction from others, which are entirely different from it" (p. 302). The "naturalistic fallacy" is traced to G. E. Moore's (1903/1993) claim that ethical terms ("good") point to non-natural, indefinable properties (although we will recognize it when we encounter it) that cannot, on pain of incoherence, be reduced to natural properties (such as human needs, desires, emotions). For example, we can always ask of something: "Is x good?" – which suggests therefore that the property of being x and the property of being good are not identical. Insofar as the property of being good cannot be identified with natural properties, it is an indefinable sui generis concept. For Moore, it is an "open question" for any natural property as to whether it is good (Casebeer, 2003. And to conflate good with natural properties is to fall prey to the naturalistic fallacy.

Taken together, "Hume's Law" and G. E. Moore's naturalistic fallacy appear to forbid grounding morality on non-moral foundations; or explicating ethical terms with natural properties. This builds a high wall between ethics and science and makes Separatists of us all.

The naturalistic fallacy is a specter that haunts ethical naturalism, although it seems to frighten psychologists the most. The debate between ethical naturalism and anti-naturalism is longstanding and beyond our competence to resolve. But we would simply note here that ethical naturalism is not helpless in this debate. MacIntrye (1959) argued, for example, that Hume was not, in any event, asserting the autonomy or morals (because he did not believe in it); nor was he making a point about logical entailment of ought by is, because he never mentions it. In fact Humeís whole Treatise is an extended example of how to violate iHumeís Law." As MacIntrye (1959) noted, "if Hume does affirm the impossibility of deriving an "ought" from an "is" then he is the first person to perform this particular impossibility" (p. 455). In MacIntyre's (1959) view, the movement from is to ought is a fallacy only if one believes that rational inference takes only one form, which is the form of a deductive syllogism. Moreover, as McKinnon (1999) points out, while descriptive facts may not determine normative prescriptions, they can certainly constrain them. What's more, the is-ought distinction and Moore's "open question" argument may be special cases of the analytical-synthetic distinction that Quine (1951) denounced as one of the dogmas of empiricism. – a "metaphysical article of faith" that cannot be sustained (Casebeer, 2003). Finally, Dewey's ethical theory provides a number of options for understanding the distinction between the desired and the desirable but in a way compatible with a broad commitment to naturalism. As Dewey (1922) put it, "a morals based on the study of human nature instead of upon disregard for it would find the facts of man continuous with those of the rest of nature and would thereby ally ethics with physics and biology" (p. 12).

But we think much of this controversy elides our present concerns. As Confederates we walk the mending wall with ethical naturalists in our joint attempt to explain moral behavior. The explanation of moral behavior will retain the language of standards, norms and reasons, so there is no intention (or possibility) of eliminating evaluative language and replacing with non-evaluative terms (Wong, 2006). For example, Wong's (2006) shows how it is possible to explain moral evaluation "through evaluative terms that are *not irreducibly moral though still evaluative and normative in character"* (p. 36, emphasis in original). In other words, we seek an explanation of morality in terms of norms, standards and reasons but as these relate to human social and psychological needs, interests and purposes (Wong, 2006). As Wong (2006) puts it, "Such an explanation, in accordance with methodological naturalism, will be responsive to our best theories of human beings. It will not rely on a priori moral truths taken as self-evident and foundational or as derived purely from logical or conceptual analysis" (p. 36).

A CONCLUDING KOHLBERGIAN POSTSCRIPT

A psychologized morality stands, then, with a methodological naturalism that attempts to ground ethical theory by what is known about "human motivation, the nature of the self, the nature of human concepts, how our reason works, how we are socially constituted, and a host of other facts about who we are and how the mind operates"

(Johnson, 1993). It rejects the notion that morality is *sui generis*; that moral properties are an irreducible part of the fabric of reality; or grounded by a priori methods or self-evident foundations (Wong, 2006). It rejects philosophical assumptions, such as the principle of phenomenalism, which chokes off access to the empirical literatures of psychology. It affirms that moral norms have regulative and functional work to do that is explicable in terms of the cultural evolutionary history of the species and the theoretical and empirical literatures of the human sciences.

We have only hinted at what the content of a psychologized morality might look like. Indeed, we are not wedded to the term, and we are not leading a movement. This is a discernible movement only in the sense that investigators are reflective about their commitment to naturalism in social science research on moral functioning. Our own work has explored the tacit, implicit and automatic aspects of moral behavior (Narvaez & Lapsley, 2005); invoked the language of cognitive schemas to understand *phronesis* and the expertise literature to understand moral skill development (Narvaez, 2006); and linked moral dispositions to neurobiologically-rooted motivational tendencies afforded by the evolutionary development of the brain (Narvaez, in press). Those interested in moral development, whether theorists, researchers, or practitioners, ought to attend to the breadth of extant empirical research bearing on moral behavior and development.

But we would like to close by returning to Kohlberg's seminal contribution to moral development. We are mindful that our reconstruction of the historical evolution of moral stage theory and our diagnosis of the current state of things, indeed, our embrace of ethical naturalism as a remedy, will be controversial. Yet we are confident that our naturalizing tendencies are in keeping with Kohlberg's own best insights about boundary issues (Kohlberg, 1971).

Kohlberg, too, was a Confederate and he embraced a kind of philosophical naturalism. He understood, for example, the implications of Piaget's genetic epistemology---that the empirical data of child development is relevant for discerning criteria for evaluating progress in science, philosophy and mathematics (Piaget); or for deciding when some moral philosophies are inadequate or unworthy of us (Kohlberg). Just as Piaget appealed to developmental criteria to dispense with unstable and inadequate epistemological positions (empiricism, rationalism), so too did Kohlberg (1969) press developmental claims against inadequate meta-theoretical positions in psychology (maturationism, associationism). And he understood that the study of development necessarily conflates descriptive claims about what is the case and evaluative claims about "good" development.

These features of Kohlberg's work are congenial with our understanding of naturalism and psychologized morality, and in this respect we claim him as a fellow traveler. Although there are surely features of our work that Kohlberg could not regard with favor, we don't think our embrace of naturalism is one of them.

"Something there is that does not love a wall," the poet says,*"that wants it down."* It is "spring mending time" in moral psychology, and we are confident of good neghbors as we walk the line of the commonboundary between etics and pycology.

REFERENCES

Casebeer, W. (2003). *Natural ethical facts*. Cambridge, MA: MIT Press.

Garfield, J. (2000). The meanings of meaning: Dimensions of the sciences of mind. *Philosophical Psychology, 13*, 421-440.

Doris, J.M. (2002). *Lack of character: Personality and moral behavior*. Cambridge: Cambridge University Press.

Doris, J.M. & Stich, S.P. (2005). As a matter of fact: Empirical perspectives on ethics. In F. Jackson (Ed)., *Oxford handbook of contemporary philosophy* (pp. 114-152). New York: Oxford University Press.

Flanagan, O. (2002). *The problem of the soul*. NY: Basic Books.

Flanagan, O. (1991). *Varieties of moral personality: Ethics and psychological realism*. Cambridge, MA: Harvard University Press.

Forrest, B. (2000). Methodological naturalism and philosophical naturalism: *Clarifying the connection*. *Philo, 3* (2), 7-29.

Hume, D. (1740/2000). *A treatise of human nature* (D.F. Norton & M.J. Norton, Eds.). Oxford: Oxford University Press.

Johnson, M. (1993). *Moral Imagination: Implications of Cognitive Science for Ethics*. Chicago: University of Chicago Press.

Killen, M. & Smetana, J. (Eds., 2006). *Handbook of moral development*. Mahwah, NJ: Lawrence Erlbaum Associates

Kohlberg, L. (1969). Stage and sequence: The cognitive developmental approach to socialization. In D. Goslin (Ed.), *Handbook of socialization theory and research* (pp. 347-480). New York: Rand McNally & Company.

Kohlberg, L. (1971). From is to ought: How to commit the naturalistic fallacy and get away with it in the study of moral development. In T. Mischel (Ed.), *Cognitive development and epistemology* (pp. 151-284). New York: Academic Press.

Kohlberg, L., Levine, C. & Hewer, A. (1983). *Moral stages: A current formulation and a response to critics*. In J.A. Meacham (Ed.), *Contributions to human development (Vol. 10)*. Basel: Karger.

Lakatos, I. (1978). Falsification and the methodology of scientific research programmes. In J. Worrall & G. Currie (Eds.), *The methodology of scientific research programmes. Imre Lakatos philosophical papers Vol. 1* (pp. 8-101). Cambridge: Cambridge University Press.

Lapsley, D. K. (in press) Moral self-identity as the aim of education. In L. Nucci & D. Narvaez (Eds). *Handbook of moral and character education*. Mahwah, NJ: Lawrence Erlbaum Associates.

Lapsley, D.K. (2006). Moral stage theory. In M. Killen & J. Smetana (Eds.), *Handbook of moral development* (pp. 37-66). Mahwah, NJ: Lawrence Erlbaum Associates

Lapsley, D.K. & Narvaez, D. (2005). Moral psychology at the crossroads. In D.K. Lapsley & F.C. Power (Eds.), *Character psychology and character education* (pp. 18-35). Notre Dame, IN: University of Notre Dame Press.

Lapsley, D.K. & Narvaez, D. (2004). A social cognitive view of moral character. In D. K. Lapsley & D. Narvaez (Eds.), *Moral development, self and identity* (pp. 189-212). Mahwah, NJ: Lawrence Erlbaum Associates.

Maxwell, B. (2007). *Psychologized morality and the varieties of ethical naturalism*. Paper presented at the annual meeting of the Association for Moral Education, New York.

MacIntyre, A. (1959). Hume on "is" and "ought". *Philosophical Review, 68*, 451-468.

McKinnon, C. (2005). Character possession and human flourishing. In D. K. Lapsley & F.C. Power (Eds.), *Character psychology and character education* (pp. 36-66). Notre Dame, IN: University of Notre Dame Press.

McKinnon, C. (1999). *Character, virtue theories and the vices*. Peterborough, Ontario: Broadview Press.

Moore, G.E. (1903/1993). *Principia ethica*. Cambridge: Cambridge University Press.

Narvaez, D. (2006). Integrative Ethical Education. In M. Killen & J. Smetana (Eds.), *Handbook of moral development* (pp. 703-733). Mahwah, NJ: Erlbaum.

Narvaez, D. (in press). Triune ethics: The neurobiological roots of our multiple moralities. *New Ideas in Psychology*.

Narvaez, D. & Lapsley, D. (2005). The psychological foundations of everyday morality and moral expertise. In D. Lapsley & Power, C. (Eds.), *Character psychology and character education* (pp. 140-165). Notre Dame: IN: University of Notre Dame Press.

Railton, P. (1989). Naturalism and prescriptivity. *Social Philosophy and Policy, 7,* 155-174.

Walker, L. J. & Hennig, K.H. (1998). Moral functioning in the broader context of personality. In S. Hala (Ed.), *The development of social cognition* (pp. 297-327). East Sussex, UK: Psychology Press.

Williams, B. (1981). Persons, character and morality. In *Moral Luck* (pp. 1-19). Cambridge: Cambridge University Press.

Wong, D.B. (2006). *Natural moralities: A defense of pluralistic relativism.* Oxford: Oxford University Press.

Daniel K Lapsley & Darcia Narvaez
University of Notre Dame, USA

ZEHAVIT GROSS

COMBATING STEREOTYPES AND PREJUDICE
AS A MORAL ENDEAVOR

The aim of this chapter is to show how combating stereotypes and discrimination is constructed as a moral endeavor within a university setting. It will present the reactions of Israeli Jewish and Arab students to one exercise, the "lemon" exercise, which is one unit in a university intervention program on conflict management for Arab and Jewish students. The principal aim of the program is to encourage coexistence among the various groups comprising Israeli society in an atmosphere of cooperation, mutual understanding and social tolerance. It enables Israeli students to reflect productively on their role in a diverse society in an educational environment that respects difference. The three-part program, designed for small groups of 20-25 students, consists of twelve weekly 1½-hour sessions offering hands-on learning, based on the personal experiences of its participants. It provides students with skills and techniques to enable them to operate within a multicultural context and to function within it as agents of change. Exercises are derived from the Anti Defamation League's "A World of Difference" program, adapted to the needs of students experiencing the complex realities of the state of Israel.

This chapter will describe and analyse one exercise and show how the process operates in practice. The workshop used what Sergiovanni (1984) calls reflective practice. In order to make students more aware of the inner processes they were undergoing in the classroom, they were asked to keep a reflective journal. The analysis is based on students' journal descriptions (40) of what occurred in the class as well as 18 semi-structure interviews held with students a year after the workshop ended.

THE EXERCISE: LEMONS AS A MEANS FOR STUDYING STEREOTYPES

I first held up a lemon and asked the students to characterize it (citrus fruit, yellow, sour, refreshing, beautiful). Then each student received a lemon and had to write down the characteristics that made their lemon better than all the others. The aim of this stage was to acquaint them with their specific lemon. Then the students broke into groups and each student had to convince the group that his or her lemon was the most beautiful lemon. This was followed by a short creative drama exercise in which the students used direct speech to hold an imaginary dialogue between the lemons. At this stage, they felt and smelled their lemons, and were becoming attached to them. Then I collect the lemons and put them all in a bag. I then took

Fritz Oser & Wiel Veugelers (eds.), Getting involved, 293–306.

some of them out of the bag, threw them on the floor and asked the students to find their lemons. To their amazement, all the students whose lemons were on the floor found their lemons and those who didn't were extremely disappointed and upset. I asked them to describe what they felt when they found or didn't find the lemon. Then I gave the class the rest of the lemons. They jumped out of their seats to find their lemons. At the end of the session, all the students had found their "original" lemon. Then I reminded them that when I entered the room with a sack of lemons, they all looked the same. At that time, they wouldn't have believed they would be able to find their lemons. I asked them to think about the purpose of the exercise and then told them that its aim was to introduce the term "stereotypical thinking," to illustrate how generalizations affect our thinking and to demonstrate the transition from a categorical to subjective perspective.

Naama wrote in her reflective journal, "We all got so attached to our lemons – this was unbelievable, can I be attached to a lemon? – that when we had to pick them out from everyone else's lemons, we were all able to find the one that originally belonged to us! The fact is that lemons don't all look the same. They all have different characteristics. I didn't realize this before – for me a lemon was a lemon. Now I can see that you cannot generalize about all lemons but rather should perceive the differences. To be honest, for me all the ultra-orthodox people who live in Bnei Brak (a religious city in Israel) look the same. I can't understand how their mothers distinguish between them."

I asked, "Can you think about another situation where you lump people together?" David answered, "Yes, all the Arabs looked the same to me until I came to this workshop where I saw individual Arabs and they look exactly like me. It is unbelievable how generalizations affect our thinking and our lives."

It is always fascinating to see the transition from a categorical to a subjective perspective. In his reflective journal, Adam wrote,

> Some of the character traits of the lemons were interesting to hear. People were very creative. Also, being able to pick my own lemon out of a bunch shows how we can really pick a piece of straw out of a haystack and recognize everyone's individuality. I think the exercise was exceptionally good, and it was interesting to see how some of the students acted when their lemon wasn't in the bunch. Some were quick to give up and convinced themselves that a different lemon was their own, which I think transmits a deeper message. Others were sure that their lemon wasn't there and they refused to take another one. They must have gotten really close to their fruit....

This quote also reflects the special atmosphere in the class.

THE CLASS AS A COMMUNITY OF PRACTICE

After this we began discussing stereotypical thinking. First we defined the term "stereotypes" (a set of beliefs about the personal attributes of a group of people) and "discrimination" (any conduct which denies individuals or groups of people equality of treatment which they may wish). Then I asked them to describe a situation when they were victims of stereotypes and prejudice.

Yussuf, a Muslim student who lives in an Arab village in the center of the country, raised his hand and said that whenever he got on a bus, people looked at him as if he were a terrorist. He could feel their eyes on his back when he boarded the bus and sense their relief when he got off. As an Israeli citizen, this gave him a bitter feeling. Sometimes he heard people saying it explicitly: "All Arabs are terrorists". He told us that two weeks before he took a taxi to the university. It was after a bus explosion in Jerusalem. The atmosphere was very tense. One of the passengers asked the taxi driver to ask to see his identity card; somebody in the back said that he looked like a terrorist. Yussuf said he had forgotten his identity card at home. Then one of the people in the taxi said that if this Arab didn't get off, he and all the others would get off. Yussuf felt that the whole taxi was against him. The driver said he knew him personally, as he drove him every morning, but nothing helped. Yussuf was so insulted that he decided to get off. It took him a few minutes to recover.

The group was shocked and felt terrible. Yussuf was one of the most vibrant active students in our group and a nice looking young man. Every lesson he came and arranged the chairs in a circle. Whenever something was needed, he was the first to volunteer. There was a terrible silence in the class. We could see that Yussuf was very upset. I asked the students for their reaction. Sarit, a Jewish girl, was the first to respond. She said, "We live in terror. This is a terrible time for all of us. I can understand the people in the taxi. I would feel the same. Yussuf, can you understand that whenever I get on a bus I pray to God that I will get off it safe and alive.... All the passengers are immediately suspect. If I see a man with an Oriental face holding a bag, I'm terrified. A few times I got off the bus before my stop because I was so afraid that someone was a terrorist." Rachel, another Jewish girl, was angry. She said she couldn't listen to Sarit who was being so rude. "Can't you have some compassion for Yussuf before telling your nightmares? Look at him – he is almost crying and you are telling stories...."

In their reflective journals there were other reactions as well. Most of the Jewish students wrote about their mixed feelings and embarrassment. The Arab students saw this as a sign that they would never be integrated into the Israeli state as equal citizens and there were also racist statements like Sarah's, who wrote: "What I felt was 'THANK G-D'! Once they start letting the 'non-dangerous' Arabs in, it will be that much harder to keep the 'dangerous' Arabs out. That, and also the fact that it will be horrible if the Arabs become too comfortable here in Israeli Jewish society. It will only lead to really bad things."

SITUATED STORIES OF EXCLUSION

Learning is always situated in specific cultural and social contexts. This story cannot be simply analyzed as a story of exclusion as a result of stereotypes. It should be understood within the unique Israeli context in which there is a constant violent conflict between Arabs and Jews (see also Sagy, 2006). Specific contexts shape the conditions for the kinds of learning that can take place. Bruner (1996) stresses that learning is a "complex pursuit of fitting a culture to the needs of its members and of fitting its members and their ways of knowing to the needs of the culture" (p. 42). "Therefore learning is not an island but the continent of culture" (p. 12). In a way, the workshop is a form of situated learning where what we study in the classroom can be understood only in this specific setting. Accordingly, learning should never be isolated, something that takes place only within an individual, because learning is inherent in ongoing interaction with a social, cultural and physical environment. The Israeli setting, where stereotypes are learned, serves as a venue for the cultural and social situatedness of learning. Lave and Wagner (1991) claim that "learning must not be seen simply as the acquisition of knowledge by individuals but as a process of social participation in a community of practice" (p. 98). Most researchers view learning as an activity that involves objective abstract knowledge acquisition. However, Lave and Wagner describe learning as a function of the activity, context and culture in which it occurs. The workshop discussed here is constructed as a community of practice where students study how to become part of a multicultural society, in practice.

CULTURAL REPRODUCTION AND RESISTANCE

The work of Antonio Gramsci (1971), Giroux (1981) and Apple (1990) is concerned with individuals' ability to critique and transform social reality and thereby counter hegemonic social structures (DeCuir & Dixson, 2004). These theorists view schools as sites of cultural and social reproduction. However, within these educational frameworks, students do not passively accept oppressive social forces. Rather they actively resist and contest these oppressive forces. Although individuals can and do consciously engage in resistance, the structure of school and the cultural hegemony that it maintains is almost always preserved (DeCuir & Dixson, 2004). Following Apple (1990), the workshop becomes a means of reproducing culture or, more accurately, of reproduction multiculturalism. The workshop became a milieu for constructing structural equality and cultural pluralism.

Specific sets of cultural norms, values, attitudes and beliefs were embedded in the ritual of the workshop. It enabled students to examine their assumptions, reflect on their group identity and connect knowledge they already had with new information they received in sessions. Students had to acknowledge the existence of stereotypes and prejudice to equip them with tools to critically assess a system of oppression in which minority groups are positioned at the lowest end of the social hierarchy; to provide them with anti-racist education; to avoid static and essentialist definitions of culture; and to be open to more dynamic and constructivist definitions.

The workshop provided voice and visibility for groups that were traditionally silenced at the university. It criticized the basic "funds of knowledge" (Olmedo, 2004) of the students and showed them to what extent they were racist and held stereo-typical and prejudiced views. Apple (1990) believes that there is a need for deeper understanding of the interconnection between lived experience and dominant social structures in order to construct a community of practice based on anti-racist knowl-edge. The students brought their social and cultural histories into the exercises and the texts we read together. At the same time, the exercises and the discussions con-stantly restructure these social and cultural identities (DeBlase, 2003, p. 282).

Stereotypes are shaped by what we read and by the social and cultural context in which we read it. The students engage discourse from the positions they occupy within the discourse of ethnicity and class. According to Gee (1990), discourse associates language with particular ways of thinking, feeling, believing, valuing and acting that can identify individuals as belonging to specific social groups. Dis-course then becomes a way of taking on a particular social role that others will recognize. These social roles in turn moderate how we learn to think, act and speak in all the various social roles we take on. This is exactly what happened during the workshop and is reflected in their personal journals. Yoav wrote, "I said in class that I was against this [the Disengagement Plan] but I'm not sure I am. After I saw the students' reactions, I thought that I had to think about it again. Perhaps I went too far. It even surprised me. In the next lesson, I took another role upon myself though I know that in this classroom, I have the role of the opponent." DeBlass (2003, p. 284) claims that individuals are not critically aware of how their social standpoints shape their readings of texts and the ways in which this interaction can work to reproduce readers' gendered sense of self.

THE FEELING OF EXCLUSION AS A MEANS TO CREATE BELONGING

In the classroom, we share our reflections on our location in the social world. Yuval-Davis, Anthias, & Kofman (2005) claim that "the notion of belonging becomes activated when there is a sense of exclusion" (p. 526). This happened to Yussuf. He told us about his feeling of exclusion in the taxi where he was suspected of being a terrorist and the moment we reacted, he got the feeling of belonging to our group. A year later in an interview, Yussuf said: "The minute David, the soldier, told me 'Don't think about them – we love you,' I felt relaxed. When I realized that in this room I'm accepted, I knew I could overcome the bitterness. I understood that I had a future in this country. The minute the group understood what I was saying and how terrible I felt, I understood that I'm not alone." Yussuf explained his feeling of belonging through space ("this room," "this country"), time ("the minute") and language.

Three basic constituents construct the sense of belonging. There is a range of identities, locations and spaces to which we feel we belong or we do not and can-not belong. Yuval-Davis et al. (2005) claim that "belonging is where the sociol-ogy of emotions interfaces with the sociology of power, where identification and participation collude in terms of aspiration and desire. Language is an important component." Bar-Tal (1997) claims that language reflects personal knowledge while it feeds a cognitive repertoire. Language as used by individuals is the carrier and transmitter of stereotypic contents (p. 511). Hence, in the classroom, we studied how to use language differently and be cautious about the socio-linguistic meaning of the words. We practiced how to use words differently and how to restructure sentences.

In many of the students' journals, there were reflections on the issue of language. For example, Shlomi, an immigrant student, wrote:

> I came out of class today extremely frustrated for a few reasons. I happen to be an extremely self-confident person who doesn't have trouble speaking up and stating my opinion when necessary. However, there is an issue about speaking up in this class that I have a problem with. I feel that word-choice is so important in this class. One has to be careful as to how one phrases whatever it is that one is trying to say because there isn't much leeway with the topics that we discuss. The Arabs can offend the Jews, the right-wingers offend the left, all because of a misunderstanding of what is trying to be said. The topics discussed are extremely serious and sensitive, and therefore word-choice is that much more important.
> With that said, I have a problem speaking up. I'm not confident enough to speak up in Hebrew in an environment like this just yet, for fear of offending someone. That's not to say that I'm conscious of speaking Hebrew – I teach in a school in Hebrew, deal with my students' parents, and speak up in all of my other classes and have no problem with it. It's just that this setting is such a sensitive setting and it's not worth me saying something that I don't mean because of "lack of better words."

Because this student is also an immigrant, he is afraid of not being understood and didn't want to offend anyone in the class. The question of language for this student is fundamental as he wanted to be part of the community but was not sure how to communicate. The change in the language gradually created a receptive climate in the classroom and the class became a "collective place" for all the students. Collective places are constructed by imagining of belonging. They produce a "natural" community of people and function as exclusionary borders of otherness (Anthias, 2002).

The fact that every week we met at the same time in the same place and shared our feelings strengthened the sense of belonging. Absences were rare and the students wrote in their journals that they tried to attend every session, as this was "precious time" or "quality time" for them.

ATTITUDE BEHAVIOR INCONSISTENCY

Though different forms of discriminatory behavior against a given outgroup should be determined by the same attitude, the literature shows attitude-behavior inconsistency: members of a minority may be discriminated against in one situation, but not in another (Ajzen & Fishbein, 1980). Different behavioral manifestations of stereotypes and prejudice can be inconsistent for various reasons, such as during a period of danger or terrorism (Yuval-Davis et al., 2005). The attitude-behavior consistency seen in Yussuf's story was not always the case. After Yussuf shared his feelings, Ansaf (an Arab student) raised her hand and told us about her bitter experience:

> Last week I was so upset. I'm in one course with very open and liberal girls. They told me during the semester how they support peace negotiations, etc., etc. and I was deeply impressed. Before the final exams, I gave my notes to one of the girls who wanted to complete the material that she was missing, and I needed it urgently. She told me she was in her room in the university dormitory and I suggested that I would come and get the notes. She said she would come to meet me in the cafeteria because they don't allow Arabs into the dormitory. I was deeply offended, of course.

In Ansaf's case, she felt a general positive attitude toward her on the part of the Jewish students, but discovered that they were not ready to let her into the dormitory because she was an Arab and thus considered dangerous. Stroebe and Insko (1989) claim that "measures of racial attitudes often leave behavior and behavior setting unspecified and even define the target of discrimination only in terms of racial or ethnic categories (p. 11). Ajzen and Fishbein (1980) explain that such discrepancies are partially because the attitudes and prejudice are usually measured at a more global level than behavior. Accordingly, Ansaf felt comfortable during the semester on a personal level with her Jewish friends.

HOW STEREOTYPES ARE PERCEIVED

The students referred to stereotypes in three different modes: social, behavioral and moral. They viewed the elimination of stereotypes as a social issue, .i.e., "If they want to become effective citizens they should avoid the use of stereotypes" or "Anti-racist behavior is crucial for the maintenance of civic society." Regarding the behavioral aspect, they wrote, "It is more pleasant when people treat each other equally" or "Using stereotypes is not aesthetic. It is inappropriate behavior, like throwing mud in your friend's face." On the moral level, the students responded on a very personal level and said explicitly that the use of stereotypes was immoral: "We are all the shadow of God so it is inhuman and immoral to discriminate or use stereotypes." Some of them also mentioned the "need to build a just society."

During the sessions, the moral aspect was the dominant factor; however, in their reflective journals the behavioral aspect was more prominent. This stems from the fact that, as Stroebe and Insko (1989) claim, the fear of public display of racism can lead to reserve racism. The public declaration is an integral part of the clarification (Raths, Harmin, & Simon, 1966; Simon, 1976). The transition from the individual choice towards the implementation of the value starts when the individual is willing to affirm the choice publicly.

THE WORKSHOP AS A MORAL ENDEAVOR

Towards the end of the workshop, the students attested that their willingness to implement the messages of the workshop was a moral decision rather than the product of cognitive knowledge. This is what makes the learning process a moral endeavour:

> At the end of the semester I started thinking to myself that I must start seeing the Arabs as equal human beings not only because I understand rationally that we must initiate peace and there isn't another option and this is the first step but rather because during the workshop I started seeing their human side. When they shared their everyday hardships. When Suha told us how her father brings her every morning to the taxi station and waits for her and then calls her thousands of times to make sure she came to the university safely, I started to look at her differently. It became a human issue. Actually I hope that they (the Arabs) will treat us as human beings who deserve to live somewhere in the world.

In the reactions of the students (both Arabs and Jews), three distinct groups could be identified: the racists, the politically correct and the humanists. The racists made comments such as "all Arabs are terrorists"; "all Arabs are liars – you cannot trust a word"; "all the Jews are killers and oppressors". The second group, the politically correct, were afraid to expose their deeper racist feelings for fear of public rebuke (this was the largest group which showed a discrepancy between what they said in class and what they later wrote on in their reflective journals). The third group was extremely human and tried not to insult or offend because of a humanistic ethic. Their consideration was a care for the future of society: "I was so shocked to hear how Michel spoke to Fatima – doesn't she think there is a limit to the way you can insult a human being? Aren't we all the shadow of God?"

Actually the infusion of anti-racist education and an anti-racist atmosphere in the classroom provides a venue in which diversity is structurally incorporated into the curriculum and the natural discourse. The more racist students made particularistic and sometimes selfish and childish statements, whereas the less racist students responded on a higher level and related to society or humanity. These three groups can perhaps be examined in light of Kohlberg's (1971) pre-conventional (the racists), conventional (politically correct) and post-conventional (the humanists) dimensions but this needs further investigation in future research.

HOW DOES THE TRANSITION FROM THE GENERAL TO THE SUBJECTIVE OCCUR?

How do the students perceive combating stereotypes in the classroom, as expressed in their reflective journals? The students indicated two main factors that helped them personally to make the transition from the general to the subjective perspective and thus to combat their own stereotypes and prejudice: the fact that they were exposed to a wide range of opinions during the sessions and the fact that they had an opportunity for direct contact with Arab or Jewish students.

THE IMPACT OF DIRECT CONTACT

Many students indicated during the sessions and in their reflective journals that the direct contact with the "other" was a meaningful learning experience for them. Usama wrote:

> I read so many terrible things about the Jews that they are cruel and greedy and it was so special to sit with a Jew and discuss things with him and look directly in his eyes. The direct speech and eye contact break the barriers. Suddenly I could see a real human being and not a monster. Not a soldier with a gun but a nice person with kind words. Sometimes they said things which irritated me but I could control myself because we became friends. The Jew was not an anonymous remote creature but someone you can laugh with and even like.

Following Williams (1947), Allport (1954) formulated the inter-group contact theory, which holds that direct face-to-face contact between rival groups can reduce prejudice and stereotypes. Allport asserts that successful and effective contact should include the following four components: equal status between the groups involved in the situation; common goals; the avoidance of competition between the groups; and an external sanction that is derived from a supreme authority. Following Allport, Amir (1969) emphasized the importance of intimate encounters, cooperative relationships, and institutional support for efforts at inter-group contact. In his view, the intimacy fostered within the group, alongside the need to cooperate, and supported by an institutional umbrella, provides complementary top-down and bottom-up paradigms for changing the atmosphere and the relationships between conflicting groups. Relating to Amir's work, Pettigrew (1998) and Mollov and Lavie (2001) emphasized the importance of the "friendship potential" emerging out of inter-group encounters.

When considering the workshop in terms of the contact hypothesis, in general, the atmosphere was very good. Equal status contacts were maintained, as the participants were all students in the same class who were collaborating in order to improve their achievements. At the weekly meetings, existential questions were analyzed that deepened the relationships between the participants. These were not merely casual encounters but rather very intimate ones, as the students shared personal information. One of the main conditions of the workshop was collaboration, which strengthened the group's social cohesion. The fact that this workshop had the institutional support of the University sanctioned the desire to function in a cooperative rather than a competitive manner.

On the other hand, direct contact may strengthen or weaken positive as well as negative held images. Alternately, it might not affect these contents at all and only confirm the previously acquired stereotypes (Bar-Tal, 1997). Bar-Tal and Teichman (2005) claim that in cases when the quality of intergroup relations is well defined, especially in situations of conflict, the encounter most frequently serves as an opportunity to validate previously acquired stereotypes" (pp. 46-47). Indeed, one of the students said, "This workshop has confirmed my ideas about the Arabs – they hate us and will never accept our existence."

Miriam wrote in her journal:

> Somehow we got onto a topic where the Arab girl was talking about her relationship to the state of Israel. She was saying how she feels comfortable living here. She used the term "State of Israel," and the Arab guy sitting next to her said sarcastically under his breath "state?" That was a shameful moment for me; that in the state of Israel, in a university, publicly, this guy had the audacity to whisper something like that. That shamed me.

As Miriam was sitting close to him and could hear directly what he was saying, this confirmed her feelings that "the Arabs will never change. They want one thing. To get rid of us."

According to Bush and Folger (2005), direct contact enables and creates what they call "a transformative conflict interaction." It "intensifies the relationships and empowers the rival parties. The conflict transformation theory claims that human beings have inherent capacities for strength and responsiveness and inherent social or moral impulses that activate these capacities. The transformative theory claims that when these capacities are activated the conflict spiral can regenerate. The critical resource in conflict transformation is the parties' own basic humanity-their essential strength, decency and compassion as human beings" (Bush & Folger, 2005, p. 54). Direct contact enables and improves the ability of the students to see the others as human beings and this kind of interaction empowers them and shifts the relationships so that the participants become "more attentive, open, trusting, and understanding of the other party – in general, shifting from self-centeredness to responsiveness to other" (Bush & Folger, 2005, p. 55). These conditions of openness and attentiveness are fundamental conditions for increased contact and this can change the group's attitude in a positive direction and combat stereotypes, prejudice and discrimination (Bar-Tal & Teichman, 2005, p. 47). In their reflective journals, the students noted that these conditions emerged as core factors in explaining their satisfaction with the workshop in general and determined the outcome of positive intergroup contacts.

MULTICULTURALISM AS A MEANS TO COMBAT STEREOTYPES AND PREJUDICES

The first question I asked myself as a facilitator was whether to conduct the workshop using an assimilationist approach; namely, to try to put all the students into a one mythical Israeli melting pot, or to use a multicultural approach that maintains the differences between the students. According to Banks (1997), in the US, the assimilationist approach was the source of the fact that many citizens lost their first culture, language and ethnic identity and some people become alienated from family and community. Multiculturalism is defined as "a social mosaic of bounded and identifiable cultures cohabiting a common territory in the context of a single dominant culture" (Rodriguez & Kitchen, 2005, p. 20). The choice of the multicultural option means to check "the extent to which boundaries as borders can encompass, rather than challenge or be challenged by boundaries of competing collective identities" (Yuval-Davis et al., 2005, p. 523). Multicultural education is built on the philosophical ideals of freedom, justice, equality and human dignity (Shealey, 2006).

At the beginning of the workshop, we discussed our expectations concerning it and I consulted with the students on the matter. The assimilationist approach was chosen by some Arab students because of their being a minority group, and also by some leftist students who thought this was an appropriate option from a civic point of view. However, most of the Jewish as well as the Arab students rejected the assimilationist option, as they felt it subordinated weak groups and silenced their unique voice.

There were Jewish students who opposed the assimilationist approach for religious reasons, as it might enhance assimilation which is considered a threat to Jewish identity. Sarit said, "Look what happened in America with the melting pot approach – the intermarriage rate in America is between 50-60%!! That is the last thing we need here in Israel."

Most of the students choose the multicultural mode not merely as a more practical choice but rather as a more ethical and moral choice. Thus, students from different backgrounds, origins, cultures and religions, learn to live with each other without fixating and naturalizing the differences between them. The question is whether differences are perceived as a problem or as an opportunity. Several students viewed differences as being a problem: "The problem is that we are very different. We come from different backgrounds. We wake up in the morning differently. I wake up in a big town and Mohammed wakes up in a small village. It's a problem. We cannot view the world the same way." Yasmin agreed: "There is a problem. We are so different from each other that I can't see the common denominator between us."

It was clear that they perceived the difference as a threat or as a problem rather than as an opportunity. When people are afraid, they tend to generalize using stereotypes as part of their defense mechanism (Bar-Tal & Teichman, 2005) against the unknown. Hence the first stage was to lessen the perceived threat and change the language in the class. The linguistic change created an atmosphere of acceptance in the classroom. In order to "market respect for diversity" (Mentz & van der Walt, 2007, p. 428), I asked the students to show me in what way they were unique and different from each other. The process of building appreciation for differences is long. Most of the students said that by the end of the workshop they had become more attentive to issues of diversity than previously. In Irvine's (2003) terminology, this represented "cultural synchronization" in the workshop between diverse students.

The implementation of multicultural education can serve as a means to assist in the creation of a community based on respect for and tolerance of diversity. The reduction of stereotypes is an integral part of multicultural education and one of its main conditions (Banks, 1997). Lemmer and Squelch (1993) describe multicultural education as education that involves development of cultural awareness, recognition and acceptance of cultural diversity, which forms a central consideration in the formulation of education policies. The aim should be the development of equity in education and transformation of the school environment to meet the needs of learners from diverse cultural, linguistic and socioeconomic backgrounds. Dantley (2002) refers to a process of "mutual accommodation" in which all the students "adapt their actions to the common goal of academic success in the course with cultural respect."

Education needs a definition of multiculturalism that will allow the construction of environments within which learners and educators can become border crossers engaged in critical and ethical reflection about what it means to bring a wider variety of cultures into dialogue with each other (Banks, 1999). During the workshop we spoke about the fact that in a modern society boundaries are never fixed and they are forms of political practice. We practiced cross-bordering and examined new forms of "multi-layered" (Yuval-Davis et al., 2005) Israeli identities. One of the fundamental messages I tried to put across in the workshop was that the failure to acknowledge the interrelatedness between multiculturalism, stereotypes and prejudice and view it as a moral enterprise prevents the educational settings to move beyond superficiality and make substantive changes to curriculum and pedagogy. Our main goal in the class is to build a community where all the groups in the class are "structurally included" (Banks, 2003) and to which they feel responsibility and allegiance. Our aim was to view multiculturalism as a value and to cultivate moral awareness. Combating discrimination was presented to the students as a moral endeavor.

REFERENCES

Ajzen, I. & Fishbein, M. (1980). *Understanding attitudes and predicting social behaviour*. Englewood Cliffs, NJ: Prentice-Hall.

Allport, G. W. (1954). *The nature of prejudice*. Reading, MA: Addison-Wesley.

Amir, Y. (1969). Contact hypothesis in ethnic relations. *Psychological Bulletin, 71*(5), 319-342.

Anthias, F. (2002). Where do I belong?: Narrating collective identity and translocational positionality. *Ethnicities, 2*(4), 491-514.

Apple, M. W. (1990). *Ideology and curriculum* (2nd ed.). Boston: Routledge & Kegan Paul.

Banks, J. A. (1997). *Educating citizens in a multicultural society*. New York: Teachers College Press.

Banks, J. A. (1999). *An introduction to multicultural education*. Boston: Allyn and Bacon.

Banks, J. A. (2003). Educating global citizens in a diverse world. Retrieved May 15, 2007, from http://www.newhorizons.org/strategies/mulicultural/banks2.htm

Bar-Tal, D. (1997). Formation and change of ethnic and national stereotypes: An integrative model. *International Journal of Intercultural Relations, 21*(4), 491-523.

Bar-Tal, D. & Teichman, Y. (2005). *Stereotypes and prejudice in conflict representations of Arabs in Israeli Jewish society.* New York: Cambridge University Press.

Bruner, J. (1996). *The culture of education.* Cambridge, MA: Harvard University Press.

Bush, R. A. B. & Folger, J. P. (2005). *The promise of mediation: The transformative approach to conflict* (rev. 2nd ed.). San Francisco: Jossey-Bass.

Dantley, M. E. (2002). Uprooting and replacing positivism, the melting pot, multiculturalism, and other impotent notions in educational leadership through an African American perspective. *Education and Urban Society, 34*(3), 334-352.

DeBlase, G. L. (2003). Missing stories, missing lives: Urban girls (re)constructing race and gender in the literacy classroom. *Urban Education, 38*(3), 279-329.

DeCuir, J. T. & Dixson, A. D. (2004). "So when it comes out, they aren't that surprised that it is there": Using critical race theory as a tool of analysis of race and racism in education. *Educational Researcher, 33*(5), 26-31.

Gee, J. P. (1990). *Social linguistics and literacies: Ideology in discourses.* London: Falmer.

Giroux, H. A. (1981). *Ideology, culture and the process of schooling.* Philadelphia: Temple University Press.

Gramsci, A. (1971). *Selections from the prison notebook.* New York: International Publishers.

Irvine, J. J. (2003). *Educating teachers for diversity: Seeing with a cultural eye.* New York: Teachers College Press.

Kohlberg, L. (1971). From is to ought: How to commit the naturalistic fallacy and get away with it in the study of moral development. In T. Mischel (Ed.), *Cognitive development and epistemology.* New York: Academic Press.

Lave, J. & Wagner, E. (1991). *Situated learning: Legitimate peripheral participation.* Cambridge: Cambridge University Press.

Lemmer, E. & Squelch, J. (1993). *Multicultural education: A teacher's manual.* Halfway House, Pretoria: Southern Book Publishers.

Mentz, K.,& van der Walt, J. L. (2007). Multicultural concerns of educators in the western cape province of South Africa. *Education and Urban Society, 39*(3), 423-449.

Mollov, B. & Lavie, C. (2001). Culture, dialogue and perception change in the Israeli-Palestinian conflict. *International Journal of Conflict Management, 12*(1), 69-87.

Olmedo, I. M. (2004). Raising transnational issues in a multicultural curriculum project. *Urban Education, 39*(3), 241-265.

Pettigrew, T. F. (1998). Intergroup contact theory. *Annual Review of Psychology, 49*, 65-85.

Raths, L. E., Harmin, M. & Simon, S. B. (1966). *Values and teaching: Working with values in the classroom.* Columbus, OH: Charles E. Merrill.

Rodriguez, A. J. & Kitchen, R. S. (Eds.). (2005). *Preparing mathematics and science teachers for diverse classrooms: Promising strategies for transformative pedagogy.* Mahwah, NJ: Lawrence Erlbaum Associates.

Sagy, S. (2006). Hope in times of threat: The case of Palestinian and Israeli-Jewish youth. In Y. Iram, H. Wahrman & Z. Gross (Eds.), *Educating towards a culture of peace* (pp. 147-160). Greenwich, CT: Information Age Publishing.

Sergiovanni, T. J. (1984). Cultural and competing perspectives in administrative theory and practice. In T. J. Sergiovanni & J. E. Corbally (Eds.), *Leadership and organizational culture: New perspectives on administrative theory and practice* (pp. 1-12). Chicago: University of Illinois Press.

Shealey, M. W. (2006). The promises and perils of "Scientifically based" Research for urban schools. *Urban Education, 41*(1), 5-19.

Simon, S. B. (1976). Values clarification vs. Indoctrination. In D. Purpel & K. Ryan (Eds.), *Moral education.* Berkeley, CA: McCutchan.

Stroebe, W. & Inkso, C. A. (1989). Stereotype, prejudice, and discrimination. In D. Bar-Tal, C. F. Grau-mann, A. W. Kruglanski & W. Strobe (Eds.), *Stereotyping and prejudice: Changing conceptions* (pp. 3-34). New York: Springer-Verlag.

Williams, R. M., Jr. (1947). *The reduction of intergroup tensions.* New York: Social Science Research Council.

Yuval-Davis, N., Anthias, F. & Kofman, E. (2005). Secure borders and safe haven and the gendered politics of belonging: Beyond social cohesion. *Ethnic and Racial Studies, 28*(3), 513-535.

Zehavit Gross
Bar-Ilan University, Tel Aviv, Israel

PART 5
RESEARCH ON RELIGIOUS INVOLVEMENT

LAWRENCE J. WALKER & JEREMY A. FRIMER

BEING GOOD FOR GOODNESS' SAKE:

Transcendence in the Lives of Moral Heroes

MORAL PSYCHOLOGY'S BLIND-SPOT

Moral psychology suffers from a grievous blind-spot. Strangely occluded from its vision is a consideration of the potential relevance of religion, spirituality, and transcendent faith to moral functioning. Kohlberg (1967) instigated and did much to perpetuate this secular skew within moral psychology and education with his insistent claim that the moral and religious domains were independent. Undoubtedly, this stance was partly motivated by the perceived need to legitimize the psychological study of morality in an antagonistic intellectual context which, at the time, widely embraced behaviorism, secular humanism, and ethical relativism. Additionally, the American constitutional requirement of separation of church and state precluded any vestige of religious influence on moral/character education programs in public schools. However, at some juncture, political and pragmatic concerns must be put aside for an impartial and open-minded investigation of the topic. The integrity of the field is on the line; investigation ought to proceed along conceptual and empirical lines, not merely ideological ones.

It is not difficult to mount the case that the domains of religion, spirituality, and faith, on the one hand (henceforth collectively referred to as transcendence), and morality, on the other hand, are intertwined in meaningful ways. However, transcendence and morality undoubtedly entail a complex relationship, one that will become increasingly apparent as this chapter unfolds. First, let us consider one direction of influence – the path from transcendence to moral functioning. All religious and spiritual traditions reference not only the vertical dimension of relating to the divine or the transcendent, but they also reference the horizontal dimension in providing explicitly moral guidelines for living a good life and interacting appropriately with others. So it would appear that religion directs and motivates individuals to moral ways of living. Indeed, history abounds with instances where religion justifies some of the most profound instances of morality (e.g., Martin Luther King, Jr., Mother Teresa, Mahatma Gandhi).

Yet, history also abounds with counter-examples, with instances of heinous immorality (e.g., the Crusades, religious terrorism) wherein religious motivation has gone terribly awry. This is simply a preliminary indication of the complexity of the relationship that is our focus here. The way in which transcendence informs moral

Fritz Oser & Wiel Veugelers (eds.), Getting involved, 309–326.
© 2008 Sense Publishers. All rights reserved.

functioning entails an unmistakable interaction, which likely rests on other variables such as cognitive distortion, integrity, identification, and so forth. It remains an open question, however, whether on balance transcendence leads individuals to do more good than bad or more bad that good. In this chapter, we will review some empirical work that informs this issue.

Having made a conceptual case for transcendence informing and motivating moral functioning, we now consider the reverse direction of influence: that morality ultimately leads individuals to transcendence. On first blush, this appears to be a more tenuous form of causal influence. "Worldly-oriented" folk (in contrast to "transcendently-oriented" ones) would rightly object to what seems to be the (pejorative) inference regarding their beliefs that would seem to be an extension of this reasoning. Let us be clear about what we are *not* saying: We are not claiming that, if only worldly folks would take a moral path, they would come to understand and embrace the transcendent. Our position is that there are a plurality of paths to mature moral functioning, both secular and transcendent. But could it be that, more often than not, the increasing abstraction and inter-relationships that accompany higher forms of moral thought prompt fundamental questions about the meaning of one's existence and the ultimate purpose of morality that remain unsatisfactorily unanswered and unanswerable by mundane observation? Might it be the case that adopting values and formulating principles eventually leads individuals to question why they internalized those values and principles in the first place, and why they should behave morally at all? The realm of the transcendent seems to be readily equipped with meaningful dialogue and to proffer answers to such questions regarding ultimate concerns.

Consistent with the above theorizing, Kohlberg (1981), somewhat surprisingly, retreated from his earlier hard-line demarcation of transcendence and morality by positing that the two converge at the apex of morality. He proposed a quasi-mystical "soft" Stage 7 that was intended to justify Stage 6 moral principles on the basis of metaethical, metaphysical, and religious epistemologies, and to help impart an element of moral motivation to his model. This bold move fell flat, however, because the abject failure to adduce adequate empirical evidence for Stage 6 (Colby & Kohlberg, 1987) left the validity of the even more abstruse Stage 7 a moot point.

In addition to the practical problems that Kohlberg encountered in trying to empirically substantiate Stage 6 and 7 reasoning, an additional problem with his proposal is conceptual. What is missing in his model is an account of the role of the transcendent in everyday morality for ordinary folk (e.g., those at the conventional level). In other words, for Kohlberg, moral thought and transcendence seemingly only interpenetrate for a very select few individuals, whereas we intuit that the two overlap considerably for virtually all who experience the transcendent.

Thus, we make two claims which will help to frame the discussion. Proposition 1 is that transcendence acts to motivate and amplify moral functioning. That is, transcendence imparts credence to moral thought and motivates individuals to carry out their judgments. However, this motivating influence occurs irrespective of how moral or immoral these judgments are in actuality; thus, it could be expected that transcendence would be associated with a considerable range of moral outcomes, both positive and negative. On the flip side, Proposition 2 is that there are various groundings for mature moral functioning, not only transcendent but also secular. Thus, we posit that, although morality may lead some individuals to concerns about transcendence, it will not do so for everyone.

In this chapter, we will begin by running a naturalistic check on our theorizing by asking whether ordinary folk conceptions concur with our framing of the relationship between transcendence and moral functioning. Then we will explore what appears to be the more obvious of the two accounts (that transcendence leads individuals to morality) with a review of some pertinent research. And finally, we will address the more difficult subject of whether or not morality necessarily leads to transcendence with the presentation of some new data that speak to the issue.

CONCEPTIONS OF THE DOMAINS

As a preliminary check on our conceptual framing of the relationship between transcendence and moral functioning, we begin by exploring naturalistic conceptions. Folk conceptions are important to examine for at least two reasons. One reason is that such conceptions do play a causal role in people's daily decision-making, emotions, and behaviors, and thus are important in explaining their psychological functioning. The second reason is that these ordinary conceptions can provide a check on the conceptual skewing that is inherent in philosophical perspectives. Flanagan (1991), for example, has advanced the notion of *minimal psychological realism* which holds that ethical theories need to be informed by an empirical account of how people understand morality and of the psychological processes involved in moral functioning. Note that this approach does not claim that folk understandings are necessarily correct; indeed, they may be in gross error. However, when there is some divergence between expert and folk conceptions (or between theory and data), it calls for some explanation and at least signals the possibility that our conceptual models may be askew.

An initial study of folk conceptions asked participants, in the context of a larger project (Walker, Pitts, Hennig, & Matsuba, 1995), to identify people whom they regarded as highly moral and to justify these nominations. Their nominations were not constrained by any preset criteria and so nominees could be historical figures or people known only personally. A content analysis of the types of moral exemplars named revealed not only the predictable categories of humanitarians, social activists, revolutionaries, and exceptional politicians, but also a sizable category comprised of religious founders (e.g., Jesus, Mohammed) and religious leaders (e.g., the pope, a chaplain). This was surprising because the instructions to participants were explicit in prompting for *moral* exemplars. Numerous other religious figures were also named (e.g., Mother Teresa, Desmond Tutu) but were classified into other categories given the nature of the justifications that participants provided for their nominations. For the present purposes, the take-home message here is that people's moral heroes are frequently religious figures.

Another content analysis examined the characteristics attributed to these moral exemplars by participants to justify their nominations. This analysis indicated that many exemplars were identified on the explicit basis of their religious and spiritual attributes, suggesting that for many people morality is defined in religious and spiritual terms. This provides a naturalistic confirmation of our most basic contention, that morality and transcendence overlap in meaningful ways. Next, we consider the nature of their intertwinement.

Prototype theory (Rosch, 1978) provides another way to examine the complex relationship between morality and transcendence. This approach to social cognition holds that concepts are better represented in terms of typical examples (or prototypes) identifying the core of the category than by definitional boundaries (the classical definition of concepts). Walker and Pitts (1998) used participants' evaluations of the attributes of moral, religious, and spiritual exemplars to explore the relationships across these domains. The critical feature of these collections of attributes for the present analysis is that, across domains, some attributes are unique in characterizing a particular domain (e.g., *just* is unique to the moral domain and *traditional* to the religious domain) whereas other attributes are shared between domains (e.g., *devout* is shared between the religious and spiritual domains). Participants in this study were asked to rate the accuracy (or prototypicality) of these attributes in describing each type of exemplar.

Prototype theory holds that participants' evaluations of unique versus shared attributes can help to explicate the relationships across these domains. Participants' ratings of the unique and shared attributes indicated that these domains are indeed related, albeit in an asymmetrical pattern – and this is a critical finding for the present analysis. The unique attributes descriptive of the moral exemplar received higher prototypicality ratings, on average, than did the attributes shared with either the religious or the spiritual exemplar. This indicates that, in people's ordinary understandings, core moral virtues and traits are relatively independent of religious and spiritual ones. In other words, to be a highly moral person, one does not *necessarily* need to manifest characteristics of either religiosity or spirituality.

In contrast, for both the religious and spiritual exemplars, their unique attributes received lower prototypicality ratings than the attributes shared with the moral exemplar. Obviously, their unique attributes are more peripheral to these concepts whereas their shared attributes are closer to their core meaning. This indicates that central to what it means to be a highly religious or spiritual person is the embodiment of moral virtues and traits.

The findings of Walker and Pitts's (1998) study can be stated more bluntly: In ordinary understandings, people believe that it is more likely that someone can function in a morally mature manner but be functionally irreligious than it is that someone can be authentically religious or spiritual but characteristically immoral in their behavior. We interpret this to be consistent with our second proposition that morality may lead individuals along different paths relative to (i.e., towards, away from) the transcendent. For some, morality prompts concerns regarding the transcendent, whereas for others, morality is not necessarily implicated and has no such effect. The findings are also consistent with our first proposition that transcendence can motivate individuals to function morally. However, the data do not address the possibility that transcendence can also lead to negative moral outcomes, by imparting "divine license" to immoral motives. In the next section we explore this issue of the motivating and amplifying effects of the transcendent on moral functioning; we defer until later sections discussion of the assertion that morality may pave the way to concerns regarding transcendence.

TRANSCENDENCE AS MORAL MOTIVATION

William James (1902), in the era of armchair psychology, argued in his classic text, *The Varieties of Religious Experience*, that the authenticity of religious faith should not be judged solely on the basis of intrapsychic experience, but also on the basis of its more objective consequences with "moral helpfulness" looming large among the evaluative criteria (Walker, 2003). James devoted a substantial proportion of *The Varieties* to an examination of the range of moral virtues that should be the practical extension of an authentic spirituality. In this section, we examine research which suggests that concerns regarding transcendence can motivate and amplify moral functioning.

In her CBC Massey Lectures, ethicist Margaret Somerville (2006) argued that connecting the self to some greater whole is a fundamental human motive.

> It is the intangible, immeasurable, numinous reality that all of us need to find meaning in life and to make life worth living – a deeply intuitive sense of relatedness or connectedness to all life, especially other people, to the world, and to the universe in which we live. One manifestation of the human spirit or human spirituality is the longing for transcendence – the strong desire to experience the feeling of belonging to something larger than ourselves. (pp. 7-8)

One explanation for this basic human motivation regarding transcendence is offered by terror management theory (Greenberg, Solomon, & Pyszczynski, 1997; Solomon, Greenberg, & Pyszczynski, 1991) which posits that the human instinct for self-preservation comes to loggerheads with the awareness of one's own inevitable death. The clash induces a sense of terror, the reaction to which is the need to transcend one's death by attaching the self to entities that exist beyond the self's mortal existence (e.g., by reaffirming one's cultural worldview).

How "longing for transcendence" manifests itself in interpersonal functioning is of particular interest for the present discussion. Not only might the need for transcendence (spirituality) directly affect the way that individuals relate to one another (Jonas, Schimel, Greenberg, & Pyszczynski, 2002), there may also exist an indirect relationship when the need for transcendence is expressed in the context of organized religion. In a religious context, two additional factors may act as moral motivators: (a) Religious concepts of omniscient overseers (e.g., a deity) may increase the extent to which individuals feel that they are being watched in everyday, ostensively private settings ("He knows if you've been bad or good ..."); and (b) for some religions, the afterlife is understood to hinge not only upon one's intrapsychic faith but also upon the uprightness of one's actions in life ("... so be good for goodness' sake!").

The notion that religion causes individuals to feel watched which, in turn, causes them to behave well was investigated by Shariff and Norenzayan (in press). Some participants were implicitly primed with religious concepts (e.g., *spirit*, *divine*, and *sacred*) in the course of a word scramble game. Those participants then behaved more generously to an anonymous stranger in an economic game than did those who were in a control priming condition. This effect was similar when the religious primes were replaced with ones representing secular moral institutions (e.g., *jury*, *police*, and *contract*). The interpretation of these results proffered here is that the priming induced participants to sense that their private actions were known which, in turn, increased incentive to behave well.

Additional research findings regarding the association of religion to moral functioning are somewhat mixed, consistent with our notion that concerns regarding the transcendent can motivate a range of moral outcomes. On the one hand, Baier and Wright (2001) conducted a meta-analysis of 60 studies and found that religious beliefs and practices exerted a moderate deterrent effect on individuals' criminal behavior; and similarly, religiosity has been found to predict a lower incidence of tax evasion (Stack & Kposowa, 2006). In terms of more obviously prosocial behaviors, Maclean, Walker, and Matsuba (2004) found that intrinsic religiosity was associated with altruism and Sosis and Ruffle (2004) found it associated with in-group cooperation. Thus, there is considerable evidence that religious faith can serve to promote good moral functioning.

On the other hand, there is ample evidence that religiosity is associated with deleterious outcomes – that religion can impart "divine license" to immoral actions. Given the strong group-identification aspect of religious affiliation, one might predict discriminatory attitudes and behaviors toward outgroups. Indeed, a typical finding is that fundamentalist religious affiliation is predictive of intolerance of minority or nonconformist groups (Burdette, Ellison, & Hill, 2005; Jackson & Esses, 1997). Batson, Schoenrade, and Ventis's (1993) review is enlightening in that regard. They found that religiosity was associated with self-reports of compassion and tolerance but not with increased compassionate and tolerate behavior toward members of outgroups; that is, there was greater concern to regard oneself as helpful than there was concern to actually be helpful.

Thus, the extant evidence is consistent with our first proposition that concerns regarding the transcendent can motivate and amplify moral action, and this can occur regardless whether those actions entail laudatory or dissolute motives. One explanation regarding these seemingly contradictory findings entails a distinction between religiosity and spirituality. It seems that strong religious affiliation and extrinsic forms of religiosity are more likely to be associated with immoral outcomes, whereas intrinsic spirituality and transcendent faith are more frequently empowering of mature moral functioning.

We now shift the discussion to begin to explore the other causal direction in this relationship – the impact of morality on concerns about transcendence. Our view is that there are various groundings for mature moral functioning; thus our second proposition is that, although morality may lead individuals to concerns about transcendence, morality does not *necessarily* do so.

COLBY AND DAMON'S SERENDIPITOUS FINDING

It was at the height of the Kohlbergian era—where morality was firmly demarcated from religious faith—that Colby and Damon (1992) reported the surprising and provocative finding regarding the significant role of faith and spirituality in the lives of moral exemplars (people who were engaged in extraordinary moral commitment and action). Their work was pivotal for a variety of reasons, one being that it heralded a paradigm shift from a focus on moral cognition (which had occupied the field for some time) to one that included broader aspects of moral personality and character. There was growing disillusionment with Kohlberg's vision of moral maturity – Stage 6 principles of justice – and it was becoming increasingly apparent that moral cognition lacked sufficient explanatory power; that is, that it was only weakly predictive of moral action – what became known as the "judgment–action gap" (Blasi, 1980; Walker, 2004). Single-variable models of moral functioning seemed to trivialize the domain. Other aspects of moral functioning, notably those pertaining to personality and motivation, needed to be incorporated into our theoretical perspectives. So Colby and Damon's study of the lives of moral exemplars represented an attempt to more fully describe moral functioning and to provide a more veridical account of moral excellence.

Colby and Damon (1992) conducted a case-study analysis of a small sample of 23 people who had been identified as leading lives of extraordinary moral commitment and action. These moral exemplars were identified on the basis of the nominations of a panel of experts who formulated a set of criteria for moral excellence and then named individuals meeting these criteria. What is particularly important here about these criteria is that they made no reference to, or even had any implication of religion, spirituality, or faith. Colby and Damon's qualitative analyses of their interviews with these moral exemplars suggested several processes in the development and maintenance of exceptional moral character, but one finding was completely unexpected: 78% of their sample of exemplars clearly attributed the value commitments underlying their moral action to their religious faith and spirituality. This appears both to challenge Kohlberg's (1967) strong demarcation and to contradict folk notions (Walker & Pitts, 1998) that exemplary moral functioning does not especially require a religious or spiritual foundation.

So what are the appropriate conclusions to draw from this serendipitous and intriguing finding? Two cautionary flags need to be raised at this point. First, Colby and Damon's study entailed an "assisted autobiography" methodology and qualitative analyses; it lacked objective measures. As a consequence, without any operationalization of their concepts, it is difficult to know exactly to what they are referring. Second, they had a small sample of American exemplars with no comparison group of participants. Among Western nations (such as North America and the countries of Europe), the United States is among the most religious and so it is not obvious that the prevalence of religious belief in Colby and Damon's sample is widely divergent from what would be found in the general population. A demographically-matched comparison group is essential and would be quite informative in that regard.

The first issue pertains to the ambiguity of Colby and Damon's provocative claim regarding the role of religious faith in moral functioning. Scholars in the psychology of religion (Hill & Hood, 1999) make important and nuanced distinctions among the concepts of religiosity, spirituality, and faith which are obscured in Colby and Damon's work. Colby and Damon noted that some exemplars explicitly based their morality on their religious beliefs (associated with a formal religion), whereas other exemplars referenced a spirituality or faith that was not amenable to encapsulation in traditional religious categories. They were left to conclude that, "although the substance of the faith and its ideals was too varied and too elusive to be captured in a final generalization, it can perhaps best be described as an intimation of transcendence" (p. 311), a tantalizing but unsatisfactory conclusion. The critical distinctions among religiosity, spirituality, and faith development figure importantly in our research which we will present later in this chapter.

The second issue with the Colby and Damon study was their lack of a comparison group. This limitation was addressed in a recent study (Matsuba & Walker, 2004, 2005) which examined the psychological functioning of a sample of young-adult moral exemplars. In this study, moral exemplars were identified on the basis of extraordinary moral commitment toward various social service organizations. A comparison group of young-adult participants was also recruited, individually matched on several demographic variables. Among the various personality constructs assessed in this study was faith development.

This assessment of faith development was based on Fowler's (1981) structural-developmental model that proposes stages of faith Fowler contends that these stages are conceptually unrelated to religiosity or religious affiliation; rather, they reflect the processes involved in individuals' meaning-making and their epistemic understanding of the transcendent. These stages can be briefly described as follows:

- Stage 1 (*intuitive–projective*): a magical, fantasy-filled period in which the young child constructs the world in a largely egocentric and episodic way.
- Stage 2 (*mythical–literal*): at this stage the child attempts to make sense of experience in narrative or concrete terms.
- Stage 3 (*synthetic–conventional*): at this stage the adolescent or adult unreflectively synthesizes and adopts the views of significant others and authorities.

— Stage 4 (*individuative–reflective*): at this stage there is the self-conscious construction of an explicit, systematic worldview.
— Stage 5 (*conjunctive*): an individual at this stage reasons in dialogical terms, embracing paradox and seeking to conjoin the truths of multiple perspectives.
— Stage 6 (*universalizing*): transcending paradox, the rare individual at this stage commits to relatedness with an all-inclusive universal community and totality of being.

The relevant finding from Matsuba and Walker's (2004) study is that their moral exemplars evidenced significantly more mature faith development than did the participants in the comparison group; and furthermore, among the large number of personality constructs assessed in this study, it was faith development that best discriminated between the exemplar and comparison groups, indicating its salience in moral functioning. There was, however, an unfortunate confound that throws the finding into some doubt: half of the exemplars were drawn from religious organizations (the other half were drawn from secular social-service organizations), whereas comparison participants were recruited from psychology classes (and the extent of their religious affiliation was not known). It is possible that the differences in faith development between moral exemplars and comparison participants might be attributable to differences in religiosity.

So, in the course of reviewing the evidence regarding the relationship between moral functioning and concerns about the transcendent, we have managed to generate numerous questions. It is in this context that we have conducted another study, examining the psychological functioning of moral exemplars, which hopefully will be more definitive in its findings.

THE PRESENT STUDY

There are three notable aspects to the study's design: (a) The study entailed a matched comparison group and objective methodology. (b) It compared two contrasting types of moral exemplars. (c) It assessed three different aspects of the transcendent domain – religiosity, spirituality, and faith. First, the critical importance of appropriately matched comparison groups and reliance on objective methodology has been argued earlier; there is no need for reiteration. Second, previous research (Colby & Damon, 1992; Matsuba & Walker, 2004) has focused on a single type of moral exemplarity, that is, caring action in the form of committed social service. It is possible that the relationship between moral functioning and religious faith may vary across different types of moral action, so in the present study we compared two quite different types of moral exemplars: brave versus caring. Third, as we have already implied, there are important distinctions among the constructs of religiosity, spirituality, and faith that need to be fleshed out in the context of empirical research. In our understanding, religiosity refers to the creedal and ritual expressions of belief and practice associated with institutional religion; spirituality refers

317

to the more personal affirmation of a higher power that is beyond oneself; whereas faith refers to the process of meaning-making and an epistemic stance toward the transcendent.

Sample

The moral exemplars identified in this study were recent recipients of a national award through the Canadian honors system. Our focus was on two contrasting types of moral exemplars: brave and caring. The 25 brave exemplars were recipients of the *Medal of Bravery*, a civilian award which recognizes individuals who have risked their lives to save others and who have persisted in their rescue attempt despite considerable danger. The 25 caring exemplars were recipients of the *Caring Canadian Award* which recognizes extraordinary volunteers who have shown long-term commitment in providing care to individuals or groups, or who have supported community service or humanitarian causes. The brave and caring exemplars were demographically alike except for the fact that the caring exemplars were substantially older than the brave exemplars (mean ages were 70 vs. 41 years), a difference that was not unexpected given that the caring exemplars were being recognized for long-term service whereas brave exemplars were being recognized for rescues in dangerous contexts in which younger people are more typically involved. Comparison groups were formed of individuals drawn from the general community. They were closely matched on a case-by-case basis to the exemplar participants in terms of the demographic variables of gender, ethnicity, age, and level of education. Thus, the total N for this study was 100.

Measures

Among other measures (see Walker & Frimer, in press, for a description of the larger project), participants completed two questionnaires and responded to a lengthy individual life-review interview which was conducted in their home. One of the questionnaires was the short 5-item *Duke Religion Index* (Koenig, Parkerson, & Meador, 1997). Two items on this self-report measure tap organizational and non-organizational religiosity (Cronbach's $\alpha = .80$) and three items tap intrinsic spirituality ($\alpha = .95$).

Participants also completed the *Personal Strivings List* (Emmons, 1999) which assesses goal motivation by prompting people to provide a list their personal strivings, that is, the things they are "typically or characteristically trying to do." These strivings can be coded for the presence of various goal-motivational themes, including spiritual self-transcendence. Examination of the scoring criteria (Emmons, 1999) for this theme revealed, however, that they conflated religious, spiritual, and moral concerns, so we developed our own scoring criteria to code religious and spiritual strivings (harkening back the distinction between religion and spirituality made by James, 1902, pp. 334-335). Religious strivings were defined as ones that explicitly refer to the beliefs, attitudes, practices, experiences, commitments, and goals of recognized religion. These could entail aspects of institutional religion (e.g., attending religious services), of private religious activities (e.g., prayer), of adherence to religious teachings (e.g., the Ten Commandments), or of beliefs and attitudes (e.g., knowledge of a relationship with a deity). In contrast, spiritual strivings were defined as ones that are oriented to transcending the self. Such strivings implicitly affirm a nonmaterial reality that is above and beyond the self; they reflect an attempt to align one's life with that reality. Spiritual strivings can take many forms, including (but not necessarily limited to) increasing one's knowledge of a higher power or metaphysical entity, developing or maintaining a relationship with a higher power, integrating the self with a transcending totality, and attempting to exercise one's spiritual beliefs in daily life. To assess these two categories of personal strivings (religious and spiritual), responses on participants' lists were independently classified for the presence/absence of the relevant motivational theme. Note that the categories are not mutually exclusive: a striving may overlap both categories or may not be codeable at all. Interrater reliability was determined by the independent coding of the data of a randomly selected subsample of 25 participants and was found to be substantial, with 100% agreement for religious strivings and 99% agreement for spiritual ones (Cohen's κ = 1.00 and .91, respectively).

Embedded within the context of the life-review interview was a lengthy series of questions tapping four aspects of faith development: (a) social perspective-taking, (b) bounds of social awareness, (c) locus of authority, and (d) form of world coherence. Participants' responses for each aspect were matched to coding criteria given in the faith coding manual (Moseley, Jarvis, & Fowler, 1993). These scored responses were then averaged to yield a faith stage score for each aspect. Interrater reliability was determined by the independent coding of the faith interviews of 25 participants and was found to be substantial, with exact agreement in faith stage scores for each aspect ranging from 80% to 96% (and with Cohen's κ_n = .78 to .96). Note that we did not assess three other aspects of faith development (viz., form of logic, symbolic function, and form of moral judgment) described by Fowler (1981). We excluded logical and symbolic processes because of their minimal relevance to the issues of interest here and we excluded moral judgment so as not to create an artifactual relationship between faith development and moral functioning. The faith coding manual (Moseley et al., 1993) does allow for the use of an abbreviated interview.

For analyses, we derived from these measures three summary indices: religiosity, spirituality, and faith development. (a) Religiosity was tapped by two scores: the overall score for extrinsic religiosity (from the *Duke Religion Index*) and by the frequency of religious strivings (from the *Personal Strivings List*). These two components of religiosity were strongly correlated (with r = .63 and p < .001); and an overall index for religiosity was generated by first standardizing each of these two scores and then averaging them. (b) Spirituality was also tapped by two scores: the overall score for intrinsic spirituality (from the *Duke Religion Index*) and by the frequency of spiritual strivings (from the *Personal Strivings List*). These two components of spirituality were moderately correlated (with $r = .42$ and $p < .001$); and an overall index for spirituality was generated by standardizing each of these two scores and then averaging them. (c) Finally, faith development was indexed by averaging the four aspect scores (Cronbach's $\alpha = .84$). Descriptive statistics for the indices of religiosity, spirituality, and faith development are presented in Table 1 for the brave and caring exemplar groups, as well as for their matched comparison groups.

Also in the course of the life-review interview, participants were asked to recall and discuss a real-life moral dilemma from their personal experience which was scored for stage of moral reasoning development, following well-established procedures in that regard (Colby & Kohlberg, 1987; Walker et al., 1995). Level of moral reasoning was indexed by the weighted average score, which is given by the sum of the percent usage at each stage weighted by the stage number. Interrater reliability was $ICC = .83$.

Results

Religiosity In order to examine differences across the groups in religiosity, a 2 (group: exemplar, comparison) × 2 (award: brave, caring) × 2 (gender) analysis of variance (ANOVA) was conducted, using the standardized religiosity scores as the dependent variable. The only significant effect revealed was for the award variable, $F(1,92) = 4.06$, $p = .04$, $\eta^2 = .04$. This relatively weak effect indicates that participants from the caring exemplar and comparison groups evidenced somewhat greater religiosity than did participants from the brave exemplar and comparison groups (Ms = 0.22 vs. -0.22). Recall that caring participants were almost a generation older than brave ones, suggesting that this effect for religiosity should be attributed to developmental or cohort factors. Indeed, there was a significant correlation between age and religiosity in this sample ($r = .30$, $p = .002$), indicating that commitment to the beliefs, practices, and goals of institutionalized religion is more pronounced among members of the older generation. Note that this analysis revealed no differences between moral exemplars and comparison participants in religiosity.

Spirituality The group × award × gender ANOVA for spirituality revealed no significant effects, indicating that on this variable there are no group differences as well.

Faith Development However, the analysis for faith development revealed a main effect for group, $F(1,92) = 8.97$, $p = .004$, $\eta^2 = .09$, which was qualified by a group × award interaction, $F(1,92) = 3.87$, $p = .05$, $\eta^2 = .04$. This interaction was examined by analyses of the simple main effects which indicated no difference in faith development between brave exemplars and their comparison group, whereas there was a substantial difference between caring exemplars and their comparison group,

$F(1,92) = 13.78, p < .001, \eta^2 = .13$. As is evident in Table 1, the caring exemplar group evidenced a more mature level of faith development (by about one-third of a stage) than did any other group.

Thus, this study revealed group differences for faith development but not for religiosity or spirituality, suggesting that faith is tapping a somewhat different facet of the domain. This notion is confirmed by the relatively modest correlation between faith and religiosity ($r = .15, p = .15$) and between faith and spirituality ($r = .29, p = .004$).

So how do we interpret this finding that caring exemplars scored higher on faith development than their comparison group? The structural-developmental measure of faith indexed in this study can best be understood as a measure of epistemic development as applied to one's worldview or understanding of the world and beyond. One possible interpretation of the evidenced relationship between faith development and moral exemplarity is that the facet of faith development that is accounting for variance in moral functioning is some feature of cognitive development as opposed to a relatedness to the transcendent. Considering that faith development was significantly correlated with stage of moral reasoning ($r = .58, p < .001$), this remains a distinct possibility (see Snarey, 1991, for a discussion of the relationships between faith and moral stages).

If cognitive-developmental level does mediate the group differences in faith development, then, we argue, these data would suggest that there may be little about transcendence, per se, that is relevant to moral exemplarity. To address this potential confound, we ran an analysis analogous to the omnibus test on faith development described above, but this time removing any covariance accounted for by stage of moral reasoning. This analysis of covariance (with stage of moral reasoning as a covariate), however, revealed that the simple main effect – caring exemplars versus their matched comparison group – remained significant although the size of the effect was somewhat reduced, $F(1,92) = 5.51, p = .02, \eta^2 = .06$. Thus, partialling out cognitive-developmental status does not eliminate the relationship between faith development and moral exemplarity.

A final proposition is that religiosity and/or spirituality might mediate the remaining relationship between faith development and moral exemplarity. However, analyses adding religiosity and spirituality as covariates indicated that neither mediated the relationship. The proportion of variance that remains explained by faith development would seem to belong to a part of the realm of transcendent faith that is not tapped by structural-developmental level, religiosity, or spirituality.

MORALITY PAVES THE WAY TO TRANSCENDENCE

This chapter has explored the relevance of religion, spirituality, and transcendent faith to moral functioning, returning to themes well-voiced by William James over a century ago. The findings of a series of studies strongly challenge the hard-line demarcation view that has been dominant in moral psychology for some time which compartmentalized these domains as independent aspects of human functioning. The evidence is now overwhelmingly abundant that these domains entail important interconnections.

The results of our research do provide a corrective response to Colby and Damon's (1992) finding regarding the claimed role of religious faith and spirituality in moral action. With a larger sample, the inclusion of appropriate comparison groups, and reliance on objective measures that operationalize religiosity, spirituality, and faith, our study indicated no differences between exemplar and comparison participants on measures of either religiosity or spirituality. Interestingly, our findings regarding the psychological functioning of moral exemplars in this regard clearly accord with Walker and Pitts's (1998) finding that, in people's ordinary understandings, mature moral functioning does not necessitate high levels of religiosity or spirituality. Our findings also accord with our second proposition that morality may but does not necessarily implicate concerns about the transcendent.

Our findings did indicate, however, that caring exemplars had a more mature level of faith development than comparison participants, whereas no such difference was found for brave exemplars. This certainly suggests that the role of faith is differentially implicated for different types of moral action. In the larger project (Walker & Frimer, in press) from which the present data are drawn, one notable and consistent finding was that personality differences between moral exemplars and comparison participants were more pronounced for caring than for brave exemplars. This may reflect that fact that caring exemplars were being recognized for long-term volunteer service which may have largely been a reflection of deeply ingrained character traits, whereas brave exemplars were being recognized for a single (albeit momentous) heroic act which may have been to a greater extent impelled by situational factors.

Interestingly, the modal stage of faith development in the present study was not particularly extraordinary given that approximately 96% of faith judgments were coded as Stage 3 or 4. Thus, the meaningful distinction between caring exemplars and other groups can be characterized primarily in terms of the qualitative contrast between these particular stages. Recall that Stage 3 individuals *passively* infuse the views of close others or authorities; the shift to Stage 4 rests on the process of *actively* and deliberatively constructing a worldview for oneself. Thus, our caring exemplars were more likely to have engaged the laborious yet critical process of constructing their own faith epistemology. This finding is congruent with moral identity theory that emphasizes the notion of personhood – the self *actively constructing* an identity under the direction of moral reasoning (Blasi, 1984).

More generally, faith development reflects the process of meaning-making and of one's epistemic standing toward the transcendent. Reasoning at the higher levels of faith development in particular displays an openness to the complexity of multiple perspectives and dimensions which is simultaneously grounded in a critical self-awareness. It entails an expanded awareness and inclusiveness of groups other than one's own. It stands prior to the social order, evaluating authority in terms of universalizable principles of relationship. It embraces complexity and ambiguity and recognizes a multidimensional reality that can be seen through different metaphors and methods as a way to deeper understanding. There is an evident working towards a transcending vision of the good. Such mature and well-developed faith provides a foundation for the expanded circle of concern that characterizes committed and caring action toward others.

An important caveat regarding moral exemplar studies such as reported here is that they have uniformly been carried out subsequent to the moral action, raising the possibility that personological and other differences are the *result* of an identity reconstructive process prompted by the action itself. This opens the question of whether identity functions predominantly in a proactive sense (akin to an operator's manual) or a reactive one (akin to a documentary) – a matter yet unresolved.

Further, there remains the question of how moral exemplar data inform our discussion on transcendence and morality. Recall that our first proposition posited that transcendence acts to amplify and motivate morally relevant (good, bad) thought, whereas our second proposition held that there are various groundings for mature moral functioning, not only transcendent but also secular. The grist for our discussion is the finding of more mature faith development among caring exemplars than other groups. There are at least three just-so stories that can be told in that regard.

One possibility is that the caring exemplars may have developed their more sophisticated faith development prior to their extraordinary moral action. This scenario is consistent with our first proposition but reticent regarding our second. Such an advanced epistemic stance may have given meaning to, and provided motivation for, the moral acts in the first place, congruent with the notion that identity may serve proactively or like an operator's manual. Several scholars (Blasi, 1990; Fernhout, 1989; Kunzman, 2003) have argued that, for many people, morality acquires its meaning primarily within the context of religious faith. It would be telling to conduct similar research with samples of immoral exemplars (such as psychopaths or terrorists) to determine the extent to which religiosity and/or faith may also lead people toward negative moral outcomes.

Another just-so story is congruent with our second proposition (that morality may lead to transcendence, albeit not necessarily so) and with the notion that identity may be a reaction to moral action. That is, the internalization of moral values and engagement in moral action may have subsequently lead the caring exemplars to explore their faith and the transcendent more seriously. This shares the spirit of Kohlberg's Stage 7, wherein the internalization of moral values and principles prompts questions regarding the ultimate purpose of morality and one's connection to the grand scheme of the universe. While Kohlberg's placing this connection at the virtually unattainable Stage 7 made such a convergence exceedingly esoteric, we argue here that the convergence of morality with larger questions about the meaning and purpose of one's existence may be far more mundane. Note that the present data are particularly supportive of our second proposition (that morality does not necessarily lead to concerns regarding the transcendent) in that one type of moral exemplar (viz., caring) did differ from their comparison group on faith development, whereas the other (viz., brave) did not. This affirms the notion that there are many paths to moral excellence, one of which may be through faith development. This remains a question for future investigation.

And the third just-so story is that the association between faith development and moral exemplarity may be spurious. There may exist a broader construct (e.g., generalized flourishing) that has caused moral functioning and faith development to co-occur. Thus it remains possible that there exists no operative relationship between the two.

In this chapter we have explored two propositions regarding the functional relationship between transcendence and moral functioning and have reviewed relevant data. The findings of our present study represent a corrective to Colby and Damon (1992) and act to clarify their assertion regarding transcendence in lives of moral exemplars. We have presented evidence that, when it comes to moral functioning, the relevant personological dimension is neither religiosity nor spirituality but, rather, faith development. In the unpacking of these data, however, we have revealed more questions than answers. The hunt is on for sources of moral motivation; it is our contention that the search ought to include the realm of that which we cannot readily discern.

ACKNOWLEDGEMENT

The research reported in this chapter was funded by grants from the Social Sciences and Humanities Research Council of Canada. We gratefully acknowledge the research assistance of Karine Burger, Sarah Breuel, and Matthew Przybylski.

REFERENCES

Baier, C. J. & Wright, B. R. E. (2001). "If you love me, keep my commandments": A meta-analysis of the effect of religion on crime. *Journal of Research in Crime and Delinquency, 38,* 3-21.

Batson, C. D., Schoenrade, P. & Ventis, W. L. (1993). *Religion and the individual.* New York: Oxford University Press.

Blasi, A. (1980). Bridging moral cognition and moral action: A critical review of the literature. *Psychological Bulletin, 88,* 1-45.

Blasi, A. (1984). Moral identity: Its role in moral functioning. In W. M. Kurtines & J. L. Gewirtz (Eds.), *Morality, moral behavior, and moral development* (pp. 128-139). New York: Wiley.

Blasi, A. (1990). How should psychologists define morality? Or, the negative side effects of philosophy's influence on psychology. In T. Wren (Ed.), *The moral domain: Essays in the ongoing discussion between philosophy and the social sciences* (pp. 38-70). Cambridge, MA: MIT Press.

Burdette, A. M., Ellison, C. G. & Hill, T. D. (2005). Conservative Protestantism and tolerance toward homosexuals: An examination of potential mechanisms. *Sociological Inquiry, 75,* 177-196.

Colby, A., & Damon, W. (1992). *Some do care: Contemporary lives of moral commitment.* New York: Free Press.

Colby, A. & Kohlberg, L. (1987). *The measurement of moral judgment* (Vols. 1-2). New York: Cambridge University Press.

Emmons, R. A. (1999). *The psychology of ultimate concerns: Motivation and spirituality in personality*. New York: Guilford.

Fernhout, H. (1989). Moral education as grounded in faith. *Journal of Moral Education, 18*, 186-198.

Flanagan, O. (1991). *Varieties of moral personality: Ethics and psychological realism*. Cambridge, MA: Harvard University Press.

Fowler, J. W. (1981). *Stages of faith: The psychology of human development and the quest for meaning*. San Francisco: Harper & Row.

Greenberg, J., Solomon, S. & Pyszczynski, T. (1997). Terror management theory of self-esteem and cultural worldviews: Empirical assessments and conceptual refinements. In M. P. Zanna (Ed.), *Advances in experimental social psychology* (Vol. 29, pp. 61-139). San Diego: Academic Press.

Hill, P. C. & Hood, R. W., Jr. (1999). *Measures of religiosity*. Birmingham, AL: Religious Education Press.

Jackson, L. M. & Esses, V. M. (1997). Of scripture and ascription: The relation between religious fundamentalism and intergroup helping. *Personality and Social Psychology Bulletin, 23*, 893-906.

James, W. (1902). *The varieties of religious experience*. New York and London: Longmans, Green, and Company.

Jonas, E., Schimel, J., Greenberg, J. & Pyszczynski, T. (2002). The Scrooge effect: Evidence that mortality salience increases prosocial attitudes and behavior. *Personality and Social Psychology Bulletin, 28*, 1342-1353.

Koenig, H. G., Parkerson, G. R., Jr. & Meador, K. G. (1997). Religion index for psychiatric research. *American Journal of Psychiatry, 154*, 885-886.

Kohlberg, L. (1967). Moral and religious education and the public schools: A developmental view. In T. Sizer (Ed.), *Religion and public education* (pp. 164-183). Boston: Houghton Mifflin.

Kohlberg, L., with Power, C. (1981). Moral development, religious thinking, and the question of a seventh stage. In L. Kohlberg, *Essays on moral development: Vol. 1. The philosophy of moral development* (pp. 311-372). San Francisco: Harper & Row.

Kunzman, R. (2003). Religion, ethics, and the implications for moral education: A critique of Nucci's *Morality and religious rules*. *Journal of Moral Education, 32*, 251-261.

Maclean, A. M., Walker, L. J. & Matsuba, M. K. (2004). Transcendence and the moral self: Identity integration, religion, and moral life. *Journal for the Scientific Study of Religion, 43*, 429-437.

Matsuba, M. K. & Walker, L. J. (2004). Extraordinary moral commitment: Young adults working for social organizations. *Journal of Personality, 72*, 413-436.

Matsuba, M. K. & Walker, L. J. (2005). Young adult moral exemplars: The making of self through stories. *Journal of Research on Adolescence, 15*, 275-297.

Moseley, R. M., Jarvis, D. & Fowler, J. W. (1993). *Manual for faith development research* (K. B. DeNicola, Rev. Ed.). Atlanta: Emory University, Center for Research in Faith and Moral Development.

Rosch, E. (1978). Principles of categorization. In E. Rosch & B. B. Lloyd (Eds.), *Cognition and categorization* (pp. 27-48). Hillsdale, NJ: Erlbaum.

Shariff, A. F. & Norenzayan, A. (in press). God is watching you: Supernatural agent concepts increase prosocial behavior in an anonymous economic game. *Psychological Science*.

Sosis, R. & Ruffle, B. J. (2004). Ideology, religion, and the evolution of cooperation: Field tests on Israeli kibbutzim. *Research in Economic Anthropology, 23*, 89-117.

Snarey, J. (1991). Faith development, moral development, and nontheistic Judaism: A construct validity study. In W. M. Kurtines & J. L. Gewirtz (Eds.), *Handbook of moral behavior and development: Vol. 2. Research* (pp. 279-305). Hillsdale, NJ: Erlbaum.

Solomon, S., Greenberg, J. & Pyszczynski, T. (1991). A terror management theory of social behavior: The psychological functions of self-esteem and cultural worldviews. In M. P. Zanna (Ed.), *Advances in experimental social psychology* (Vol. 24, pp. 93-159). San Diego: Academic Press.

Somerville, M. (2006). *The ethical imagination: Journeys of the human spirit*. Toronto: House of Anansi Press.

Stack, S. & Kposowa, A. (2006). The effect of religiosity on tax fraud acceptability: A cross-national analysis. *Journal for the Scientific Study of Religion, 45*, 325-351.

Walker, L. J. (2003). Morality, religion, spirituality—The value of saintliness. *Journal of Moral Education, 32*, 373-384.

Walker, L. J. (2004). Gus in the gap: Bridging the judgment–action gap in moral functioning. In D. K. Lapsley & D. Narvaez (Eds.), *Moral development, self, and identity* (pp. 1-20). Mahwah, NJ: Erlbaum.

Walker, L. J. & Frimer, J. A. (in press). Moral personality of brave and caring exemplars. *Journal of Personality and Social Psychology*.

Walker, L. J. & Pitts, R. C. (1998). Naturalistic conceptions of moral maturity. *Developmental Psychology, 34*, 403-419.

Walker, L. J., Pitts, R. C., Hennig, K. H. & Matsuba, M. K. (1995). Reasoning about morality and real-life moral problems. In M. Killen & D. Hart (Eds.), *Morality in everyday life: Developmental perspectives* (pp. 371-407). Cambridge, UK: Cambridge University Press.

Lawrence J. Walker & Jeremy A. Frimer
University of British Columbia, Vancouver, Canada

KIRSI TIRRI, PETRI NOKELAINEN & KRISTIINA HOLM

ETHICAL SENSITIVITY
OF FINNISH LUTHERAN 7TH - 9TH GRADERS

ABSTRACT

This study examined ethical sensitivity self-evaluations of two Finnish urban schools 7th - 9th grade students (n = 249) with the Ethical Sensitivity Scale Questionnaire (ESSQ). The ESSQ is based on Narvaez operationalization of ethical sensitivity (2001): (1) Reading and expressing emotions, (2) taking the perspectives of others, (3) caring by connecting to others, (4) working with interpersonal and group differences, (5) preventing social bias, (6) generating interpretations and options and (7) identifying the consequences of actions and options. Three research questions were formulated: Are there any differences in the self-reported ethical sensitivity between (1) Lutheran non-confirmed and confirmed; (2) female and male; and (3) academically average and above average students? Results showed that more data (also cross-cultural) and further statistical analyses are needed to prove the usefulness of the ESSQ in practice. Results regarding the first question showed that those students who have had more religious education at school, and also were confirmed as Lutherans, self-reported higher ethical skills than their younger and non-confirmed peers. Results regarding the second question showed clearly that female students estimated their ethical skills higher than their male peers. Results regarding the third question showed that more academically gifted students estimated their ethical skills higher than average ability students.

ETHICAL SENSITIVITY AS AN IMPORTANT COMPONENT IN MORALITY

According to Bebeau, Rest and Narvaez (1999), morality is built upon four basic component processes. These processes include moral sensitivity, moral judgment, moral motivation and moral character. The components of moral sensitivity, moral motivation and moral character have been studied less than the component of moral judgment.

Most of the studies in the area of moral development have based their theory on the cognitive-developmental theory of Lawrence Kohlberg (e.g., 1969). The Defining Issues Test (DIT) is a well-documented measure of moral judgment that has been used all over the world (Rest, 1986). The index most frequently used is the "P score", which reflects the principled reasoning (Stages 5 and 6 in Kohlberg's

Fritz Oser & Wiel Veugelers (eds.), Getting involved, 327–341.
327

theory) of a person. Kohlberg's procedures have been criticized for lack of diversity in the moral dilemmas that have been used in the interviews (Yussen, 1977). The hypothetical dilemmas can also be seen as being too abstract and removed from the daily experiences of most people (Straughan, 1975). Recognition of these aspects of hypothetical dilemmas has led educational researchers to study real-life moral problems identified by people (Walker, de Vries & Trevethan, 1987). The research conducted in this area shows that the adolescents formulate dilemmas, which are very different from the hypothetical dilemmas used by Kohlberg and his colleagues to assess moral reasoning (Yussen, 1977; Binfet, 1995). Most of the dilemmas formulated by Kohlberg focus on issues of ownership, public welfare and life-and-death. In Yussen's (1977) study, the moral dilemma themes, formulated by adolescents, focused most frequently on interpersonal relations. Colangelo (1982) and Tirri (1996) found the same tendency with gifted adolescents.

Andreani and Pagnin provided a comprehensive review of the literature in their article (1993, 539-553). According to these authors, the gifted students are presumed to have a privileged position in the maturation of moral thinking because of their precocious intellectual growth. Terman's (1925) sample of gifted children showed superior maturity in moral development in choosing socially constructive activities and in rating misbehaviour.

In the 1980's, Karnes and Brown (1981) made an initial investigation on moral development and the gifted, using Rest's DIT. Their sample included 233 gifted students (9-15 years of age) who were selected for a gifted programme. The results of the DIT were compared to the students' results in a test that measured their intellectual ability (WISC-R). The empirical results of the study showed positive correlation between the two tests. According to the researchers, intellectually gifted children appear to reach a relatively high stage of moral reasoning earlier than their chronological peers (Karnes & Brown, 1981, 54).

Other studies of moral judgment using DIT scores have shown that gifted adolescents scored higher than their peers as a group (Tan-Willman & Gutteridge, 1981; Janos & Robinson, 1985; Narvaez, 1993). However, the data with high-achieving adolescents has indicated that the relationship between apparent academic talent and moral judgment scores is more complex. According to Narvaez's study, high academic competence is necessary for an unusually high P score, but it does not necessarily predict it. The high achievers may have average to high moral judgment scores, whereas low achievers cannot be high scorers in moral judgment (Narvaez, 1993).

Morality includes other components besides moral judgment, as measured by DIT scores. Real-life moral dilemmas also require moral sensitivity and moral motivation (Narvaez, 1993). Before an individual can make responsible moral judgments, he or she needs to identify real-life moral dilemmas in different contexts. A broad conception of morality requires more than just skill in abstract reasoning. Affective and social factors play a vital role in moral conduct. The few empirical studies available have contradictory results on the relationships between general intelligence, social competence, and altruism (Abroms, 1985). Earlier studies on deviant behaviour and crime among the gifted have also shown that there is no necessary relationship between morality and intelligence (Brooks, 1985; Gath, Tennenth & Pidduck, 1970). Furthermore, earlier studies show that there are qualitative differences in the moral reasoning of gifted adolescents (Tirri & Pehkonen, 2002).

DEFINITION AND OPERATIONALIZATION
OF THE ETHICAL SENSITIVITY SCALE

According to Muriel Bebeau and her colleagues (1999, 22), moral sensitivity

...is the awareness of how our actions affect other people. It involves being aware of the different possible lines of action and how each line of action could affect the parties involved (including oneself). Moral sensitivity involves imaginatively constructing possible scenarios (often from limited cues and partial information), knowing cause-consequent chains of events in the real world, and having empathy and role taking skills. Moral sensitivity is necessary to become aware that a moral issue is involved in a situation.

To respond to a situation in a moral way, a person must be able to perceive and interpret events in ways that lead to ethical action. The person must be sensitive to situational cues and must be able to visualize various alternative actions in response to that situation. A morally sensitive person draws on many aspects, skills, techniques and components of interpersonal sensitivity. These include taking the perspective of others (role taking), cultivating empathy for a sense of connection to others, and interpreting a situation based on imagining what might happen and who might be affected. Ethical sensitivity is closely related to a new suggested intelligence type, social intelligence, which can be defined as the ability to get along well with others and get them to cooperate with you (Albrecht, 2006; Goleman, 2006).

We acknowledge that numerous tests of ethical sensitivity exists, but most of them are very context-specific, for example, relating to medicine and dental education (Bebeau, Rest & Yamoor, 1985) or to racial and gender intolerance (Brabeck, Rogers, Sirin, Handerson, Ting & Benvenuto, 2000). Darcia Narvaez (2001) has operationalized ethical sensitivity to include seven sets of skills that operate on a more general level: Reading and expressing emotions, taking the perspectives of others, caring by connecting to others, working with interpersonal and group differences, preventing social bias, generating interpretations and options, and identifying the consequences of actions and options. Those ethical skills have guided our Ethical Sensitivity Scale (ESS) instrument development work.

GOALS OF THE RESEARCH

In this study, we have two research goals: *The first research goal* is to present an initial 28 –item version of the Ethical Sensitivity Scale Questionnaire (ESSQ). *The second research goal* is to answer the following three questions: Are there any differences in the self-reported ethical sensitivity between (1) Lutheran non-confirmed and confirmed students; (2) female and male students; and (3) academically average and above average students?

METHOD

Sample

The non-probability sample ($N = 249$) was collected with the Ethical Sensitivity Scale Questionnaire (ESSQ) during the autumn semester 2006, from two secondary schools in Finland. One of the schools was located in Helsinki (Southern Finland, capital of Finland with about 560,000 inhabitants) and the other one was located in Jyväskylä (Central Finland, about 165,000 inhabitants). Each respondent was personally invited to complete a paper and pencil version of the questionnaire. Participants were asked to evaluate their attitude towards the statements measuring ethical sensitivity.

The sample consists of seventh ($n = 85$, 34%), eighth ($n = 81$, 33%) and ninth ($n = 82$, 33%) grade students of which 132 (53 %) are females and 116 (47 %) are males. The age median in the sample is 14 years. The ninth-grade students in the sample had been confirmed in the Lutheran Church. The students were further classified into two groups: Academically (1) average ($n = 114$, 46.7 %, self-reported grade point average $6.4 < GPA < 8.5$) and (2) above average ($n = 130$, 53.3 %, $8.5 \leq GPA \leq 10.0$) students.

Ethical Sensitivity Scale Questionnaire

ESSQ is based on Narvaez's operationalization of ethical sensitivity (2001). Its main purpose is to scale the pupils' orientations on ethical issues. The ESSQ measures the following seven dimensions of ethical sensitivity: (1) Reading and expressing emotions, (2) taking the perspectives of others, (3) caring by connecting to others, (4) working with interpersonal and group differences, (5) preventing social bias, (6) generating interpretations and options and (7) identifying the consequences of actions and options. The instrument consists of 28 items on a Likert-scale from 1 (*totally disagree*) to 5 (*totally agree*) (Table 1.).

The ESSQ items were designed to apply to people from different backgrounds and cultures. This allows us to use the instrument in a multicultural society and in cross-cultural studies. The statements described the issues and values that the respondent considered important for him or her. Each of the seven dimensions was operationalized in the questionnaire with four statements. For example, the first category, Reading and expressing emotions, was measured with the item ess1_1 "In conflict situations, I am able to identify other persons' feelings." All the items, with means and standard deviations, are listed in Table 2.

Table 1. Measurement model of the Ethical Sensitivity Scale Questionnaire (ESSQ).

Dimension	Factor	Items	M (SD)	α
1 Reading and express-ing emotions	ESS_1	es1_1, es1_2, es1_3, es1_4	3.9 (0.6)	.54
2 Taking the perspec-tives of others	ESS_2	es2_5, es2_6, es2_7, es2_8	3.7 (0.7)	.71
3 Caring by connect-ing to others	ESS_3	es3_9, es3_10, es3_11, es3_12	3.9 (0.7)	.78
4 Working with inter-personal and group differences	ESS_4	es4_13, es4_14, es4_15, es4_16	3.4 (0.7)	.75
5 Preventing social bias	ESS_5	es5_17, es5_18, es5_19, es5_20	3.5 (0.5)	.50
6 Generating interpre-tations and options	ESS_6	es6_21, es6_22, es6_23, es6_24	3.6 (0.6)	.69
7 Identifying the con-sequences of actions and options	ESS_7	es7_25, es7_26, es7_27, es7_28	3.3 (0.6)	.65

Statistical Analyses

The first stage of the analysis describes the psychometric properties of the seven dimensions of the ESSQ. The analysis techniques we apply here are non-parametric Spearman rank order correlations to study statistical dependencies between the indicators and parametric Cronbach's alpha values, that estimate how well the items co-operate within each dimension.

The second stage of the analysis answers the three research questions with a non-parametric Mann-Whitney U–test. The first research question, "Are there any differences in the ethical sensitivity between Lutheran non-confirmed and confirmed students?", was addressed with the confirmation status (confirmed/non-confirmed) as a grouping variable. The second research question, "Are there any differences in the ethical sensitivity between female and male students?", was addressed with gender (male/female) as a grouping variable. The third research question, "Are there any differences in the ethical sensitivity between academically average and above average students?", was addressed with average school grade (average school success: 6.5 - 8.4; and above average school success: 8.5 – 10.0) as a grouping variable.

Table 2. ESSQ items

Item	Label	M (SD)
es1_1	In conflict situations, I am able to identify other persons' feelings.	3.8 (0.7)
es1_2	I am able to express my different feelings to other people.	3.9 (0.9)
es1_3	I notice if someone working with me is offended by me.	4.0 (0.9)
es1_4	I am able to express to other people if I am offended or hurt because of them.	3.7 (1.0)
es2_5	I am concerned about the wellbeing of my partners.	3.3 (0.9)
es2_6	I take care of the wellbeing of others and try to improve it.	3.7 (0.9)
es2_7	In conflict situations, I do my best to take actions that aim at maintaining good personal relationships.	3.9 (0.9)
es2_8	I try to have good contact with all the people I am working with.	4.0 (0.9)
es3_9	I am able to cooperate with people who do not share my opinions on what is right and what is wrong.	3.8 (0.9)
es3_10	I tolerate different ethical views in my surroundings.	3.9 (0.9)
es3_11	I think it is good that my closest friends think in different ways.	4.1 (0.9)
es3_12	I also get along with people who do not agree with me.	3.9 (0.8)
es4_13	I take other peoples' points of view into account before making any important decisions in my life.	3.5 (1.0)
es4_14	I try to consider an other person's position when I face a conflict situation.	3.2 (1.0)
es4_15	When I am working on ethical problems, I consider the impact of my decisions on other people.	3.3 (0.9)
es4_16	I try to consider other peoples' needs, even in situations concerning my own benefits.	3.5 (0.9)
es5_17	I recognize my own bias when I take a stand on ethical issues.	3.3 (0.8)
es5_18	I realize that I am tied to certain prejudices when I assess ethical issues.	3.6 (0.9)
es5_19	I try to control my own prejudices when making ethical evaluations.	3.7 (0.9)
es5_20	When I am resolving ethical problems, I try to take a position evolving out of my own social status.	3.2 (0.8)
es6_21	I contemplate on the consequences of my actions when making moral decisions.	3.6 (0.9)

es6_22	I ponder on different alternatives when aiming at the best possible solution to an ethically problematic situation.	3.6 (0.9)
es6_23	I am able to create many alternative ways to act when I face ethical problems in my life.	3.5 (0.8)
es6_24	I believe there are several right solutions to ethical problems.	3.8 (0.9)
es7_25	I notice that there are ethical issues involved in human interaction.	3.6 (0.9)
es7_26	I see a lot of ethical problems around me.	3.3 (1.0)
es7_27	I am aware of the ethical issues I face at school.	3.6 (0.9)
es7_28	I am better than other people in recognizing new and current ethical problems.	2.9 (0.9)

RESULTS

Psychometric Properties of the ESSQ

The first task of the statistical analysis was to investigate the psychometric properties of the Ethical Sensitivity Scale items. Inter-item correlations between the items were investigated for the sample with the nonparametric correlation coefficient (Spearman rho). The seven dimensions are measured by 28 items, producing 378 inter-item correlations when diagonal and double-presentations are omitted ($N_{i-i\ corr}$ = (N_{items} × (N_{items} - 1)) / 2). The absolute value correlations in the sample ($n = 249$) range from .001 to .55 ($M = .22$, $SD = .10$). Three correlations were above |.50| and thus considered large, according to Cohen (1988), as they share more than 25 per cent of their variance ($.5^2 = .25$). On the average, the items share only five per cent of their variance with other items ($.22^2 = .05$). The result of an inter-item correlation analysis shows that the items measuring ethical sensitivity do not share enough common variance in the sample to proceed to an exploratory factor analysis.

Psychometric properties of the ESSQ items were further studied with reliability analysis (Cronbach, 1970). The results are presented in Table 1. "3 Caring by connecting to others" and "4 Working with interpersonal and group differences" scales had the highest reliabilities ($\alpha = .78$; $\alpha = .75$) while "1 Reading and expressing emotions" and "5 Preventing social bias" scales had the lowest reliabilities ($\alpha = .54$; $\alpha = .50$). Alpha values depend heavily on the dimensionality of the scale. Higher inter-item reliability is achieved with one-dimensional constructs. The second issue affecting reliability negatively is the fact that high abstraction level concepts are more difficult to operationalize into intuitive items.

The results of initial ESSQ dimensionality testing show that more data (generalizability study with data splitting requires at least 400 observations) and further statistical analyses (EFA, CFA) are needed to prove the usefulness of the ESS model in practice.

Research Question 1: Ethical sensitivity related differences between Lutheran non-confirmed and confirmed students

The first research task was to analyze if students' responses to the ESSQ items are statistically dependent on their Lutheran confirmation experience. We used a dichotomous variable "confirmation" with values (1 = confirmed, 2 = non-confirmed) as the grouping variable in a non-parametric group mean rank difference test (Mann-Whitney U). The first group members, non-confirmed students, came from classes seven and eight ($n = 166$). The second group includes ninth-grade students ($n = 82$) who have been confirmed in the Lutheran church. Group differences are comparable, as both females and males were equally represented in the two sub groups. Using confirmation, as a grouping factor is as equal as using a 15-year-old cut-off point (Finnish church law defines 15 years as the earliest age for confirmation).

According to the first research question, we aim to explain the differences between the two groups, with religious teaching available for those who are confirmed. However, we fully acknowledge that some error enters into the analysis, as the highly abstract ESS items are more demanding for the younger students. We have analyzed this error source by comparing the standard deviations of all three age groups' answers to single items. Results did not show any significant differences between the younger and older students' response tendencies to 28 ESS items. Figure 1 shows firstly that the unanimity in response tendency is not related to the grade, as all three lines are close to each other in most items. Secondly, items related to the fifth (Preventing social bias) dimension of the ESS have the lowest standard deviations, indicating the smallest disagreement among the students.

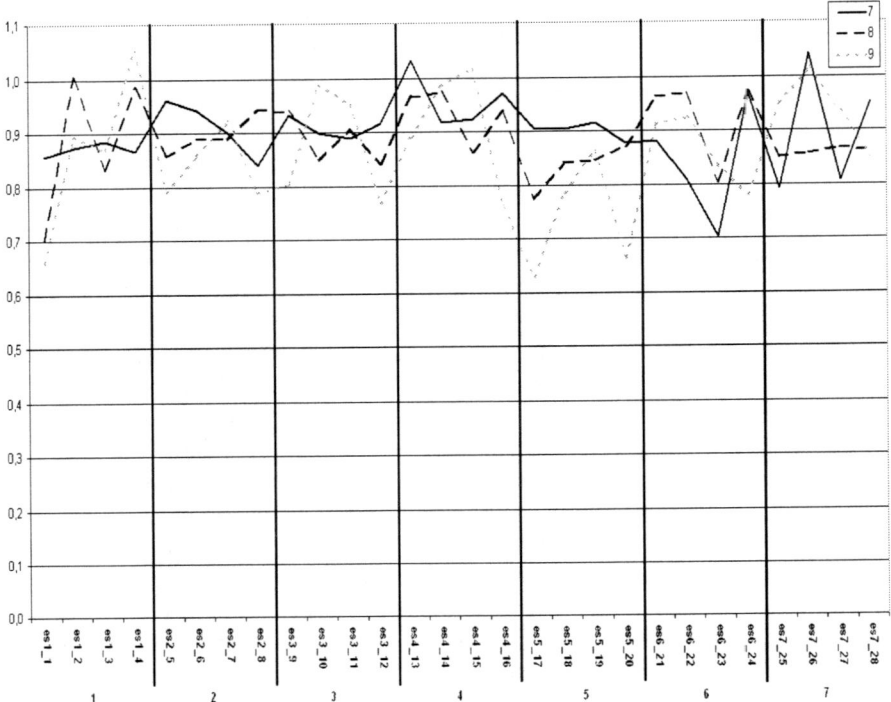

Figure 1. Comparison of disagreement (measured with SD, values close to zero indicate smaller disagreement) between the three age groups on the seven ESSQ dimensions.

Overall results presented in Table 3 show that those students who have had more re-ligious education at school, and also were confirmed in the Lutheran church, self-re-ported higher ethical skills than their younger and non-confirmed peers. On a more detailed level, we see that confirmed students ($M = 3.9$, $SD = 0.6$) report statistically significantly higher skills on taking the perspectives of others than non-confirmed students ($M = 3.7$, $SD = 0.7$), $Z(1, n = 248) = -2.382$, $p = .017$. For the other six scales, the group mean ranks do not differ statistically significantly, indicating that there is at least a 5 per cent or higher possibility to have similar or larger difference between the two groups' responses, if we assume that they come from the same population (i.e., null hypothesis is true).

However, when we examine the results presented in Table 3 on a more detailed level, we learn that in six scales out of seven those students who have confirmed in the Lutheran church have higher self-reported ethical skills than their non-con-firmed peers.

Table 3. Comparison of non-confirmed and confirmed students' responses to the ESSQ.

	Confirmed (n = 82)	Non-confirmed (n = 166)	
Scale	*M (SD)*	*M (SD)*	*Z (p)*
1 Reading and expressing emotions	3.9 (0.6)	3.8 (0.6)	-1.622 (.105)
2 Taking the perspectives of others	3.9 (0.6)	3.7 (0.7)	-2.382 (.017)
3 Caring by connecting to others	4.0 (0.7)	3.9 (0.7)	-0.756 (.450)
4 Working with interpersonal and group differences	3.5 (0.7)	3.3 (0.7)	-1.931 (.053)
5 Preventing social bias	3.5 (0.4)	3.4 (0.6)	-1.500 (.134)
6 Generating interpretations and options	3.7 (0.6)	3.6 (0.6)	-1.857 (.063)
7 Identifying the consequences of actions and options	3.3 (0.7)	3.3 (0.6)	-0.294 (.769)

Research Question 2: Gender related differences in ethical sensitivity

To answer the second research question, we compared female and male students' self-reported ethical sensitivity skills. A non-parametric group mean rank difference test (Mann-Whitney U) was applied to a dichotomous grouping variable, "gender" (1 = female, 2 = male). Group differences are comparable, as both genders were equally represented in the sample (female n = 132, 53.2 % and male n = 116, 46.8 %) (Table 4.).

Overall results show clearly that on all but one dimension ("Identifying the consequences of actions and options") female participants estimated their ethical skills higher than males. Female students were more likely to read and express emotions ($M = 4.0$, $SD = 0.5$) than their male peers ($M = 3.7$, $SD = 0.6$), $Z(1, n = 248) = -3.138$, $p = .002$. Female students were more likely to take the perspectives of others ($M = 3.9$, $SD = 0.6$) than male students ($M = 3.5$, $SD = 0.6$), $Z(1, n = 248) = -4.514$, $p < .001$. Female students were also more caring, by connecting to others ($M = 4.1$, $SD = 0.6$), than male students ($M = 3.7$, $SD = 0.7$), $Z(1, n = 248) = -4.270$, $p < .001$. Females in this sample self-reported themselves as more effective workers with interpersonal and group differences ($M = 3.5$, $SD = 0.6$) than males ($M = 3.2$, $SD = 0.7$), $Z(1, n = 248) = -4.348$, $p < .001$. Table 4 shows that the difference between female and male respondents was smallest in dimensions five (Preventing social bias) and seven (Identifying the consequences of actions and options).

Table 4. Gender-related differences in students' responses to ESSQ.

	Female (n = 132)	Male (n = 116)	
Scale	*M (SD)*	*M (SD)*	*Z (p)*
1 Reading and express-ing emotions	4.0 (0.5)	3.7 (0.6)	-3.138 (.002)
2 Taking the perspec-tives of others	3.9 (0.6)	3.5 (0.6)	-4.514 (<.001)
3 Caring by connecting to others	4.1 (0.6)	3.7 (0.7)	-4.270 (<.001)
4 Working with inter-personal and group differences	3.5 (0.7)	3.2 (0.7)	-4.348 (<.001)
5 Preventing social bias	3.5 (0.6)	3.4 (0.5)	-2.115 (.034)
6 Generating interpreta-tions and options	3.7 (0.6)	3.5 (0.7)	-2.683 (.007)
7 Identifying the conse-quences of actions and options	3.3 (0.6)	3.3 (0.7)	-0.125 (.900)

Research Question 3: Academic giftedness related differences in ethical sensitivity

The last research task was to compare academically average and above average students' responses to ethical sensitivity scales. Respondents were asked to report their grade point average (GPA) on the following six point scale: (1) = 4.0 – 5.4 ($n = 1$, .4 %); (2) = 5.5 – 6.4 ($n = 3$, 1.2 %); (3) = 6.5 – 7.4 ($n = 23$, 9.3 %); (4) = 7.5 – 8.4 ($n = 91$, 36.7 %); (5) = 8.5 – 9.4 ($n = 119$, 48.0 %); (6) = 9.5 – 10.0 ($n = 11$, 4.4 %). As the research task was to analyze differences between average and above average students, we recoded a new two-class variable with a cut-off point of 8.5, and left out the analysis the two lowest GPA classes 1 and 2 (containing only four students,

1.6 % of all responses). The new "GPA2class" variable (1 "averageGPA" = 6.4 < GPA < 8.5, n = 114, 46.7 %; 2 "highGPA" = 8.5 ≤ GPA ≤ 10.0, n = 130, 53.3 %) was the grouping variable in a non-parametric group mean rank difference test (Mann-Whitney U). Group differences were related to gender to some extent as female students were slightly over represented in the "highGPA" group (n_{female_total} = 132, 53.2%; $n_{female\_highGPA}$ = 72, 64.3%) and male students were over represented in the "averageGPA" group (n_{male_total} = 116, 46.8 %; $n_{male\_averageGPA}$ = 90, 68.2 %). However, the bias is not too large (about ten per cent) to prevent further comparison of the two groups. (Table 5.)

Table 5. Academic achievement (GPA) related differences in students' responses to ESSQ.

Scale	Average academic achievement (n = 114) M (SD)	Above average academic achievement (n = 130) M (SD)	Z (p)
1 Reading and expressing emotions	3.9 (0.5)	3.9 (0.6)	-0.397 (.691)
2 Taking the perspectives of others	3.6 (0.6)	3.9 (0.6)	-3.715 (<.001)
3 Caring by connecting to others	3.9 (0.7)	4.0 (0.7)	-1.994 (.046)
4 Working with interpersonal and group differences	3.3 (0.6)	3.4 (0.8)	-0.953 (.341)
5 Preventing social bias	3.4 (0.5)	3.5 (0.6)	-1.429 (.153)
6 Generating interpretations and options	3.5 (0.6)	3.8 (0.6)	-3.668 (<.001)
7 Identifying the consequences of actions and options	3.3 (0.6)	3.4 (0.7)	-1.290 (.197)

Overall results regarding the third question showed that more academically gifted students estimated their ethical skills higher than average ability students. Those students who reported high GPA (M = 3.9, SD = 0.6) were clearly more likely to consider the perspectives of others than average GPA students (M = 3.6, SD = 0.6).

This result was statistically significant, $Z(1, n = 244)= -3.715, p < .001$. High GPA students also felt that they were more skilful in generating interpretations and options ($M = 3.8, SD = 0.6$) than their average GPA peers ($M = 3.5, SD = 0.6$), $Z(1, n = 244)= -3.668, p < .001$. Average GPA students self-reported slightly weaker skills in taking the perspectives of others ($M = 3.9, SD = 0.7$) than their above average GPA peers ($M = 4.0, SD = 0.7$). The difference was statistically small, but significant, $Z(1, n = 244) = -1.994, p = .046$.

CONCLUSIONS

In this paper, we presented a 28-item Ethical Sensitivity Scale Questionnaire (ESSQ) and tested its psychometric properties with a sample consisting of 249 Finnish Lutheran urban schools' 7th - 9th grade students.

We discussed theoretical issues related to ethical sensitivity as an important component in morality and presented a definition and operationalization of the ethical sensitivity in the form of an Ethical Sensitivity Scale Questionnaire (ESSQ).

The ESSQ is based on the work of Narvaez (2001) and its main purpose is to scale the pupils' orientations on ethical issues. The ESSQ measures the following seven dimensions of ethical sensitivity: (1) Reading and expressing emotions, (2) considering the perspectives of others, (3) caring by connecting to others, (4) working with interpersonal and group differences, (5) preventing social bias, (6) generating interpretations and options, and (7) identifying the consequences of actions and options.

We answered the three research questions with a statistical analysis: Are there any differences in the self-reported ethical sensitivity between (1) Lutheran non-confirmed and confirmed students; (2) female and male students; and (3) academically average and above average students?

Results regarding the first question showed that those students who have had more religious education at school and also were confirmed in the Lutheran church, self-reported higher ethical skills than their younger and non-confirmed peers. This finding supports our initial hypothesis that ninth graders, who have had more religious education at school and alsowere confirmed, assess themselves more as ethically sensitive than their younger and less educated peers.

Results regarding the second question showed clearly that female students estimated their ethical skills higher than their male peers. This tendency can be explained by the types of items measuring ethical sensitivity skills. The majority of them measure caring ethics with emotional and social intelligence. In earlier Finnish studies, both 6th and 9th grade girls were shown to be more care-oriented in their moral orientation than their same age male peers who were clearly justice-oriented (Tirri, 2003).

Results regarding the third question showed that more academically gifted students estimated their ethical skills as higher than the opinions of average ability students. This finding supports other researchers' notion that gifted students have a privileged position in the maturation of moral thinking because of their precocious intellectual growth (Andreani & Pagnin, 1993; Karnes & Brown, 1981; Terman, 1925).

Results regarding the psychometric properties of the ESSQ showed that more data (also cross-cultural) and further statistical analyses are needed to prove its usefulness in practice. Also, generalizability of the results would benefit from a more convincing empirical sample. However, this study proved that the ESSQ is a promising ethical sensitivity measurement instrument that can be applied to various learning contexts both in traditional face-to-face and online learning environments. It can also be used together with our previously developed Spiritual Sensitivity Scale Questionnaire (SSSQ, Tirri, Nokelainen & Ubani, 2006). Our current research activity is targeted towards collecting a more representative empirical sample to test the psychometric validity of the ESSQ.

In the future, the seven item shortened version of the ESSQ is to be included as the tenth dimension in our Multiple Intelligences Profiling Questionnaire (MIPQ, Tirri, K., Komulainen, Nokelainen & Tirri, H., 2002). MIPQ operationalizes Howard Gardner's MI theory's (1983; 1999) nine intelligences: (1) Linguistic, (2) Logical-mathematical, (3) Musical, (4) Spatial, (5) Bodily-kinesthetic, (6) Interpersonal, (7) Intrapersonal, (8) Naturalistic and (9) Existential intelligence.

REFERENCES

Abroms, K. (1985). Social giftedness and its relationship with intellectual giftedness. In J. Freeman (Ed.), *The psychology of gifted children* (pp. 201-218). Chichester: Wiley & Sons.

Albrecht, K. (2006). *Social intelligence. The new science of success.* San Francisco, CA: Jossey-Bass.

Andreani, O. & Pagnin, A. (1993). Nurturing the moral development of the gifted. In K. Heller, F. Mönks, & H. Passow (Eds.), *International handbook of research and development of giftedness and talent* (pp. 539-553). Oxford: Pergamon Press.

Bebeau, M., Rest, J., & Yamoor, C. (1985). Measuring dental students' ethical sensitivity. *Journal of Dental Education, 49*(4), 225-235.

Bebeau, M., Rest, J. & Narvaez, D. (1999). Beyond the promise: A perspective on research in moral education. *Educational Researcher, 28*(4), 18-26.

Binfet, J. (1995). *Identifying the themes in student-generated moral dilemmas.* A paper presented at the annual meeting of the American Educational Research Association, April 18th, 1995, San Francisco, CA.

Brabeck, M., Rogers, L., Sirin, S., Handerson, J., Ting, K. & Benvenuto, M. (2000). Increasing ethical sensitivity to racial and gender intolerance in schools: Development of the racial ethical sensitivity test (REST). *Ethics and Behavior,10*(2), 119-137.

Brooks, R. (1985). Delinquency among gifted children. In J. Freeman (Ed.), *The psychology of gifted children* (pp. 297-308). London: Wiley.

Cohen, J. (1988). *Statistical power analysis for the behavioral sciences.* Second edition. Hillsdale: Lawrence Erlbaum Associates.

Colangelo, N. (1982). Characteristics of moral problems as formulated by gifted adolescents. *Journal of Moral Education, 11*(4), 219-232.

Cronbach, L. J. (1970). *Essentials of psychological testing.* Third edition. New York: Harper & Row.

Gardner, H. (1983). *Frames of mind.* New York: Basic Books.

Gardner, H. (1999). *Intelligence reframed: multiple intelligences for the 21st century.* New York: Basic Books.

Gath, D., Tennent, G. & Pidduck, R. (1970). Psychiatric and social characteristics of bright delinquents. *British Journal of Psychology, 116,* 515-516.

Goleman, D. (2006). *Social intelligence.* New York: Bantam Books.

Janos, P. & Robinson, N. (1985). Psychosocial development in intellectually gifted children. In F. Horowitz, & M. O'Brien (Eds.), *The gifted and talented: Developmental perspectives* (pp. 149-195). Washington, DC: American Psychological Association.

Karnes, F. & Brown, K. (1981) Moral development and the gifted: An initial investigation. *Roper Review, 3,* 8-10.

Kohlberg, L. (1969). Stage and sequence: The cognitive-developmental approach to socialization. In D. A. Goslin (Ed.) *Handbook of socialization theory and research* (pp. 347-480). Chicago: Rand McNally.

Narvaez, D. (2001). *Ethical sensitivity. Activity booklet 1.* Retrieved March 2 2007 from http://www.nd.edu/~dnarvaez/

Narvaez, D. (1993). High achieving students and moral judgment. *Journal for the Education of the Gifted, 16*(3), 268-279.

Narvaez, D., Endicott, L. & Bock, T. (2002). *Constructing ethical expertise: A skills-based approach to moral education.* Paper submitted and under revision.

Rest, J. (1986). *Moral development: Advances in research and theory.* New York: Praeger.

Straughan, R. (1975). Hypothetical moral situations. *Journal of Moral Education, 4*(3), 183-189.

Tan-Willman, C. & Gutteridge, D. (1981). Creative thinking and moral reasoning in academically gifted secondary school adolescents. *Gifted Child Quarterly. 25*(4), 149-153.

Terman, L. (1925). *Genetic studies of genius: Vol. 1. Mental and physical traits of a thousand gifted children.* Stanford, CA: Stanford University Press.

Tirri, K. (1996). *The themes of moral dilemmas formulated by preadolescents.* Resources in Education ED 399046.

Tirri, K. (2003). The moral concerns and orientations of sixth- and ninth-grade students. *Educational Research and Evaluation, 9*(1), 93-108.

Tirri, K., Komulainen, E., Nokelainen, P. & Tirri, H. (2002). Conceptual modeling of self-rated intelligence-profile. *Proceedings of the 2nd International Self-Concept Research Conference.* Sydney: University of Western Sydney, Self Research Center.

Tirri, K., Nokelainen, P. & Ubani, M. (2006). Conceptual definition and empirical validation of the spiritual sensitivity scale. *Journal of Empirical Theology, 19(1),* 37-62.

Tirri, K. & Pehkonen, L. (2002). The moral reasoning and scientific argumentation of gifted adolescents. *The Journal of Secondary Gifted Education, 13*(3), 120-129.

Walker, L., de Vries, B. & Trevethan, S. (1987). Moral stages and moral orientations in real-life and hypothetical dilemmas. *Child Development, 58,* 842-858.

Yin, R. (1994). *Case study research,* Vol. 5. 2nd edition. Thousand Oaks, CA: Sage.

Yussen, S. (1977). Characteristics of moral dilemmas written by adolescents. *Developmental Psychology, 13*(2), 162-163.

Kirsi Tirri, Petri Nokelainen & Kristina Holm
University of Helsinki, Finland

ELINA HELLA

PHENOMENOGRAPHY
AND THE VARIATION THEORY OF LEARNING
AS TOOLS FOR UNDERSTANDING RELIGION

INTRODUCTION

This paper focuses on how the diversity of religious and secular traditions and variation in their beliefs and values can be dealt with as a challenge for students' understanding of religion and religious issues in religious education. Opportunities and critical conditions for learning about religion as a subject matter in religious education (RE) are analysed from the theoretical framework of a qualitative research approach called 'phenomenography' (Marton, 1981) and the principles of the 'Variation Theory of Learning' (e.g., Marton & Booth, 1997; Bowden & Marton, 1998; Marton et al., 2004) which has been developed within the phenomenographic research tradition.

Phenomenographic research investigates qualitative variation in understanding of a particular phenomenon within a group, in order to find educationally critical aspects for learning about that phenomenon (Marton & Booth, 1997). Phenomenographic pedagogy focuses on improving learning as a qualitative change towards wider, more complex understanding of the phenomenon and its aspects as a whole (Marton & Booth, 1997). The Variation Theory of Learning focuses on how qualitatively different ways of understanding a particular phenomenon are linked to an individual learner's perceptual abilities to discern aspects of that phenomenon. The theory identifies variation as a necessary condition for learning. It emphasises that for learning to take place, variation in the aspects of that which is to be learned, the object of learning, must be experienced (Marton et al., 2004: Marton & Pang, 2006). Variation theory introduces the concept of *dimension of variation*, an aspect along which it is possible to experience variation and make comparisons and distinctions in order to discern a meaning of a particular phenomenon. These dimensions are seen as critical aspects of learning about the particular phenomenon in question. Thus, they can be used as an educational tool to expand students' awareness of different aspects of religion(s) and spirituality. Based on this theory, in order to discern a certain religious tradition or a religious worldview, one must be aware of different religious worldviews in relation to non-religious worldviews. In other words, variation in the dimension of worldviews must be experienced.

This chapter suggests that the Variation Theory of Learning serves as a peda-

Fritz Oser & Wiel Veugelers (eds.), Getting involved, 343–355.

gogical tool for teachers to help their students to relate to a specific subject matter of religious education and to discern the critical aspects the object of learning (see, Marton et al., 2004). Suggestions of how to use variation of educationally critical aspects of understanding religion as the object of learning in religious education classrooms are outlined. These suggestions are based on an empirical study on variation in understanding of Lutheranism in terms of teachers' and students' discernement of its meaning (Hella, 2007a; Hella 2007b). Furthermore, the implications of using variation as a tool for understanding religion amongst the plurality of beliefs and values of different religious and secular traditions in order to educate the global citizens are discussed.

PHENOMENOGRAPHIC RESEARCH SPECIALISATION

Phenomenographic research started in the 1970's when a group of Swedish educational researchers began to study qualitative differences in students' learning of the subject matter. The term 'phenomenography' comes from the Greek words 'phainomein' (phenomenon) and 'graphein' (to describe) (Marton & Booth, 1997). It was introduced by Ference Marton (1981) as a qualitative research specialisation that is concerned to investigate variation in the experiences of certain aspects of the world. In the 1990's, the question of theoretical underpinnings of phenomenography was explicated and theoretical insights into 'what is a way of experiencing the world' and 'what is learning' were developed. This period became known as the phase of 'new phenomenography' (Pang, 2003).

Phenomenographic pedagogy focuses on learning from the learners' perspective: how the subject matter to be taught and learned is understood by the learner (e.g, Ramsden, 1988; Marton, Hounsell & Entwistle, 1997). The basic unit of phenomenographic research, a way of experiencing or understanding something, which is defined as an internal, non-dualistic relationship between the person and the world (Marton & Booth, 1997). Therefore, learning is seen as a qualitative change in this relationship towards wider, more complex understanding of part-whole relationships of particular phenomenon (Marton & Booth, 1997). The focus is neither on the psychological aspects of the learner, nor on the learning process, strategies, skills or competences in general, but on the content as it appears to the learner in the relationship between the two. Learners' different ways of understanding the same subject matter serves as the basis for teaching that aims at developing the learner's understanding of that which is to be learned. The phenomenographic research approach has its pedagogical focus on the educationally critical aspects of a particular subject matter, which are revealed by qualitative differences in the ways in which the learners understand the meaning of that subject matter (Marton & Booth, 1997). The theoretical explication of these empirical findings within phenomenography has led to the development of the Variation Theory of Learning.

RELATIONALITY IN THE PHENOMENOGRAPHIC TRADITION AND ITS IMPLICATIONS TO RESEARCH ON RELIGIOUS EDUCATION

In the phenomenographic research tradition, the concept 'relation' appears in the non-dualistic ontological view of the relation between the person and the world (see, e.g., Marton & Booth, 1997). Epistemologically, this means that all knowledge is constituted in this experiential relationship between the two. Thus, when doing research, this relation has fundamental effects on our understanding of knowledge constitution (Bowden, 2005), as well as on our understanding of the relationship between learning and teaching (e.g., Marton, 1988; Ramsden, 1988; Trigwell & Prosser, 1999). In this section, the concept of relationality within phenomenography and the Variation Theory of Learning is elaborated in three different ways: onto-logically, epistemologically and pedagogically.

Relational Ontology and Epistemology

In the phenomenographic tradition, ontology and epistemology are viewed in terms of a non-dualistic relational perspective, according to which there is an internal re-lationship between the person and the world, and this relationship reflects both the one who experiences the world and the world experienced (Marton & Booth, 1997). Thus, the question of knowledge constitution is based on changes in this internal relationship. Reality is seen in terms of totality of all the possible ways of experi-encing it. Thus, that which is called 'Lutheranism', for example, is seen as a totality of all the possible ways of experiencing it.

Epistemologically relationality means that the person has access to the world through her/his own way of experiencing the world (Marton & Booth, 1997). Ac-cording to this view, we cannot know the world or aspects of it, such as the substance to the concept of 'Lutheranism' *per se*, but we can gain knowledge of it through our own experience of it and by relating to others' experiences of it. So when one becomes aware of new aspects of Lutheranism, there is a qualitative change between one's old experience of Lutheranism and one's present experience of Lutheranism: Lutheranism appears different from one's earlier experience of it. Because the experiential relation-ship is different from the earlier experience, the person her-/himself has changed.

Relationality in phenomenographic research

Bowden (2005) has referred to the concept of relationality to describe how knowledge in phenomenographic research practice is constituted. In line with relational ontol-ogy and epistemology, the notion of relationality describes how knowledge gained through phenomenographic research is co-constituted in the relationships between the researcher, the subjects and the phenomenon, such as religion. Bowden (2005) describes relationality in phenomenographic research as presented in *Figure 1*.

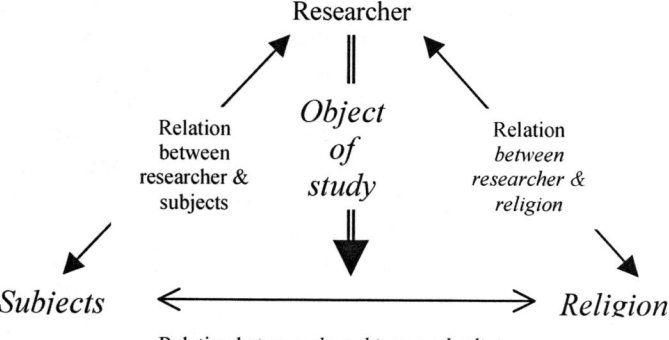

Figure 1. Application of Bowden's (2005, 13) model of phenomenographic relationality.

The object of phenomenographic study is not the phenomenon of religion *per se*, but the phenomenon as it appears to the people who experience it. However, the researcher's own relationship with the phenomenon and with the people participating in the study affects the way in which the object of study appears to the researcher. Thus, it is important for the researcher to acknowledge the relationship between these aspects influencing the way in which the outcomes of the study are constituted.

From the phenomenographic standpoint it is important to be aware that we gain knowledge, whether about religious phenomena as expressed in religious practices or about their underlying theological ideas, through relating to different understandings of those phenomena or ideas. Knowledge of religion in the school is constituted from the understandings of religious adherents' within religious traditions and mediated by interdisciplinary, academic research. In this sense, students should be aware of the 'contested' nature of knowledge; different understandings of religion at different levels which constitute the knowledge of religion with which teaching is supposed to help students to connect.

Relational teaching and learning about religion

In the phenomenographic research tradition, teaching and learning are seen as fundamentally related and this connection is expressed by talking about a 'teaching-learning' process: teaching is focused on enhancing student learning, thus the aims for teaching should be defined in terms aims for student learning (Prosser & Trigwell, 1999).

According to Marton (1988) the question of how people learn is necessarily a question of what they learn, because what is learned (the outcome or the result) and how it is learned (the act or the process) are internally related aspects of learning and thus cannot be separated from each other. This characterises the relational nature of learning. Rather than focusing on learning in general, phenomenography is always concerned with learning about a particular content. The phenomenographic pedagogy is simultaneously a 'pedagogy of content' (Marton, 1986) and a 'pedagogy of learning', and these two are fundamentally related (Marton & Booth, 1997). Prior phenomenographic studies show that people who were asked to describe their understanding or learning described it in terms of the content towards which their awareness was directed, rather than in terms of the act or process of understanding (e.g., Marton, 1988; Ahlberg, 2004). Instead of making pre-assumptions about the general character of religious understanding or spiritual awareness/consciousness as distinct forms of awareness, the phenomenographic perspective focuses on understanding concepts of 'religion' or 'spirituality', 'transcendence' or 'God' as experienced by different people. Understanding of religion is thus characterised as understanding of a particular object related to the concept of religion in a particular learning context. However, certain key features can be applied to understanding religion in a more general sense. Therefore, it is possible to learn about religion by relating different ways of understandings to each other in different contexts.

Several empirical studies illustrate the internal relationship between experiences and actions: the way in which teachers understand the subject matter influences the way they approach it in their teaching and their students' understandings of that subject matter (e.g., Prosser & Trigwell, 1999; Martin et al., 2000). Therefore, the way in which teachers understand a subject matter or a concept, such as religion, and the intentionality with which they approach it in their teaching can be seen as a critical precondition for their students' understanding of that subject matter in religious education. From the phenomenographic perspective, the teaching-learning process is seen as relational activity between the teacher, learner, the content, and the learning context of particular time and place. Prosser and Trigwell (1999) offer a relational, constitutionalist model of learning and teaching: a particular learning situation is constituted from different aspects within the teaching-learning context. They describe how variation in students' and teachers' experiences of their situation is related to variation in their prior experiences, which brings to the foreground those aspects of awareness that lead to variations in approaches to learning and teaching and to variations in the outcomes. These aspects are simultaneously present in teaching-learning situations, some more to the foreground of students' and teachers' awareness than others in the particular moment.

The relational model of the teaching-learning activity highlights the importance of the internal relationships between different aspects as constitutive of teaching-learning of religion in the religious education classroom. Phenomenographic pedagogy is focused on developing more effective teaching in terms of enhancing learning that is meaningful and results in qualitatively changed ways of seeing an aspect of the world (see, e.g., Trigwell et al., 2005). In order to improve learning, as widening of students' understanding of certain content of religious education, it is important to acknowledge how the learning situation appears to the learner as a whole, how the teaching situation appears to the teacher and how the two are related to each other. Entwistle et. al. (2000) conclude, on the basis of an empirical study of conceptions and beliefs about 'good teaching', that a sophisticated conception of teaching implies expanded awareness of the relationship between teaching and learning and the strategic alertness to classroom events. Marton & Booth (1997) have described good teaching in terms of pedagogy that depends on connections between the awareness of teachers and learners:

> Teachers mould experiences for their students with the aim of bringing about learning, and the essential feature is that *the teacher takes part of the learner'* (p. 179, original emphasis)

PHENOMENOGRAPHIC METHODS

The phenomenographic approach aims to uncover different ways of experiencing something, such as Lutheranism in the data presented in this chapter (Hella, 2007a; 2007b), typically through semi-structured interviews or writing assignments with open questions. A way of understanding/experiencing something as a basic unit of phenomenographic research consists of two analytical aspects which are intertwined in the experience (Marton & Pong, 2005, 336): 1) *the referential aspect,* a particular meaning of something, such as Lutheranism delimited by the studied group of people, and 2) *the structural aspect,* the combination of features discerned and focused upon by these people.

The results of qualitatively different ways of experiencing something are presented in categories of description, the relationships of which form a hierarchical system, called the 'outcome space' (e.g., Marton, 1994). The categories are logically related to each other in such a way that the more developed ways of experiencing a particular phenomenon include the less developed understandings (Marton & Booth, 1997). Differences in the ways of experiencing Lutheranism, for example, mean differences in those features or aspects that are discerned and focused upon and related to each other as well as to the overall meaning of it.

Understanding of religion is approached from the learner's perspective as s/he relates to the phenomenon of religion (see, e.g. Dahlin, 1989). Therefore, the relationship between the person and religion is not approached psychologically by making *a priori* assumptions of cognitive and affective or social aspects of that relationship to guide the researcher's focus on the object of study (see, e.g., Marton, 1996). Because the focus is on the ways in which the learners' direct their awareness to and focus on that which they perceive as a 'religion', such distinctions are not constructed by the researcher; rather they can only be analytically discerned by the researcher if they are discerned by the learner. Furthermore, phenomenographic categories do not form a typology of separate meanings of religion, for example, or a typology of different individuals who relate to it; rather they show how ways of understanding of religion differ in terms of differences in aspects discerned and focused upon, and how they are related in the experiences verbally expressed by the people who participate in the study.

VARIATION THEORY OF LEARNING

The Variation Theory of Learning has been developed within the phenomenographic research tradition (see, Marton et al., 2004). According to the theory, to learn something, the learner has to discern the critical aspects of what is to be learned (Marton & Pang, 2006). Based on Brentano's notion of intentionality, learning is always learning about something, thus, in education it is necessary to define what is to be learned – the object of learning (Marton et al., 2004). According to Marton, Tsui & Runesson (2004, 4). The object of learning refers to a capability, such as understanding, and to a specific object, such as a particular subject matter to be learned. To avoid arbitrary learning amongst the students, teachers should define the object of learning, the aims for what kind of abilities students are supposed to develop in relation to a particular content (Marton et al., 2004). In addition, teachers should be aware of the critical differences between the ways in which students understand the subject matter in question in order to define what students should learn (Marton, Tsui & Runesson, 2004). How students and teachers understand the object of learning influences what constitutes the conditions for learning in the classroom, the shared space of learning between the learner, the context, and the object of learning (Marton, Tsui & Runesson, 2004).

Differences in what aspects are discerned at the same time are important for learning, because in order to experience or understand something in a certain way, certain aspects must be discerned at the same time (Runesson, 2006). Different ways in which the same phenomenon is experienced or understood depend on what aspects are being discerned (Marton & Booth, 1997; Runesson, 2006). Differences in seeing something in a certain situation are due to different aspects that appear to the fore of awareness to different people according to limitations in perception (Marton & Pang, 2006). The possibility for the learner to discern and focus on these aspects is critical for learning. Knowing and understanding thus has to do with ability to discern the critical aspects, which is possible only through the experience of variation (Runesson, 2006). Every feature discerned corresponds to simultaneous variation experienced in the dimension which and object is compared with something else (Marton & Pong, 2005, 336). In order to discern a feature it must be invariant against the background of other variants (Marton, Tsui & Runesson, 2004). For example, to discern an aspect of a particular religious tradition, for example, the learner must experience variation, corresponding to that aspect: one cannot understand the meaning of 'religion', if there was only one religion. Different ways of understanding the phenomenon of religion are due to differences in discerned aspects in the dimension of religion.

EXAMPLES OF PHENOMENOGRAPHIC STUDIES IN RELIGIOUS EDUCATION

In this section, I provide two examples of phenomenographic studies of variation in understanding of Lutheranism in Finnish upper secondary school. The first study

ELINA HELLA

is an example of a phenomenographic study concerned with Finnish students' understandings of Lutheranism (Hella, 2007a). The data consisted of 63 students' responses to a writing task together with complementary interviews of 11 students. The second study explored how meanings of Lutheranism were constituted as expressed by Finnish teachers of religious education (Hella, 2007b). Implications for religious education were discussed in terms of what students and teachers could learn from the different ways in which students understand Lutheranism. The studies explored different ways in which the meaning of Lutheranism was constituted in students' and teachers' awareness by focusing on the following questions:
– What are the key meanings of Lutheranism as expressed?
– How are the meanings of Lutheranism constituted?

Each way of understanding Lutheranism was analysed in terms of two analytical aspects according to phenomenographic procedure: the overall meaning of Lutheranism in focus of awareness and the corresponding dimension within which the aspect had been discerned from an alternative aspect through experienced variation. The results of the different ways in which students understood Lutheranism were presented in categories of description, which formed a hierarchical outcome space. The hierarchy described an increasing complexity of logical relationships between the aspects related to the overall meaning of Lutheranism; the higher in the hierarchy, the more specific and developed distinctions were made by the students in discerning the meanings and aspects of Lutheranism. Thus, the higher categories are also logically inclusive of the lower level categories, as shown in *Table 1*. The relationships between the categories show how awareness of Lutheranism expands from the first to the last category: the development of discernment of the complex relationships between different aspects of Lutheranism that are simultaneously focused upon. The structural aspect describes how the meaning of Lutheranism is constituted by what is focused upon and what is as background of awareness. Meanings were discerned in terms of distinctions made in the corresponding dimension of variation.

The key differences between students' understandings can be described in terms of variation in focus across the five main aspects represented in each category, according to which Lutheranism was discerned as: 1) religion vs. non-religion, 2) religious tradition (cultural differences, 3) true vs. nominal Christian way of life, 4) personal vs. mediated relationship with God 5) Core of Faith: Mercy/freedom vs. guilt.

According to *Category 1*, Lutheranism was discerned as a religion in terms of distinguishing between religious and non-religious phenomena. *Category 2* described how Lutheranism was discerned as a Finnish religiosity or a cultural way of life in terms of external distinctions between features of Finnish Christianity in relation to other religious traditions and their religious customs. In *Category 3*, the distinction between living as a true or real believer vs. living as a nominal Chris-

Table 1. Variation in Finnish students' ways of understanding Lutheranism represented in inclusive hierarchy of descriptive categories (Hella, 2007a)

CATEGORY	DIMENSIONS OF VARIATION				
	Religion vs. non-religion	Religious tradition (cultural differences)	True vs. nominal Christian way of life	Personal vs. mediated relationship with God	Core of Faith: Mercy/freedom vs. guilt
1	X				
2	X	X			
3	X	X	X		
4	X	X	X	X	
5	X	X	X	X	X

tian was based on the external perception of consistency between knowledge of Lutheran beliefs and a practical way of living. In *Category 4*, understanding of Lutheranism as a personal relationship with God was discerned in terms of variation in the Image of God: the distinction experienced between individual images of God related to Lutheranism and a more institutionally mediated, for example, such as that instituted within the Roman Catholic Church. Finally, in *Category 5*, the view of Lutheranism as faith in salvation as a gift from God is based on the experienced variation between the internal aspects of faith. A distinction was made between mercy and freedom vs. guilt and despair in terms of which Lutheran faith was perceived as relieving in its nature. This way of experiencing Lutheranism showed how the experienced core of the Lutheran faith was seen simultaneously as a core of Lutheranism (Figure) discerned against the background (Ground) according to 'figure-ground structure' of gestalt psychology introduced by Gurwich (1964).

The key differences between *teachers' understandings* were described in terms of variation in focus across the four main aspects represented in each category: 1) historical, 2) socio-cultural, 3) doctrinal and 4) spiritual aspect, by which the key meaning of Lutheranism was discerned. These corresponding meanings identified Lutheranism as a 1) historical movement based on faith of Martin Luther; 2) social practices within Lutheran culture; 3) the doctrine of justification as a basis for life and 4) the theological viewpoint to Christian answers to spiritual questions.

There was a relationship between students' and teachers' understandings. The same thematic key aspects focused upon by the students appear in different, more discerned and elaborate form in teachers' understandings. Thus, there is sequence from variation in students' understandings to variation in teachers' understandings, which represents the phenomenographic idea of widening of collective awareness of the same content.

In light of the Variation Theory of Learning, dimensions of variation are the critical aspects for learning of Lutheranism as they mark the line of development in understanding, from relatively undiscerned understanding of Lutheranism towards more nuanced and complex understanding of Lutheranism as a whole. Thus, dimensions of variation serve as tools for teachers to identify students' understandings by revealing the distinctions these students were able to make to discern the meaning of Lutheranism. Being informed about the level of students' ability to discern meanings, teachers' could better evaluate and adapt the teaching aims to enhance students' understanding towards more awareness of Lutheranism. The dimensions of variation mark the critical differences between understandings of Lutheranism. Therefore, they can guide a teacher to identify what dimensions of Lutheranism are open for students in the group, and what dimensions need to be opened up in teaching so that it would be possible for the students to see new aspects of Lutheranism.

EDUCATIONAL IMPLICATIONS FOR RELIGIOUS EDUCATION

This paper argues for a relational approach to religious education from the perspective of phenomenographic research approach and the Variation Theory of Learning. What makes some aspects of religion as the object of learning more critical than others is determined by two aspects: 1) the educational aims for desired learning outcomes – which include students skills and competences in relation to religion – and 2) students' abilities to discern and engage with religion. Both aspects determine that which is educationally critical for students to know about a particular religion and what is required from teaching to create the necessary conditions for students' learning about that religion to successfully take place in accordance with the educational aims. Phenomenography describes the educationally critical aspects between individual ways of understandings of a particular content of religious education, variation in the collective understanding of the subject matter. By comparing different individual ways of experiencing a particular religious content, critical differences between the individual ways of understanding the religious content in the study group are revealed to the teacher. These differences mark the educationally critical aspects by which teacher can identify the phase of learning of an individual in terms of what aspects should be discerned to develop understanding of that particular phenomenon. The hierarchical relationships between the phenomenographic categories illustrate how learning proceeds from undifferentiated understanding of religious content as a whole towards more differentiated understanding of the complex relations between the whole and its aspects.

Due to the contested nature of knowledge about religion, which is mediated in many levels, the task of defining the critical aspects of what should be learned about religion is challenging for the teacher. In Hella's study (2007b) teachers' main focus on the theological questions of Lutheranism addressed the importance of the ontological questions about the existence or absence of transcendental reality - that are inherent in meanings generally given to religion and spirituality. Thus, the study supports the argument that the search for truth about the ultimate order-of-things, represented in both religious and secular traditions, should be considered educationally critical for teaching of religious education in order to promote students' understandings of different religious and secular worldviews. Such an approach relates the horizon of religion to teachers' and students' horizons in an informed manner (Wright, 2000). Phenomenography may help to define the central, 'prototypical features' of religious traditions (Flood, 1999; see also Wright, 2007) by making explicit the most critical features focused upon by different groups of people and bring them into a dialogue with each other.

Furthermore, it is crucial for learning that the necessary conditions of perceptual learning are met, in order to build a 'shared space' for teachers and students to learn from each others ways of understanding of religion as a subject matter. This means that variation must be experienced in the critical aspects of the object of learning. In such a way, religious education can make it possible for the students to learn *about* religion and learn *from* religion to develop as persons in relation to the way things are in the world. (Hella & Wright, 2007). Variation theory focuses on how the educationally critical aspects could be used systemically as a didactic tool to enhance individual understanding of religion as the object of learning. In order to discern a certain aspect of the world, such as Lutheran Christianity, one must be aware of different perspectives to Christianity by experiencing contrasts between Catholic and Lutheran viewpoints, for example. In other words, variation in the dimension of Christianity must be experienced. To understand the distinctive nature of Christianity as a world faith or a belief system in relation to others, variation in the dimension of world faiths must be experienced against the background of seeing the distinction between religious and non-religious or secular worldviews. These critical aspects, or dimensions of variation, serve as a teaching tool to help both teachers and students to make sense of diversity of ways in which the same religious issue may appear to the students, as it is approached from various perspectives. Dimensions of variation can thus be used as a tool for expanding students' awareness of religion and spirituality.

CONCLUDING REMARKS

Students are challenged to make sense of the plurality of beliefs and values within and between religious and secular traditions in current multi-cultural encounters between societies. Religious education can help students to discern the meaning of a particular religious feature or tradition by bringing students into relationship with the religious feature (invariant) in question through exposing them to experience variation in that aspect by means of contrast with an alternative aspect (variant). Hence, students can make sense of the diversity of worldviews by comparing similarities and differences between two contrasting perspectives by which it is possible to discern one from the other. Even though a non-confessional form of religious education, such as Evangelical Lutheran RE in Finland, does not aim to help students to find a personal relationship with God or transcendence, it is important to be aware that such a relationship is deeply meaningful for many religious adherents as it identifies the core of the tradition they belong to. This may help students to understand the 'religious' and 'spiritual' aspects of the world and build up their own worldviews based on awareness of different ways of relating to the ultimate questions addressed by religious traditions. However, it is of equal importance to focus on secular worldviews to see the contrasts between religious and non-religious worldviews. Focusing on different ways of understanding human-God relationship by contrasting views of Muslims and Christians, for example, may help students to search for and reflect on different worldviews of others as well as their own and to live in harmony with others. Such harmony should not be based on ignorance of the differences between people's beliefs and values. Rather, religious education has a key role in helping learners to develop a deep understanding of fundamental differences between varying understandings of the ultimate nature of (transcendent) reality that underlie different beliefs and values according to which people live their lives. This calls for a duty to help students to engage with variation in the accounts of reality in order to make it possible for them to discern and make judgments between worldviews in relation to their own lives and to live responsibly with others as global citizens amongst the plurality of beliefs and moral values.

REFERENCES/BIBLIOGRAPHY

Ahlberg, K. (2004). SYNVÄNDOR - universitetsstudenters berättelser om kvalitativa förändringar av sätt att erfara situationers mening under utbildningspraktik. [View-Turns – University Students' Narratives of Qualitative Changes in Ways of Experiencing Meaning of situations during Educational placement.]Göteborg: Acta Universitatis Gothoburgensis.

Bowden, J. (2005). Reflections on the phenomenographic team research process. In J. A. Bowden. & P. Green (Eds.), *Doing developmental phenomenography* (pp. 11–33). Melbourne: RMT University.

Dahlin, B. (1989). *Religionen, skälen och livets mening. En fenomenografisk och existensfilosofisk studie av religonsundervisningen villkor.* [Religion, Soul and Meaning of Life. A phenomenographic and existential study of the conditions for religious education.] Göteborg Studies in Educational Sciences 73.Göteborg: Acta Universitatis Gothonburgensis.

Entwistle, N., Skinner, D. Entwistle, D. & Orr, S. (2000). Conceptions and beliefs about "good teaching": An integration of contrasting research areas, *Higher Education Research & Development, 19* (1), 5–25.

Flood, G. (1999). *Beyond phenomenology: Rethinking the study of religion.* London: Cassell.

Gurwitsch, A. (1964). *The field of consciousness.* Pittsburgh, PA: Duquesne University Press.

Hella, E. (2007a). Variation in Finnish students' understandings of Lutheranism and its implications for religious education: A phenomenographic study. *British Journal of Religious Education.* (In press)

Hella, E. (2007b). Variation in Finnish religious education teachers' understandings of Lutheranism: A phenomenographic study. In Tirri, K. & Ubani, M. (Eds.), *Giftedness and holistic education. Yearbook 2007 of the Department of Practical Theology.* Publications of the Department of Practical Theology 111 (pp. 109–124). Helsinki: University of Helsinki.

Hella, E. & Wright, A. (2007). Learning 'about' and learning 'from' religion: Phenomenography, the variation theory of learning and religious education in Finland and the UK. *British Journal of Religious Education* (In press)

Martin, E., Prosser, M., Trigwell, K., Ramsden, P. & Benjamin, J. (2000). What university teachers teach and how they teach it. *Instructional Science, 28* (5), 387–412.

Marton, F. (1981). Phenomenography: Describing conceptions of the world around us. *Instructional Science 10*, 177–200.

Marton, F. (1988) Describing and improving learning. In R. Schmeck (Ed.), *Styles and strategies of learning* (pp. 53–82). New York: Plenum.

Marton, F. (1994) Phenomenography. In Husén T.& Postlethwaite T.N. (Eds.), *The international encyclopedia of education 8*, 2nd Edition. (pp. 4424–4429). Oxford: Pergamon

Marton, F., & Booth, S. (1997). *Learning and awareness*. Mahwah, N.J.: Lawrence Erlbaum.

Marton, F. & Pang, M.F. (2006). On some necessary conditions of learning, *The Journal of The Learning Sciences, 15* (2), 193–220.

Marton, F. & Pong, Y.Y. (2005). On the description unit of phenomenography, *Higher Education Research & Development, 24* (3), 335–348.

Marton, F., Hounsell, D. & Entwistle, N. (Eds.) (1997). *The experience of learning: Implications for teaching and studying in higher education*. Edinburgh: University of Edinburgh Centre for Teaching, Learning and Assessment.

Marton, F., Tsui, A.B.M. & Runesson, U. (2004). The Space of Learning. In F. Marton, A. Tsui et al., *Classroom discourse and the space of learning* (pp. 3–40). Mahwah, N.J.: Lawrence Erlbaum.

Marton, F., Tsui, A.B.M. with Chik, P.P.M., Ko, P.Y., Lo, M.L., Mok, I.A.C., Ng, F.P., Pang, M.F., Pong, W.Y., Runesson, U. (2004). *Classroom discourse and the space of learning*. Mahwah, N.J: Lawrence Erlbaum.

Pang, M. F. (2003). Two faces of variation: on continuity in the phenomenographic movement. *Scandinavian Journal for Educational Research, 47*(2), 145–156.

Prosser, M. & Trigwell, K. (1999). *Understanding learning and teaching: the experience in higher education*. Buckingham: SRHE/Open University.

Ramsden, P. (1988). Studying learning: Improving teaching. In P. Ramsden (Ed.), *Improving learning: New perspectives* (pp. 13–31). London: Kogan Page.

Runesson, U. (2006). What is possible to learn? On variation as necessary conditions for learning. *Scandinavian Journal of Educational Research, 50* (4), 397–410.

Trigwell, K. Prosser, M. & Ginns, P. (2005). Phenomenographic pedagogy and a revised approaches to teaching inventory, *Higher Education Research & Development, 24* (3), 349–350

Wright, A. (2000). The spiritual education project. In M. Grimmitt, (Ed.), *Pedagogies of religious education: Case studies in the development of good pedagogic practice* (pp. 170–187). Great Wakering, Essex: McCrimmons.

Wright, A. (2007). Contextual religious education and the actuality of religions. *British Journal of Religious Education* (In press).

Elina Hella
University of Helsinki, Finland

PART 6
**CONFLICTS BETWEEN ETHICAL INVOLVEMENT
AND ECONOMIC ENGAGEMENT**

KLAUS BECK

MORAL JUDGMENT IN ECONOMIC SITUATIONS

Towards Systemic Ethics

MORAL UNIVERSALISM AND MORAL DOMAINS

In many societies, whether traditional or modern, whether religious or secular, it is common sense that moral rules are considered to be valid universally, i.e. they claim obedience at any time and in any place. Prominent examples are the Ten Command-ments, especially the ban of killing human beings or the ban of lying. Respect for the dignity of man or the claim to fulfil a promise, the principle of equal justice under the law or the ban of theft – all these principles are also good instances for moral rules of unrestricted validity. And, of course, the Golden Rule ("Treat others as you want to be treated") as well as Kant's Categorical Imperative (first formula-tion: "Act only according to that maxim whereby you can at the same time will that it should become a universal law." 1785/1993, 30) has to be mentioned in this list of prototypes of universal moral rules.

Though everybody spontaneously seems to agree that these rules are particu-larly suitable candidates for principles to be observed in any situation (including economic contexts), we also know that in our real world this demand is not at all respected consequently. For all of them we experience, and even many of us agree with, exceptions: Killing human beings is "allowed" in times of war as is "allowed" in some countries as death penalty, in some as infanticide. To lie is worldwide ac-cepted in cases of emergency, particularly in cases of personal endangering and also, not rarely, in cases of economic negotiations. Respect for the dignity of hu-man beings often goes lost in political election campaigns when rivalling opponents vilify each other or in the diverse forms of modern slavery (e.g. temps in building industry, forced prostitution) or, sad to say, also if a person suffers from serious mental disability.

To go further with our examples "we" feel free to brake a promise if our coun-terpart on her or his part doesn't obey this rule or if otherwise a good stroke of business is missed or if certain "higher reasons" might force us to abstain from fulfilling it as is dramatically discussed in the famous poem of Friedrich Schiller, "The Hostage" ("Die Buergschaft"). As to the equality under the law we all could tell examples in which we had the strong feeling that e.g. prominent film stars or top managers have not been prosecuted as consequently as the so-called normal tax payer. Furthermore, many people seem to accept that at least for some top terror-

Fritz Oser & Wiel Veugelers (eds.), Getting involved, 359–370.

ists the presumption of innocence is not valid, i.e. that they have lost the right to be treated as someone who is not guilty as long as he or she is not sentenced by a judge (catchword "Guantanamo").

As opposed to moral rules of this type all of which are cases of *"material ethics"* (Scheler 1913/2000) in that they command to put a "concrete" value into practice it is not as easy to show that the Categorical Imperative which commands to follow a *formal* procedure when deciding on a moral issue is also not taken as strictly as its author had intended it to be. The reason is that the Categorical Imperative in each of its three versions[1] does not offer a clear and distinct criterion for moral decision. As Christian Schnoor (1989) in an extensive and careful analysis shows even none of Kant's own seven instances of the application of his Categorical Imperative is free of mistakes and in none of these cases a solution can be derived by application of the Categorical Imperative (see also Petrovich 1986).

The same problem of under-determination applies to all procedural imperatives (e.g. Rawls' "veil of ignorance" (1972) or Habermas' ethics of discourse (1981)) because their prescription of an ultimately open ended process of decision making on principle fails to come to a definite conclusion. Even more, procedural imperatives – besides Kant's Categorical Imperative which is an example for ethics of conviction – usually are generated in the context of consequentialistic ethics ("ethics of responsibility") which, in turn, presuppose comprehensive knowledge of *consequences* and *conditions* of our actions we – in principle – never can arrive at: As to the *consequences* of our actions we often do not even have sufficient knowledge of the *immediate* social effects including side-effects of our verbal and non-verbal behavior (think, e.g., of teachers and their effects on students), let alone *medium* and *long-term* consequences.[2] And as to *conditions* universal ethics postulate that reasons *for* or consequences *of* our actions be acceptable for everybody concerned whether empirically or as a virtual human being (Rawls' version) or by consensus of an ideal communication community (Habermas' version).

Looking at all variants of universal moral principles we have to state that they cannot help to decide whether an individual act at a unique space-time-locus is morally allowed or forbidden because, by definition, they do not take into account the special situational context. Think, e.g., of Kohlberg's Heinz-Dilemma where the question is asked whether Heinz should steel a drug for his seriously ill wife. For most people it depends on very many side conditions what a morally acceptable solution looks like. Not only the fact whether Heinz either loves his wife or thinks of divorce is morally relevant for many people when deciding this conflict. Also the question whether he is going to be a successful theft (may be he is a disabled person or he lacks of a good idea how to get into the pharmacy and, important enough, how to get out again with the drug or he is afraid not to find the drug between all the other drugs), furthermore the question whether Heinz and his wife have young children for whom the wife can't care nor Heinz can if he were captured and set into prison and so on.[3]

To put it short: The social world is not only a rich multifaceted arrangement which is difficult to understand in terms of causality and which is complicated in terms of acting successfully because of the unlimited number of factors working; it is to the same extent difficult to be judged in terms of morality and complicated in terms of doing the right. From this point of view it seems futile and vain from the very first to hope that some few general moral rules or principles were sufficient to regulate (in the strict sense of the word) social interaction in an ethical sufficient manor. This raises the questions whether there are "moral domains" subject to different principles and – the topic of this paper – whether economy might be reconstructed as such a domain.[4]

DESIGN OF THE STUDY AND A BASIC HYPOTHESIS

In a six years longitudinal study we collected moral judgment data from insurance apprentices and clerks by administering four different domain related stories.[5] Two of them deal with business problems, one focusing on a market situation, i.e. a bargaining process between an insurance male clerk and a female client, the other focusing on an in-company team situation where an employee has to decide upon forging or not an account to help his superior escaping from a temporary shortage of money he needs to pay for his new house.

Analogously to Kohlberg's method (cf. Colby/Kohlberg 1987) we varied the situational context step by step changing the social relation between the protagonists from neutral to warm and accepting, turning it to hostile, then changing the consequences of possible decisions from harmless to extremely serious and modifying the perspectives from the point of view of an involved actor to a neutral third person, e.g. a judge. In doing so, administering partly Kohlberg's Moral Judgment Interview (Colby/Kohlberg 1987), partly a questionnaire (sensu Gibbs/Widaman 1982), we diversified more or less slightly the moral content of the situation bringing changing value conflicts into the play as shown in Fig. 1.

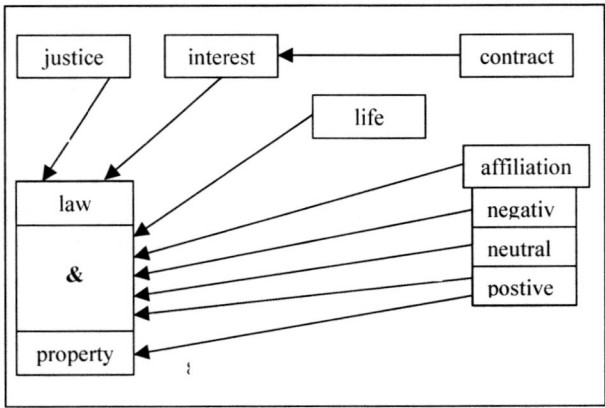

Fig. 1: Value conflicts constituting different situations

From the point of view of moral universalism these variations of situation should not make any difference. The universal principle commands how to judge the core conflict out of respect for the individual circumstances. One and the same moral principle has to be applied no matter whether people involved love or hate each other, whether the consequences of their actions are serious or small and, of course, whether one is personally involved or not.

In Kohlberg's psychological turn of this ethical view (cf. Beck 1990) a person assessing the different variations of the conflict story will normally judge on the basis of her or his stage of moral development which is nothing else than an individual universal principle. Only during transition phases when a person moves up to a higher stage of moral reasoning it might occur that two different principles come into the play. From this follows that – as a central hypothesis – it is expected that every person in our study by and large should make use of the same principle across the variations of our conflict stories, i.e. the distribution of principles used should not vary subject to the changes of value conflicts as shown in Fig. 1.

In our cohort design (cf. Fig. 2) we included every year a new group keeping track of it until the end of the study after six years. All in all, 174 persons were included. The members of the first group have been interviewed or questioned respectively six times, those of the second group five times and so forth. Thus, we got from the first group 6 times 17, that is 102, data sets, from the second (5 x 41 =) 205 and so on. Every year we administered the same dilemma stories including all variations of contexts as shown in Fig. 1. So, all in all we should have collected 673 data sets. Of course, there was a certain amount of drop outs, some of them only partially if they attended only one of the two yearly sessions. This is the reason that on the following charts the numbers of cases are varying within limited boundaries. Only cases with full data on the respective questions are reported.

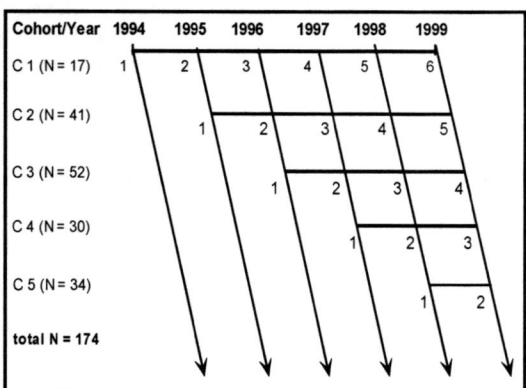

Fig. 2: Design of the longitudinal study

Our interviewees as well as the persons, who produced written comments (i.e. decisions and reasons) in the questionnaire, had no pressure in deliberating the circumstances relevant for them and they have been stimulated by follow-up questions to work out their best solutions.

MORAL JUDGMENTS IN CONTEXT

To get a first insight into the processes of moral reasoning look at Fig. 3.1. The horizontal line is divided up along Kohlberg's stages 1 to 5. The vertical line represents the percentage of judgments based on the different principles.

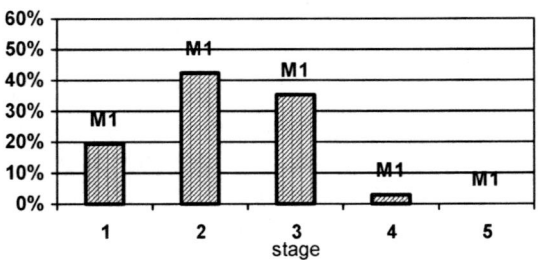

M1: affiliation (neutral) vs. law/property

Figure 3.1. Distribution of moral principles used in judging conflicts in economy: market situation (N = 431)

In the first variant of the market situation, M1, dealing with the male insurance clerk and the female client the two conflicting values "affiliation" and "law in connection with property" had to be deliberated. As can be seen, about 20 % of the decisions have been based on Kohlberg's stage 1, 42 % on stage 2 an so on. Now, the situation has been changed: The female client was depicted as a very attractive and charming young woman (M2). The distribution of principles used as grounds for the new decision shift, at least a bit, down to stage 1 (see Fig. 3.2).

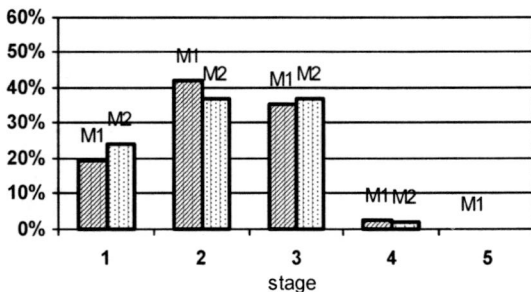

M1: affiliation (neutral) vs. law/property M2: affiliation (postive) vs. law/property

Figure 3.2. Distribution of moral principles used in judging conflicts in economy: market situation (N = 431 data sets)

In the next situation (see Fig. 3.3) the client was characterized as unfriendly and cold (M3). Again, the reasons for judgment shift down. In the next step we opposed "affiliation" to "property", the latter in the sense of benefit vs. loss (M4). Here occurs a dramatic change in the distribution of reasons towards stage 2 judgments. The same is true with "life" vs. "law and property" (M5) and again with "law" vs. "justice" (M6) as well as with "contract" vs. "interest" (M7).

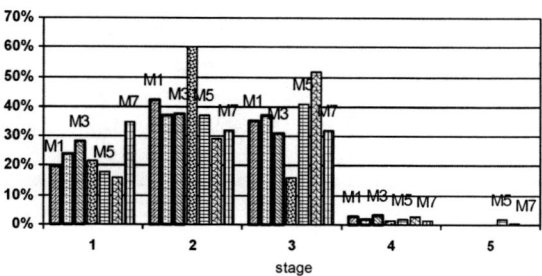

M1: aff. (neutral) vs. law/prop. M2: aff. (pos.) vs. law/prop. M3: aff. (neg.) vs. law/prop. M4: aff. (neutral) vs. prop. M5: life vs. law/prop. M6: law vs. justice M7: contract vs. interest

Figure 3.3. Distribution of moral principles used in judging conflicts in economy: market situation (N = 418 ... 445 data sets)

Now, Fig. 3.4 shows a comparison between judgment reasons used in the *market* and in the *team* situation, again both embedded in the context of an insurance company.

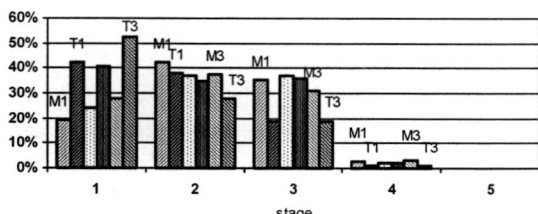

M1/T1: aff. (neutral) vs. law/prop. M2/T2: aff. (pos.) vs. law/prop. M3/T3: aff. (neg.) vs. law/prop.

Figure 3.4. Distribution of moral principles used in judging conflicts in economy: market situation (N = 420 ... 458 data sets)

Looking at the starting constellations, neutral or unbiased "affiliation" vs. "law and property", there is obviously a big difference in the two distributions (M1 vs. T1). In the team situation (T1) more than twice as much persons as in the market situation (M1) choose a stage 1-priciple to solve this team conflict. Nearly the same constellations occur with the next pairs of value conflicts in the two different situational settings (M2 vs. T2 and M3 vs. T3).[6] It is not only that the type of affiliation (neutral, positive, negative) alters the moral interpretation of given situations. Additionally, affiliation plays obviously a different role in moral judgment procedures due to the varying situational context, in our example the market and the team context.[7]

To extend these findings to the other distributions of judgments across the four conflict constellations within the market situation (M4 to M7) as opposed to the team situation (T4 to T7) Fig. 3.5 shows the respective frequencies. Looking at the neighboring pairs of columns (M4/T4, M5/T5 etc.) it can easily been detected that there are considerable discrepancies in the use of moral principles *between* (M vs. T) as well as *within* situational contexts (M1 vs. M2 vs. M3 etc.).

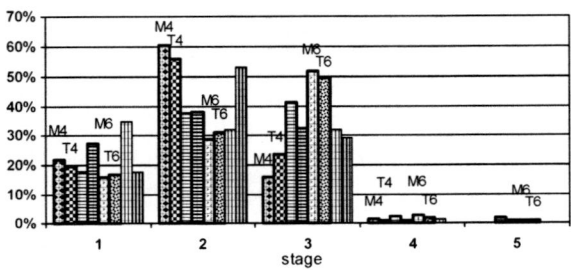

M4/T4: aff. (neutral) vs. prop. M5/T5: life vs. law/prop.
M6/T6: law vs. justice M7/T7: contract vs. interest

Figure 3.5. Distribution of moral principles used in judging conflicts in economy market situation (N = 418 ... 450 data sets)

As the varying distributions suggest individuals draw on different moral rules or principles when facing different constellations of circumstances. Doubtlessly the range of principles they have at their disposal (cf. Rest 1979) depends on the state of their individual moral development. The more sophisticated it is the more possibilities to adapt to varying circumstances are given. We analyzed the individual range of principles used by one and the same person at a particular time. Fig. 4 shows the numbers. Only 1,5 % are judging upon only one principle be it of stage 1, 2, 3, 4, or 5. But nearly 64 % make use of *three* different principles. This is not at all in line with Kohlberg's hypothesis. And from the point of view of ethical universalism this state of moral practice must look like degeneration into the moral slum of Sodom and Gomorrah.

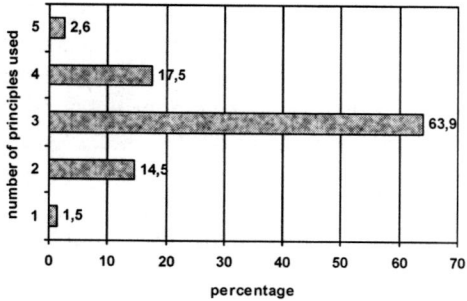

Figure 4. Number of different principles (Kohlberg's stages) used in judging different issue
conflicts in two situations (N = 502 data sets)

To give a least quantitative evidence for the practice of moral differentiation along changing situations we computed an individual average per person across all judgments he or she produced for the market story and for the team story (see Fig. 5.1 and 5.2). Of course, the numbers of Kohlberg's stages are of ordinal scale quality which does not allow for the computation of arithmetic means. Nevertheless, the means offer *virtual tentative indicators* for the extent of variation of judgment behavior in different contexts.

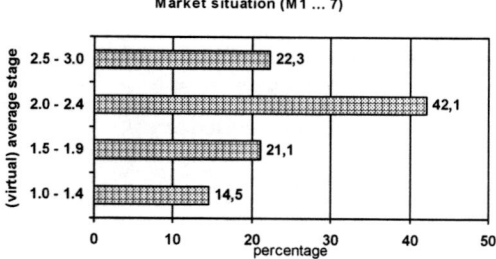

Figure 5.1. Distributions of judgments across all variants of the market situation
(virtual average stages; N = 166 persons)

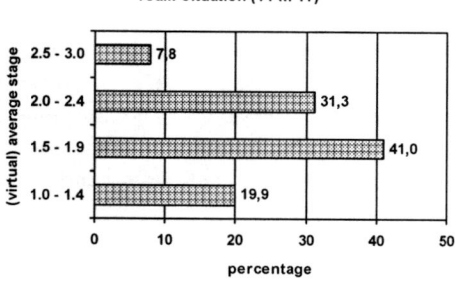

Figure 5.2. Distributions of judgments across all variants of the team situation
(virtual average stages; N = 166 persons)

Across all versions of the market story M1 to M7 about 21 % of our insurance people get an average stage score between 1,5 and 1,9. But across all versions of the team situation T1 to T7 41 % get an average stage score in the same interval (1,5 to 1,9). Again, the "*average stage score*" is a pure virtual number without empirical correspondence. But nevertheless it can be used as *indicator* for the interindividual as well as the intraindividual tendency to draw on different moral ideas along with the change of circumstances.

To sum up, it can be said that presumably most people differentiate between types of situations (or problems or conflicts) when they – under standard conditions: spontaneously and unconsciously – choose a moral principle to produce a moral decision or valuation. We suppose that people interpret and reconstruct situations along a hierarchy of fundamental social functions and that they tend to choose a respective moral principle which in turn can approximately be described in terms of Kohlberg's theory. The basic types are shown in Fig. 6.

Social function	Prototypical types of social roles	Moral orientation approx. to Kohlberg's ...
controversy	victor, victim	Stage 1
competition	winner, loser	Stage 2
cooperation	colleague, partner	Stage 3
coordination	professional, manager	Stage 4
constitution	legislator, top manager	Stage 5

Figure 6. Basic types of situations with respective moral principles

According to this typology the standard economic situation seems to be of the competition type. In a sense this is an appropriate sight, especially when one is about to characterize the overarching ample social subsystems. But as we have seen "economy" – in the common sense of this term – is not at all homogenous in terms of moral regulation. Everyday life in companies is socially multi-faceted including different basic types of social functions. Hence, for "economy" in a colloquial sense there is of course no universal moral rule for the regulation of all types of social conflicts. And, as a matter of fact, people in "economy" do not obey one and only one general moral rule but – in adaptation to changing circumstances – they refer to adequate moral principles which ensure systemic functionality and at the same time dependability and – ultimately – social peace.

INDIVIDUAL MORALITY AND ETHICS OF ECONOMY

Contrary to ethical universalism we can look at our western mass societies as systems which are subdivided into subsystems like legislation, jurisdiction, politics, welfare, traffic, culture, education, religion, economy etc. Each subsystem contributes to the overarching suprasystem by producing its special output: laws and rulings by legislation, law-based sentences by jurisdiction, goods and services by economy and so on. In this sense subsystems have emerged during centuries and have developed their own "logics" and, at the same time, their own morals. So, e.g., the prevalent moral principle within the subsystem welfare might be something like Kohlberg's stage 3-principle whereas in the subsystem economy, as mentioned above, the leading moral idea should be to seeking for one's own benefit (a principle similar to Kohlberg's stage 2).

Of course, in accordance with social systems theory (cf. Parsons 1951), subsystems are not separated in locally or temporally disjunctive areas of life. Rather, the notion stands for the pure regulative idea (Kant) of functional coherence of social aggregates. In the empirical world they are multilaterally interwoven (like in that what is meant by the colloquial "economy"). To human beings they occur in the shape of situations, i.e. by "gestalt" of appearances of temporarily stable constellations of persons and matters. Under a socio-moral aspect and from the point of view of human beings, situations are constituted by constellations of postulations and expectations in connection with sanctions. Individuals can be seen as role occupants who fulfil (or not fulfil) expectations which in turn are nothing else than the quintessence of subsystemic logics and morals – the other side of the same medal.

To put it in terms of sociology (see Fig. 7): Individuals are integrated in our modern societies by roles which they overtake and which they play in the different subsystemic settings. They enter different subsystems where they act as role players and where they meet other role players, different from subsystem to subsystem. This is fundamentally distinct from the early times of mankind when people lived in small communities, hordes and tribes, into which they were integrated as whole persons and where their moral behavior was watched by everybody and where they were sanctioned by the whole group.

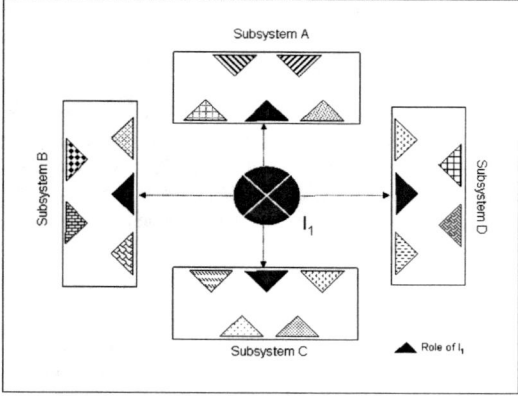

Figure 7. Integration of individuals into subsystems

As the examples of conflict stories mentioned above have shown the "economy" provides not only one type of situations. Besides *competition* ("market") and *cooperation* situations ("team") especially managers will have to process *coordination* and *constitution* situations when organizing production processes or implementing corporate cultures. However, the fundamental and prototype situation of economy in the sense of systems theory is still *competition*. From a moral point of view in *competition situations* it is commanded to act as a role player who is seeking for his or her own benefit. Economy is based on the idea of supplying the demand of people to satisfy their needs. As already Adam Smith, the famous Scottish economist and moralist, in the 18th century stated it is not the good motive ("benevolence") which forces the butcher, baker or brewer to offer his goods and services but his interest in his own benefit. In striving for profit he simultaneously fulfils the task of supplying people though this is not the standard motive of his acting (1776/1904). At the same time he is saving resources because competition forces him to produce at lowest cost, i.e. by using the least amount of input of material, energy and work.

Ethically speaking it is of course completely unacceptable to sign the principle of seeking for benefit into a universal law. On the other hand it would be completely unacceptable as well to stigmatize this principle as morally deficient by nature. On the contrary, in certain situations it is morally commanded to ground actions on it. When and where this is the case depends on the subsystemic context and the role an individual has to play in it. Thus, instead of universalism we are in need of elaboration of a subsystemic relativism.

NOTES

1 Second formulation (Kant 1785/1993, 36): "Act in such a way that you treat humanity, whether in your own person or in the person of any other, always at the same time as an end and never simply as a means". – Third formulation (ibid. 43): "Every rational being must so act as if he were through his maxim always a legislating member in the universal kingdom of ends."

2 As a prominent example think of friar Bertold Schwarz who is said to be the inventor of gunpowder. Is he responsible for the consequences followed by the use of his invention?

3 For further discussion see Evans (1985).

4 From another perspective Carol Gilligan has put this question, too (1982).

5 For details see Beck et al. (1999).

6 Interestingly enough and unexpectedly, it is the team situation in which our young clerks and apprentices tend to make use of lower stage principles than in the market situation. The reasons for this finding are not investigated here because the focus of our considerations is on the problem of ethical diversity. For an interpretation see Beck 1996.

7 Statistically spoken there is an interaction "context x affiliation".

REFERENCES

Beck, K. (1990). Philosophische Ethik als Basis moralpsychologischer Theoriebildung? Ein Beitrag zur Kohlberg-Kant-Kritik. In P. Strittmatter (Hrsg.) *Zur Lernforschung: Befunde - Analysen - Perspektiven.* Festschrift anlässlich des 60. Geburtstags von Gunther Eigler. Weinheim: Deutscher Studien Verlag, 7-23

Beck, K. (1996). *The segmentation of moral judgment of adolescent students in Germany - Findings and problems.* Pap. pres. at the Annual Meeting of the American Educational Research Association (AERA), New York, NY, April 9, 1996 (ERIC Document Reproduction Service No. ED 396 229)

Beck, K. et al. (1999). Homogeneity of moral judgment? - Apprentices solving business conflicts. *Journal of Moral Education, 28,* 429-443

Colby, A. & Kohlberg, L. (1987). *The measurement of moral judgment.* Cambridge, MA, USA: Cambridge Univ. Pr.

Evans, Ch. (1985). Kohlberg's moral judgment interview: Is there a need for additional research? In S. Mogdil & C. Mogdil, (Eds.) *Lawrence Kohlberg. Consensus and controversy.* Ohiladelphia, USA: Falmer Pr., 471-480

Gibbs, J. C. & Widaman, K. (1982). *Social intelligence: Measuring the development of sociomoral reflection.* Englewood Cliffs, N. J.. Prentice Hall

Gilligan, C. (1982). *In a different voice. Psychological theory and women's development.* Cambridge, Mass., USA: Havard Univ. Pr.

Habermas, J. (1981). *Theorie des kommunikativen Handelns* (3. Aufl.). Frankfurt a. M.: Suhrkamp 1985

Kant, I.; [1785] (1993). *Grounding for the metaphysics of morals* (3rd ed.). Translated by J.W. Ellington. Indianapolis, IN: Hackett

Parsons, T. (1951). *The social system.* Glencoe, IL: Free Pr.

Petrovich, O. (1986). Moral autonomy and the theory of Kohlberg. In: S. Mogdil & C. Mogdil (Eds.). *Lawrence Kohlberg. Consensus and controversy.* Philadelphia,: Falmer Pr., 85-106

Rawls, J. (1972). *A theory of justice* (4. print).. Cambridge, MA: Belknap Press of Harvard Univ. Pr.

Rest, J.R. (1979). *Development in judging moral issues.* Minneapolis, MN: Univ. of Minnesota Pr.

Schnoor, Ch. (1989). *Kants Kategorischer Imperativ als Kriterium der Richtigkeit des Handelns.* Tübingen: Mohr

Scheler, M. [1913] (2000). *Der Formalismus in der Ethik und die materiale Wertethik* (7. Aufl.) Bonn: Bouvier

Smith, A. [1776] (1904). *An inquiry into the nature and causes of the wealth of nations.* London: Methuen.

Klaus Beck
Johannes Gutenberg University, Mainz, Germany

GERHARD MINNAMEIER

EDUCATION FOR BUSINESS ETHICS

Options and restrictions from a systematic point of view

BUSINESS ETHICS AS AN EDUCATIONAL PROBLEM

Business ethics has been a prominent topic for many years, with its perceived importance fuelled by (purportedly) growing corruption, labour exploitation, illegal environmental pollution and the like in a globalised world. Apart from calls for controls, a lack of ethical conduct and commitment is often stated, combined with the quest for moral education and training as well as the establishment of ethical codes in industry.

It may be asked, however, how far ethical awareness and commitment can or should go. On the one hand, it is certainly important to teach young professionals ethical standards, but on the other hand, the ones adhering to these standards might be the ones to lose out economically (which cannot really be "professional" from the business point of view). This raises the question, whether it can be morally justified to teach business professionals that they have to leave out chances for the sake of higher ends, but to their own economical detriment and to the advantage of their (relatively) "immoral" competitors. Most proponents of business ethics seem to answer in the affirmative, but some do not. These different views are going to be presented and discussed in Section 2 in the context of what might be called an educational trilemma in the field of vocational education and training.

However, at the heart of the matter there seems to be an even deeper problem which concerns the relation between ethics and economics as such. As the analysis in Section 2 reveals, most theoreticians believe that ethics is superior to economics and that economical activity should be curbed or guided by suitable ethical rules and principles. Contrary to this position, the relation between ethics and economics may also be looked at from a different angle, which shall be explicated in Section 3. According to this view, economics – maybe surprisingly – turns out to provide means to solve genuinely ethical problems.

This deeper look at the relation between ethics and economics reveals that ethical curbing of economic rationality may not only be unnecessary, but may even be morally wrong and to the detriment of ethical adjustment in a mass society or in global contexts. What this consequence would mean for business ethical guidance shall be analysed in Section 4 in which the notion of moral segmentation (which is introduced in Section 2) will be further scrutinised and eventually rejected.

Fritz Oser & Wiel Veugelers (eds.), Getting involved, 371–381.

The present analysis entails that those who call for ethical commitment beyond economic rationality are wrong and that, accordingly, those who claim to act according to highly moral principles may be equally wrong and misguided. This (perhaps unexpected) result leads to a differentiated view on educational goals and the question of moral action that are going to be outlined in the final Section 5 of this paper.

AN EDUCATIONAL TRILEMMA AND THE IDEA OF MORAL SEGMENTATION

The most part of business and economic ethics has emphasised a growing importance of ethical guidance for actors in the field, based on the view that the rationality of business would have to be sided or even supervised by an ethical rationality. In German speaking countries, for instance, there are discursive approaches based on – broadly speaking – Rawlsian or Habermasian principles in the sense of the ideal communication situations that should bring about fair solutions for moral conflicts (e.g. Steinmann & Löhr 1994; Ulrich 1990) or post-modern approaches with a cultural focus (Koslowski 1992). And there is also a more Kantian view which stresses the ethical dignity and responsibility of the moral person (Zabeck 1991; 2002). Whatever the theoretical foundation, theoreticians in these camps demand the ethical curbing or mediating of "pure" economic thought and action.

Zabeck, e.g., argues that the idea of *homo oeconomicus* suspends human beings from their moral duty to confine themselves for the sake of others (see 1991, 544; 2002, 486). Against this orientation he maintains that a moral point of view is indispensable, because the individual would always have to act as a whole person and according to his or her own free will (in the Kantian sense) as opposed to perceived external economic requirements. He says:

> Those who act in a professional function, with which they try to identify, will be confronted with tasks that may appear morally questionable to them or may even be suited to weigh heavily on their conscience. An awareness of values that has been sharpened by business education could contribute to a critical attitude as to whether certain instructions or assignments by a superior ought to be heeded. Refusal may lead to devastating social and economic consequences for the individual. Even if rules and rationales for ethical conflict resolution have been acquired in vocational education, a considerable risk of conflict would remain, of which the individual can, however, not be relieved. (Zabeck 1991, 561; transl. G. M.; see also Zabeck 2002, 500)

If this is to be taken seriously and looked at from a Kohlbergian perspective, an educational trilemma emerges, as Beck et al. (1996, 199) point out (see Figure 1). Supposing – as will be discussed below – that success in business requires Stage 2 reasoning, there is a trade-off between economic efficiency and morality, and being moral (also in the sense of the above-mentioned approaches) would be tantamount to vocational "dequalification" or even "disqualification" and, conversely, professionality in business terms would imply a rather narrow moral scope (see A and B in Figure 1). Apart from these two options it might be possible to develop different points of view in, broadly speaking, vocational contexts on the one hand and public or private contexts on the other. This is the idea of moral segmentation or differentiation[1] (see Beck 2003; Beck et al. 1996; 1999; 2002; Rest 1979), an alternative which would allow the individual to adapt to different situations, however at the expense of cross-situational identity and integrity (C). Whatever one thinks of these alternatives, educating people toward moral segmentation or a stable Stage 2 orientation would preclude moral views and actions as demanded by the ethical approaches presented above. The question is, whether this trade-off between moral and ethical orientation can be avoided in some way.

+ Fostering moral competence
- Hampering professional competence

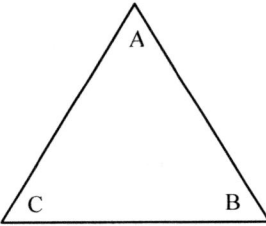

+ Supporting moral segmentation
- Inconsistent personality (identity crisis?)

+ Enhancing professional competence
- Reducing moral competence (stagnation/regression)

Figure 1. An educational trilemma

ETHICS AND ECONOMICS – A FURTHER PROBLEM AS THE SOLUTION

It is often the case that solutions constitute new problems, but in the present case a new problem may lead to a way out of the above-mentioned predicament. This new problem is that neither universalistic ethical approaches nor post-modern culturally based ethics seem to take us very far in the economic context. As for the former, it has long been clear that universalism as such eventually turns out as a cultural concept of universal ethics with no ultimately universalistic basis (see e.g. Buchanan 1977, 123-147; also Homann 1990, 160-162; Sandel 1982). This has been conceded by Rawls himself (see Rawls 1999, Chapt. 18 and 22)[2] and is the received view today.

The resulting problem is that none of the approaches discussed so far provides a suitable ethical basis for a global world. Universalism seems to be seriously flawed in itself and culturally based ethics is inherently limited (see also Minnameier 2000). Not even globally oriented approaches from this camp like, e.g., Michael Walzer's (1994) concept of "thick" [inner-cultural] und "thin" [cross-cultural] ethics can, to my mind, solve the problem, since in this view all is down to contingent agreements or contingently shared moral principles. What we are in need of, however, is to get a systematic handle on the ethical regulation of cross-cultural relations.

Luckily there seems to be at least one way, which we could go. The basic idea is that there is no use searching for a new overarching ethical supernorm that would help us as a foil to negotiate ethical problems and evaluate possible solutions. Rather could we start – as all post-universalistic approaches in fact do – from the values and norms that people already have and take these as input in an economic analysis which aims at rules and regulations that would best implement the normativity of the grass roots, under the restriction of given concurrent claims. That is, the generated solutions should be acceptable for everyone given the views and orientations of all other players in the game.

Of course, this ethical input is not ready at hand, such that it would just need to be "filled" into the economic "mills", but has to be generated and condensed in public debates and across the layers modern societies have brought about. This is part of the process of sharpening ethical problems and claims on the one hand as well as analysing what deficits we perceive and at what price (and how) they could possibly be removed. In other words, economics could help us to attain a "universal" point of view, if we stopped looking out for an ultimate "first" principle from which to derive concrete conclusions and start with concrete views of different people(s) which we subject to an economic analysis in order to find rules complemented with sanctions that would appear to be acceptable for all (under the premise of all conceivable alternatives). Therefore, it would not be necessary that everybody accepts the content of what is decided, acceptance may only be on condition that non-acceptance would eventually produce outcomes that one would rather decline.

For this reason, Homann paraphrases this approach as ethics with economic means and calls it "interaction economics" (see e.g. 2001, 23). This is the idea of a self-regulating process in which ethics is *input* for discourses on institutional reforms to address perceived moral deficiencies. Accordingly, ethics is to be driven "from below", from the grass-roots, and not derived "from above", from universal moral principles. All that is needed is transparency and a societal organisation that ensures that ethical claims are carried "upwards" in a process in which they are analysed and transformed (i.e. implemented) into suitable regulations.[3] The upward movement can be modelled as a multistage process that proceeds from certain actions at one level to the level of action conditions and so forth. When business people, e.g., are in a predicament as described above, they ought not to counter practices they dislike with practices they themselves deem fair (because this undermines their business), but try to change the rules so that all have to do what is fair. This process of negotiating rules, again, takes place under certain conditions, which means that here, too, we can distinguish between actions and action conditions. And like before, there may be a point where it makes no sense anymore to act as if the conditions were differently, so that the activity would have to shift to shape those conditions (and so forth). In other words, a discussion about certain action conditions takes place in a certain context which has its own action conditions and which can itself be subjected to a meta-discourse on how to set or modify these conditions.

In the downward direction, the political will of the people has to be implemented in suitable regulations and secured by appropriate sanctions (which are then the new conditions in the lower contexts).because human interaction is shaped and guided in a way that is optimal for all in the given circumstances. Moreover, these optima are "optimal" in a sense superior to so-called Pareto optima, because the setting of societal rules allows us to attain states in which all partners reach a higher level of satisfaction then they would if they had to negotiate one by one in an open market situation.

Hence, "economics" is not (simply) to be equated with "market economy", just as "satisfaction" is not to be equated with "personal benefit". Interaction economics is not based on a self-interested version of *homo oeconomicus*, but on an open concept of "utility", or "benefit". This wide notion benefit covers everything that people may take to belong to a "good life" (see e.g. Becker 1976; see also Homann 1999, p. 64). There is no prescription whatsoever as to specific contents of what is thought to be beneficial.

Now what is the ethical impact of interaction economics on morality in business or in a larger framework of public life? Three important consequences can be drawn (see also Minnameier 2004; 2005a):

1. It is a matter of ethics (and of respect for others) that one should basically accept current regulations and their outcomes, since it is impossible to refer to an ethical principle that is prior in the sense of universalism or in the sense of Kohlberg's Stage 6.
2. This does not mean that any rule has to be accepted for its own sake. As has been explained, normative claims are input in the process of inventing and implementing intelligent institutions that ensure what we – i.e. those taking part in this process – consider morally adequate. In precisely this way, thousands or millions of globalisation critics, e.g., help to shape a better global world, not to return to pre-global times.
3. Ethical input is to be put into the institutions. Especially under the conditions of mass societies and a globalised world, ethics as direct action is neither sound (see (1)) nor efficient, because this kind or "moral behaviour" will definitely be exploited by competitors (which, by the way, reduces costs for the consumers). Hence ethics is not to be put into our actions (in the market), but into the conditions of action, i.e. the institutions and regulations that ensure moral behaviour of all (on pain of suitable penalties).

These aspects entail the solution to the educational trilemma introduced in the previous section, since it is neither ethically justified nor practically necessary that the individual acts against common (business) practices for the sake of morality and for the price of personal disadvantages. What this suggested solution means in the Kohlbergian framework is to be analysed in the following section.

MORAL SEGMENTATION REVISITED

Klaus Beck has suggested that moral segmentation could provide a way out of the educational trilemma, if we accept that segmentation does not imply a split moral mind, but the insight that we live in different social frameworks with different moral requirements. Although Beck refers, in part, to Homann's approach, his view contrasts rather sharply in certain respects with the solution developed above.

Beck's solution to the trilemma is straightforward. He suggests dropping the assumption of structured wholeness and that we accept that individuals develop different perspectives in different domains, according to the specific conditions they find and the particular roles they take on (see Beck 1996, p. 137; 2003, p. 287). This is also spelt out, to some extent, with respect to certain contexts in which people should stick to specific (Kohlbergian) stage principles (see Colby & Kohlberg 1987). For instance, in business they should reason in terms of Stage 2 (seeking one's benefit in mutual exchange), in the family context Stage 3 is thought to be appropriate (caring and sharing), and in political contexts one should reason in terms of Stage 4 or Stage 5, depending on whether existing rules have to be applied or new ones contrived (see Beck 1999).

The notion of domain specific (moral) concepts is certainly appropriate in some way, but in the sense of a classifying pattern with corresponding contexts and stage principles it seems to me too rigid in various respects. First of all, it may be questioned whether such a pattern would – as Beck holds – be compatible with our idea of an integrated mind and personality. He says that personal identity would be brought about on the level of meta-cognition which holds together the differentiated spectrum of moral orientations (see 1996, p. 137). However, if we assume a meta-cognitive link, how would that have to be understood? In particular, it would be interesting to know whether this would not imply (or constitute) a meta-moral principle that justifies our first order moral decisions. If this is the case, then there is no moral segmentation or differentiation in any deeper sense, since this move reduces first order principles to mere moral *content* put in the *form* of the second order principle. If, however, meta-cognition in the present context is to be understood merely as knowledge or awareness that one in fact – and so to speak "deliberately" – follows different principles in different situations, then I do not see, how this overcomes the problem of a "split mind" (indeed, this would make the split explicit for the individual).

Secondly, fixed correspondence rules between roles or contexts on the one hand and moral stage principles on the other would free business people from all responsibility, because in their role as business people and as professionals they are – according to Beck – bound to follow Kohlberg Stage 2. Of course, he also believes that those people might make moral claims as to the shaping of economic conditions and argues that they would then be in a different – namely political – context (1999, 21-22). But still, this reasoning misses the point. It puts the whole burden of inventing and implementing suitable institutions on politicians or governments and the political processes in which they are situated. However, especially in times of globalisation no government can pass legislation without the compliance and initiative of other bodies, in particular multi-nationally operating companies. On the other hand, companies must also have a vital interest in providing stable conditions, developing markets, establishing good relations with governments in developing countries, keeping old and gaining new clients or consumers, having highly qualified and motivated workers at their disposal and so on. For all these vital interests and also for securing the future of the company (which is at least as relevant for company executives as it is for political leaders) companies have to play a pro-active role in the forming of social order and global co-operation (see Homann [2004a] for more on this point).

Thirdly, if business people have to act strategically to maximise profits for their shareholders in order to keep the value of the firm high and secure the companies future, the question arises, whether all other people in all other (non-economic) contexts would not have to act in exactly the same way, i.e. trying to reach their goals as efficiently and effectively as possible. Under the wide and open notion of "benefit" (see above) there is no systematic difference between, say, producing cost-*efficiently* and reducing global warming *efficiently*. Both aim at the highest possible effect with the least input of scarce resources. The only real difference is that in the economy it is not the companies who decide upon the ultimate goals; this is rather mediated by the market and market regulation (so that, again, values are input in these contexts). However, if Stage 2 is thought appropriate for business especially on grounds of the strategic orientation that is necessary, and if the need of strategic thinking is ubiquitous, then there is no reason why this kind of strategic reasoning should not be equally relevant, mutatis mutandis, for all other possible contexts. Hence, Stage 2 would have be a universal guideline, which obviously leads us into an ethical fallacy of some sort.

The point, to my mind, is that strategic reasoning is indeed a universal requirement – or principle of rationality – and should therefore not be equated with Kohlberg Stage 2. Stage 2 is a restricted view in which only personal benefits and those of one's counterparts are considered – which is, of course, important in business practice, but obviously not the whole story (see the above arguments). Conversely, strategic thinking is important in relation to all moral orientations, especially in the context of differentiating between moral action within certain situations or under certain institutions and contexts in which the conditions of action have to be altered so as to establish new rules and regulations. It is pointless and detrimental for individuals to follow ethical ideals as long as they are likely to be exploited by other players. Strategic rationality would require them to put their efforts into suitable regulations that allow them to be "moral" without being exploited, rather than "fighting against windmills". This aspect of morality has long been overlooked (see Homann 2004b).

The result of the present analysis can be summed up as follows: Ethical differentiation does not mean moral segmentation in a strict sense (that would endanger the individual's integrity). This is what Beck also holds. Above and beyond his conception of moral adaptation I have, however, tried to show that differentiation cannot follow a clear role-like differentiation of contexts. The differences obviously have to more subtle, not relating to (superficial) organisational features, but to the deeper question of what is the moral point of a given problem and how this meshes with the situation of the reflecting individual, in particular whether he or she is in a position that affords direct action or whether there is a need to change the conditions of those actions in the first place. This latter point takes us straight to the following discussion of the educational impact of the present analysis.

HOW TO BE MORAL IN BUSINESS WITHOUT LOSING OUT

There are several important consequences of our approach that can be organised in three categories: (1) aspects that have already been discussed above, (2) further consequences to be derived, (3) consequences for business ethics above and beyond educational goals.

As for the first point, it should once again be stressed that (young) adults, and in particular (young) professionals, should know or learn how to differentiate between situations in which direct moral action works and situations in which it is likely to be exploited so that these situations require changing the conditions of action in terms of rules and sanctions. What seems to be important, also for a healthy personality that is moral on the one hand, but not self-destructive (or complacent) on the other hand, is to make clear what one wants and also how this is best attained. In terms of moral evaluation, a "good will" seems to be most important for many people – and idea that we also inherited from Kant[4] –, but moral efficiency in the sense of the outcome of moral action of any kind should, to my mind, rank equally high. Not only conscience is important, but also strategy.

Secondly, Kohlberg Stage 2 turns out not to be enough, not even in business. Of course, business professionals have to negotiate good deals in their daily practice, but they also have to be able to form reliable alliances, co-operate with partners inside and outside the firm, deal with their clients' and other interaction partners' moral claims and find ways to address them, contribute to the shaping of statutory regulations and social relations to secure their markets, labour force and general future (see e.g. Becker-Olsen et al. 2006; Marin & Ruiz 2007). All this requires reflected thinking on the part of business people, their ability and willingness to co-operate with all sorts of stakeholders.

To achieve this, fostering moral development would be required. And it seems to be important for two different reasons: On the one hand, business people have to be able and motivated to bring about ethical progress in the sense of interaction economics. On the other hand, rules and regulations should not only be understood as restrictions, but have to be accepted for what they are. In this respect it would at least be helpful, if people comprehended why rules are set they way they are, and this requires moral understanding on the part of the acting individuals.

However, even people at Kohlberg Stage 6 could act in morally inadequate ways, when they follow their own guidelines, ignorant of what may really be incorporated in the rules that a person at Stage 6 might possibly break. It is the arrogance of overestimating one's own moral powers combined with the chief criterion of a good will (see above) that could easily make defectors from the outside point of view. However, this is only an argument against the idea that Stage 6 is the most elaborated form of moral reasoning (which was already implicitly rejected in the above critique of moral universalism). Hence, and if one still adheres to the idea of moral stages, there might be a kind – or more kinds – of moral reasoning beyond the assumed end-point of Stage 6 (for more on this see e.g. Minnameier 2000; 2001; 2005a and b).

Whatever the "true" moral stage taxonomy may be and whatever moral development may ultimately head for, the present discussion entails that moral development could still be the general aim of education (Kohlberg & Mayer 1987), besides and despite all the talk of domain specifity. The strategic orientation and a consequent differentiation of action and conditions of action would ensure that even highly developed individuals would not (have to) be less proficient in business than their perhaps more inconsiderate competitors.

Thirdly, rules in society in general have to be such that – ideally – all individuals actually do what they ought to do from the overall societal point of view (which is itself gained from the analysis of normative input), independently of what their own moral orientation is. This is the gist and thrust of statutory and other regulations. Put into the framework of action and conditions of action, moral education is the action that educators can take. However, if they do not reach their goals and if it is not for the quality of education but for the impossibility of getting learners where we would like them to be, then this no case of educational action anymore (which is or has been obviously futile [in the given circumstances]), but one of changing the conditions. Conditions might be altered either in the sense of providing more opportunities for moral learning or setting suitable limits to the actions of morally incompetent individuals (or both).

This does not mean that in the end maladapted people are forced into patterns they do not accept or understand. Quite to the contrary, such rules can also be understood in the sense that they set the individuals free to act according to their own moral views and convictions, rather then reprimanding them and demanding them to adopt moral principles that they simply do not have. Rules can indeed provide freedom in that everybody not only can but should follow his or her individual morality – within the institutional constraints they encounter and which they on their part can also try to alter.

NOTES

1 It should be noted that Beck prefers the notion of differentiation since he believes it can manifest itself without producing personal inconsistency (see discussion further below in the text).

2 These are his papers "Justice as Fairness: Political not Metaphysical" (1985) and "The Domain of the Political and Overlapping Consensus" (1989). In a later publication he referred to his theory of justice as a "moral conception" and explained that "(i)n saying that a conception is moral, I mean ... that its content is given by certain ideals, principles and standards; and that these norms articulate certain values, in this case political values" (1993, 11).

3 Nota bene that the organisation of societies is thought to evolve in the same way so that a certain type of societal organisation is no precondition in the sense of a condition sine qua non.

4 He begins the opening section of his „Grundlegung der Metaphysik der Sitten" with the words: „Es ist überall nichts in der Welt, ja überhaupt auch außer derselben zu denken möglich, was ohne Einschränkung für gut könnte gehalten werden, als allein ein guter Wille" (1968, 393).

REFERENCES

Beck, K. (1996). "Berufsmoral" und "Betriebsmoral": Didaktische Konzeptualisierungsprobleme einer berufsqualifizierenden Moralerziehung. In K. Beck, W. Müller, T. Deißinger & M. Zimmermann (Eds.) *Berufserziehung im Umbruch – Didaktische Herausforderungen und Ansätze zu ihrer Bewältigung*. Weinheim, Deutscher Studien Verlag.

Beck, K. (1999). Wirtschaftserziehung und Moralerziehung – ein Widerspruch in sich? Zur Kritik der Kohlbergschen Moralentwicklungstheorie. *Pädagogische Rundschau*, 53, 9-28.

Beck, K. (2003). Ethischer Universalismus als moralische Verunsicherung? Zur Diskussion um die Grundlegung der Moralerziehung. *Zeitschrift für Berufs- und Wirtschaftspädagogik*, 99, 274-298.

Beck, K., Brütting, B., Lüdecke, S., Minnameier, G., Schirmer, U. & Schmid, S. N. (1996). Zur Entwicklung moralischer Urteilskompetenz in der kaufmännischen Erstausbildung: Empirische Befunde und praktische Probleme. In K. Beck & H. Heid (Eds.) *Lehr-Lern-Prozesse in der kaufmännischen Erstausbildung: Wissenserwerb, Motivierungsgeschehen und Handlungskompetenzen*. Stuttgart: Steiner.

Beck, K., Dransfeld, A., Minnameier, G. & Wuttke, E. (2002). Autonomy in heterogeneity? Development of moral judgement behaviour during business education. In K. Beck (Ed.) *Teaching-learning processes in vocational education – Foundations of modern training programmes*. Frankfurt/Main: Lang.

Beck, K., Heinrichs, K., Minnameier, G. & Parche-Kawik, K. (1999). Homogeneity of moral judgement? Apprentices solving business conflicts. *Journal of Moral Education*, 28, 429-443.

Becker, G.S. (1976). *The economic approach to human behavior*. Chicago: University of Chicago Press.

Becker-Olson, K. L., Cudmore, B. A. & Hill, R. P. (2006). The impact of perceived corporate social responsibility on consumer behavior. *Journal of Business Research*, 59, 46–53.

Buchanan, J.M. (1977). *Freedom in constitutional contract: Perspectives of a political economist*. College Station, Texas A & M: University Press.

Colby, A. & Kohlberg, L. (1987). *The measurement of moral judgment, Vol. I: Theoretical foundations and research validation*. Cambridge MA: Cambridge University Press.

Homann, K. (1990). Demokratie und Gerechtigkeitstheorie – James M. Buchanans Kritik and John Rawls. In B. Biervert, K. Held & J. Wieland (Eds.) *Sozialphilosophische Grundlagen ökonomischen Handelns*. Frankfurt/Main: Suhrkamp.

Homann, K. (1994). Ethik und Ökonomik – Zur Theoriestrategie der Wirtschaftsethik. In K. Homann (Ed.) *Wirtschaftsethische Perspektiven I: Theorie, Ordnungsfragen, Internationale Institutionen*. Berlin: Duncker & Humblot.

Homann, K. (1999). Das Problem der "Instrumentalisierung" der Moral in der Wirtschaftsethik. In B.N. Kumar, M. Osterloh & G. Schreyögg (Eds.) *Unternehmensethik und die Transformation des Wettbewerbs: Shareholder-Value – Globalisierung – Hyperwettbewerb.* Stuttgart: Schäffer-Poeschel.

Homann, K. (2001). Ökonomik: Fortsetzung der Ethik mit anderen Mitteln. In G. Siebeck (Ed.) *Artibus ingenuis:Beiträge zu Theologie, Philosophie, Rechtswissenschaft und Wirtschaftswissenschaft.* Tübingen: Mohr Siebeck.

Homann, K. (2004a). Gesellschaftliche Verantwortung der Unternehmen – Philosophische, gesellschaftstheoretische und ökonomische Überlegungen. In U. Schneider & P. Steiner (Eds.) *Betriebswirtschaftslehre und gesellschaftliche Verantwortung – Mit Corporate Social Responsibility zu mehr Engagement.* Wiesbaden: Gabler.

Homann, K. (2004b). Das Problem des Sollens. In U. Dierse (Ed.): *Joachim Ritter zum Gedenken.* Stuttgart: Steiner. Mainz: Akademie der Wissenschaften und der Literatur. Wiesbaden: Gabler.

Kant, I. (1968): Kants Werke (Akademie Textausgabe), Bd. IV. Berlin: de Gruyter.

Kohlberg, L. & Mayer, R. (1987). Development as the aim of education. In L. Kohlberg (Ed.): *Child psychology and childhood education: A cognitive-developmental view.* New York: Longman, 45-85.

Koslowski, P. (1992). Der homo oeconomicus und die Wirtschaftsethik. In P. Koslowski (Ed.): *Neuer Entwicklungen in der Wirtschaftsethik und Wirtschaftsphilosophie.* Berlin: Springer.

Marin, L. & Ruiz, S. (2007). "I need you too!" Corporate identity attractiveness for consumers and the role of social responsibility. *Journal of Business Ethics, 71,* 245-260.

Minnameier, G. (2000). *Strukturgenese moralischen Denkens – Eine Rekonstruktion der Piagetschen Entwicklungslogik und ihre moraltheoretischen Folgen.* Münster: Waxmann.

Minnameier, G. (2001). A new "stairway to moral heaven"? A systematic reconstruction of stages of moral thinking based on a Piagetian "logic" of cognitive development. *Journal of Moral Education, 30,* 317-337.

Minnameier, G. (2004). Ethics and economics, friends or foes? An educational debate. *Journal of Moral Education, 33,* 359-369

Minnameier, G. (2005a). Wer Moral hat, hat die Qual, aber letztlich keine Wahl! Homanns (Wirtschafts)Ethik im Kontext der Wirtschaftsdidaktik. *Zeitschrift für Berufs- und Wirtschaftspädagogik, 101,* 19-42.

Minnameier, G. (2005b) Developmental progress in ancient Greek ethics. *European Journal of Developmental psychology, 2,* 71-99.

Rawls, J. (1971). *A theory of justice.* Cambridge MA: Harvard University Press.

Rawls, J. (1993). *Political liberalism.* New York: Columbia University Press.

Rawls, J. (1999). *Collected papers,* ed. by S. Freeman. Cambridge MA: Harvard University Press.

Rest, J. R. (1979). *Development in judging moral issues.* Minneapolis, Minnesota: University of Minnesota Press.

Sandel, M. (1982). *Liberalism and the limits of justice.* Cambridge MA: Cambridge University Press.

Steinmann, H. & Löhr, A. (1994). Grundlagen der Unternehmensethik. 2. Aufl. Stuttgart: Poeschel.

Ulrich, P. (1990). Integrative Wirtschaftsethik: Grundlagen einer lebensdienlichen Ökonomie. Bern: Haupt.

Walzer, M. (1994). *Thick and thin: Moral arguments at home and abroad.* Notre Dame: University of Notre Dame Press.

Zabeck, J. (1991). Ethische Dimensionen der "Wirtschaftserziehung", *Zeitschrift für Berufs- und Wirtschaftspädagogik, 87,* 534-562.

Zabeck, J. (2002). Moral im Dienste betrieblicher Zwecke? Anmerkungen zu Klaus Becks Grundlegung einer kaufmännischen Moralerziehung, *Zeitschrift für Berufs- und Wirtschaftspädagogik, 98,* 485-503.

Gerhard Minnameier
Aachen Insitute of Technology, Germany

Printed in the United States
127091LV00005BC/31/P

9 789087 906351